SUPERMAN
ACTION COMICS
VOL. 1 INVISIBLE MAFIA

SUPERMAN
ACTION COMICS
VOL. 1 INVISIBLE MAFIA

BRIAN MICHAEL BENDIS
writer

RYAN SOOK
PATRICK GLEASON
YANICK PAQUETTE
WADE VON GRAWBADGER
artists

ALEJANDRO SANCHEZ
BRAD ANDERSON
NATHAN FAIRBAIRN
colorists

JOSH REED
letterer

RYAN SOOK
collection cover artist

PATRICK GLEASON and BRAD ANDERSON
RYAN SOOK
STEVE RUDE
original series covers

SUPERMAN created by **JERRY SIEGEL** and **JOE SHUSTER**
SUPERBOY created by **JERRY SIEGEL**
By special arrangement with the Jerry Siegel family

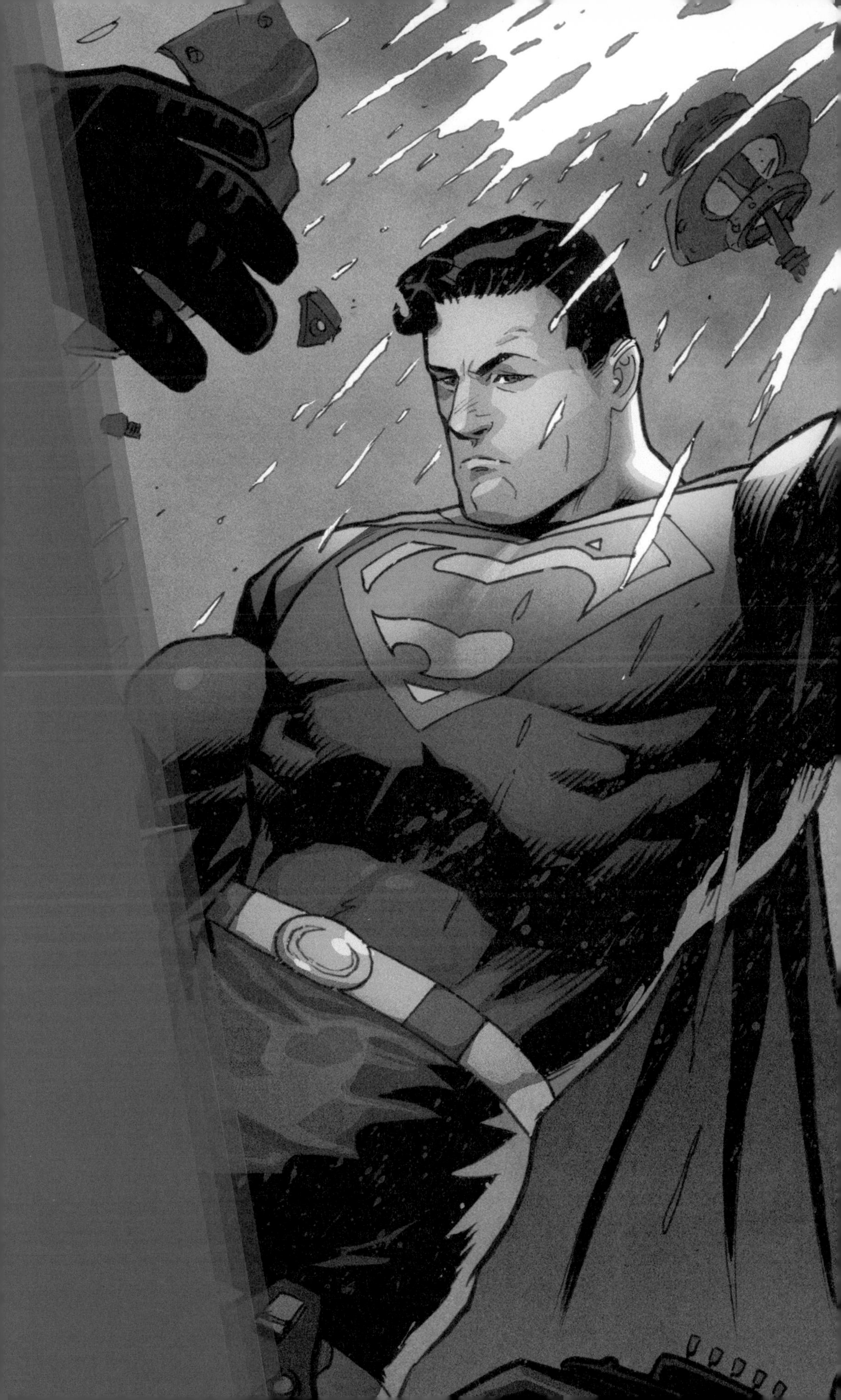

MIKE COTTON Editor – Original Series
JESSICA CHEN Associate Editor – Original Series
JEB WOODARD Group Editor – Collected Editions
SCOTT NYBAKKEN Editor – Collected Edition
STEVE COOK Design Director – Books
SHANNON STEWART Publication Design
TOM VALENTE Publication Production

BOB HARRAS Senior VP – Editor-in-Chief, DC Comics
PAT McCALLUM Executive Editor, DC Comics

DAN DiDIO Publisher
JIM LEE Publisher & Chief Creative Officer
BOBBIE CHASE VP – New Publishing Initiatives & Talent Development
DON FALLETTI VP – Manufacturing Operations & Workflow Management
LAWRENCE GANEM VP – Talent Services
ALISON GILL Senior VP – Manufacturing & Operations
HANK KANALZ Senior VP – Publishing Strategy & Support Services
DAN MIRON VP – Publishing Operations
NICK J. NAPOLITANO VP – Manufacturing Administration & Design
NANCY SPEARS VP – Sales
MICHELE R. WELLS VP & Executive Editor, Young Reader

SUPERMAN: ACTION COMICS VOL. 1: INVISIBLE MAFIA

DC Comics, 2900 West Alameda Ave., Burbank, CA 91505
Printed by LSC Communications, Owensville, MO, USA. 10/4/19. First Printing.
ISBN: 978-1-4012-9478-6

Library of Congress Cataloging-in-Publication Data is available.

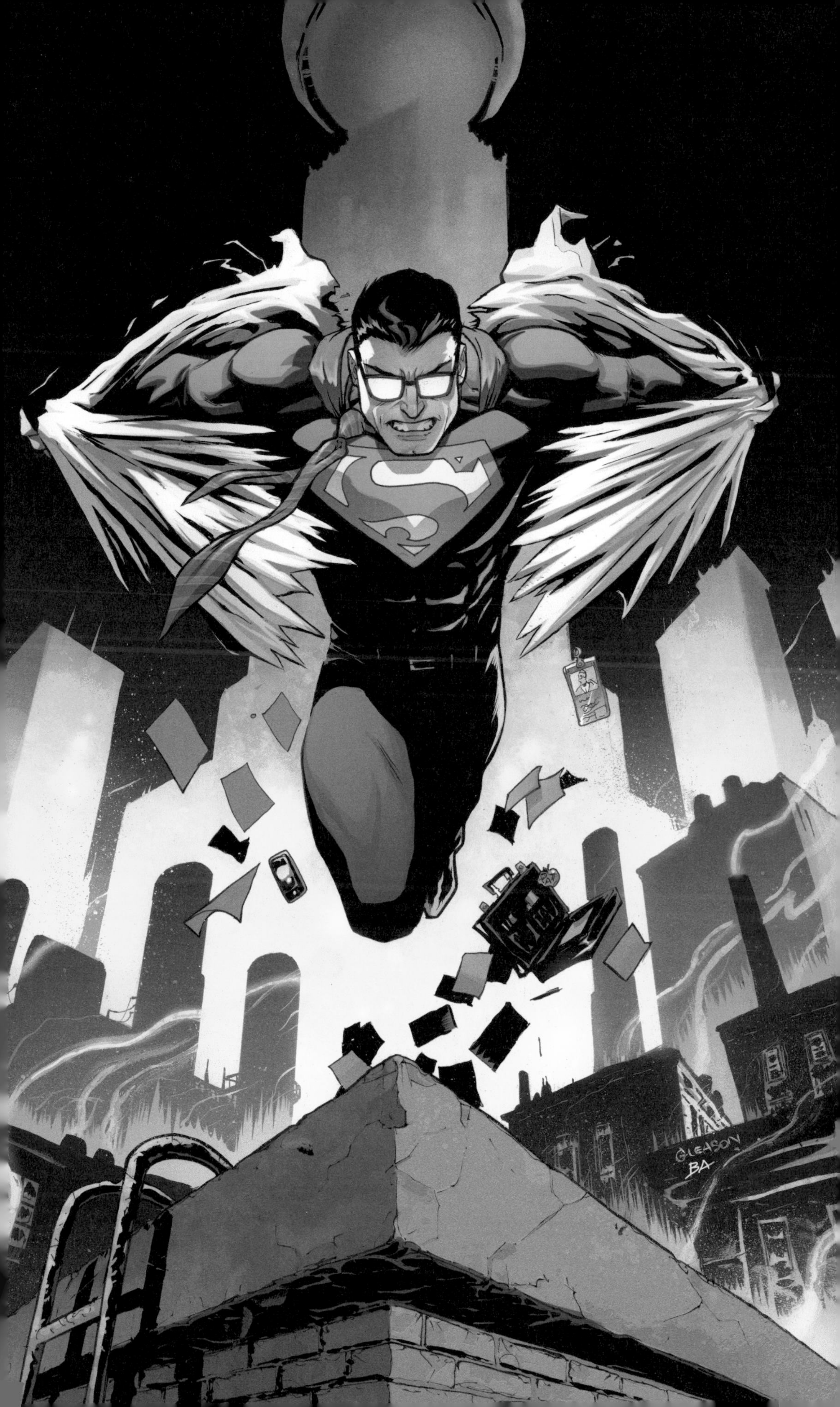
GLEASON
BA

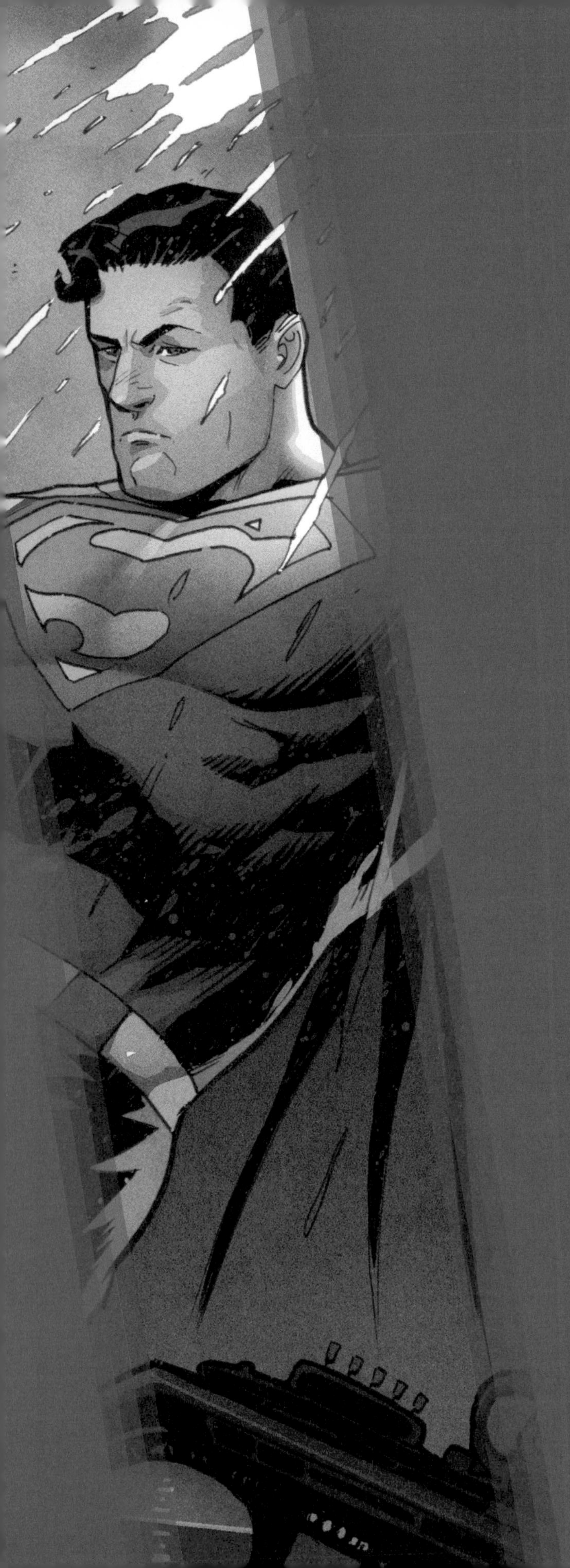

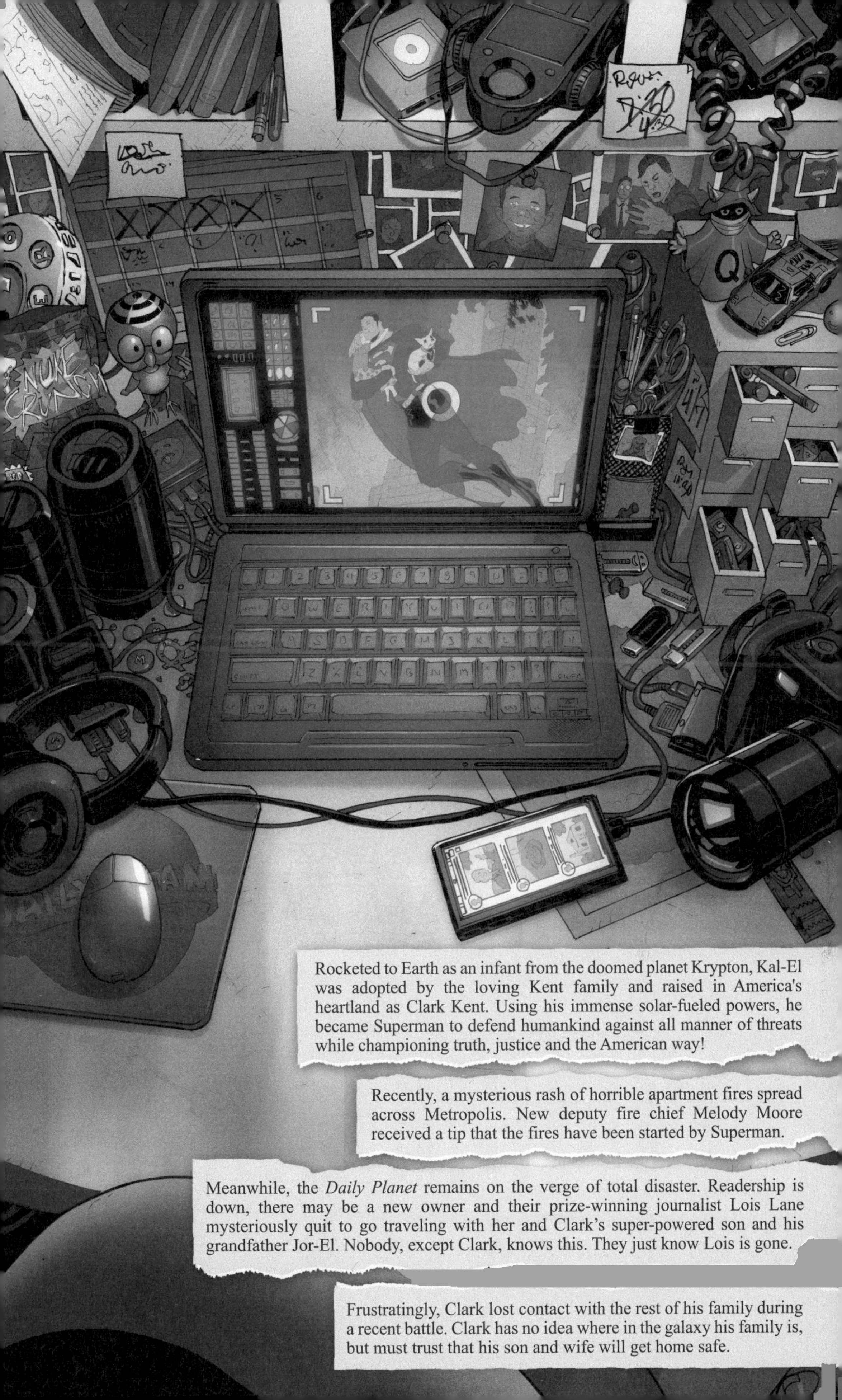
NUKE CRUNCH
Q
Rocketed to Earth as an infant from the doomed planet Krypton, Kal-El was adopted by the loving Kent family and raised in America's heartland as Clark Kent. Using his immense solar-fueled powers, he became Superman to defend humankind against all manner of threats while championing truth, justice and the American way!
Recently, a mysterious rash of horrible apartment fires spread across Metropolis. New deputy fire chief Melody Moore received a tip that the fires have been started by Superman.
Meanwhile, the *Daily Planet* remains on the verge of total disaster. Readership is down, there may be a new owner and their prize-winning journalist Lois Lane mysteriously quit to go traveling with her and Clark's super-powered son and his grandfather Jor-El. Nobody, except Clark, knows this. They just know Lois is gone.
Frustratingly, Clark lost contact with the rest of his family during a recent battle. Clark has no idea where in the galaxy his family is, but must trust that his son and wife will get home safe.

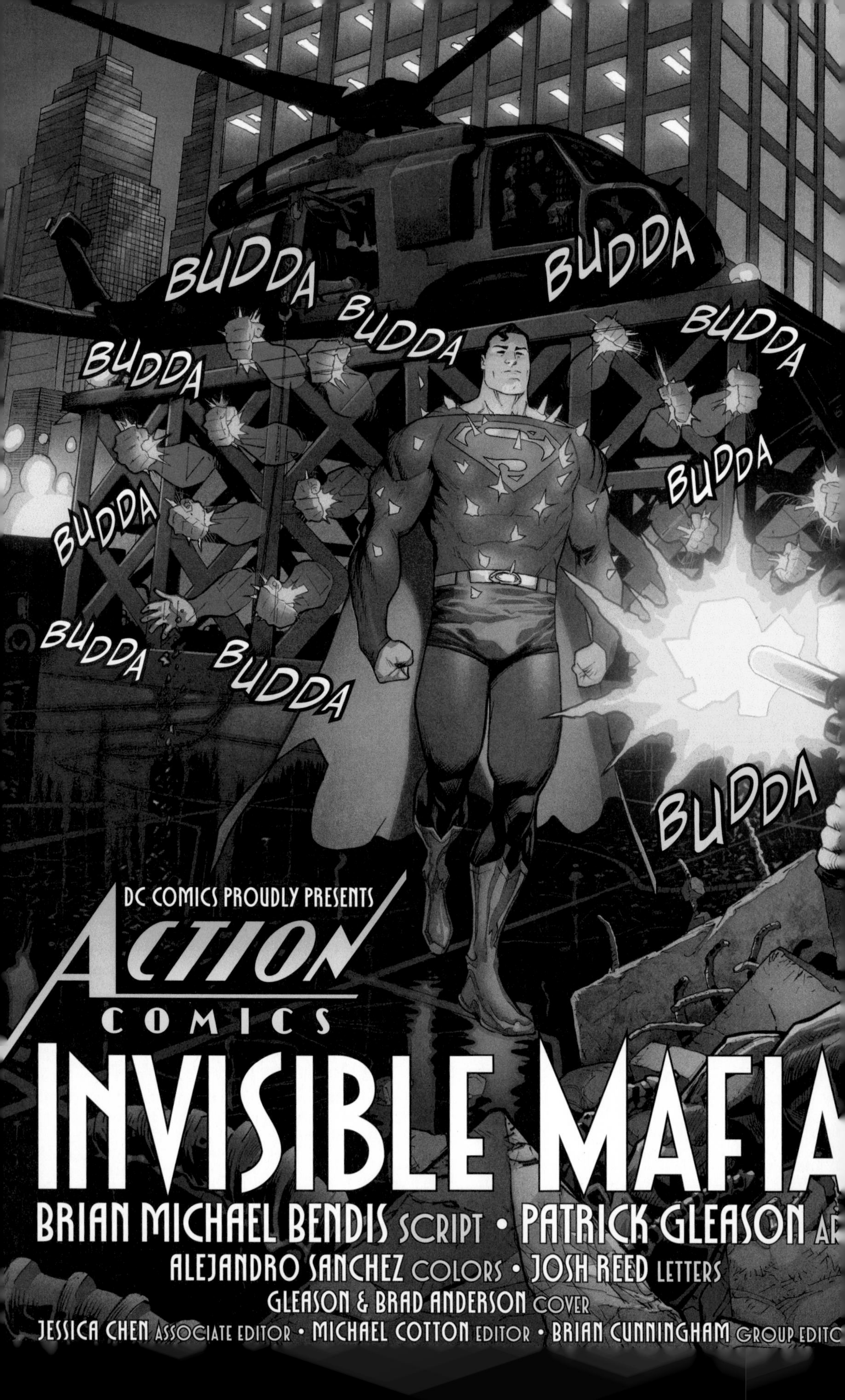

BUDDA
BUDDA
BUDDA
BUDDA
BUDDA
BUDDA
BUDDA
BUDDA
BUDDA
BUDDA
DC COMICS PROUDLY PRESENTS
ACTION COMICS
INVISIBLE MAFIA
BRIAN MICHAEL BENDIS SCRIPT • PATRICK GLEASON AR
ALEJANDRO SANCHEZ COLORS • JOSH REED LETTERS
GLEASON & BRAD ANDERSON COVER
JESSICA CHEN ASSOCIATE EDITOR • MICHAEL COTTON EDITOR • BRIAN CUNNINGHAM GROUP EDITO

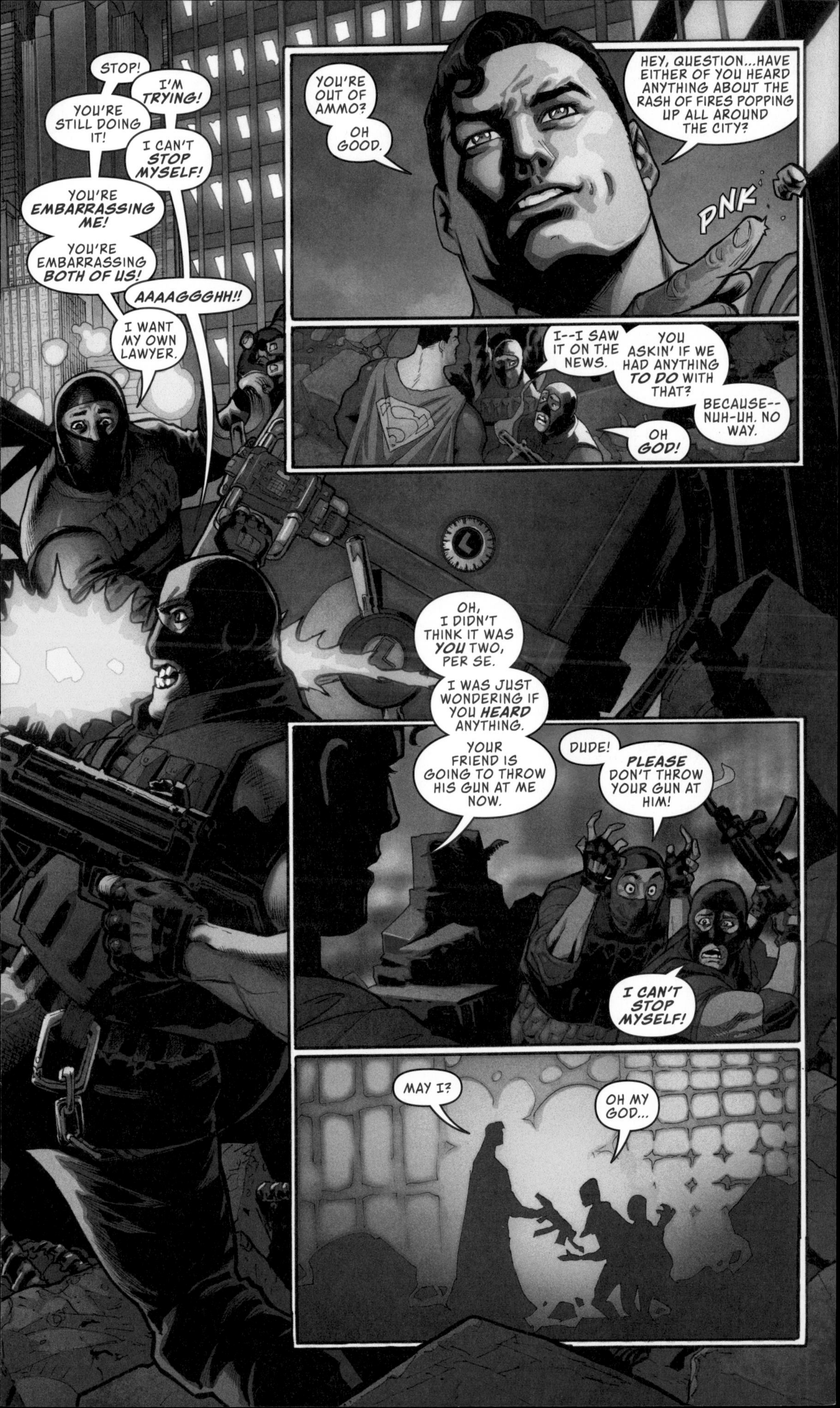
STOP!
I'M TRYING!
YOU'RE STILL DOING IT!
I CAN'T STOP MYSELF!
YOU'RE EMBARRASSING ME!
YOU'RE EMBARRASSING BOTH OF US!
AAAAGGGHH!!
I WANT MY OWN LAWYER.
YOU'RE OUT OF AMMO?
OH GOOD.
HEY, QUESTION...HAVE EITHER OF YOU HEARD ANYTHING ABOUT THE RASH OF FIRES POPPING UP ALL AROUND THE CITY?
PNK
I--I SAW IT ON THE NEWS.
YOU ASKIN' IF WE HAD ANYTHING TO DO WITH THAT?
BECAUSE--NUH-UH. NO WAY.
OH GOD!
OH, I DIDN'T THINK IT WAS YOU TWO, PER SE.
I WAS JUST WONDERING IF YOU HEARD ANYTHING.
YOUR FRIEND IS GOING TO THROW HIS GUN AT ME NOW.
DUDE!
PLEASE DON'T THROW YOUR GUN AT HIM!
I CAN'T STOP MYSELF!
MAY I?
OH MY GOD...

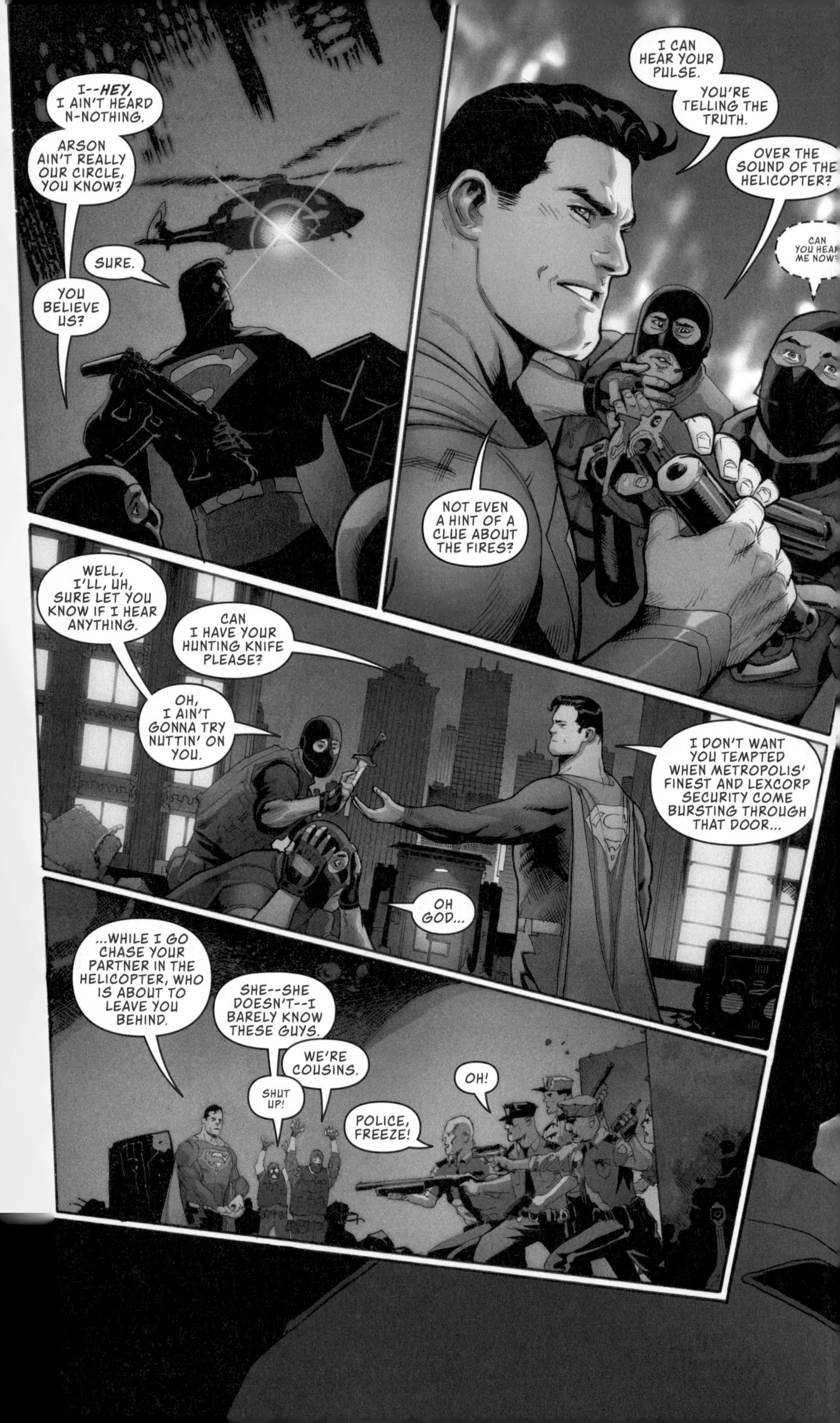
I--*HEY,* I AIN'T HEARD N-NOTHING.
ARSON AIN'T REALLY OUR CIRCLE, YOU KNOW?
SURE.
YOU BELIEVE US?
I CAN HEAR YOUR PULSE.
YOU'RE TELLING THE TRUTH.
OVER THE SOUND OF THE HELICOPTER?
NOT EVEN A HINT OF A CLUE ABOUT THE FIRES?
WELL, I'LL, UH, SURE LET YOU KNOW IF I HEAR ANYTHING.
CAN I HAVE YOUR HUNTING KNIFE PLEASE?
OH, I AIN'T GONNA TRY NUTTIN' ON YOU.
I DON'T WANT YOU TEMPTED WHEN METROPOLIS' FINEST AND LEXCORP SECURITY COME BURSTING THROUGH THAT DOOR...
OH GOD...
...WHILE I GO CHASE YOUR PARTNER IN THE HELICOPTER, WHO IS ABOUT TO LEAVE YOU BEHIND.
SHE--SHE DOESN'T--I BARELY KNOW THESE GUYS.
WE'RE COUSINS.
SHUT UP!
OH!
POLICE, FREEZE!

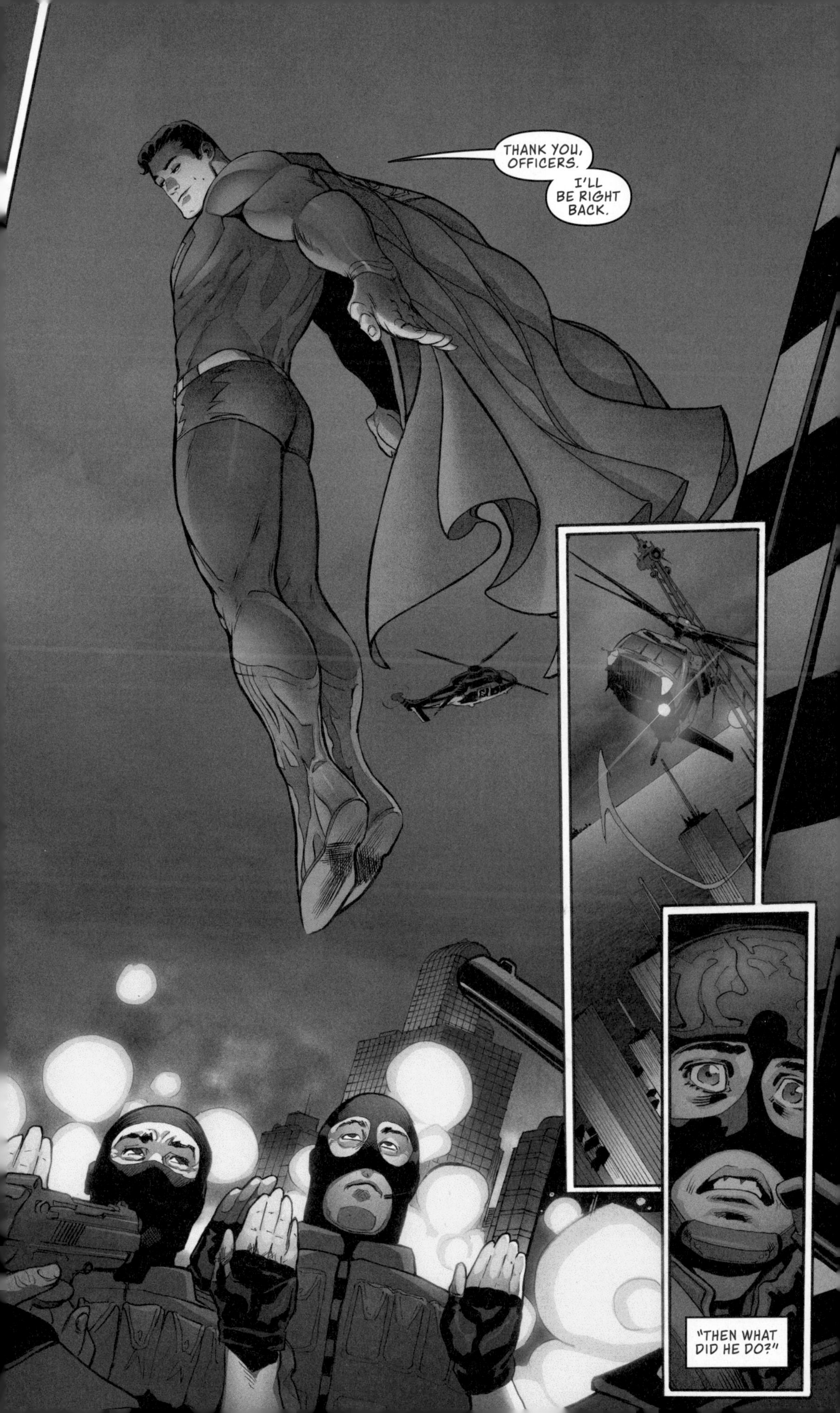
THANK YOU, OFFICERS.
I'LL BE RIGHT BACK.
"THEN WHAT DID HE DO?"

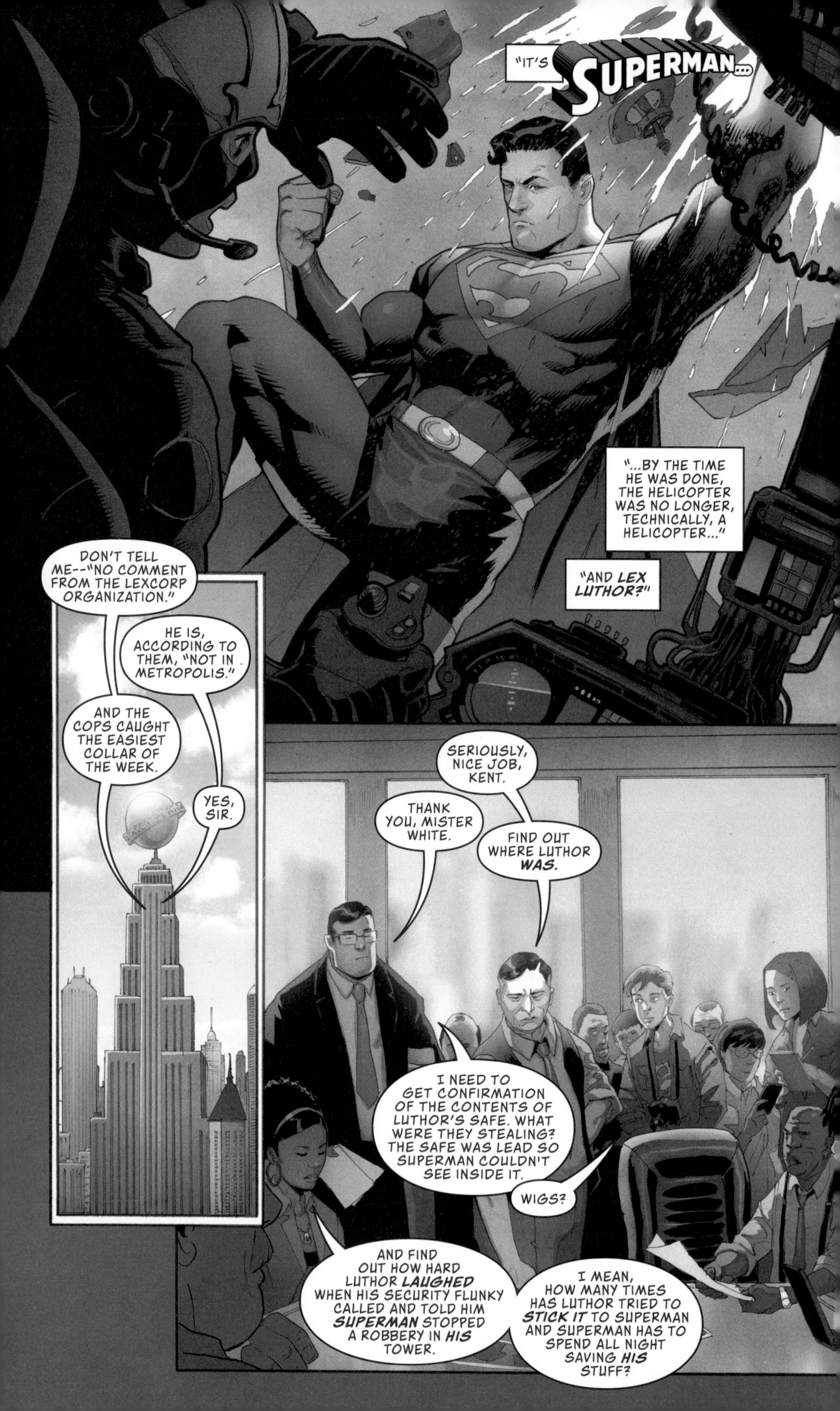
"IT'S SUPERMAN...
"...BY THE TIME HE WAS DONE, THE HELICOPTER WAS NO LONGER, TECHNICALLY, A HELICOPTER..."
"AND LEX LUTHOR?"
DON'T TELL ME--"NO COMMENT FROM THE LEXCORP ORGANIZATION."
HE IS, ACCORDING TO THEM, "NOT IN METROPOLIS."
AND THE COPS CAUGHT THE EASIEST COLLAR OF THE WEEK.
YES, SIR.
SERIOUSLY, NICE JOB, KENT.
THANK YOU, MISTER WHITE.
FIND OUT WHERE LUTHOR WAS.
I NEED TO GET CONFIRMATION OF THE CONTENTS OF LUTHOR'S SAFE. WHAT WERE THEY STEALING? THE SAFE WAS LEAD SO SUPERMAN COULDN'T SEE INSIDE IT.
WIGS?
AND FIND OUT HOW HARD LUTHOR LAUGHED WHEN HIS SECURITY FLUNKY CALLED AND TOLD HIM SUPERMAN STOPPED A ROBBERY IN HIS TOWER.
I MEAN, HOW MANY TIMES HAS LUTHOR TRIED TO STICK IT TO SUPERMAN AND SUPERMAN HAS TO SPEND ALL NIGHT SAVING HIS STUFF?

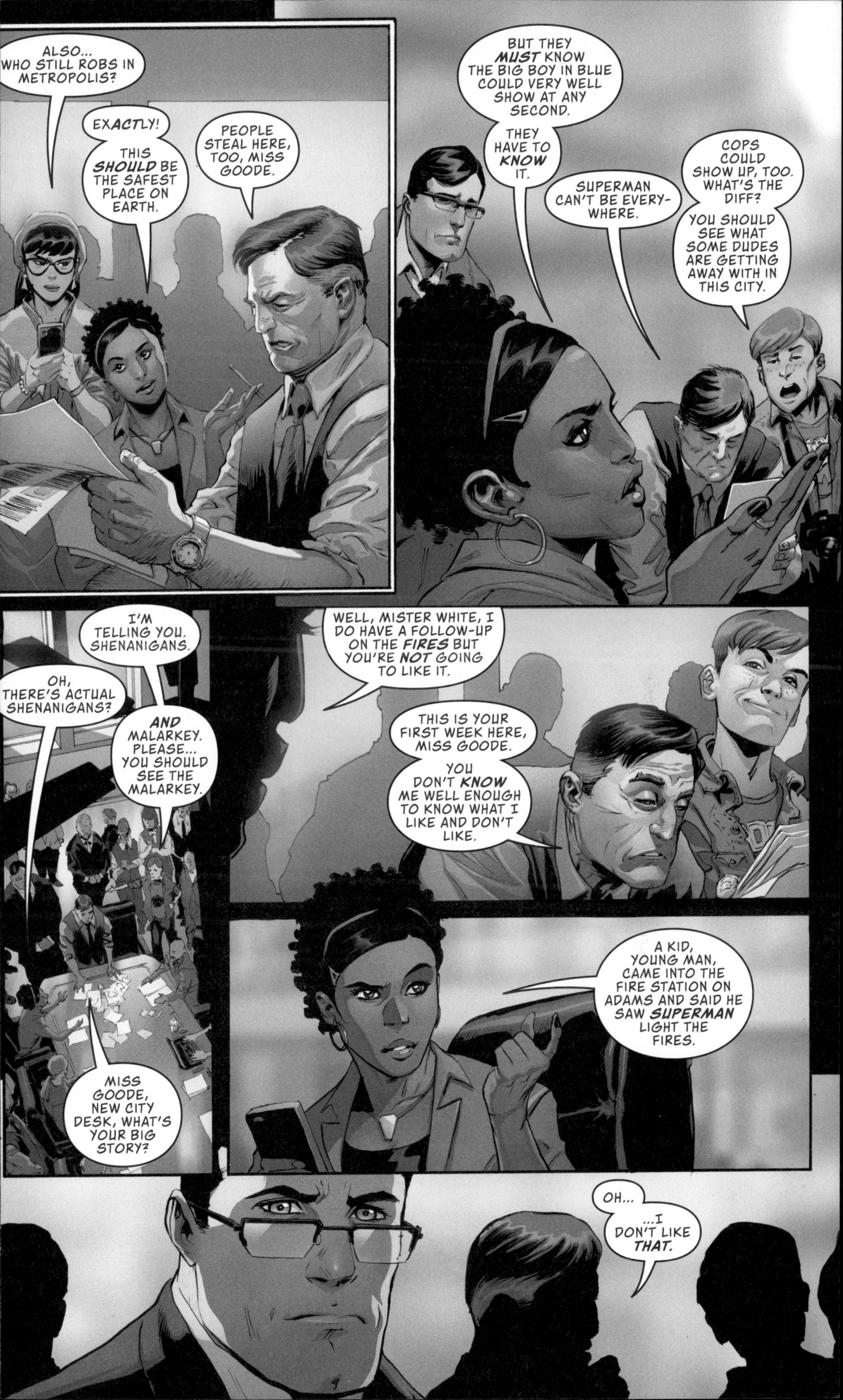

ALSO... WHO STILL ROBS IN METROPOLIS?
EXACTLY!
THIS SHOULD BE THE SAFEST PLACE ON EARTH.
PEOPLE STEAL HERE, TOO, MISS GOODE.
BUT THEY MUST KNOW THE BIG BOY IN BLUE COULD VERY WELL SHOW AT ANY SECOND.
THEY HAVE TO KNOW IT.
SUPERMAN CAN'T BE EVERY-WHERE.
COPS COULD SHOW UP, TOO. WHAT'S THE DIFF?
YOU SHOULD SEE WHAT SOME DUDES ARE GETTING AWAY WITH IN THIS CITY.
I'M TELLING YOU. SHENANIGANS.
OH, THERE'S ACTUAL SHENANIGANS?
AND MALARKEY. PLEASE... YOU SHOULD SEE THE MALARKEY.
MISS GOODE, NEW CITY DESK, WHAT'S YOUR BIG STORY?
WELL, MISTER WHITE, I DO HAVE A FOLLOW-UP ON THE FIRES BUT YOU'RE NOT GOING TO LIKE IT.
THIS IS YOUR FIRST WEEK HERE, MISS GOODE.
YOU DON'T KNOW ME WELL ENOUGH TO KNOW WHAT I LIKE AND DON'T LIKE.
A KID, YOUNG MAN, CAME INTO THE FIRE STATION ON ADAMS AND SAID HE SAW SUPERMAN LIGHT THE FIRES.
OH...
...I DON'T LIKE THAT.

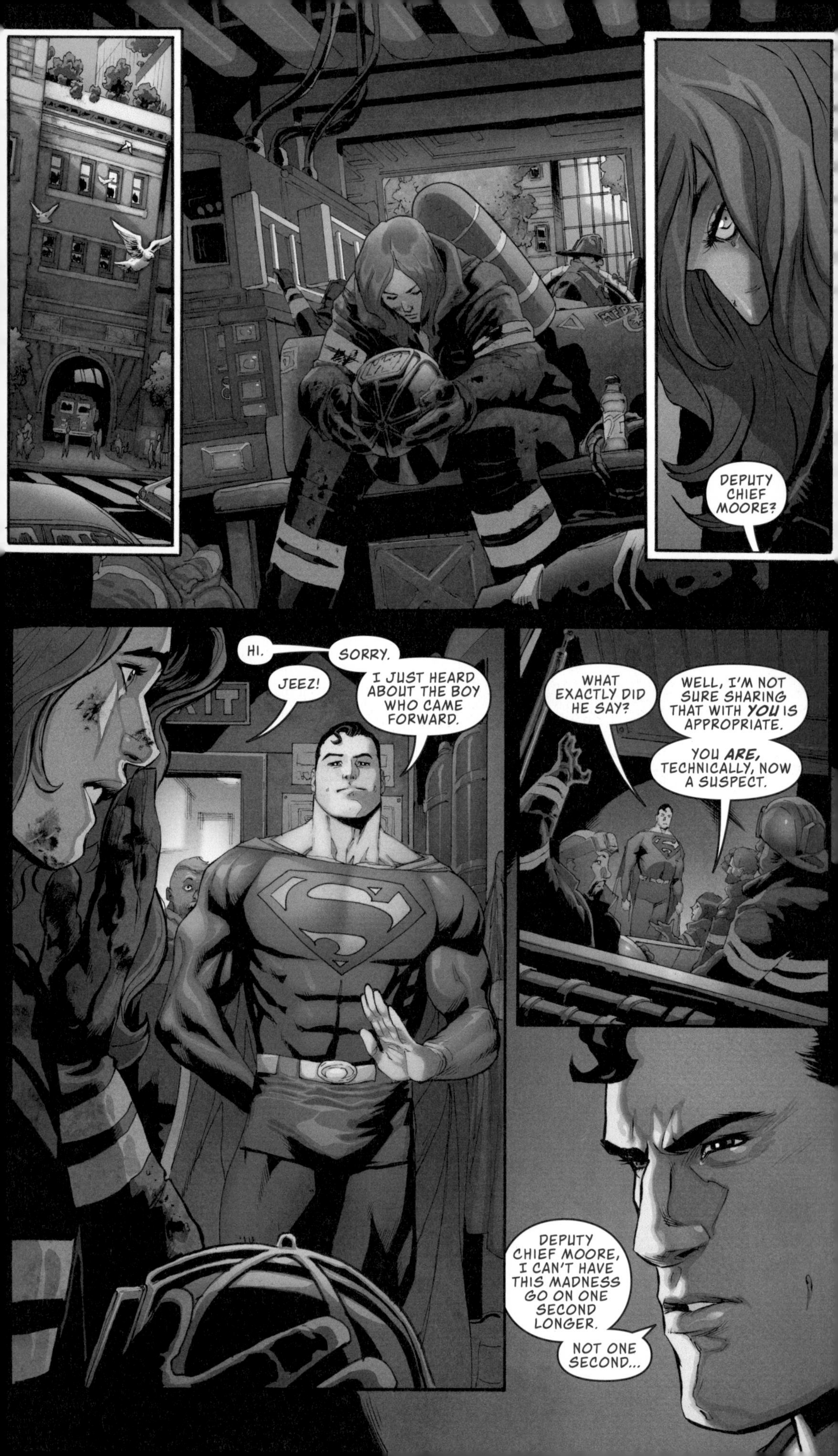
DEPUTY CHIEF MOORE?
HI.
SORRY.
JEEZ!
I JUST HEARD ABOUT THE BOY WHO CAME FORWARD.
WHAT EXACTLY DID HE SAY?
WELL, I'M NOT SURE SHARING THAT WITH YOU IS APPROPRIATE.
YOU ARE, TECHNICALLY, NOW A SUSPECT.
DEPUTY CHIEF MOORE, I CAN'T HAVE THIS MADNESS GO ON ONE SECOND LONGER.
NOT ONE SECOND...

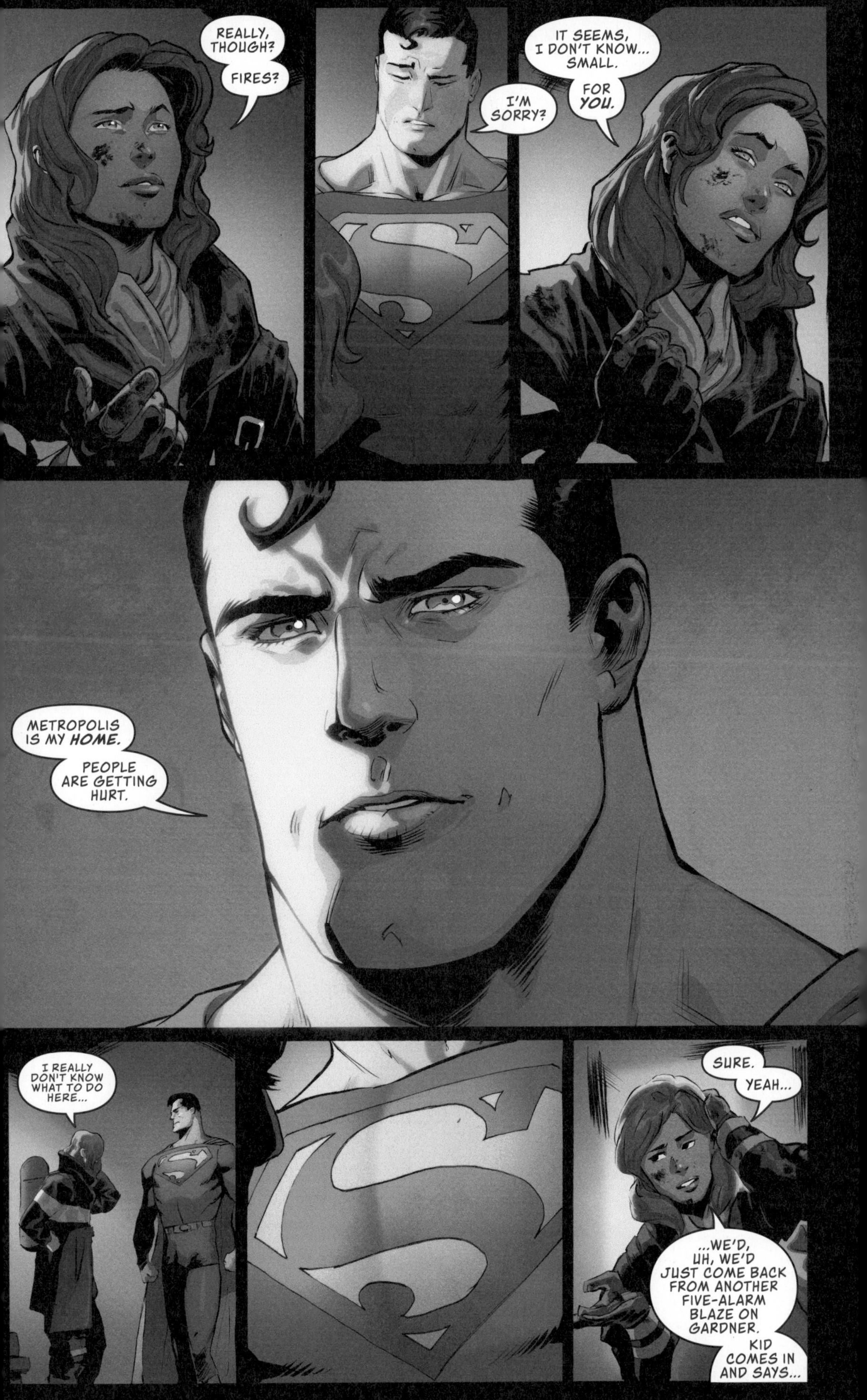
REALLY, THOUGH?
FIRES?
I'M SORRY?
IT SEEMS, I DON'T KNOW... SMALL.
FOR *YOU*.
METROPOLIS IS MY *HOME*.
PEOPLE ARE GETTING HURT.
I REALLY DON'T KNOW WHAT TO DO HERE...
SURE.
YEAH...
...WE'D, UH, WE'D JUST COME BACK FROM ANOTHER FIVE-ALARM BLAZE ON GARDNER.
KID COMES IN AND SAYS...

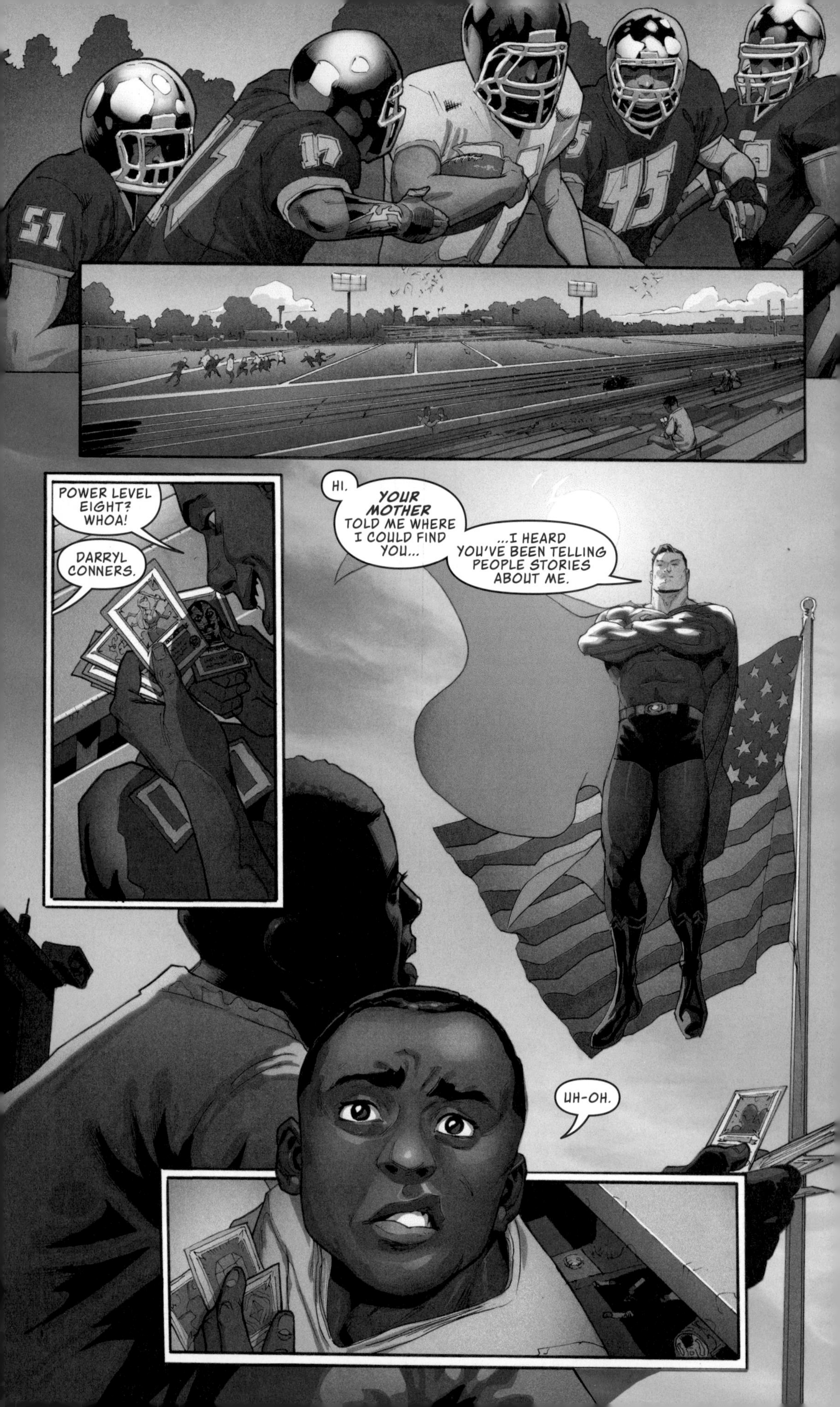
POWER LEVEL EIGHT? WHOA!
DARRYL CONNERS.
HI.
YOUR MOTHER TOLD ME WHERE I COULD FIND YOU...
...I HEARD YOU'VE BEEN TELLING PEOPLE STORIES ABOUT ME.
UH-OH.

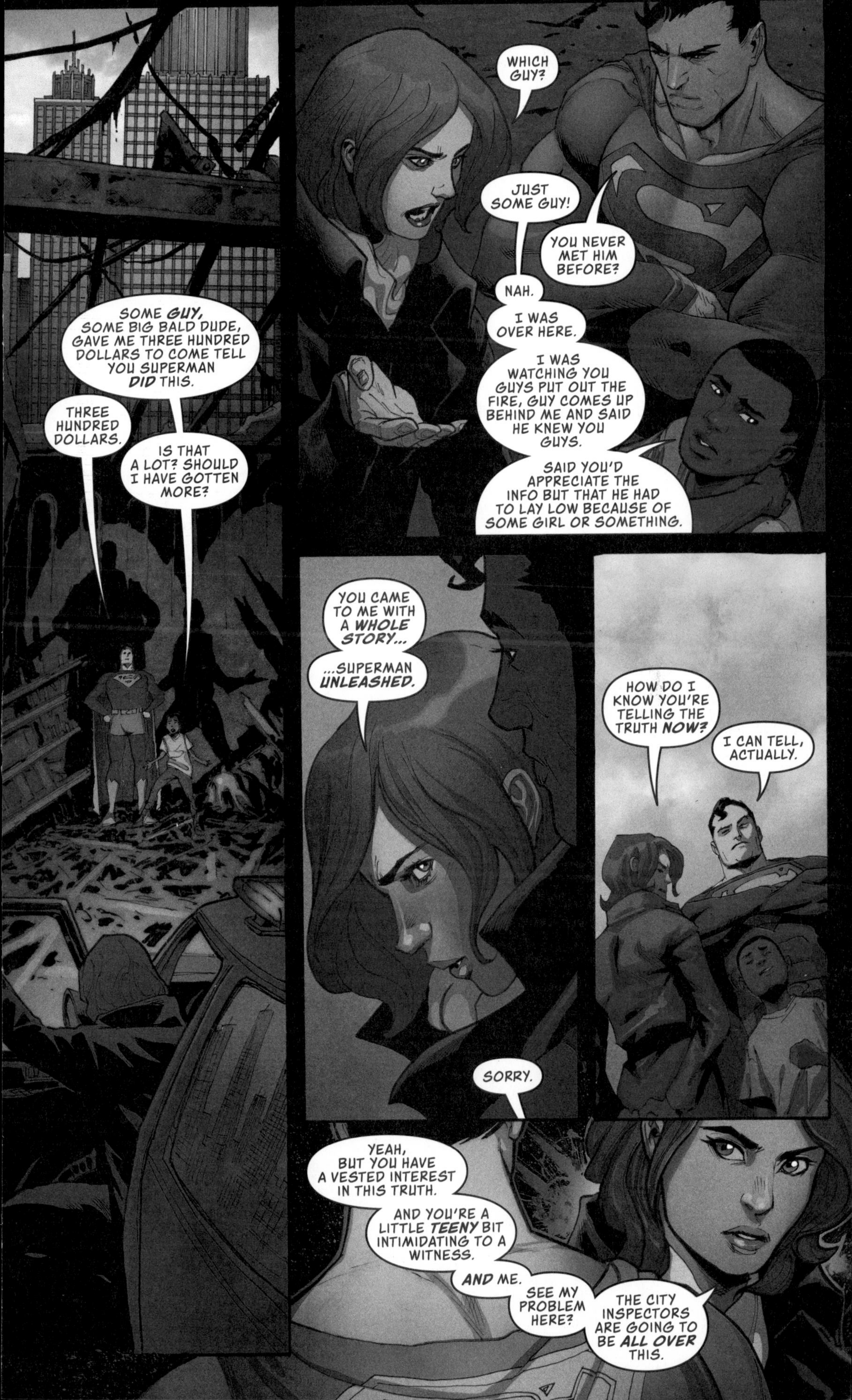
SOME GUY, SOME BIG BALD DUDE, GAVE ME THREE HUNDRED DOLLARS TO COME TELL YOU SUPERMAN DID THIS.
THREE HUNDRED DOLLARS.
IS THAT A LOT? SHOULD I HAVE GOTTEN MORE?
WHICH GUY?
JUST SOME GUY!
YOU NEVER MET HIM BEFORE?
NAH.
I WAS OVER HERE.
I WAS WATCHING YOU GUYS PUT OUT THE FIRE, GUY COMES UP BEHIND ME AND SAID HE KNEW YOU GUYS.
SAID YOU'D APPRECIATE THE INFO BUT THAT HE HAD TO LAY LOW BECAUSE OF SOME GIRL OR SOMETHING.
YOU CAME TO ME WITH A WHOLE STORY...
...SUPERMAN UNLEASHED.
HOW DO I KNOW YOU'RE TELLING THE TRUTH NOW?
I CAN TELL, ACTUALLY.
SORRY.
YEAH, BUT YOU HAVE A VESTED INTEREST IN THIS TRUTH.
AND YOU'RE A LITTLE TEENY BIT INTIMIDATING TO A WITNESS.
AND ME.
SEE MY PROBLEM HERE?
THE CITY INSPECTORS ARE GOING TO BE ALL OVER THIS.

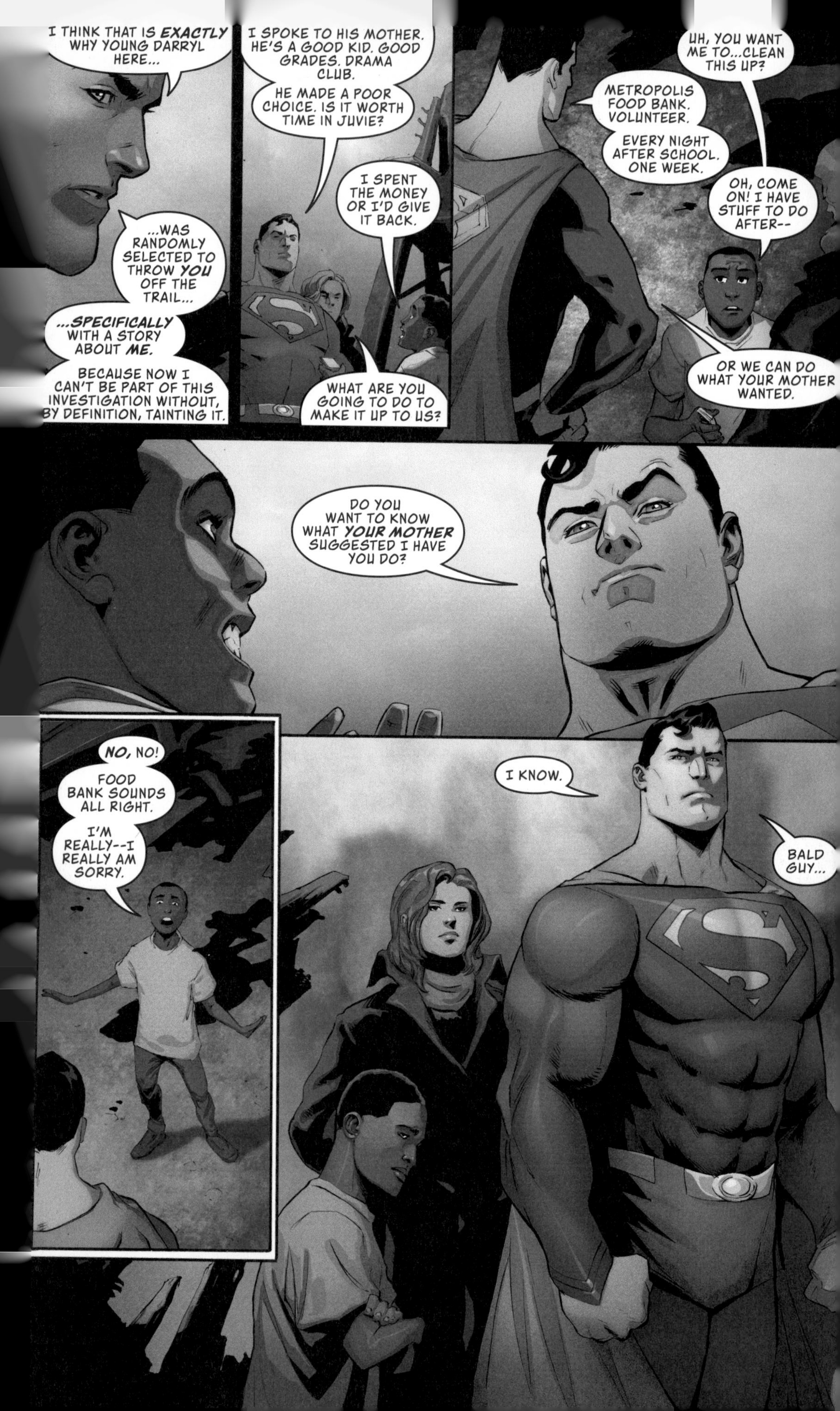

I THINK THAT IS EXACTLY WHY YOUNG DARRYL HERE...
...WAS RANDOMLY SELECTED TO THROW YOU OFF THE TRAIL...
...SPECIFICALLY WITH A STORY ABOUT ME.
BECAUSE NOW I CAN'T BE PART OF THIS INVESTIGATION WITHOUT, BY DEFINITION, TAINTING IT.
I SPOKE TO HIS MOTHER. HE'S A GOOD KID. GOOD GRADES. DRAMA CLUB.
HE MADE A POOR CHOICE. IS IT WORTH TIME IN JUVIE?
I SPENT THE MONEY OR I'D GIVE IT BACK.
WHAT ARE YOU GOING TO DO TO MAKE IT UP TO US?
UH, YOU WANT ME TO...CLEAN THIS UP?
METROPOLIS FOOD BANK. VOLUNTEER.
EVERY NIGHT AFTER SCHOOL. ONE WEEK.
OH, COME ON! I HAVE STUFF TO DO AFTER--
OR WE CAN DO WHAT YOUR MOTHER WANTED.
DO YOU WANT TO KNOW WHAT YOUR MOTHER SUGGESTED I HAVE YOU DO?
NO, NO! FOOD BANK SOUNDS ALL RIGHT.
I'M REALLY--I REALLY AM SORRY.
I KNOW.
BALD GUY...

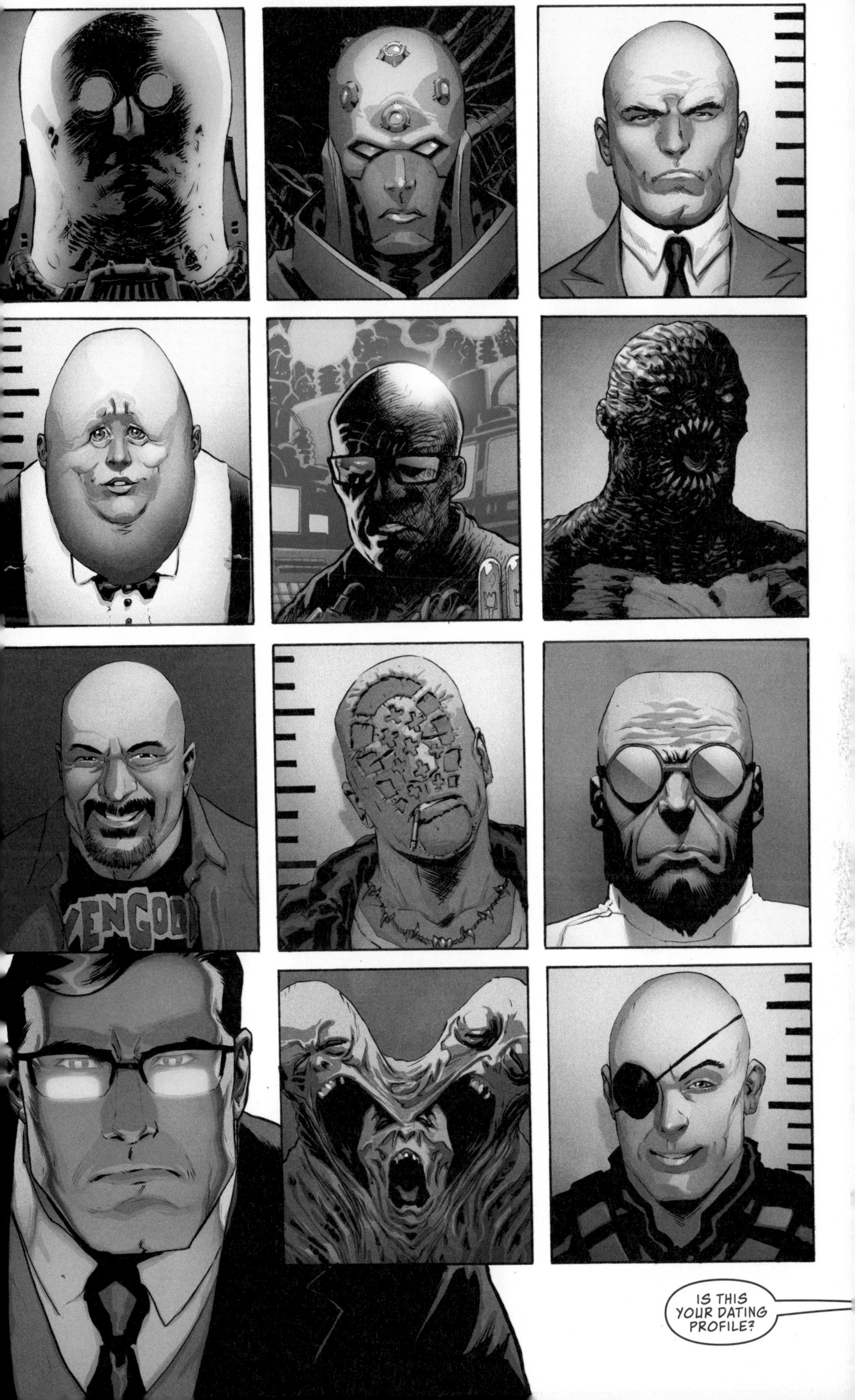
IS THIS YOUR DATING PROFILE?

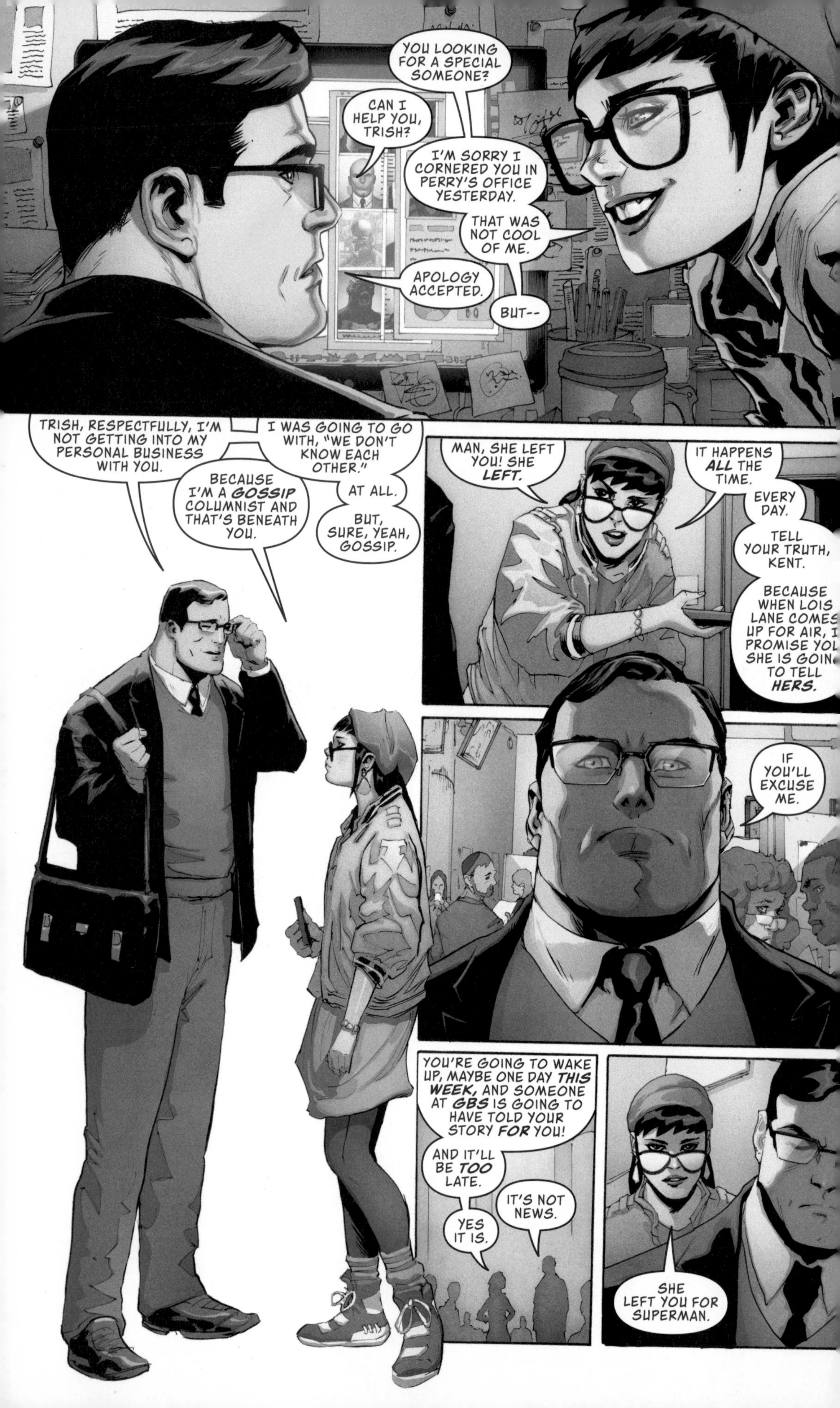

CAN I HELP YOU, TRISH?
YOU LOOKING FOR A SPECIAL SOMEONE?
I'M SORRY I CORNERED YOU IN PERRY'S OFFICE YESTERDAY.
THAT WAS NOT COOL OF ME.
APOLOGY ACCEPTED.
BUT--
TRISH, RESPECTFULLY, I'M NOT GETTING INTO MY PERSONAL BUSINESS WITH YOU.
BECAUSE I'M A GOSSIP COLUMNIST AND THAT'S BENEATH YOU.
I WAS GOING TO GO WITH, "WE DON'T KNOW EACH OTHER."
AT ALL.
BUT, SURE, YEAH, GOSSIP.
MAN, SHE LEFT YOU! SHE LEFT.
IT HAPPENS ALL THE TIME.
EVERY DAY.
TELL YOUR TRUTH, KENT.
BECAUSE WHEN LOIS LANE COMES UP FOR AIR, I PROMISE YOU SHE IS GOING TO TELL HERS.
IF YOU'LL EXCUSE ME.
YOU'RE GOING TO WAKE UP, MAYBE ONE DAY THIS WEEK, AND SOMEONE AT GBS IS GOING TO HAVE TOLD YOUR STORY FOR YOU!
AND IT'LL BE TOO LATE.
IT'S NOT NEWS.
YES IT IS.
SHE LEFT YOU FOR SUPERMAN.

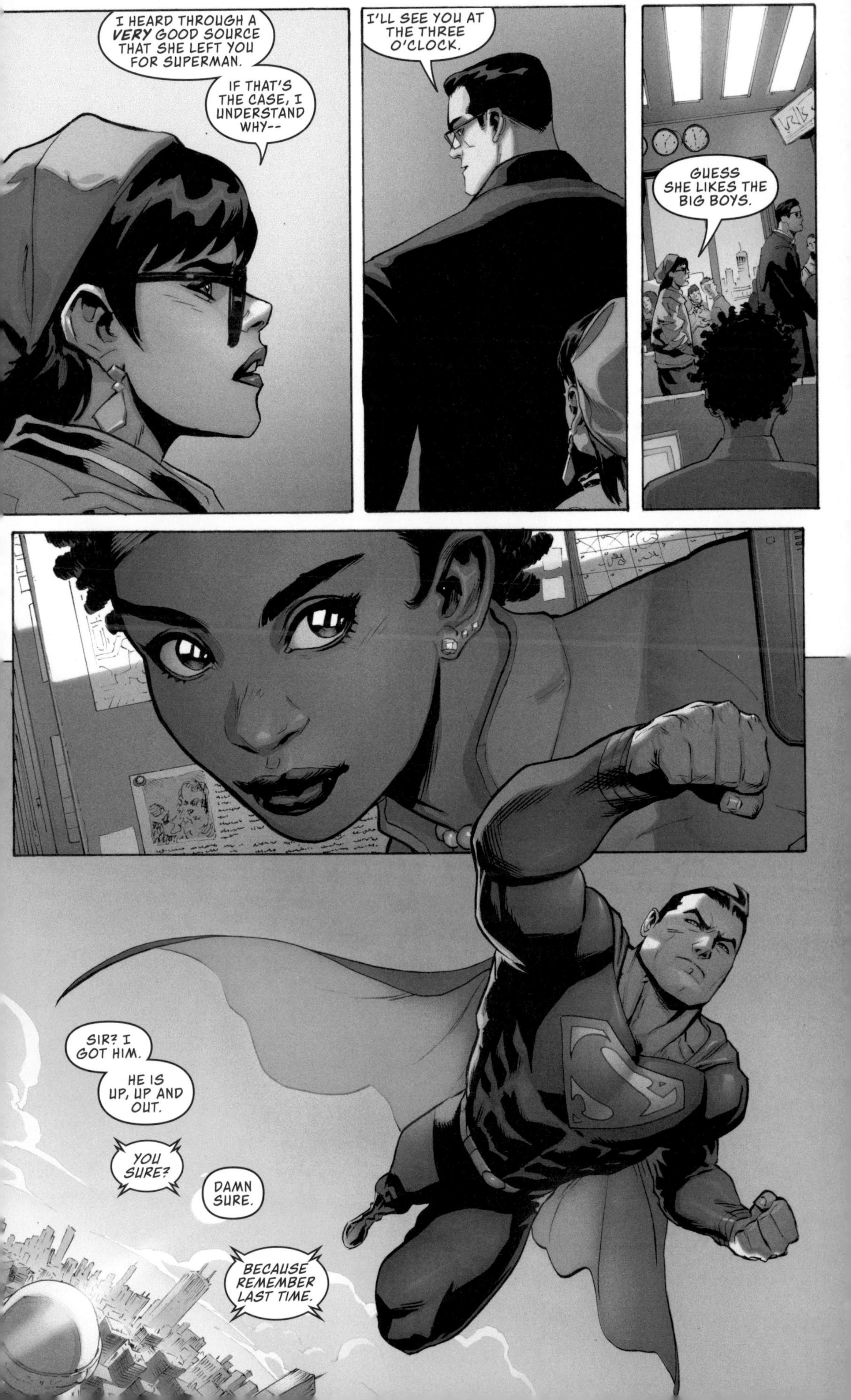
I HEARD THROUGH A VERY GOOD SOURCE THAT SHE LEFT YOU FOR SUPERMAN.
IF THAT'S THE CASE, I UNDERSTAND WHY--
I'LL SEE YOU AT THE THREE O'CLOCK.
GUESS SHE LIKES THE BIG BOYS.
SIR? I GOT HIM.
HE IS UP, UP AND OUT.
YOU SURE?
DAMN SURE.
BECAUSE REMEMBER LAST TIME.

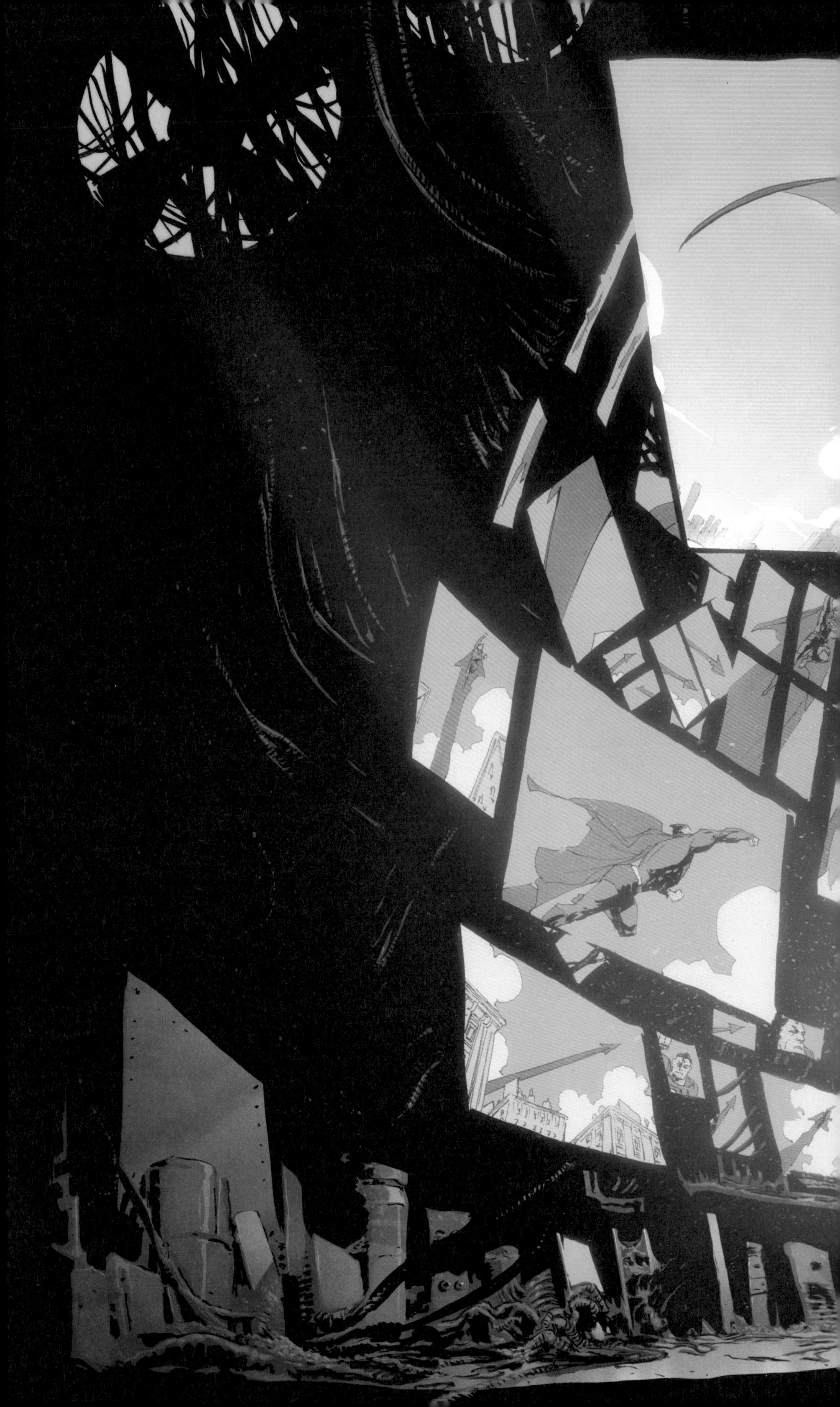

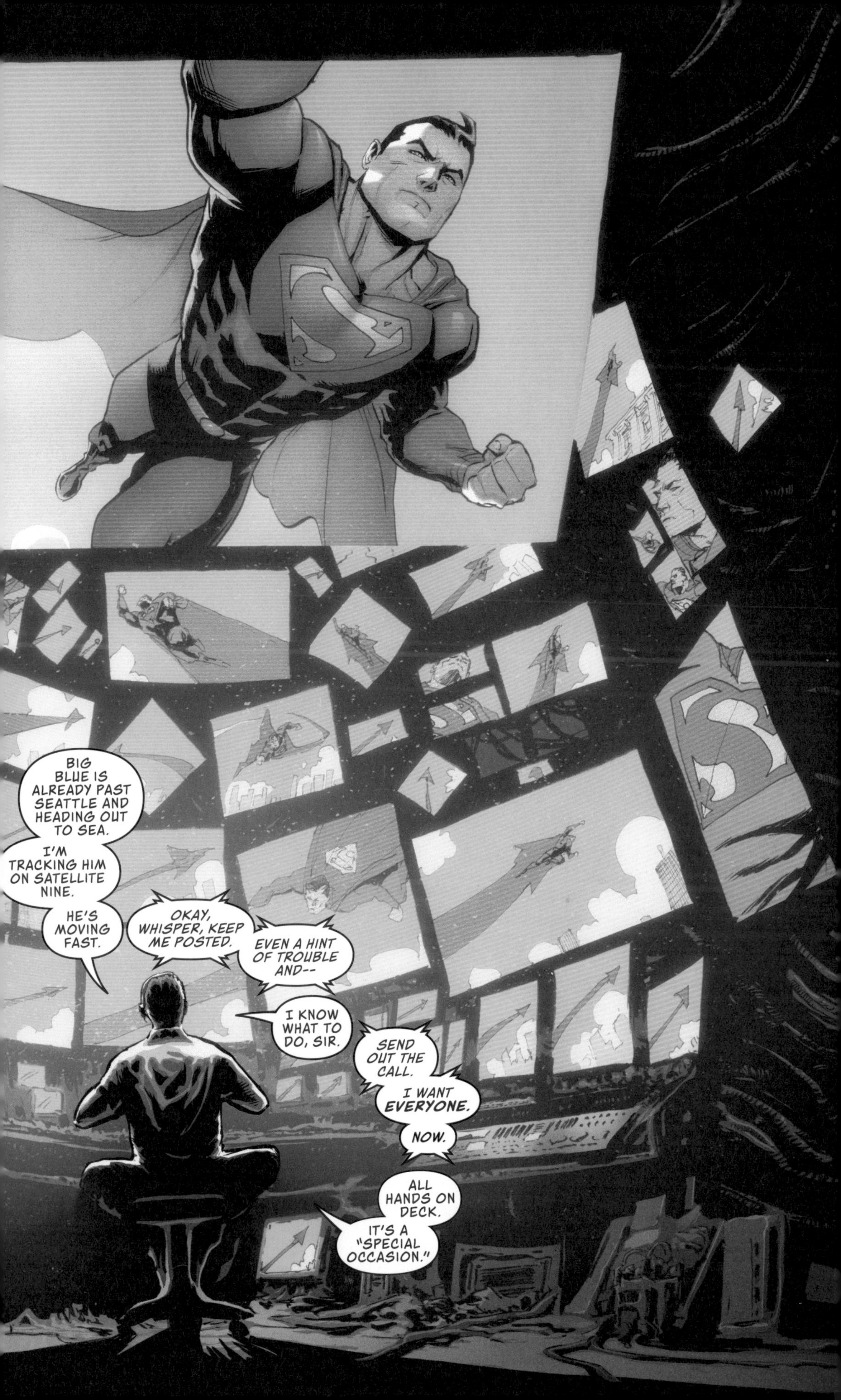
BIG BLUE IS ALREADY PAST SEATTLE AND HEADING OUT TO SEA.
I'M TRACKING HIM ON SATELLITE NINE.
HE'S MOVING FAST.
OKAY, WHISPER, KEEP ME POSTED.
EVEN A HINT OF TROUBLE AND--
I KNOW WHAT TO DO, SIR.
SEND OUT THE CALL.
I WANT EVERYONE.
NOW.
ALL HANDS ON DECK.
IT'S A "SPECIAL OCCASION."

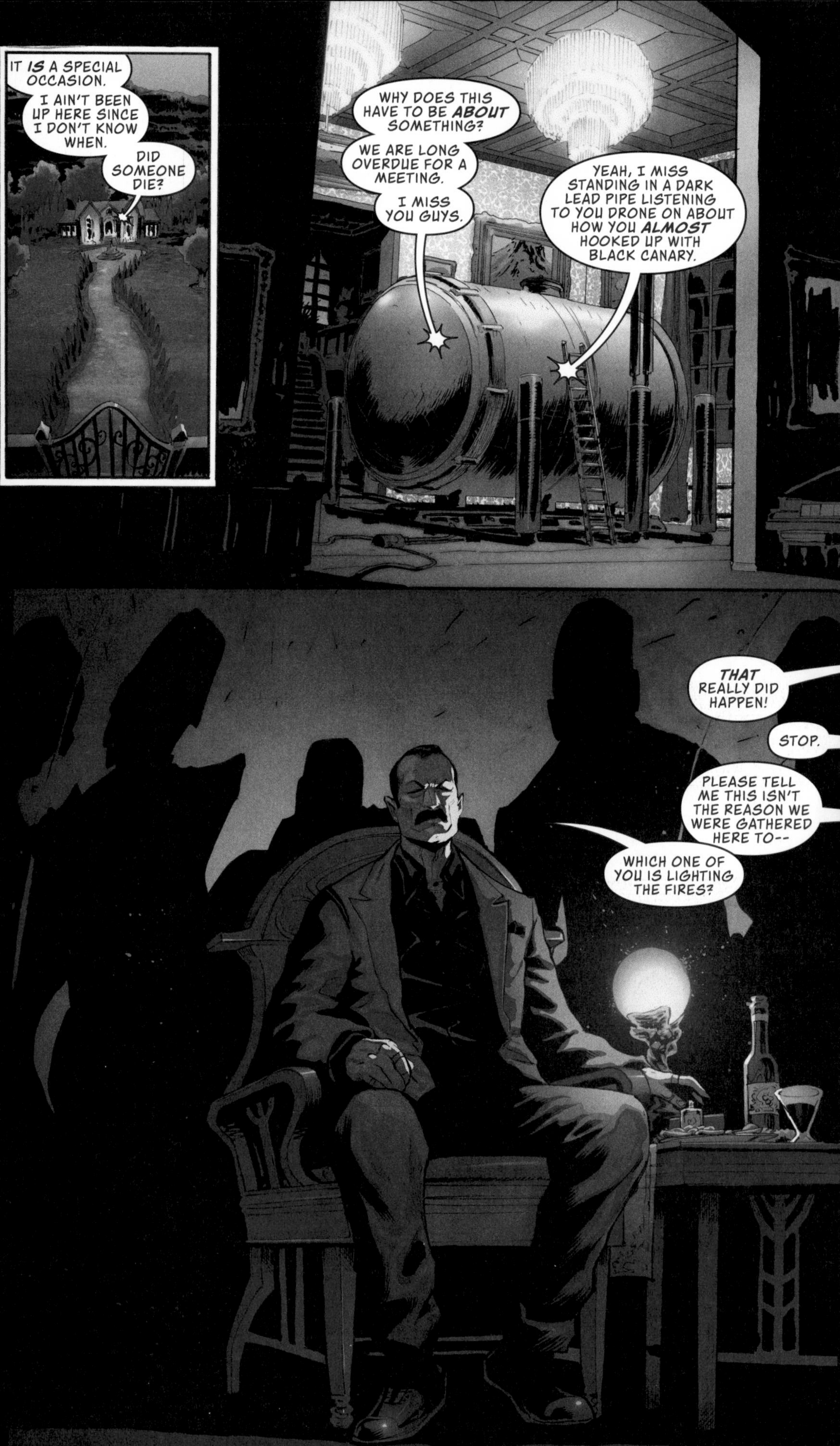
IT IS A SPECIAL OCCASION.
I AIN'T BEEN UP HERE SINCE I DON'T KNOW WHEN.
DID SOMEONE DIE?
WHY DOES THIS HAVE TO BE ABOUT SOMETHING?
WE ARE LONG OVERDUE FOR A MEETING.
I MISS YOU GUYS.
YEAH, I MISS STANDING IN A DARK LEAD PIPE LISTENING TO YOU DRONE ON ABOUT HOW YOU ALMOST HOOKED UP WITH BLACK CANARY.
THAT REALLY DID HAPPEN!
STOP.
PLEASE TELL ME THIS ISN'T THE REASON WE WERE GATHERED HERE TO--
WHICH ONE OF YOU IS LIGHTING THE FIRES?

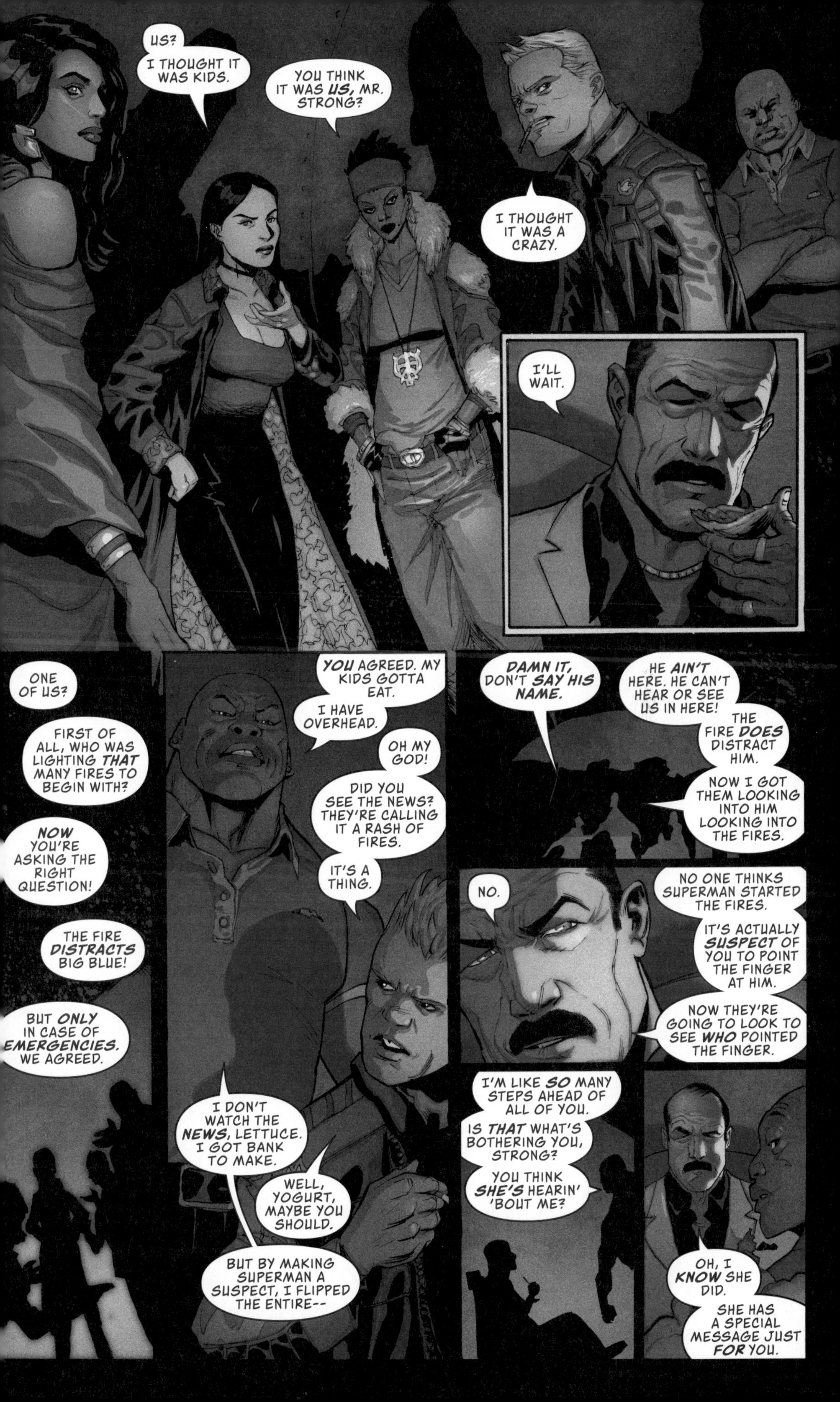
US?
I THOUGHT IT WAS KIDS.
YOU THINK IT WAS US, MR. STRONG?
I THOUGHT IT WAS A CRAZY.
I'LL WAIT.
ONE OF US?
FIRST OF ALL, WHO WAS LIGHTING THAT MANY FIRES TO BEGIN WITH?
NOW YOU'RE ASKING THE RIGHT QUESTION!
THE FIRE DISTRACTS BIG BLUE!
BUT ONLY IN CASE OF EMERGENCIES. WE AGREED.
YOU AGREED. MY KIDS GOTTA EAT.
I HAVE OVERHEAD.
OH MY GOD!
DID YOU SEE THE NEWS? THEY'RE CALLING IT A RASH OF FIRES.
IT'S A THING.
I DON'T WATCH THE NEWS, LETTUCE. I GOT BANK TO MAKE.
WELL, YOGURT, MAYBE YOU SHOULD.
BUT BY MAKING SUPERMAN A SUSPECT, I FLIPPED THE ENTIRE--
DAMN IT, DON'T SAY HIS NAME.
HE AIN'T HERE. HE CAN'T HEAR OR SEE US IN HERE!
THE FIRE DOES DISTRACT HIM.
NOW I GOT THEM LOOKING INTO HIM LOOKING INTO THE FIRES.
NO.
NO ONE THINKS SUPERMAN STARTED THE FIRES.
IT'S ACTUALLY SUSPECT OF YOU TO POINT THE FINGER AT HIM.
NOW THEY'RE GOING TO LOOK TO SEE WHO POINTED THE FINGER.
I'M LIKE SO MANY STEPS AHEAD OF ALL OF YOU.
IS THAT WHAT'S BOTHERING YOU, STRONG?
YOU THINK SHE'S HEARIN' 'BOUT ME?
OH, I KNOW SHE DID.
SHE HAS A SPECIAL MESSAGE JUST FOR YOU.

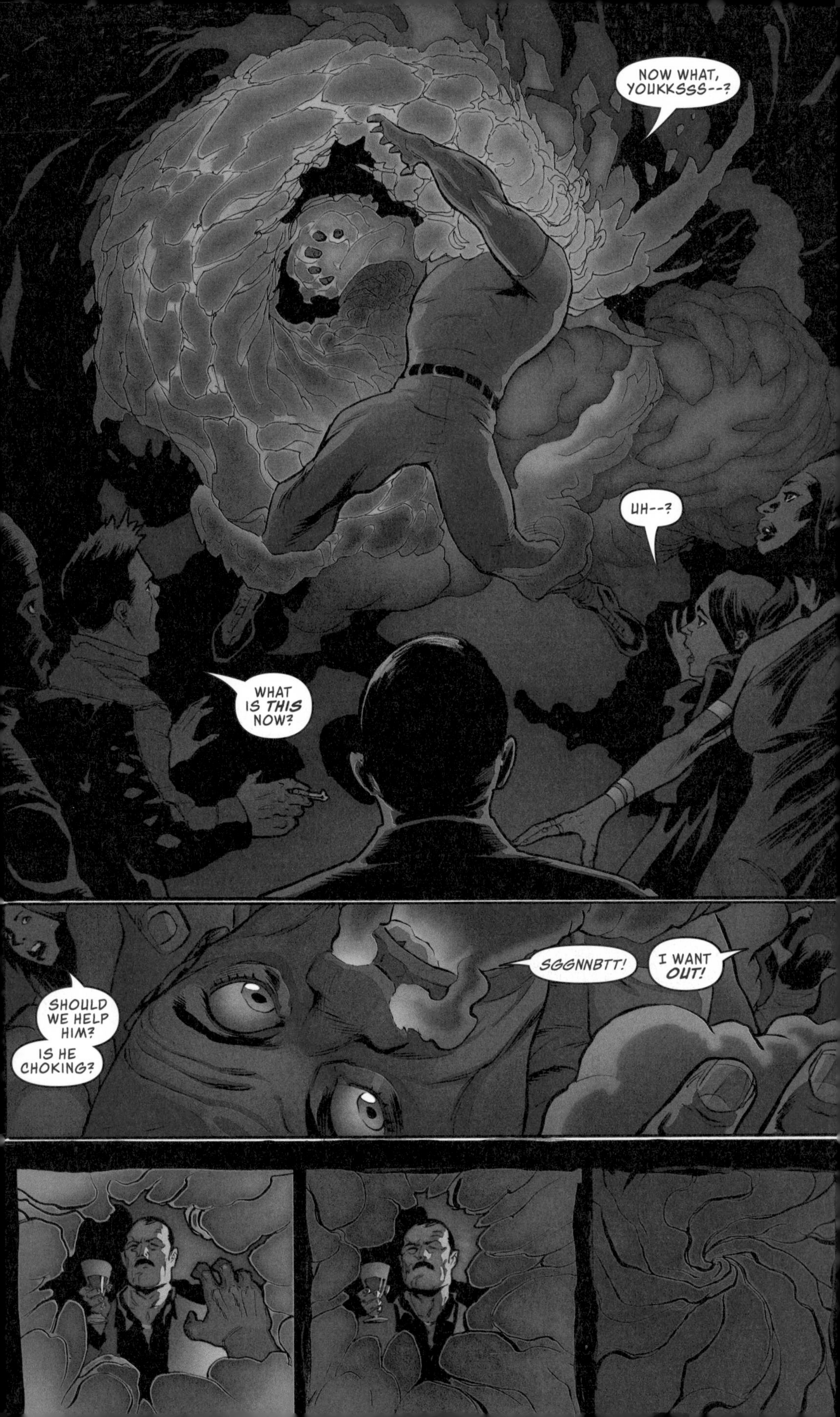
NOW WHAT, YOUKKSSS--?
UH--?
WHAT IS THIS NOW?
SHOULD WE HELP HIM?
IS HE CHOKING?
SGGNNBTT!
I WANT OUT!

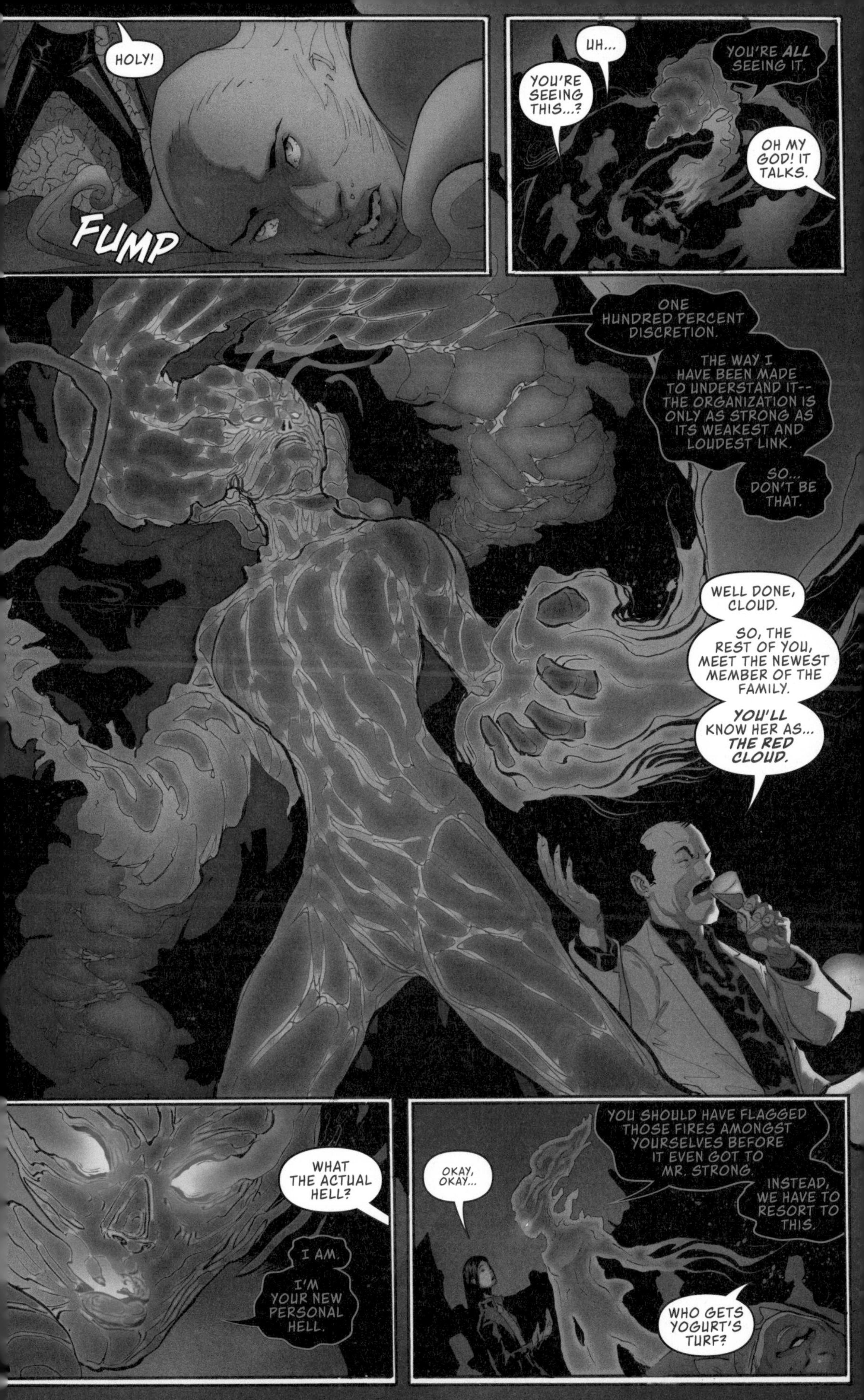
HOLY!
FUMP
UH...
YOU'RE SEEING THIS...?
YOU'RE ALL SEEING IT.
OH MY GOD! IT TALKS.
ONE HUNDRED PERCENT DISCRETION.
THE WAY I HAVE BEEN MADE TO UNDERSTAND IT-- THE ORGANIZATION IS ONLY AS STRONG AS ITS WEAKEST AND LOUDEST LINK.
SO... DON'T BE THAT.
WELL DONE, CLOUD.
SO, THE REST OF YOU, MEET THE NEWEST MEMBER OF THE FAMILY.
YOU'LL KNOW HER AS... THE RED CLOUD.
WHAT THE ACTUAL HELL?
I AM.
I'M YOUR NEW PERSONAL HELL.
OKAY, OKAY...
YOU SHOULD HAVE FLAGGED THOSE FIRES AMONGST YOURSELVES BEFORE IT EVEN GOT TO MR. STRONG.
INSTEAD, WE HAVE TO RESORT TO THIS.
WHO GETS YOGURT'S TURF?

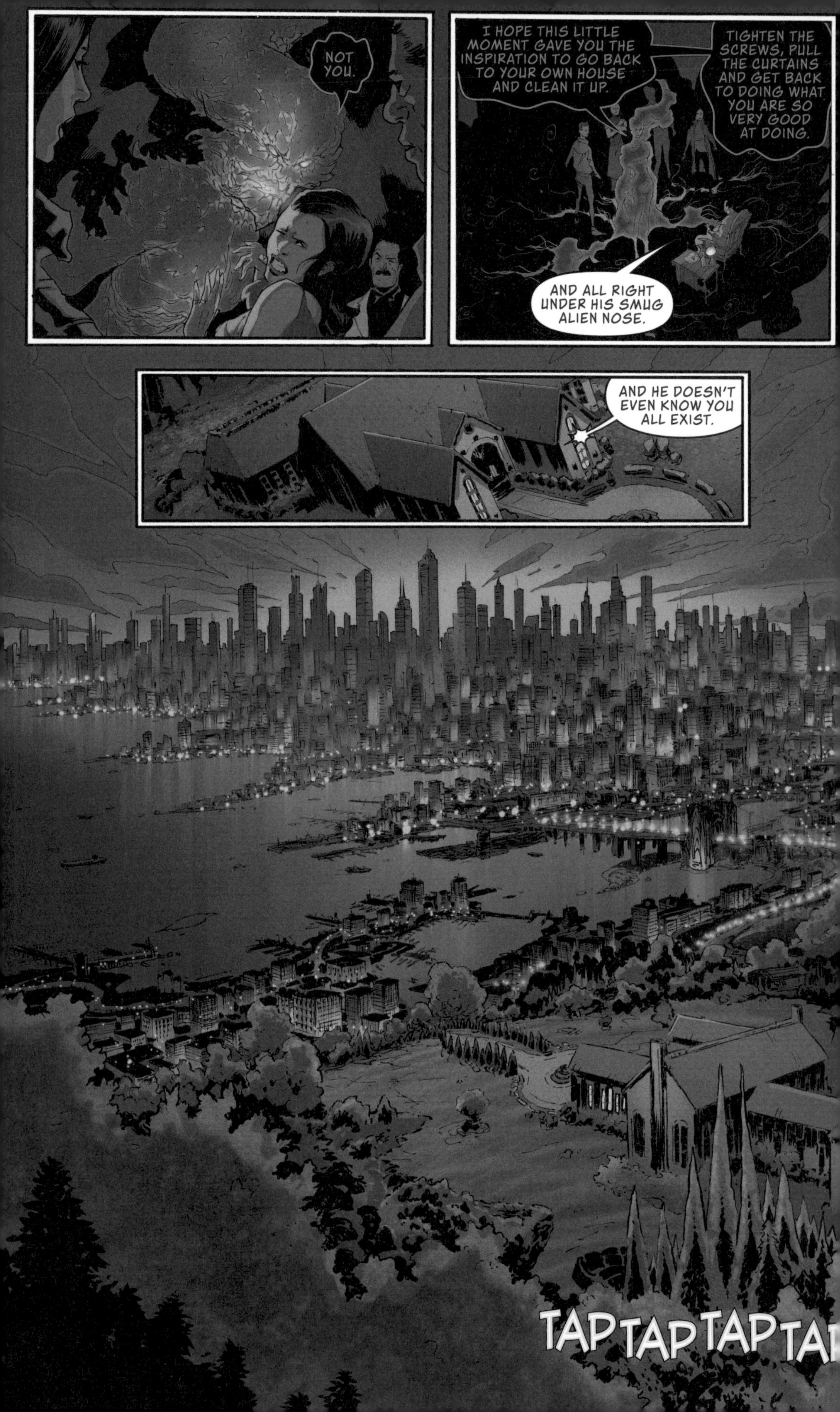
NOT YOU.
I HOPE THIS LITTLE MOMENT GAVE YOU THE INSPIRATION TO GO BACK TO YOUR OWN HOUSE AND CLEAN IT UP.
TIGHTEN THE SCREWS, PULL THE CURTAINS AND GET BACK TO DOING WHAT YOU ARE SO VERY GOOD AT DOING.
AND ALL RIGHT UNDER HIS SMUG ALIEN NOSE.
AND HE DOESN'T EVEN KNOW YOU ALL EXIST.
TAPTAPTAPTAP

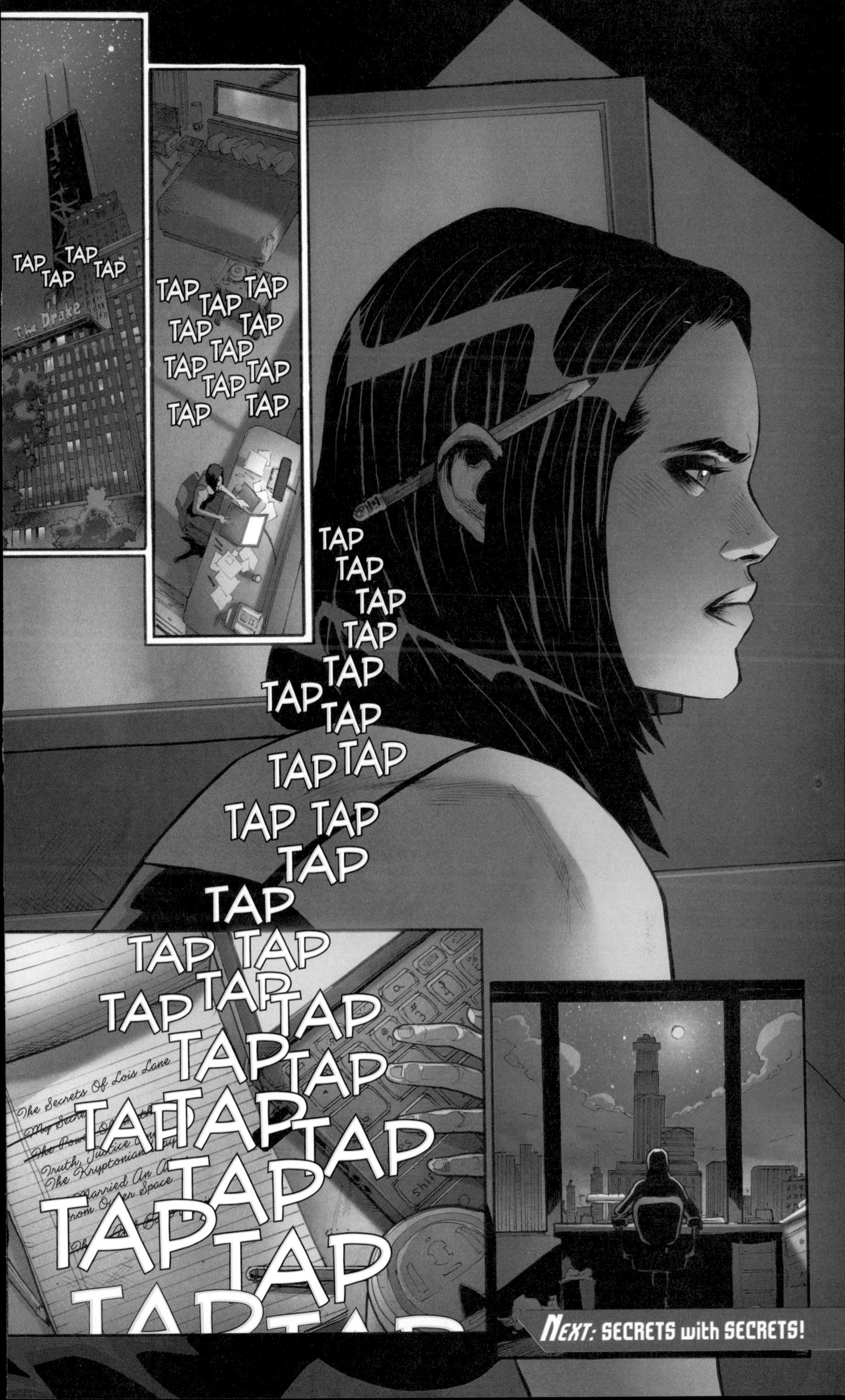

TAP TAP TAP TAP
The Drake
TAP TAP TAP
TAP TAP
TAP TAP
TAP TAP TAP
TAP TAP
TAP
TAP
TAP
TAP
TAP TAP
TAP
TAP TAP
TAP TAP
TAP
TAP
TAP TAP
TAP TAP TAP
TAP TAP
The Secrets Of Lois Lane
TAP TAP TAP TAP
TAP TAP
TAP TAP
NEXT: SECRETS with SECRETS!

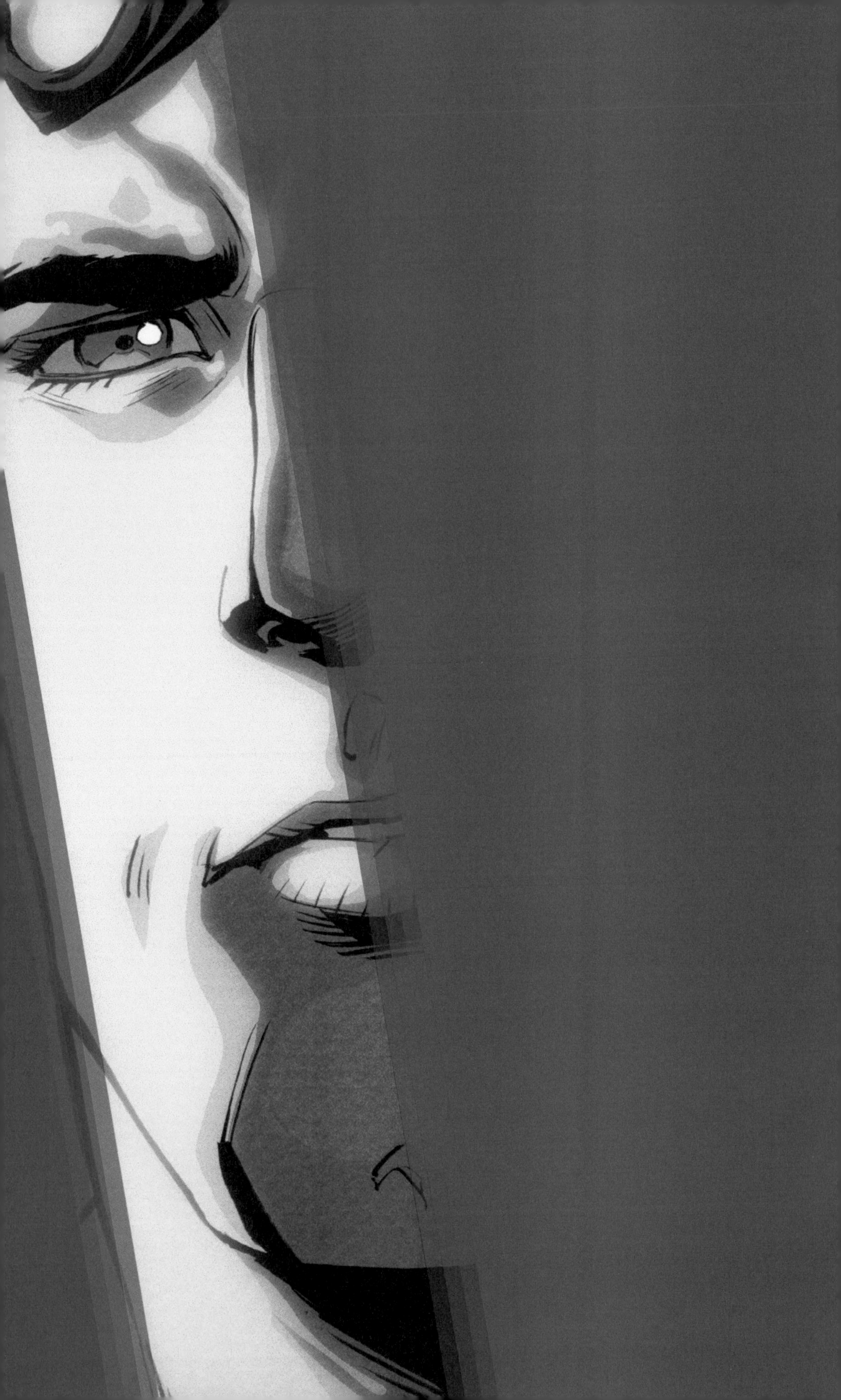

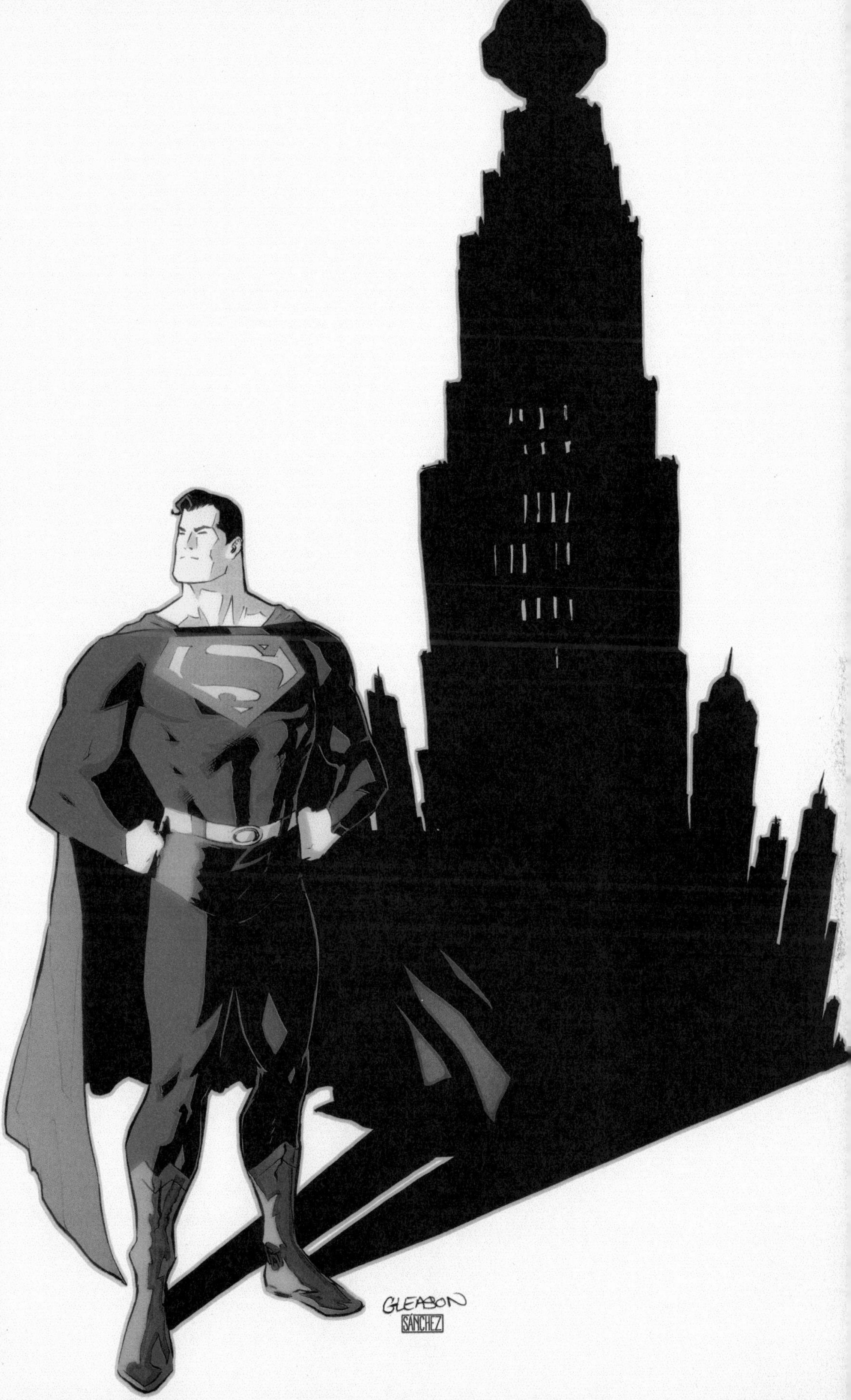
GLEASON
SÁNCHEZ

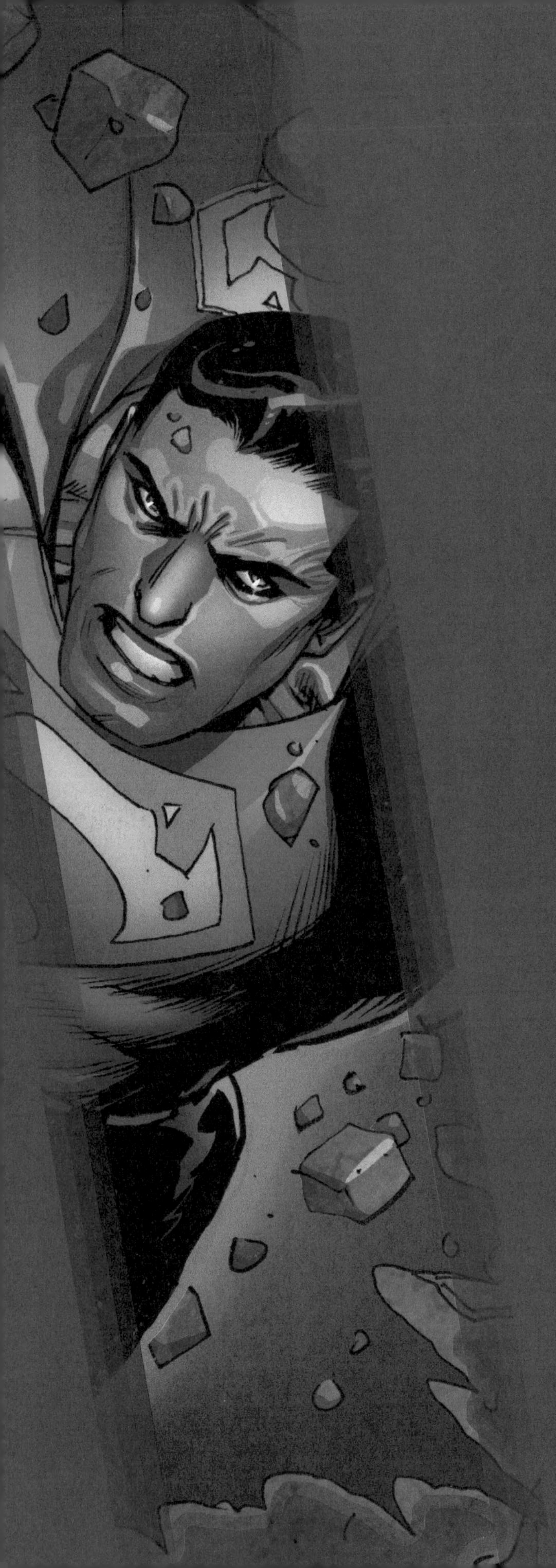

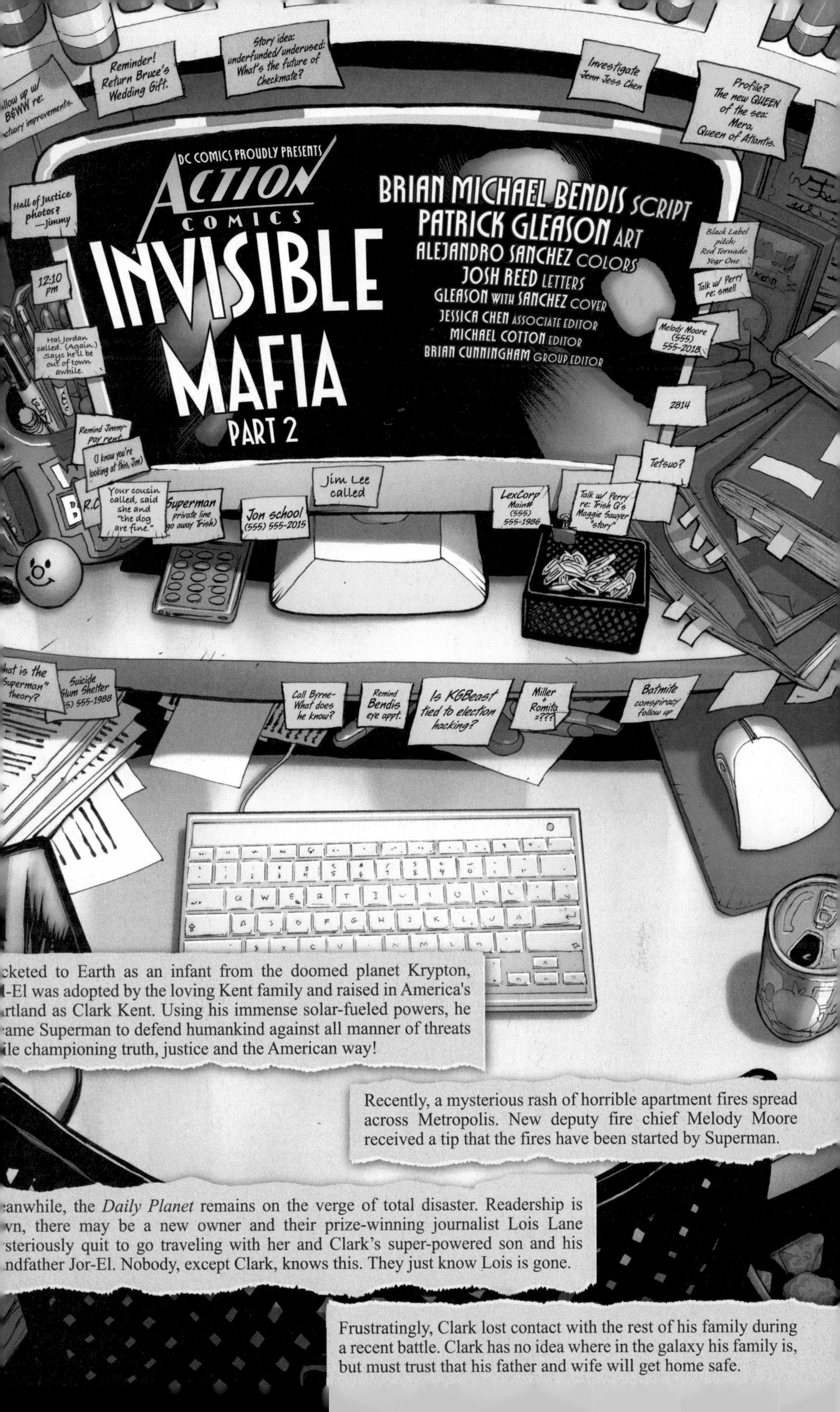

DC COMICS PROUDLY PRESENTS
ACTION COMICS
INVISIBLE MAFIA
PART 2
BRIAN MICHAEL BENDIS SCRIPT
PATRICK GLEASON ART
ALEJANDRO SANCHEZ COLORS
JOSH REED LETTERS
GLEASON WITH SANCHEZ COVER
JESSICA CHEN ASSOCIATE EDITOR
MICHAEL COTTON EDITOR
BRIAN CUNNINGHAM GROUP EDITOR
llow up w/ BEWW re: ctuary improvements.
Reminder! Return Bruce's Wedding Gift.
Story idea: underfunded/underused: What's the future of Checkmate?
Investigate Jenn Jess Chen
Profile? The new QUEEN of the sea: Mera, Queen of Atlantis.
Hall of Justice photos? —Jimmy
12:10 pm
Hal Jordan called. (Again.) Says he'll be out of town awhile.
Remind Jimmy- pay rent
(I know you're looking at this, Jim)
Your cousin called, said she and "the dog are fine."
Superman private line (go away Trish)
Jon school (555) 555-2015
Jim Lee called
LexCorp Main# (555) 555-1986
Talk w/ Perry re: Trish Q's Maggie Sawyer "story"
Tetsuo?
2814
Melody Moore (555) 555-2018
Talk w/ Perry re: smell
Black Label pitch: Red Tornado: Year One
hat is the Superman" theory?
Suicide Slum Shelter 5) 555-1988
Call Byrne- What does he know?
Remind Bendis eye appt.
Is KGBeast tied to election hacking?
Miller + Romita =???
Batmite conspiracy follow up
ckteted to Earth as an infant from the doomed planet Krypton, -El was adopted by the loving Kent family and raised in America's rtland as Clark Kent. Using his immense solar-fueled powers, he ame Superman to defend humankind against all manner of threats ile championing truth, justice and the American way!
Recently, a mysterious rash of horrible apartment fires spread across Metropolis. New deputy fire chief Melody Moore received a tip that the fires have been started by Superman.
anwhile, the Daily Planet remains on the verge of total disaster. Readership is wn, there may be a new owner and their prize-winning journalist Lois Lane steriously quit to go traveling with her and Clark's super-powered son and his ndfather Jor-El. Nobody, except Clark, knows this. They just know Lois is gone.
Frustratingly, Clark lost contact with the rest of his family during a recent battle. Clark has no idea where in the galaxy his family is, but must trust that his father and wife will get home safe.

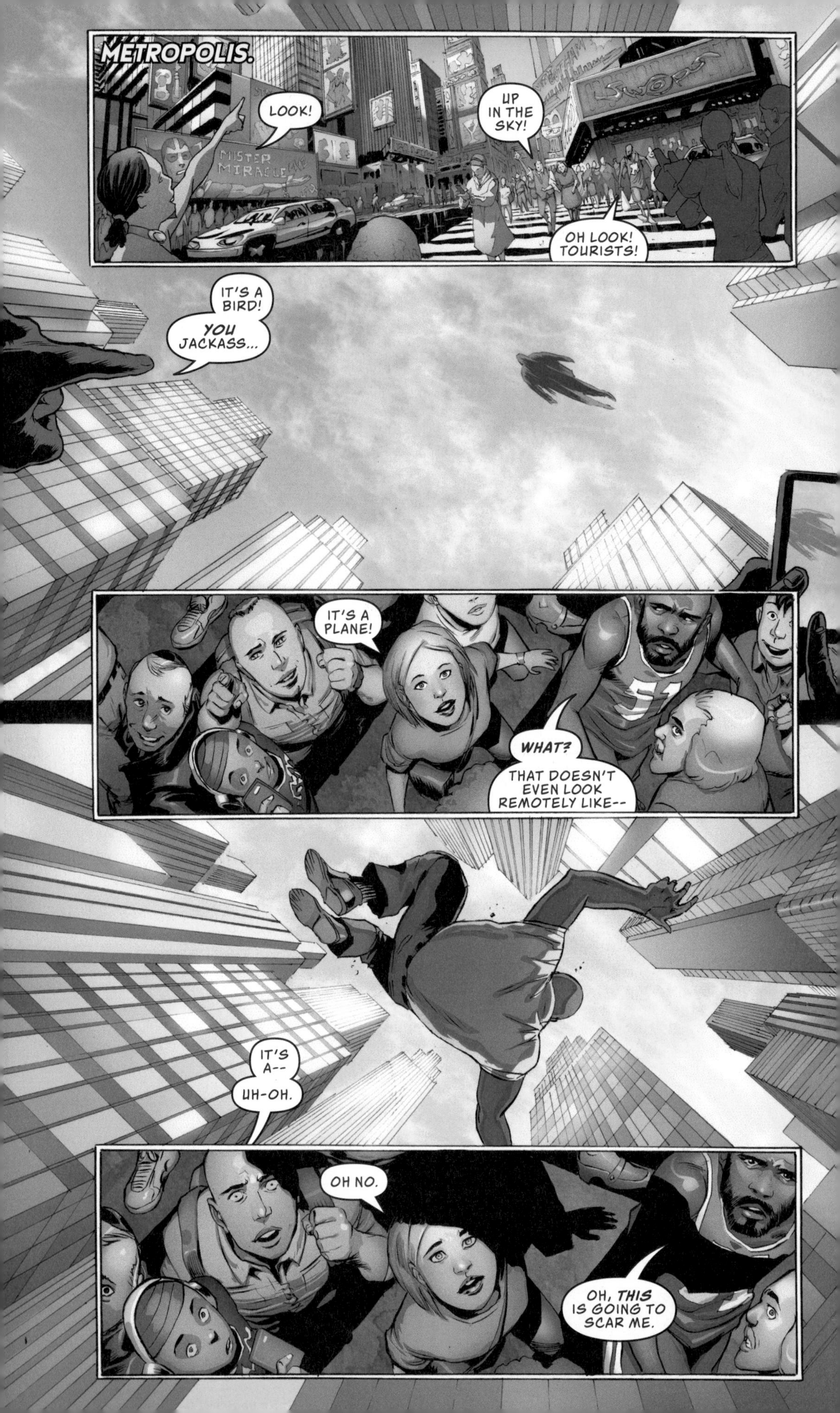
METROPOLIS.
LOOK!
UP IN THE SKY!
OH LOOK! TOURISTS!
IT'S A BIRD!
YOU JACKASS...
IT'S A PLANE!
WHAT?
THAT DOESN'T EVEN LOOK REMOTELY LIKE--
IT'S A--
UH-OH.
OH NO.
OH, THIS IS GOING TO SCAR ME.

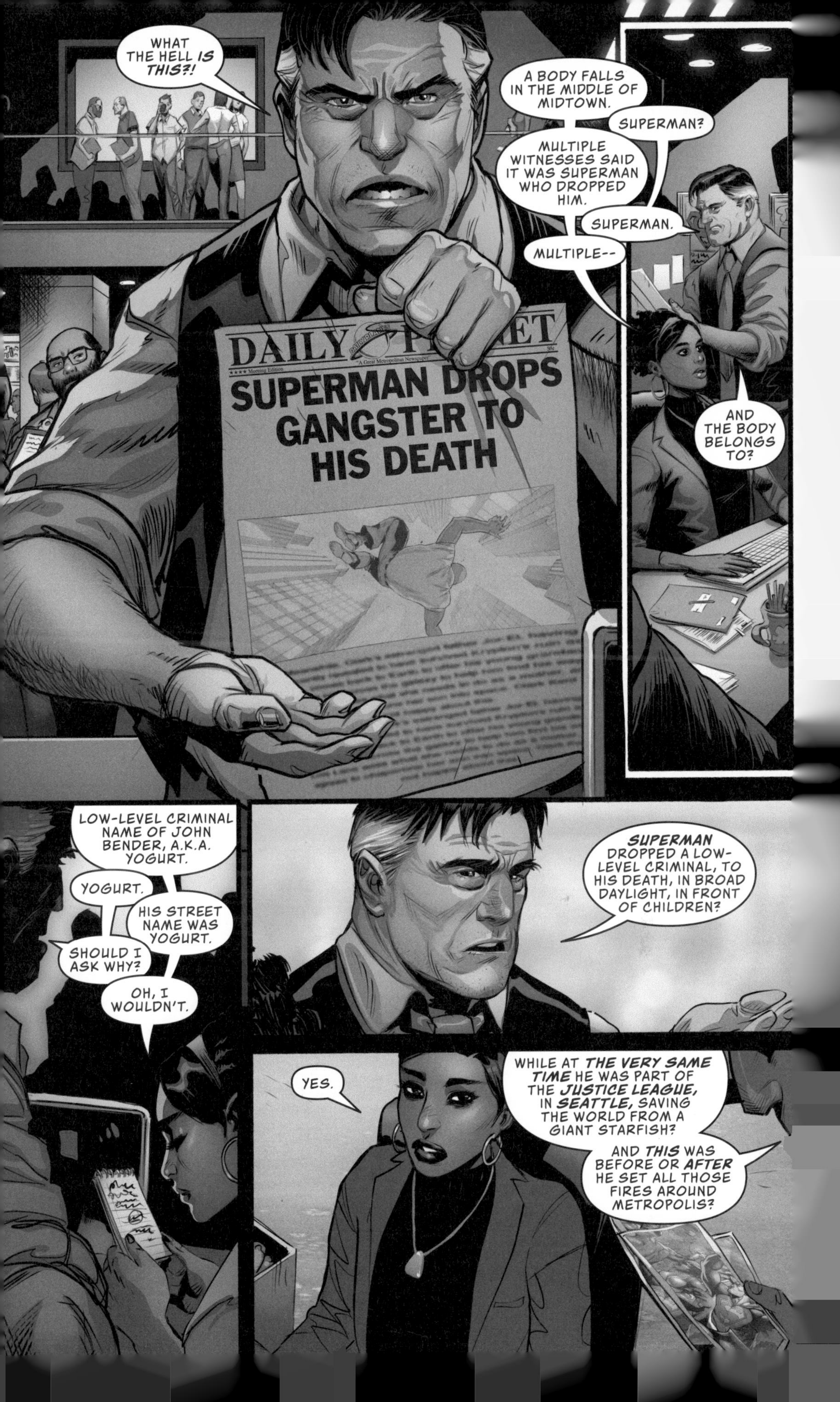
WHAT THE HELL IS THIS?!
DAILY PLANET
A Great Metropolitan Newspaper
Morning Edition
SUPERMAN DROPS GANGSTER TO HIS DEATH
A BODY FALLS IN THE MIDDLE OF MIDTOWN.
SUPERMAN?
MULTIPLE WITNESSES SAID IT WAS SUPERMAN WHO DROPPED HIM.
SUPERMAN.
MULTIPLE--
AND THE BODY BELONGS TO?
LOW-LEVEL CRIMINAL NAME OF JOHN BENDER, A.K.A. YOGURT.
YOGURT.
HIS STREET NAME WAS YOGURT.
SHOULD I ASK WHY?
OH, I WOULDN'T.
SUPERMAN DROPPED A LOW-LEVEL CRIMINAL, TO HIS DEATH, IN BROAD DAYLIGHT, IN FRONT OF CHILDREN?
YES.
WHILE AT THE VERY SAME TIME HE WAS PART OF THE JUSTICE LEAGUE, IN SEATTLE, SAVING THE WORLD FROM A GIANT STARFISH?
AND THIS WAS BEFORE OR AFTER HE SET ALL THOSE FIRES AROUND METROPOLIS?

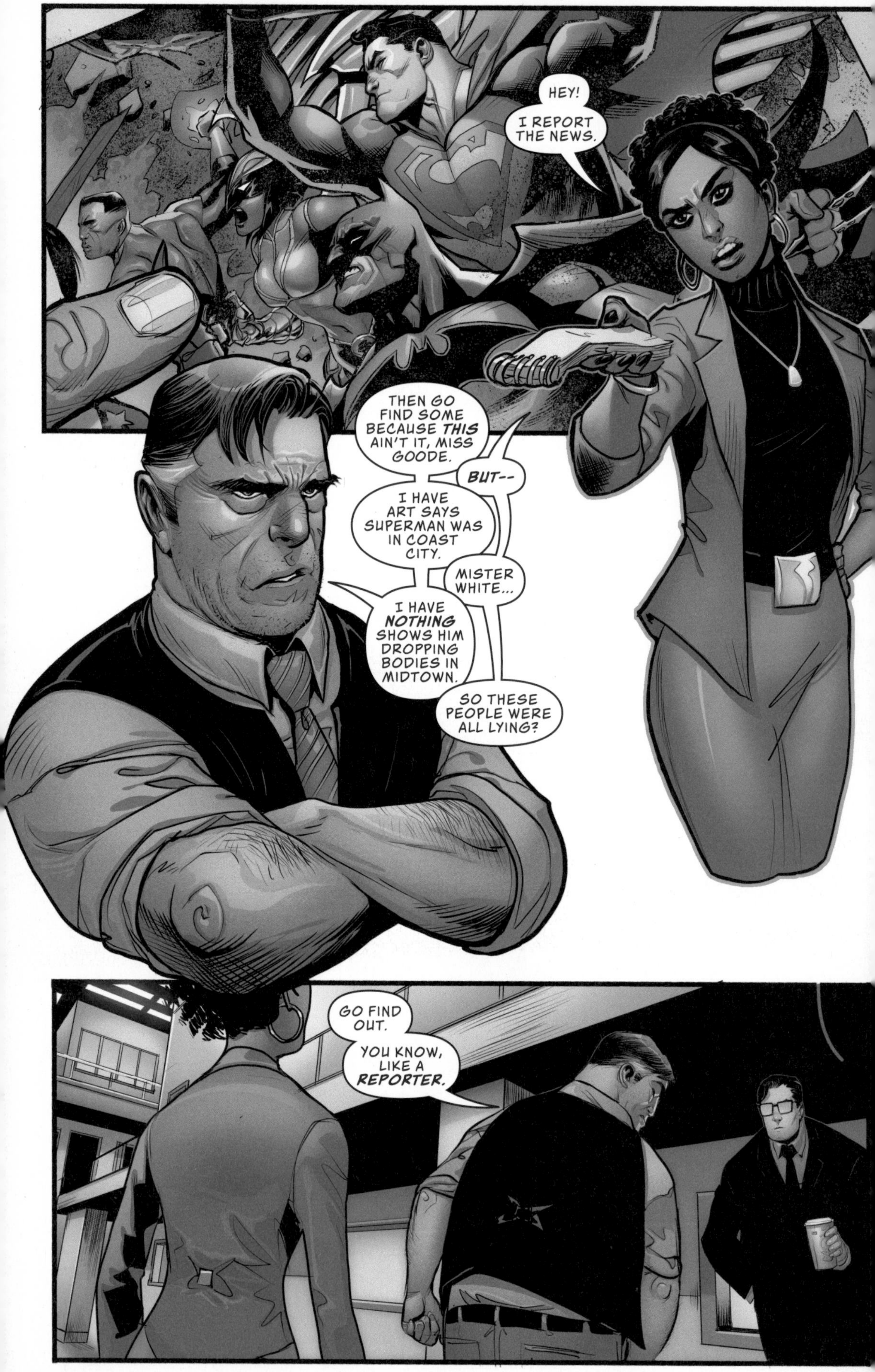
HEY!
I REPORT THE NEWS.
THEN GO FIND SOME BECAUSE THIS AIN'T IT, MISS GOODE.
BUT--
I HAVE ART SAYS SUPERMAN WAS IN COAST CITY.
MISTER WHITE...
I HAVE NOTHING SHOWS HIM DROPPING BODIES IN MIDTOWN.
SO THESE PEOPLE WERE ALL LYING?
GO FIND OUT.
YOU KNOW, LIKE A REPORTER.

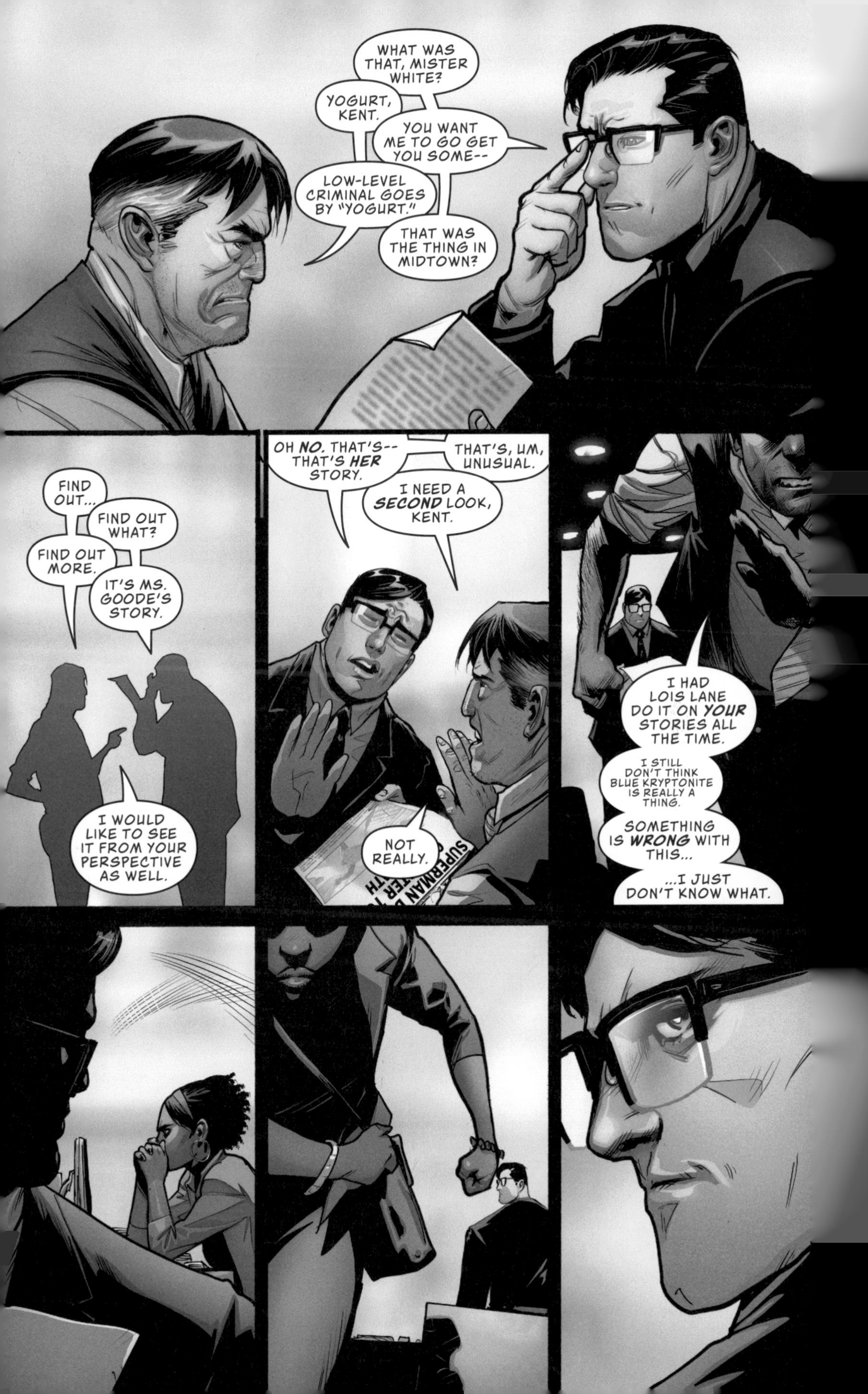
WHAT WAS THAT, MISTER WHITE?
YOGURT, KENT.
YOU WANT ME TO GO GET YOU SOME--
LOW-LEVEL CRIMINAL GOES BY "YOGURT."
THAT WAS THE THING IN MIDTOWN?
FIND OUT...
FIND OUT WHAT?
FIND OUT MORE.
IT'S MS. GOODE'S STORY.
I WOULD LIKE TO SEE IT FROM YOUR PERSPECTIVE AS WELL.
OH NO. THAT'S-- THAT'S HER STORY.
THAT'S, UM, UNUSUAL.
I NEED A SECOND LOOK, KENT.
NOT REALLY.
I HAD LOIS LANE DO IT ON YOUR STORIES ALL THE TIME.
I STILL DON'T THINK BLUE KRYPTONITE IS REALLY A THING.
SOMETHING IS WRONG WITH THIS...
...I JUST DON'T KNOW WHAT.

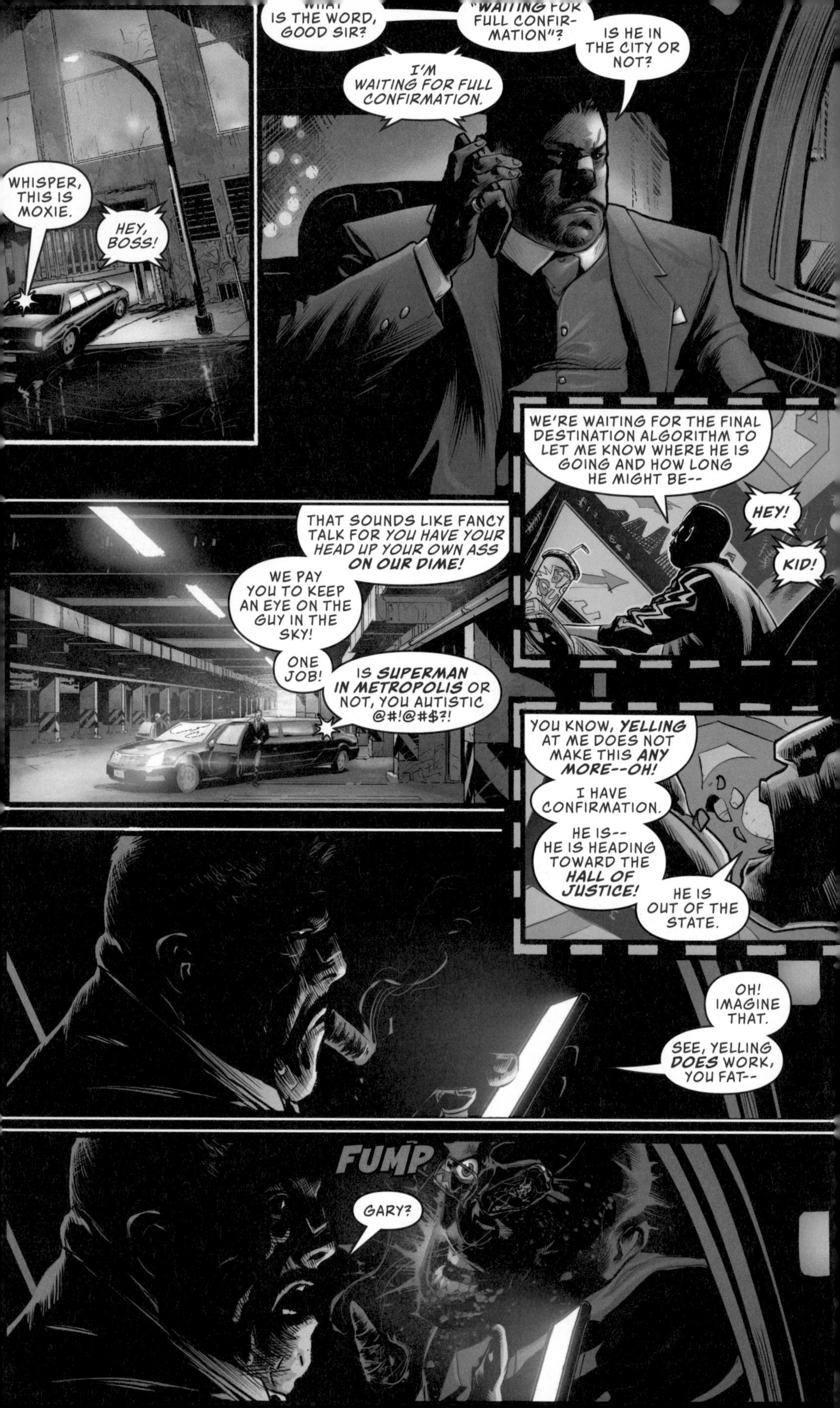
WHISPER, THIS IS MOXIE.
HEY, BOSS!
IS THE WORD, GOOD SIR?
I'M WAITING FOR FULL CONFIRMATION.
"WAITING FOR FULL CONFIRMATION"?
IS HE IN THE CITY OR NOT?
WE'RE WAITING FOR THE FINAL DESTINATION ALGORITHM TO LET ME KNOW WHERE HE IS GOING AND HOW LONG HE MIGHT BE--
HEY!
KID!
THAT SOUNDS LIKE FANCY TALK FOR YOU HAVE YOUR HEAD UP YOUR OWN ASS ON OUR DIME!
WE PAY YOU TO KEEP AN EYE ON THE GUY IN THE SKY!
ONE JOB!
IS SUPERMAN IN METROPOLIS OR NOT, YOU AUTISTIC @#!@#$?!
YOU KNOW, YELLING AT ME DOES NOT MAKE THIS ANY MORE--OH!
I HAVE CONFIRMATION.
HE IS-- HE IS HEADING TOWARD THE HALL OF JUSTICE!
HE IS OUT OF THE STATE.
OH! IMAGINE THAT.
SEE, YELLING DOES WORK, YOU FAT--
FUMP
GARY?

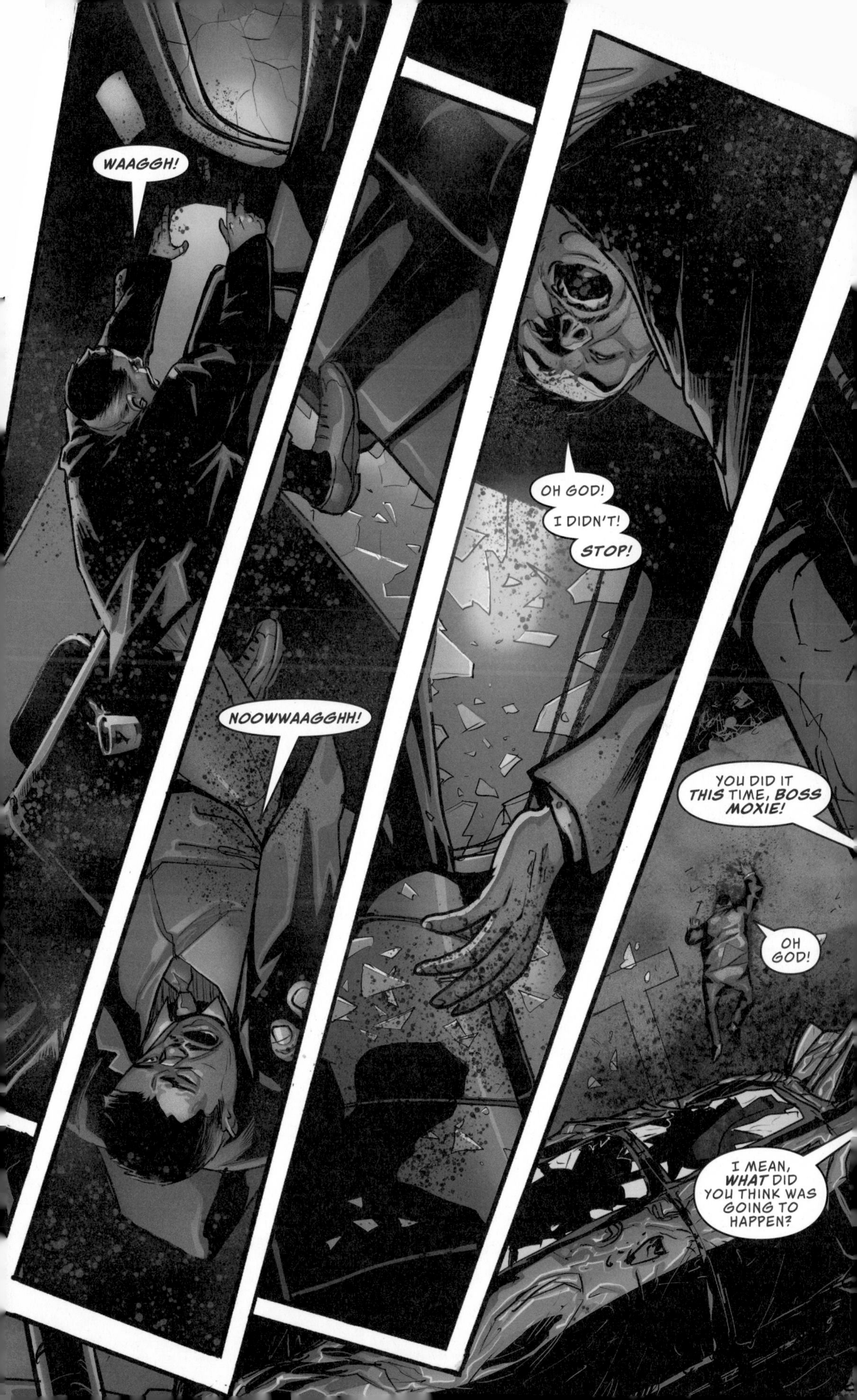
WAAGGH!
NOOWWAAGGHH!
OH GOD!
I DIDN'T!
STOP!
YOU DID IT THIS TIME, BOSS MOXIE!
OH GOD!
I MEAN, WHAT DID YOU THINK WAS GOING TO HAPPEN?

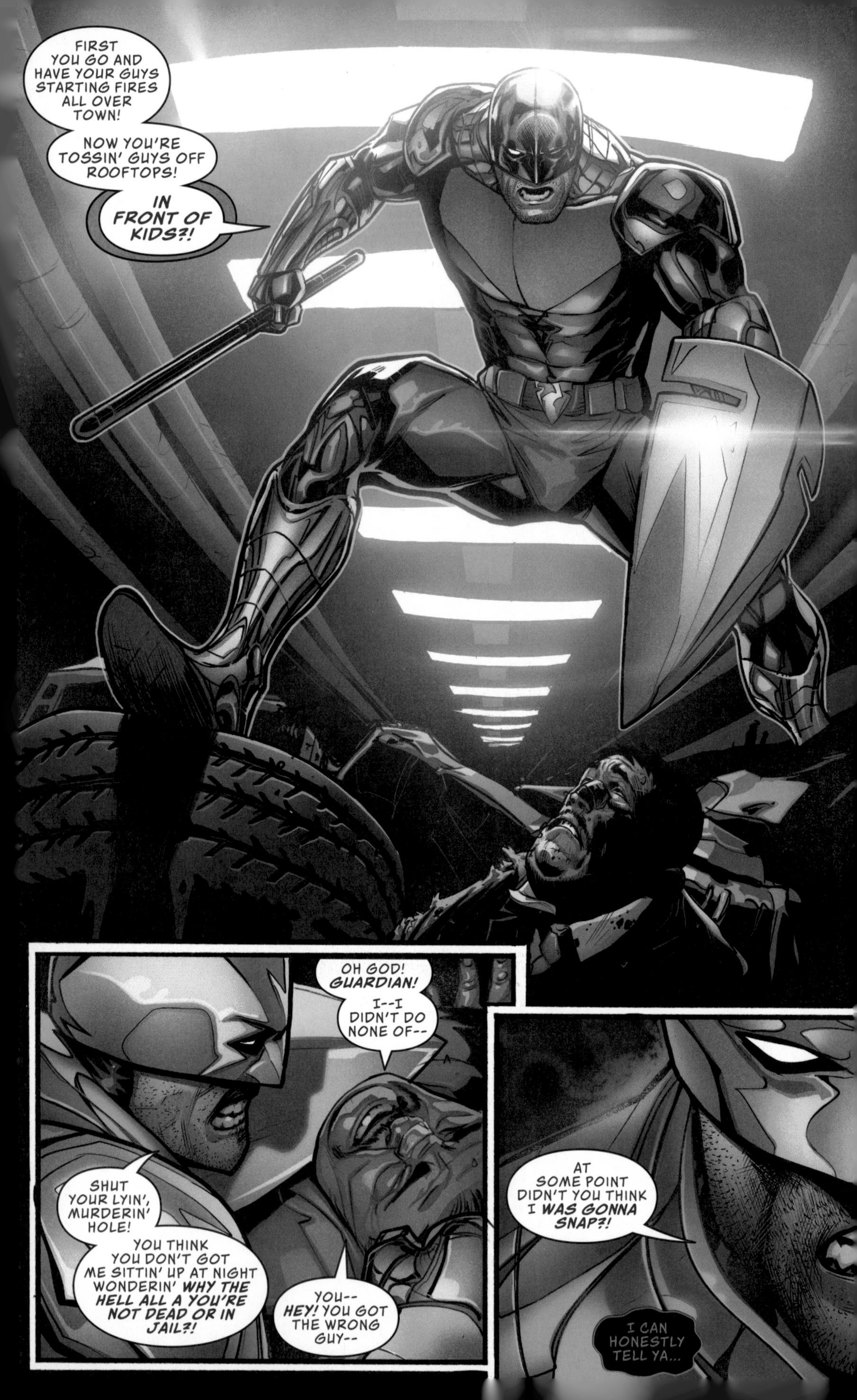
FIRST YOU GO AND HAVE YOUR GUYS STARTING FIRES ALL OVER TOWN!
NOW YOU'RE TOSSIN' GUYS OFF ROOFTOPS!
IN FRONT OF KIDS?!
OH GOD! GUARDIAN!
I--I DIDN'T DO NONE OF--
SHUT YOUR LYIN', MURDERIN' HOLE!
YOU THINK YOU DON'T GOT ME SITTIN' UP AT NIGHT WONDERIN' WHY THE HELL ALL A YOU'RE NOT DEAD OR IN JAIL?!
YOU-- HEY! YOU GOT THE WRONG GUY--
AT SOME POINT DIDN'T YOU THINK I WAS GONNA SNAP?!
I CAN HONESTLY TELL YA...

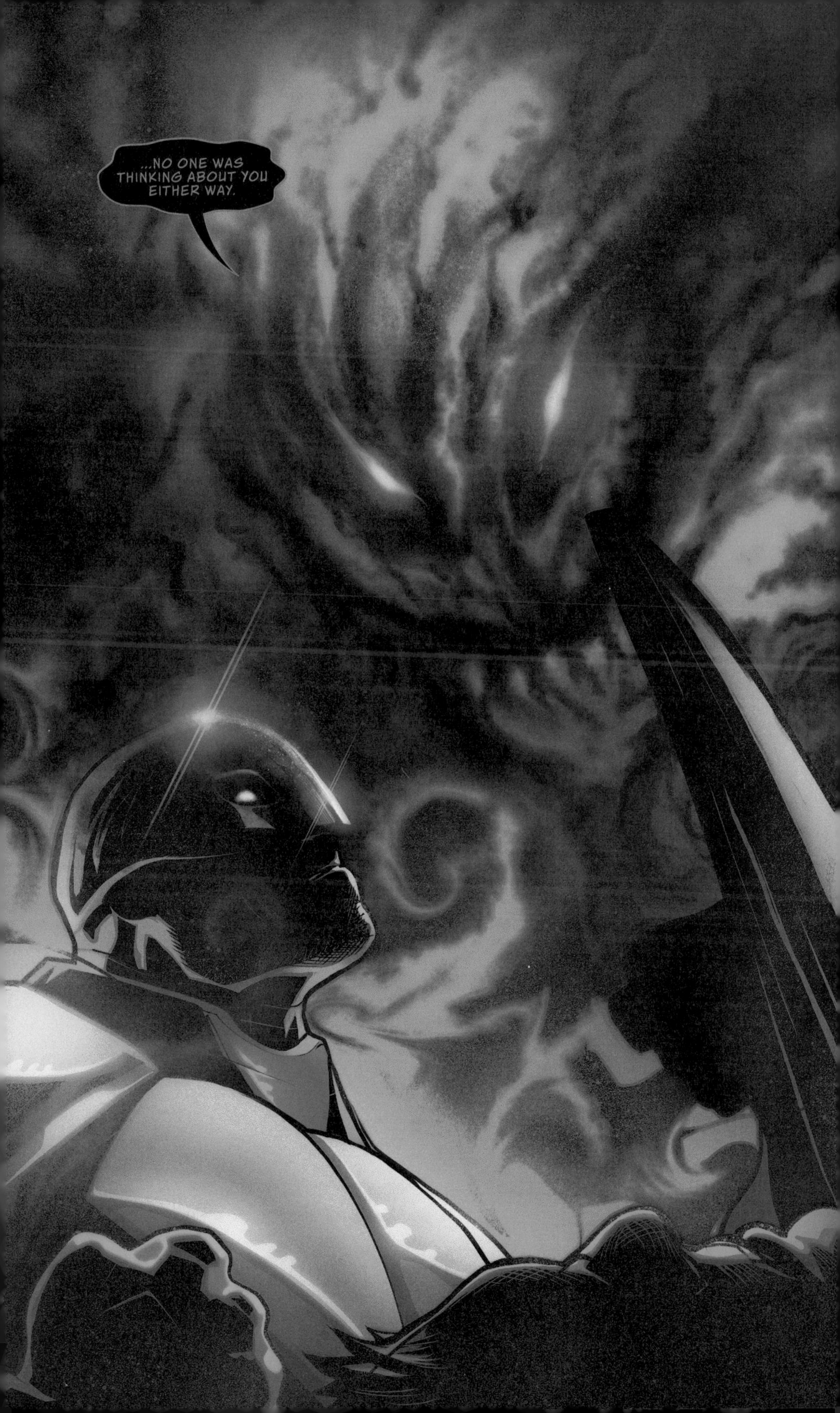
...NO ONE WAS THINKING ABOUT YOU EITHER WAY.

METROPOLIS GENERAL HOSPITAL.

OKAY, I'M HERE!

UH, HI.

I'M THE ATTENDING DOCTOR.

HI. MAGGIE SAWYER. METROPOLIS SPECIAL CRIMES.

THAT WAS FAST.

WE WERE IN THE CAFETERIA.

IT'S BEEN THAT KIND OF WEEK.

DAMN! IT *IS THE* GUARDIAN!

I WAS *HOPING* IT WAS A FAKE.

THIS-- *THIS* IS HEART-BREAKING.

HE WAS A COP ONCE, RIGHT?

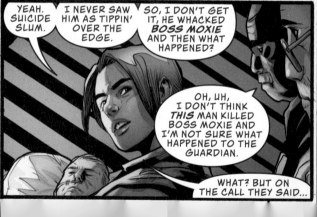

YEAH. SUICIDE SLUM.

I NEVER SAW HIM AS TIPPIN' OVER THE EDGE.

SO, I DON'T GET IT, HE WHACKED *BOSS MOXIE* AND THEN WHAT HAPPENED?

OH, UH, I DON'T THINK *THIS* MAN KILLED BOSS MOXIE AND I'M NOT SURE WHAT HAPPENED TO THE GUARDIAN.

WHAT? BUT ON THE CALL THEY SAID...

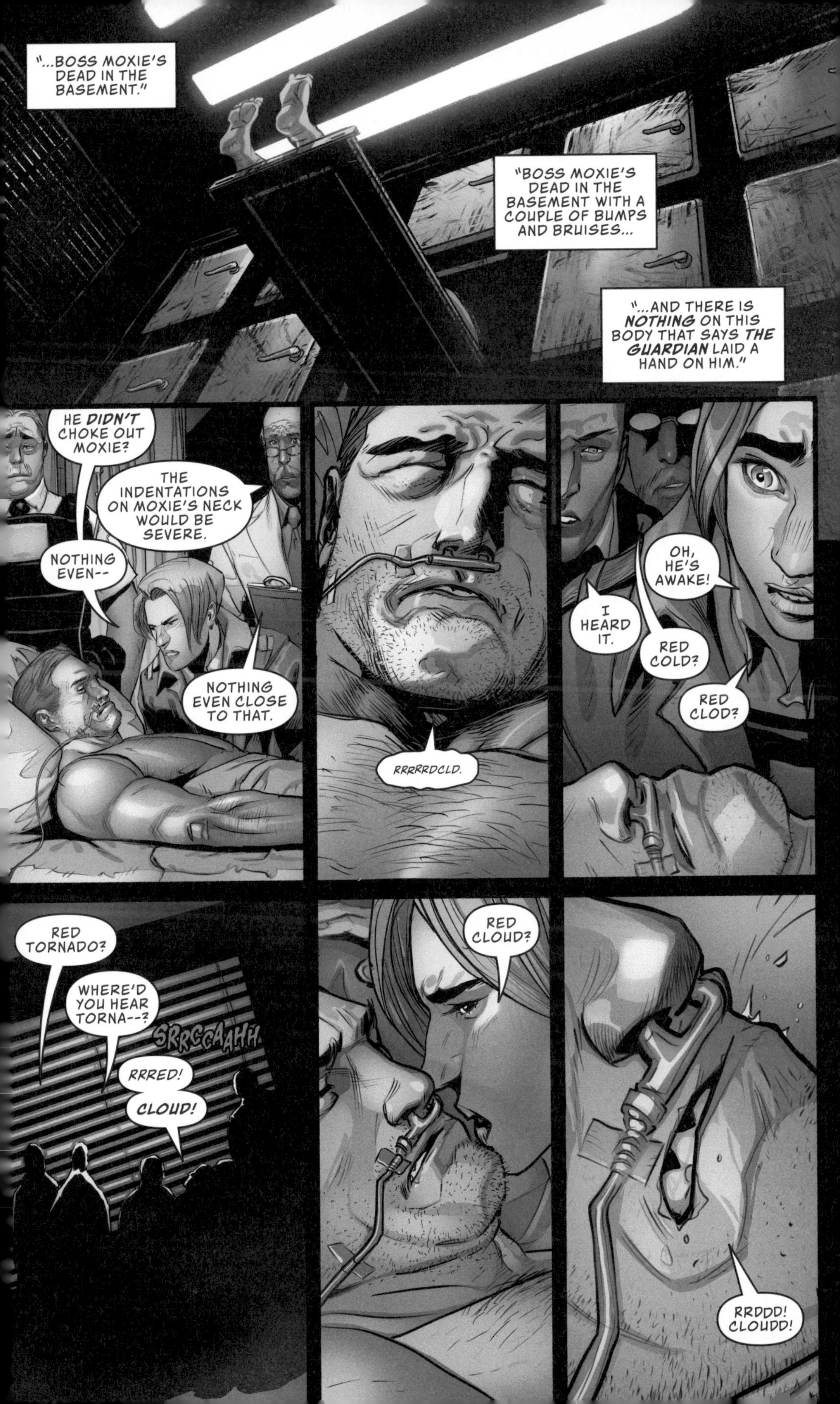
"...BOSS MOXIE'S DEAD IN THE BASEMENT."
"BOSS MOXIE'S DEAD IN THE BASEMENT WITH A COUPLE OF BUMPS AND BRUISES...
"...AND THERE IS NOTHING ON THIS BODY THAT SAYS THE GUARDIAN LAID A HAND ON HIM."
HE DIDN'T CHOKE OUT MOXIE?
THE INDENTATIONS ON MOXIE'S NECK WOULD BE SEVERE.
NOTHING EVEN--
NOTHING EVEN CLOSE TO THAT.
RRRRRDCLD.
OH, HE'S AWAKE!
I HEARD IT.
RED COLD?
RED CLOD?
RED TORNADO?
WHERE'D YOU HEAR TORNA--?
SRRCCAAHH
RRRED!
CLOUD!
RED CLOUD?
RRDDD! CLOUDD!

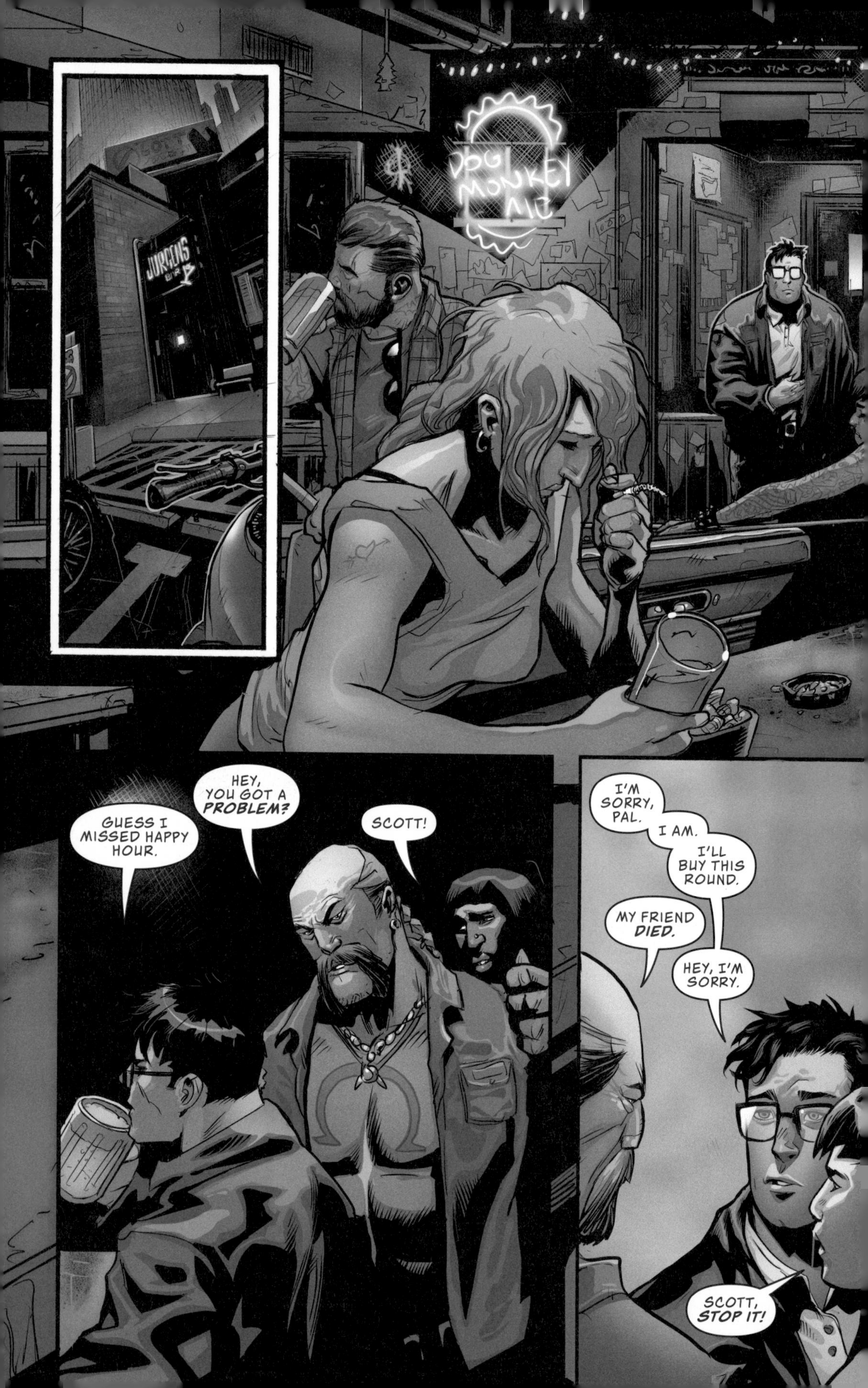
JURGENS
DOG MONKEY ALE
GUESS I MISSED HAPPY HOUR.
HEY, YOU GOT A PROBLEM?
SCOTT!
I'M SORRY, PAL.
I AM.
I'LL BUY THIS ROUND.
MY FRIEND DIED.
HEY, I'M SORRY.
SCOTT, STOP IT!

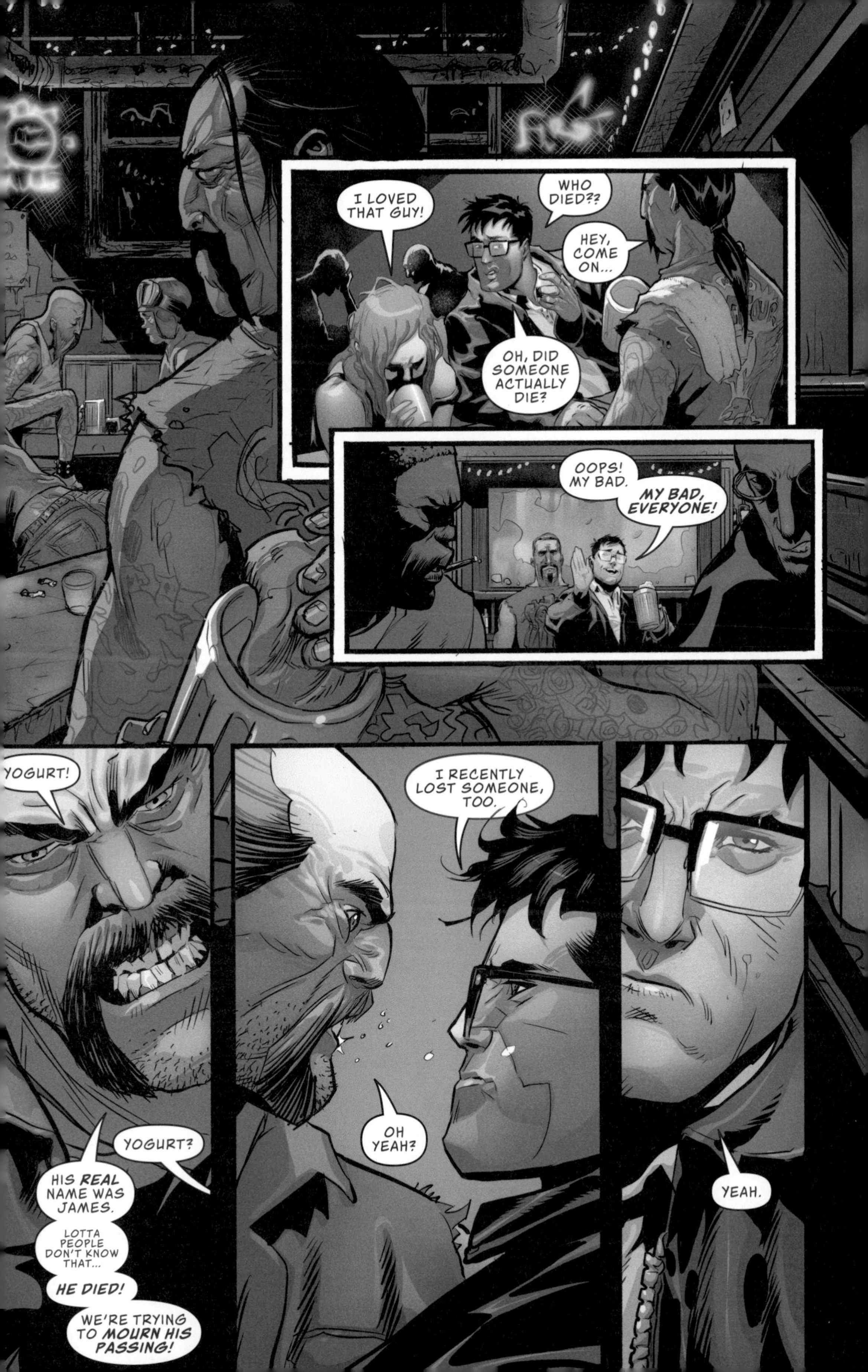
I LOVED THAT GUY!
WHO DIED??
HEY, COME ON...
OH, DID SOMEONE ACTUALLY DIE?
OOPS! MY BAD.
MY BAD, EVERYONE!
YOGURT!
I RECENTLY LOST SOMEONE, TOO.
YOGURT?
HIS REAL NAME WAS JAMES.
LOTTA PEOPLE DON'T KNOW THAT...
HE DIED!
WE'RE TRYING TO MOURN HIS PASSING!
OH YEAH?
YEAH.

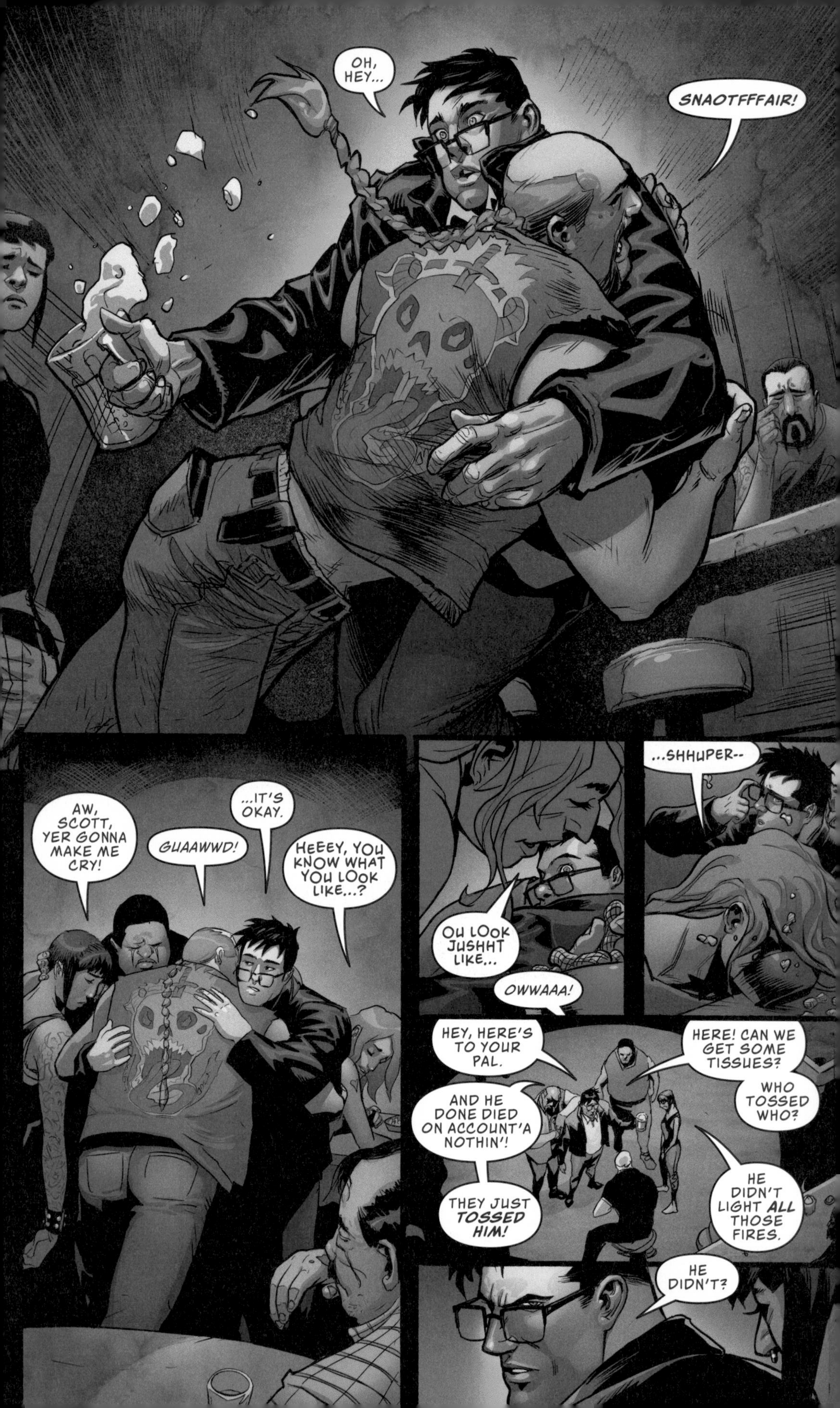
OH, HEY...
SNAOTFFFAIR!
AW, SCOTT, YER GONNA MAKE ME CRY!
GUAAWWD!
...IT'S OKAY.
HEEEY, YOU KNOW WHAT YOU LOOK LIKE...?
OU LOOK JUSHHT LIKE...
OWWAAA!
...SHHUPER--
HEY, HERE'S TO YOUR PAL.
AND HE DONE DIED ON ACCOUNT'A NOTHIN'!
THEY JUST TOSSED HIM!
HERE! CAN WE GET SOME TISSUES?
WHO TOSSED WHO?
HE DIDN'T LIGHT ALL THOSE FIRES.
HE DIDN'T?

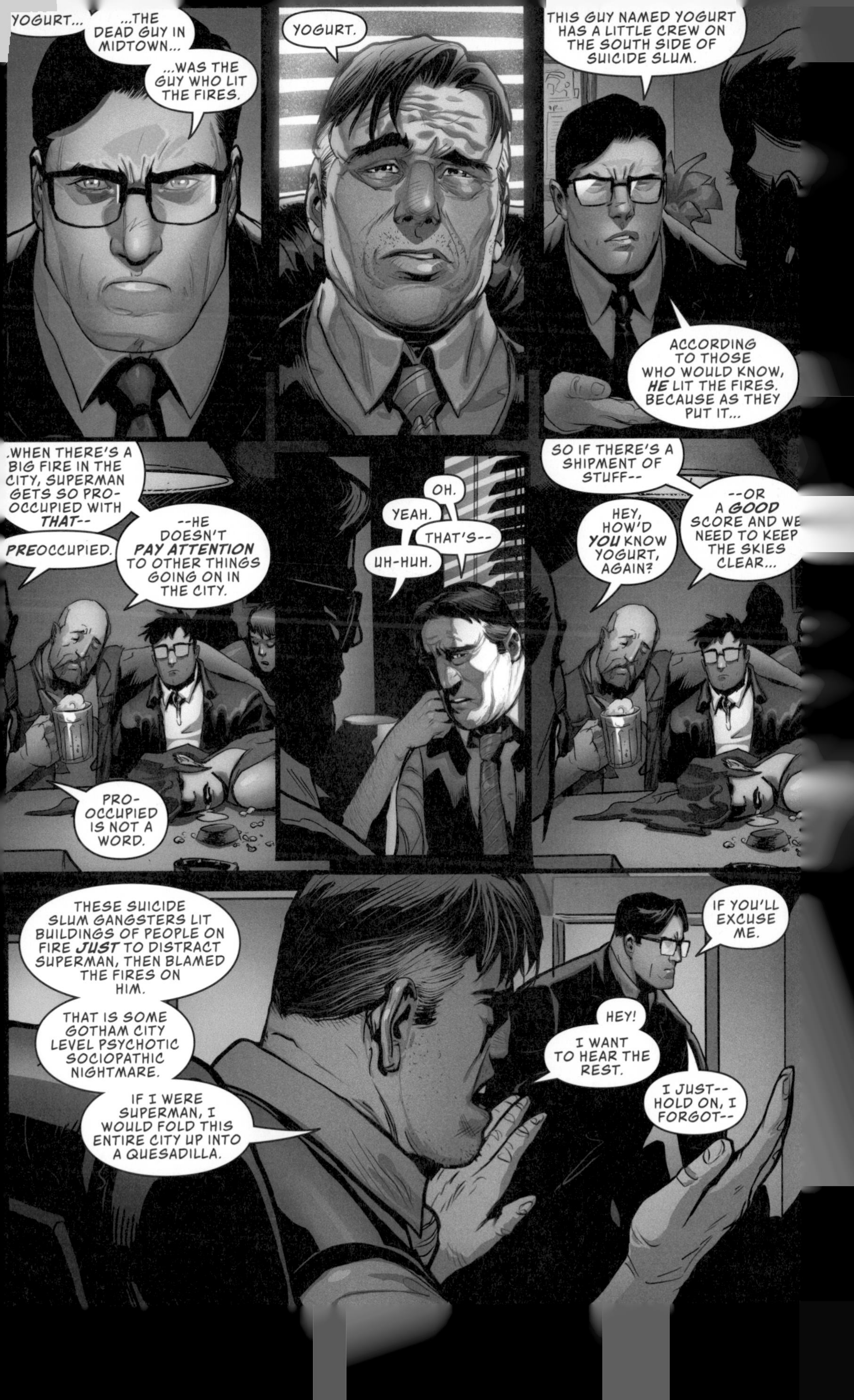

YOGURT...
...THE DEAD GUY IN MIDTOWN...
...WAS THE GUY WHO LIT THE FIRES.
YOGURT.
THIS GUY NAMED YOGURT HAS A LITTLE CREW ON THE SOUTH SIDE OF SUICIDE SLUM.
ACCORDING TO THOSE WHO KNOW, HE LIT THE FIRES. BECAUSE AS THEY PUT IT...
...WHEN THERE'S A BIG FIRE IN THE CITY, SUPERMAN GETS SO PRO-OCCUPIED WITH THAT--
PREOCCUPIED.
--HE DOESN'T PAY ATTENTION TO OTHER THINGS GOING ON IN THE CITY.
PRO-OCCUPIED IS NOT A WORD.
OH.
YEAH.
THAT'S--
UH-HUH.
SO IF THERE'S A SHIPMENT OF STUFF--
--OR A GOOD SCORE AND WE NEED TO KEEP THE SKIES CLEAR...
HEY, HOW'D YOU KNOW YOGURT, AGAIN?
THESE SUICIDE SLUM GANGSTERS LIT BUILDINGS OF PEOPLE ON FIRE JUST TO DISTRACT SUPERMAN, THEN BLAMED THE FIRES ON HIM.
THAT IS SOME GOTHAM CITY LEVEL PSYCHOTIC SOCIOPATHIC NIGHTMARE.
IF I WERE SUPERMAN, I WOULD FOLD THIS ENTIRE CITY UP INTO A QUESADILLA.
IF YOU'LL EXCUSE ME.
HEY!
I WANT TO HEAR THE REST.
I JUST--HOLD ON, I FORGOT--

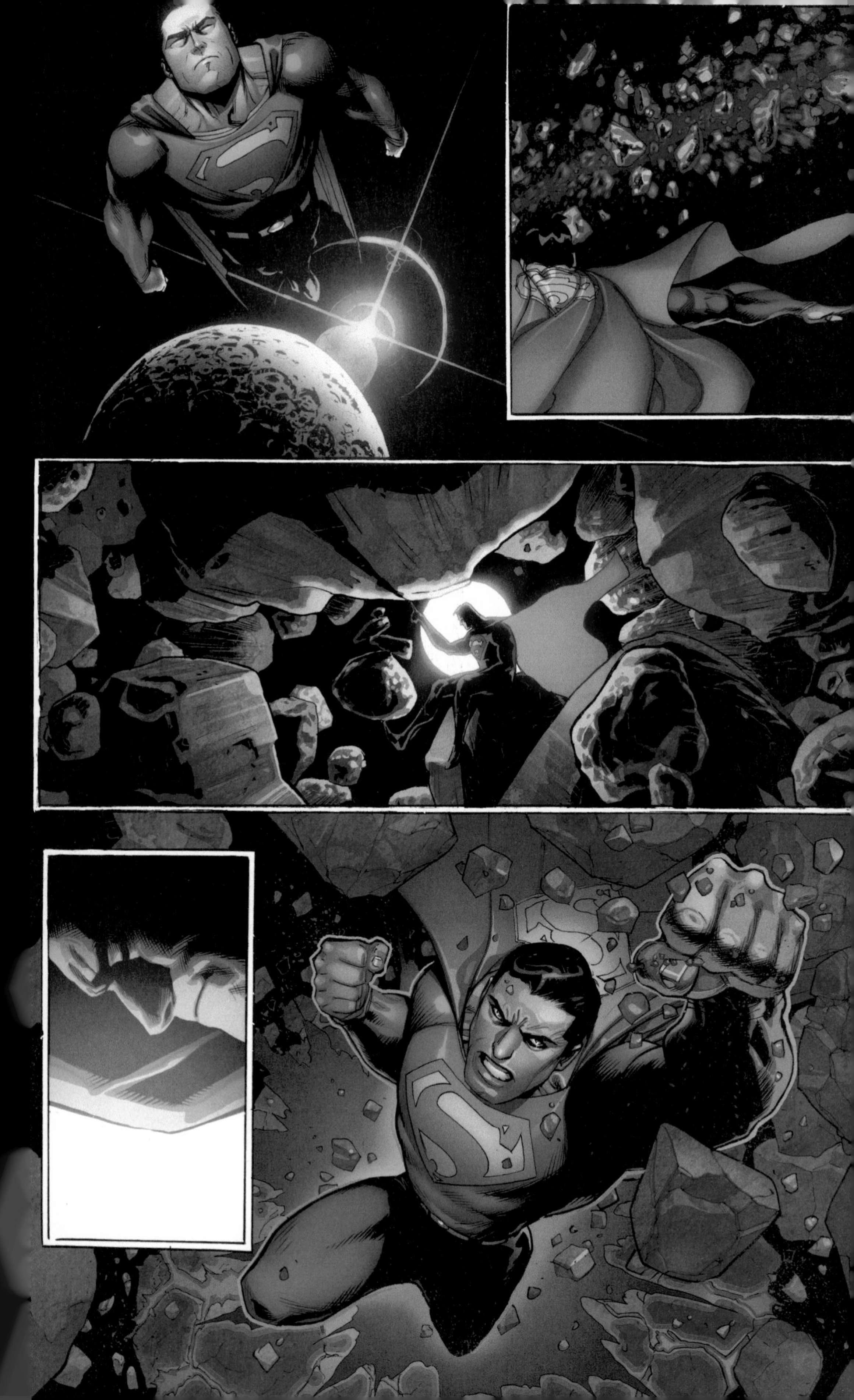

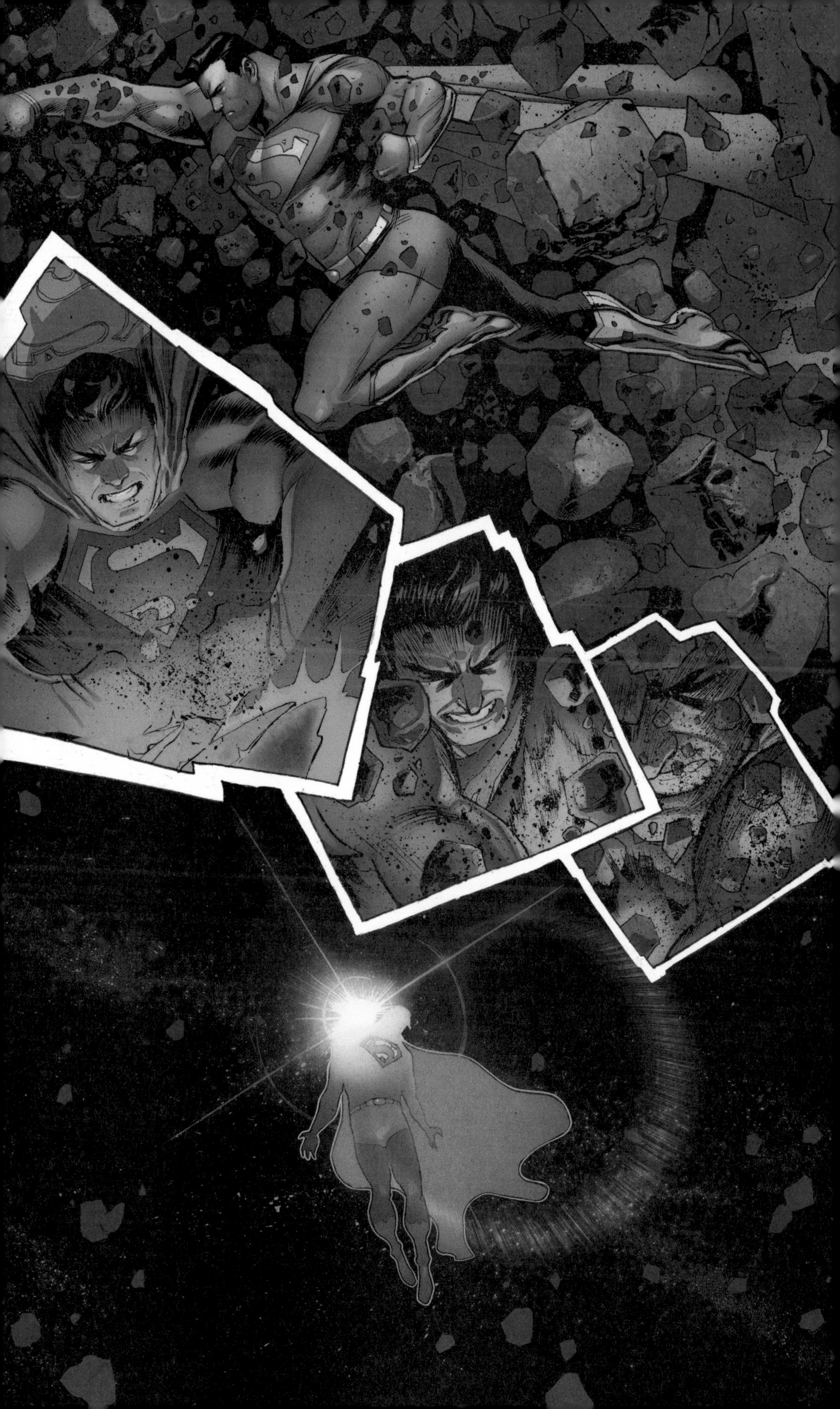

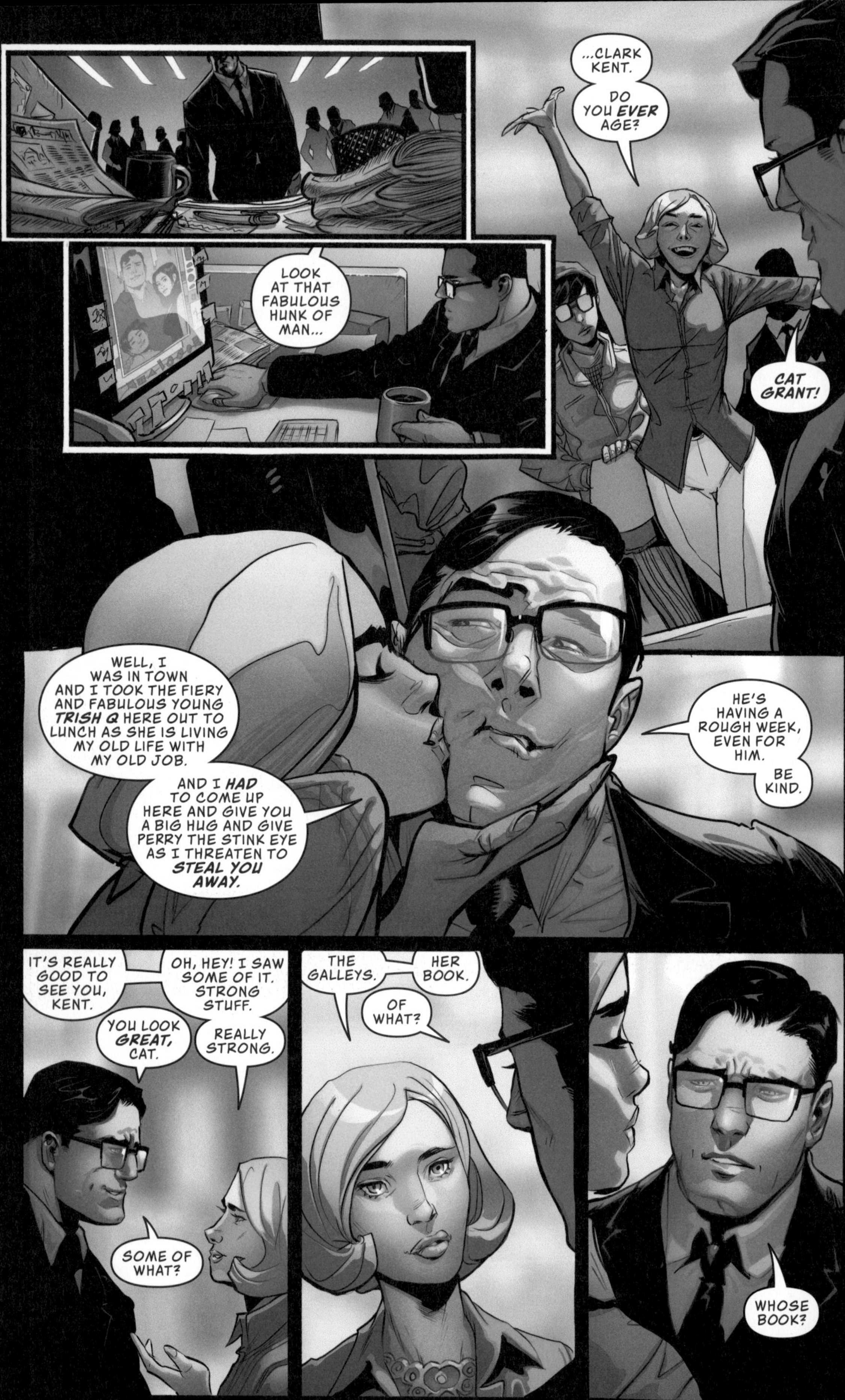

LOOK AT THAT FABULOUS HUNK OF MAN...
...CLARK KENT.
DO YOU EVER AGE?
CAT GRANT!
WELL, I WAS IN TOWN AND I TOOK THE FIERY AND FABULOUS YOUNG TRISH Q HERE OUT TO LUNCH AS SHE IS LIVING MY OLD LIFE WITH MY OLD JOB.
AND I HAD TO COME UP HERE AND GIVE YOU A BIG HUG AND GIVE PERRY THE STINK EYE AS I THREATEN TO STEAL YOU AWAY.
HE'S HAVING A ROUGH WEEK, EVEN FOR HIM.
BE KIND.
IT'S REALLY GOOD TO SEE YOU, KENT.
YOU LOOK GREAT, CAT.
OH, HEY! I SAW SOME OF IT. STRONG STUFF.
REALLY STRONG.
SOME OF WHAT?
THE GALLEYS.
HER BOOK.
OF WHAT?
WHOSE BOOK?

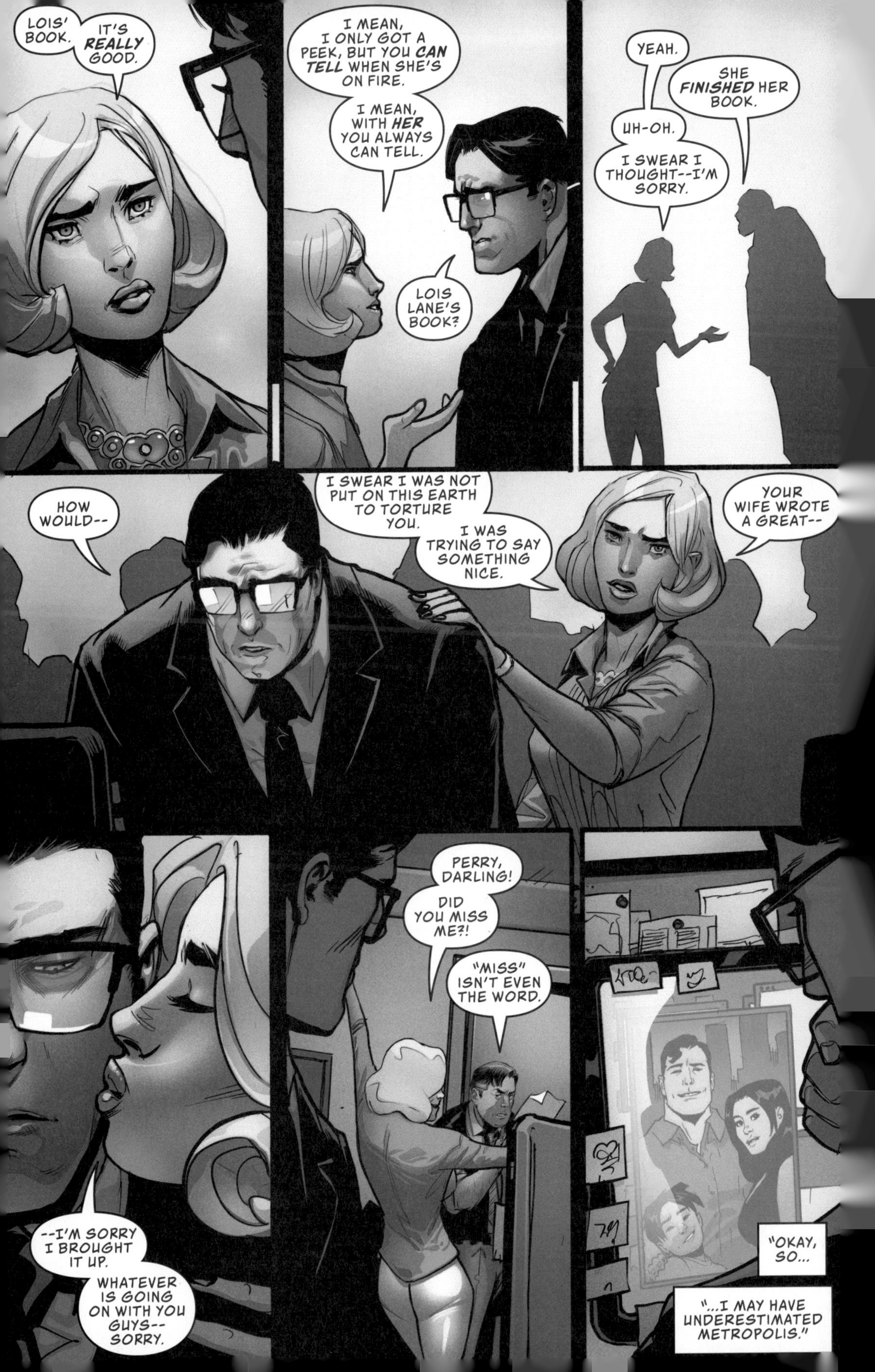
LOIS' BOOK.
IT'S REALLY GOOD.
I MEAN, I ONLY GOT A PEEK, BUT YOU CAN TELL WHEN SHE'S ON FIRE.
I MEAN, WITH HER YOU ALWAYS CAN TELL.
LOIS LANE'S BOOK?
YEAH.
SHE FINISHED HER BOOK.
UH-OH.
I SWEAR I THOUGHT--I'M SORRY.
HOW WOULD--
I SWEAR I WAS NOT PUT ON THIS EARTH TO TORTURE YOU.
I WAS TRYING TO SAY SOMETHING NICE.
YOUR WIFE WROTE A GREAT--
--I'M SORRY I BROUGHT IT UP.
WHATEVER IS GOING ON WITH YOU GUYS--SORRY.
PERRY, DARLING!
DID YOU MISS ME?!
"MISS" ISN'T EVEN THE WORD.
"OKAY, SO...
"...I MAY HAVE UNDERESTIMATED METROPOLIS."

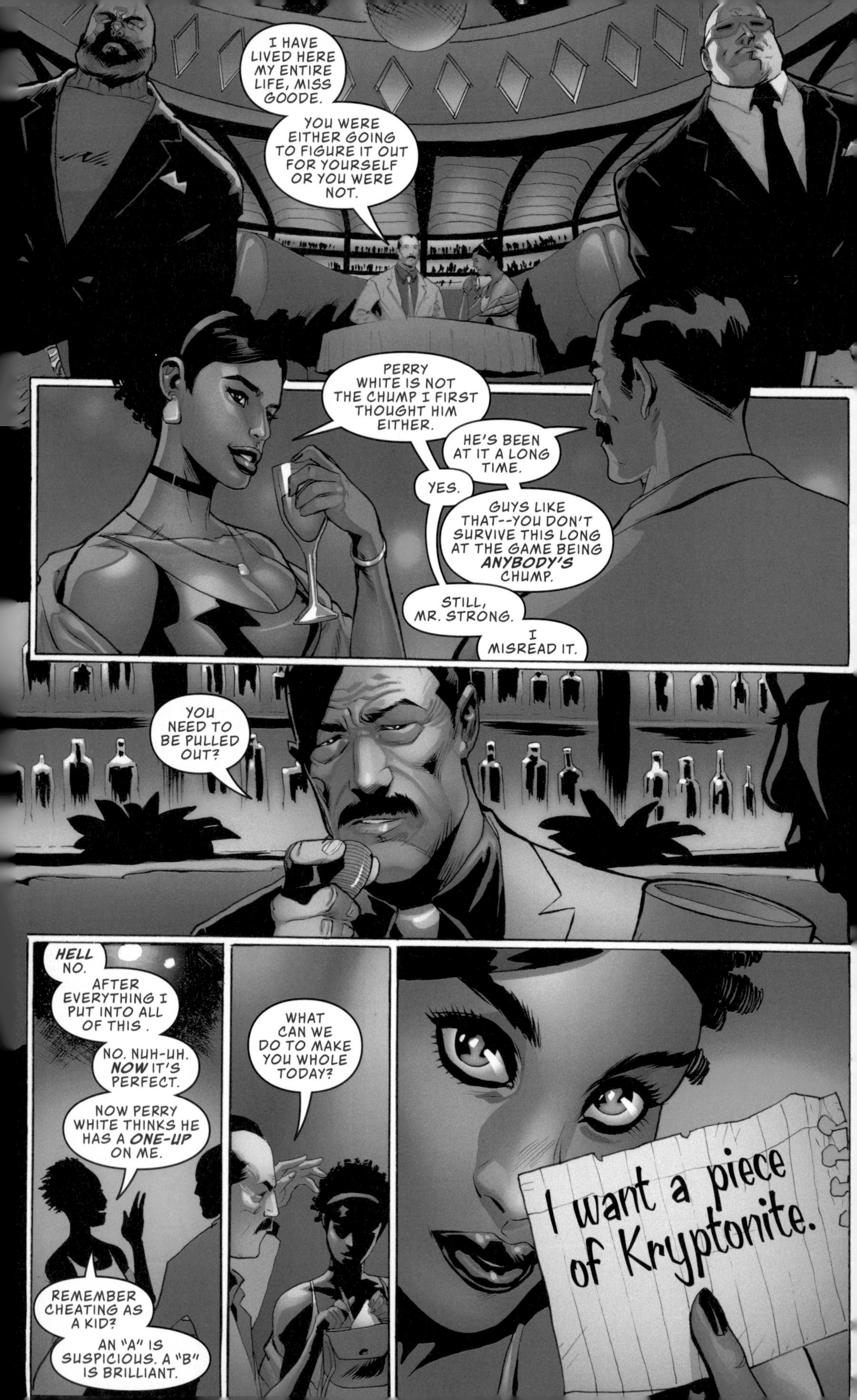
I HAVE LIVED HERE MY ENTIRE LIFE, MISS GOODE.
YOU WERE EITHER GOING TO FIGURE IT OUT FOR YOURSELF OR YOU WERE NOT.
PERRY WHITE IS NOT THE CHUMP I FIRST THOUGHT HIM EITHER.
HE'S BEEN AT IT A LONG TIME.
YES.
GUYS LIKE THAT--YOU DON'T SURVIVE THIS LONG AT THE GAME BEING ANYBODY'S CHUMP.
STILL, MR. STRONG.
I MISREAD IT.
YOU NEED TO BE PULLED OUT?
HELL NO.
AFTER EVERYTHING I PUT INTO ALL OF THIS .
NO. NUH-UH. NOW IT'S PERFECT.
NOW PERRY WHITE THINKS HE HAS A ONE-UP ON ME.
REMEMBER CHEATING AS A KID?
AN "A" IS SUSPICIOUS. A "B" IS BRILLIANT.
WHAT CAN WE DO TO MAKE YOU WHOLE TODAY?
I want a piece of Kryptonite.

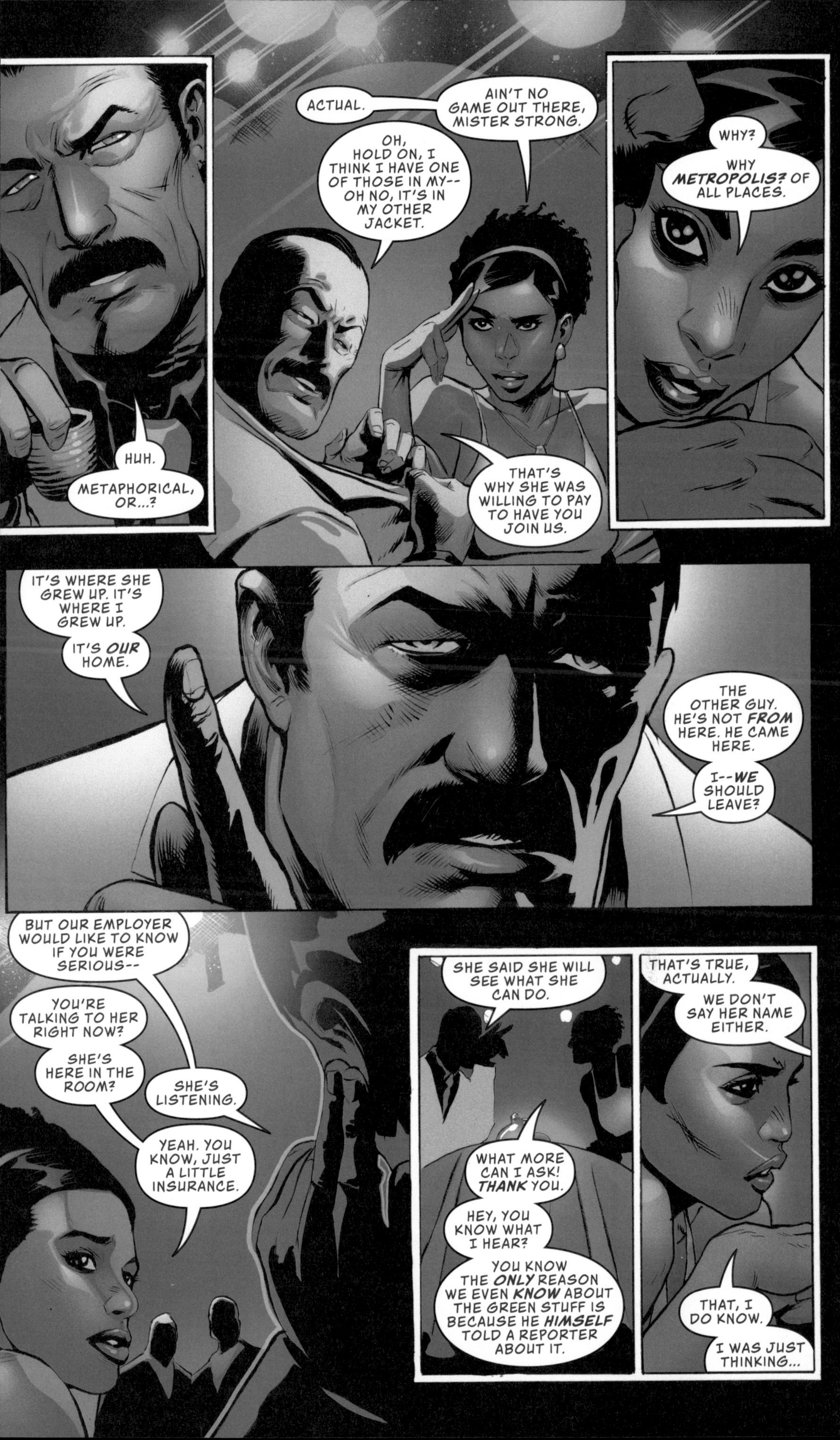
AIN'T NO GAME OUT THERE, MISTER STRONG.
ACTUAL.
OH, HOLD ON, I THINK I HAVE ONE OF THOSE IN MY-- OH NO, IT'S IN MY OTHER JACKET.
HUH.
METAPHORICAL, OR...?
THAT'S WHY SHE WAS WILLING TO PAY TO HAVE YOU JOIN US.
WHY?
WHY METROPOLIS? OF ALL PLACES.
IT'S WHERE SHE GREW UP. IT'S WHERE I GREW UP.
IT'S OUR HOME.
THE OTHER GUY. HE'S NOT FROM HERE. HE CAME HERE.
I--WE SHOULD LEAVE?
BUT OUR EMPLOYER WOULD LIKE TO KNOW IF YOU WERE SERIOUS--
YOU'RE TALKING TO HER RIGHT NOW?
SHE'S HERE IN THE ROOM?
SHE'S LISTENING.
YEAH. YOU KNOW, JUST A LITTLE INSURANCE.
SHE SAID SHE WILL SEE WHAT SHE CAN DO.
WHAT MORE CAN I ASK! THANK YOU.
HEY, YOU KNOW WHAT I HEAR?
YOU KNOW THE ONLY REASON WE EVEN KNOW ABOUT THE GREEN STUFF IS BECAUSE HE HIMSELF TOLD A REPORTER ABOUT IT.
THAT'S TRUE, ACTUALLY.
WE DON'T SAY HER NAME EITHER.
THAT, I DO KNOW.
I WAS JUST THINKING...

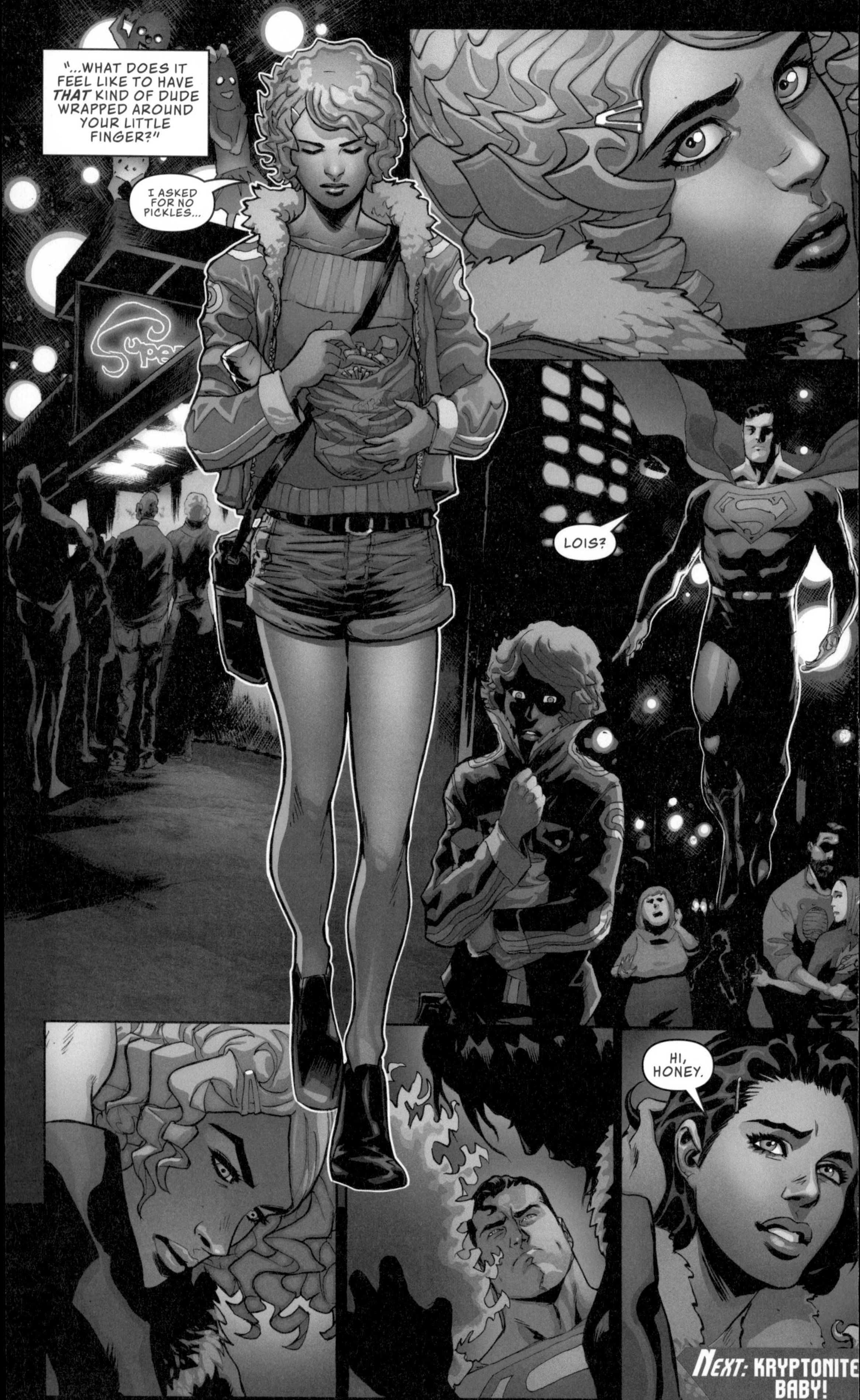
"...WHAT DOES IT FEEL LIKE TO HAVE *THAT* KIND OF DUDE WRAPPED AROUND YOUR LITTLE FINGER?"
I ASKED FOR NO PICKLES...
LOIS?
HI, HONEY.
NEXT: KRYPTONITE BABY!

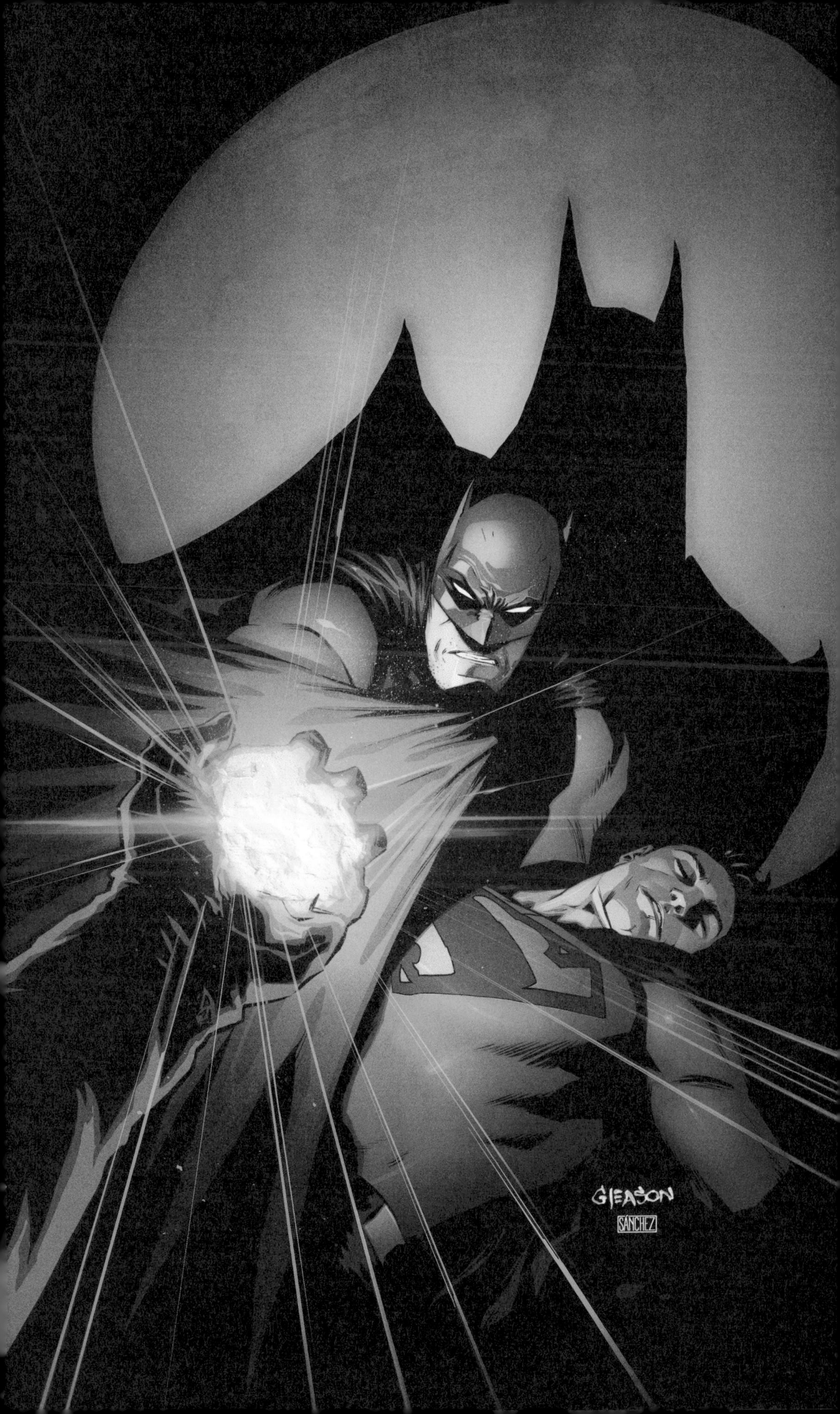
GLEASON
SÁNCHEZ

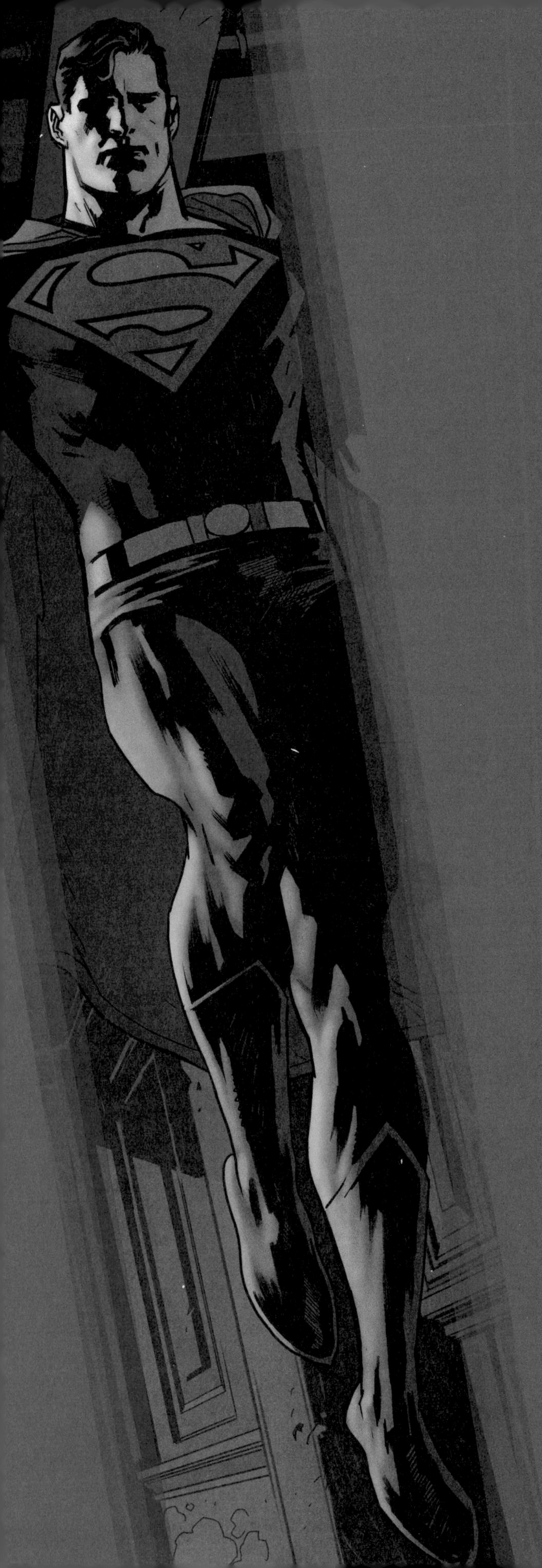

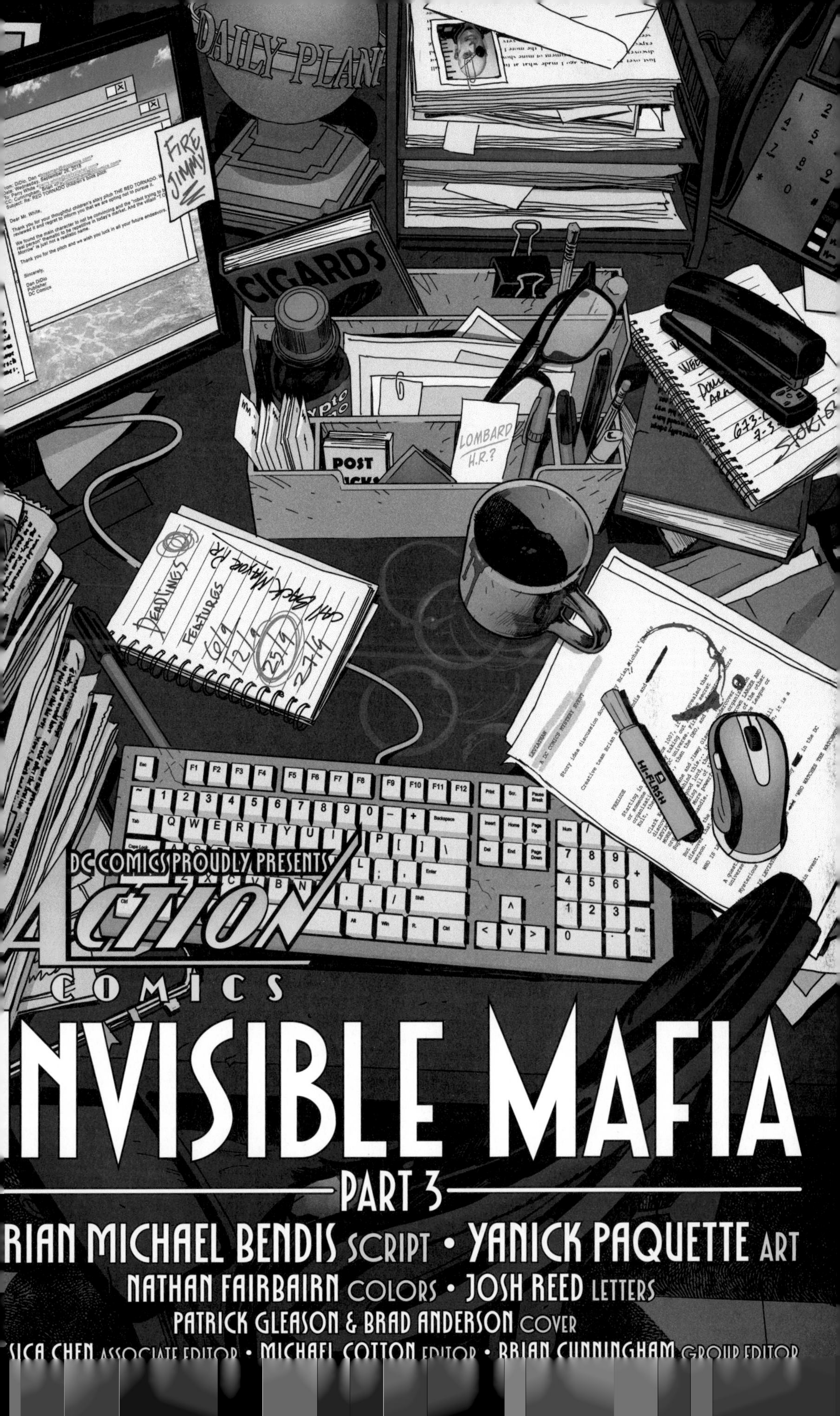
DAILY PLAN
FIRE JIMMY
CIGARDS
LOMBARD H.R.?
POST
DEADLINES
FEATURES
Call Back Mayor P.R.
HI-FLASH
DC COMICS PROUDLY PRESENTS
ACTION COMICS
NVISIBLE MAFIA
PART 3
RIAN MICHAEL BENDIS SCRIPT • YANICK PAQUETTE ART
NATHAN FAIRBAIRN COLORS • JOSH REED LETTERS
PATRICK GLEASON & BRAD ANDERSON COVER
SICA CHEN ASSOCIATE EDITOR • MICHAEL COTTON EDITOR • BRIAN CUNNINGHAM GROUP EDITOR

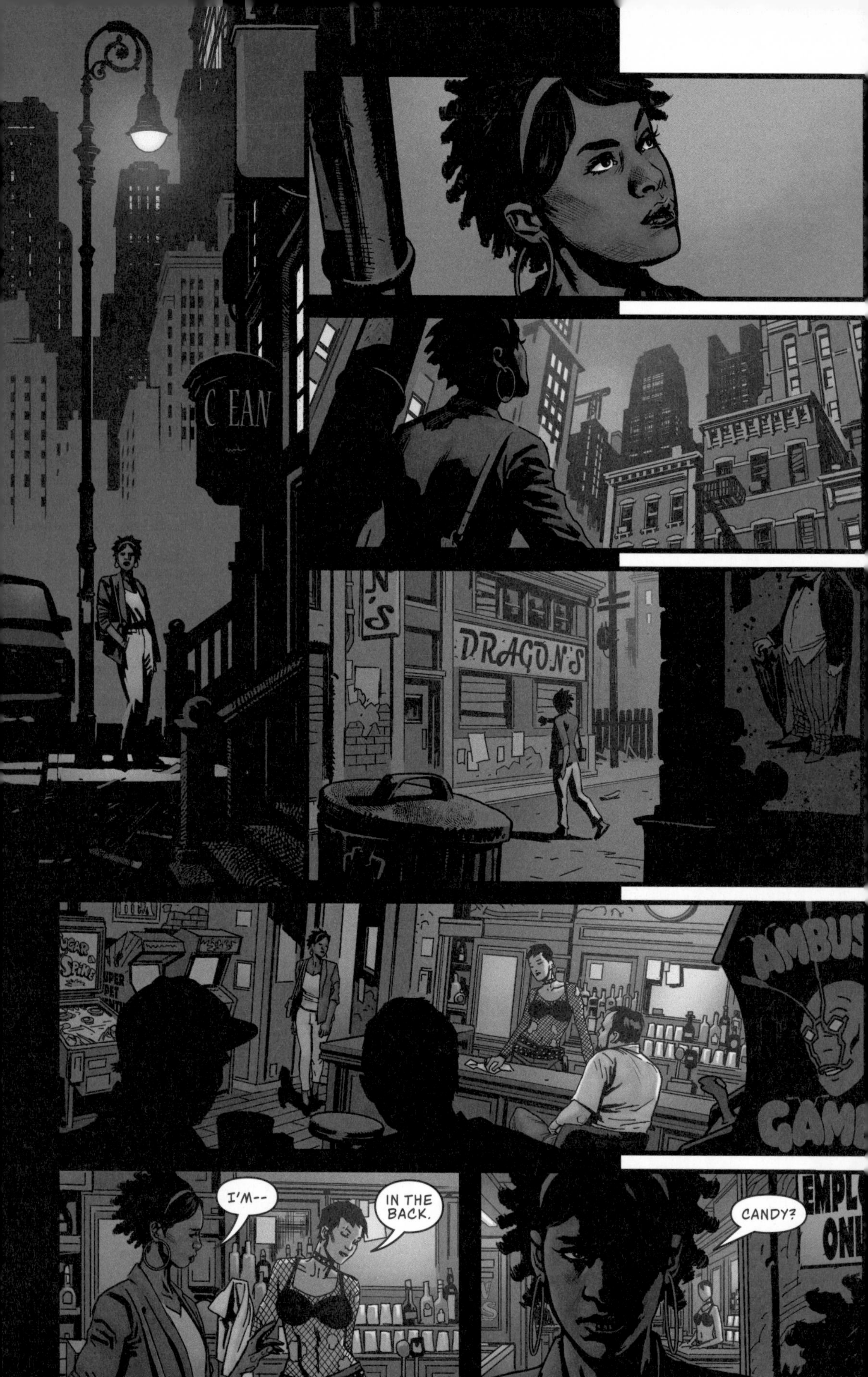
DRAGON'S
I'M--
IN THE BACK.
CANDY?

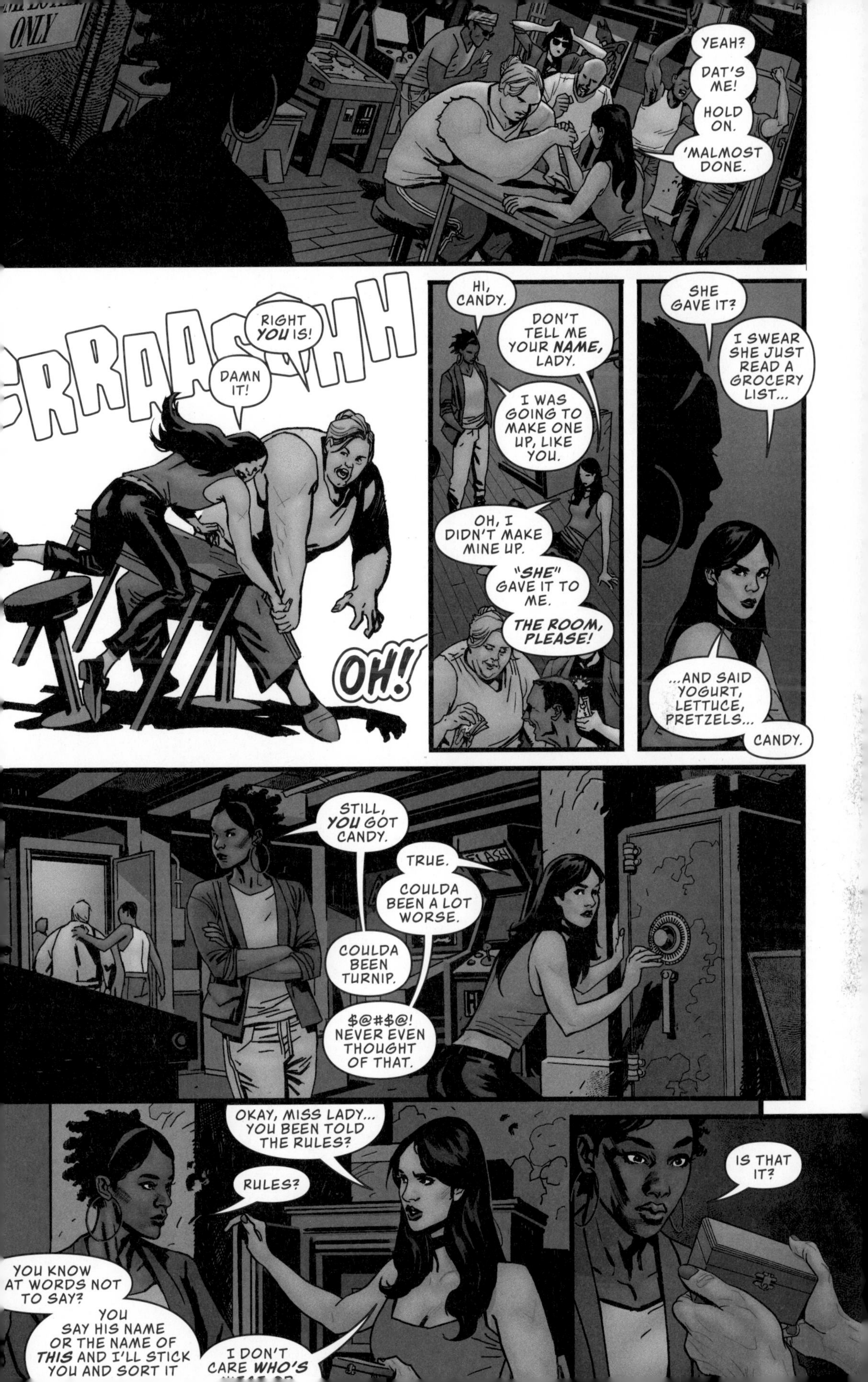
ONLY
YEAH? DAT'S ME! HOLD ON. 'MALMOST DONE.
CRRAASSHH
RIGHT *YOU* IS!
DAMN IT!
OH!
HI, CANDY.
DON'T TELL ME YOUR *NAME,* LADY.
I WAS GOING TO MAKE ONE UP, LIKE YOU.
OH, I DIDN'T MAKE MINE UP.
"SHE" GAVE IT TO ME.
THE ROOM, PLEASE!
SHE GAVE IT?
I SWEAR SHE JUST READ A GROCERY LIST...
...AND SAID YOGURT, LETTUCE, PRETZELS...
CANDY.
STILL, *YOU* GOT CANDY.
TRUE.
COULDA BEEN A LOT WORSE.
COULDA BEEN TURNIP.
$@#$@! NEVER EVEN THOUGHT OF THAT.
OKAY, MISS LADY... YOU BEEN TOLD THE RULES?
RULES?
IS THAT IT?
YOU KNOW
AT WORDS NOT TO SAY?
YOU SAY HIS NAME OR THE NAME OF *THIS* AND I'LL STICK YOU AND SORT IT
I DON'T CARE *WHO'S*

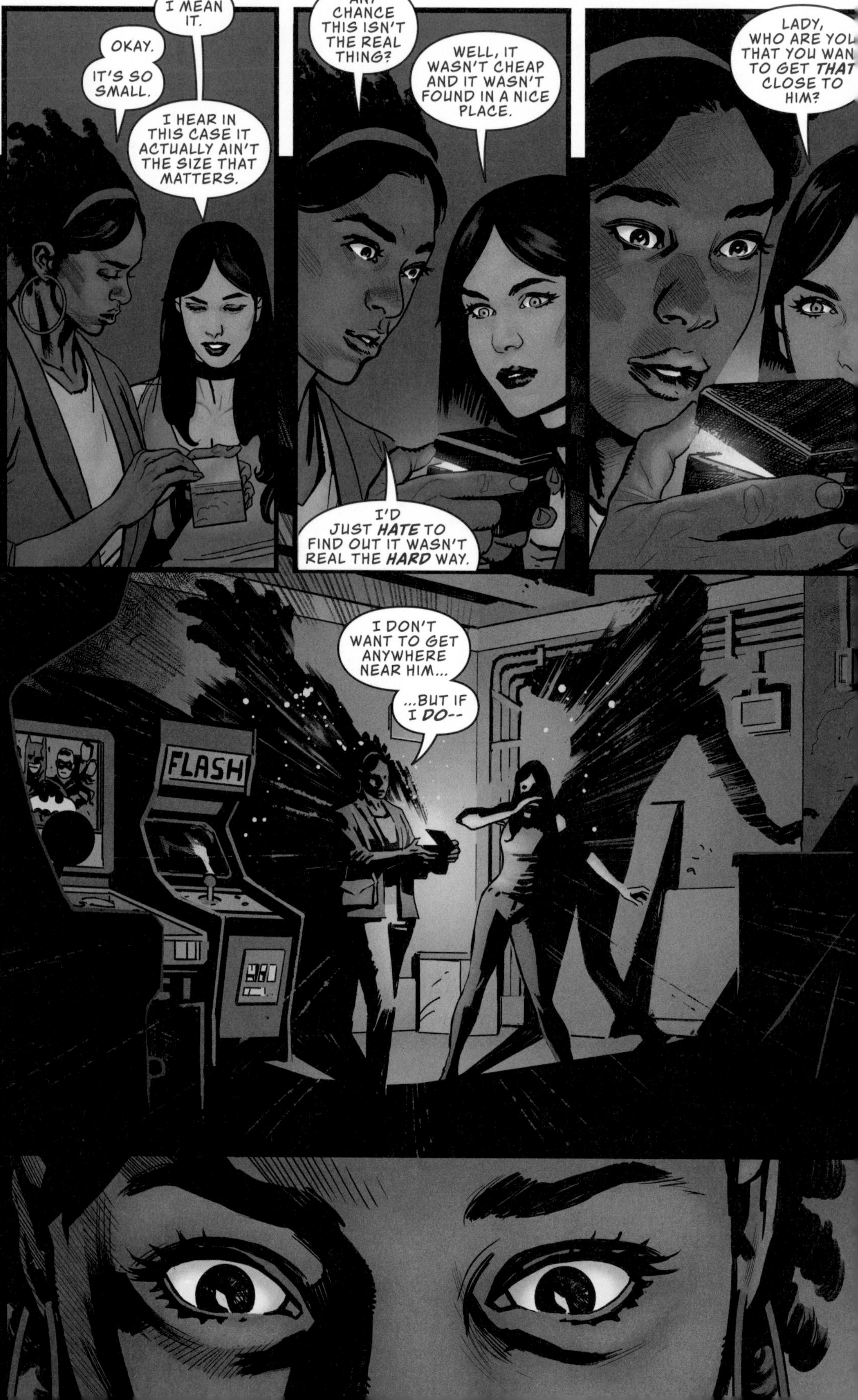
I MEAN IT.
OKAY.
IT'S SO SMALL.
I HEAR IN THIS CASE IT ACTUALLY AIN'T THE SIZE THAT MATTERS.
ANY CHANCE THIS ISN'T THE REAL THING?
WELL, IT WASN'T CHEAP AND IT WASN'T FOUND IN A NICE PLACE.
I'D JUST HATE TO FIND OUT IT WASN'T REAL THE HARD WAY.
LADY, WHO ARE YOU THAT YOU WANT TO GET THAT CLOSE TO HIM?
I DON'T WANT TO GET ANYWHERE NEAR HIM...
...BUT IF I DO--
FLASH

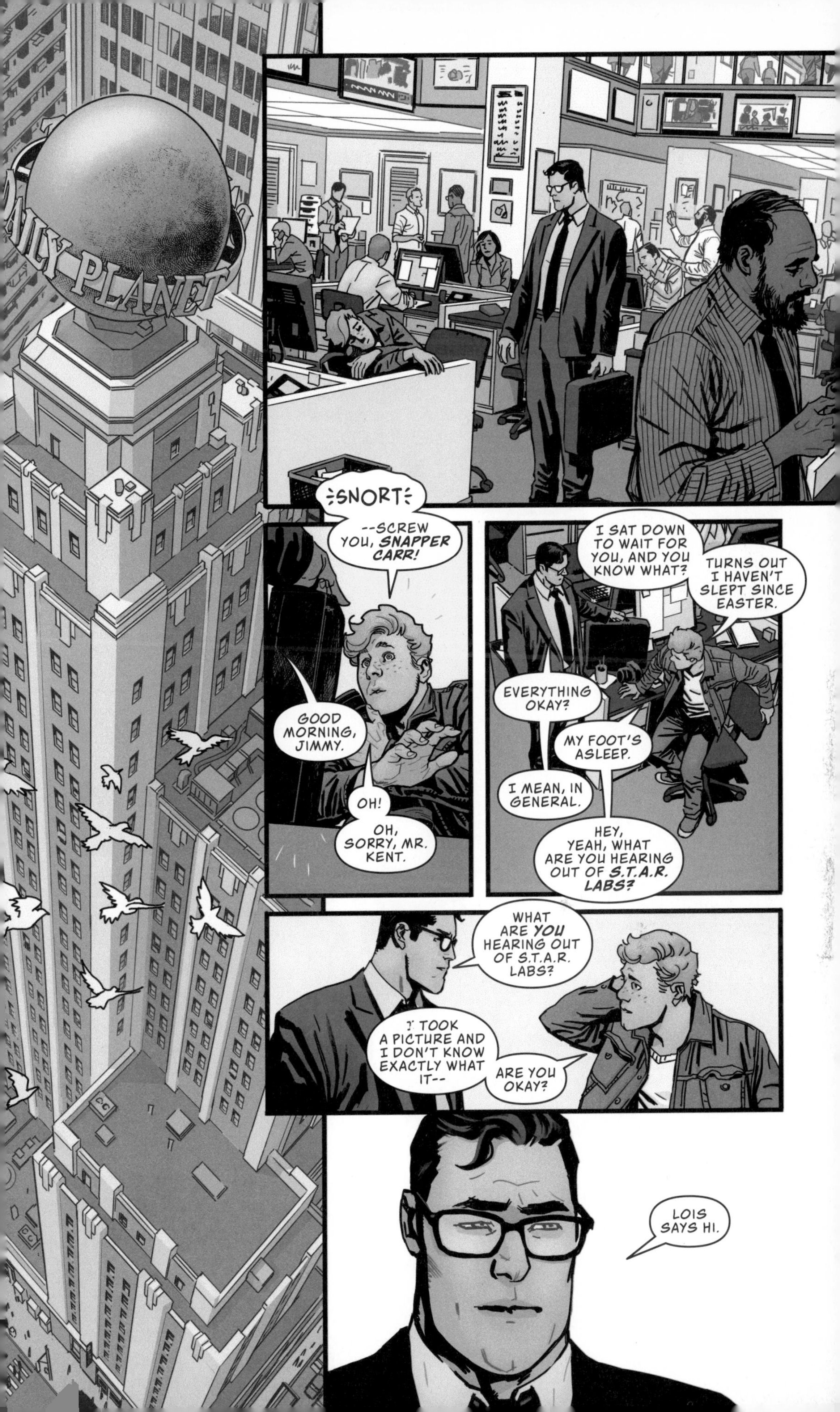
DAILY PLANET
SNORT
--SCREW YOU, SNAPPER CARR!
GOOD MORNING, JIMMY.
OH!
OH, SORRY, MR. KENT.
I SAT DOWN TO WAIT FOR YOU, AND YOU KNOW WHAT?
TURNS OUT I HAVEN'T SLEPT SINCE EASTER.
EVERYTHING OKAY?
MY FOOT'S ASLEEP.
I MEAN, IN GENERAL.
HEY, YEAH, WHAT ARE YOU HEARING OUT OF S.T.A.R. LABS?
WHAT ARE YOU HEARING OUT OF S.T.A.R. LABS?
I TOOK A PICTURE AND I DON'T KNOW EXACTLY WHAT IT--
ARE YOU OKAY?
LOIS SAYS HI.

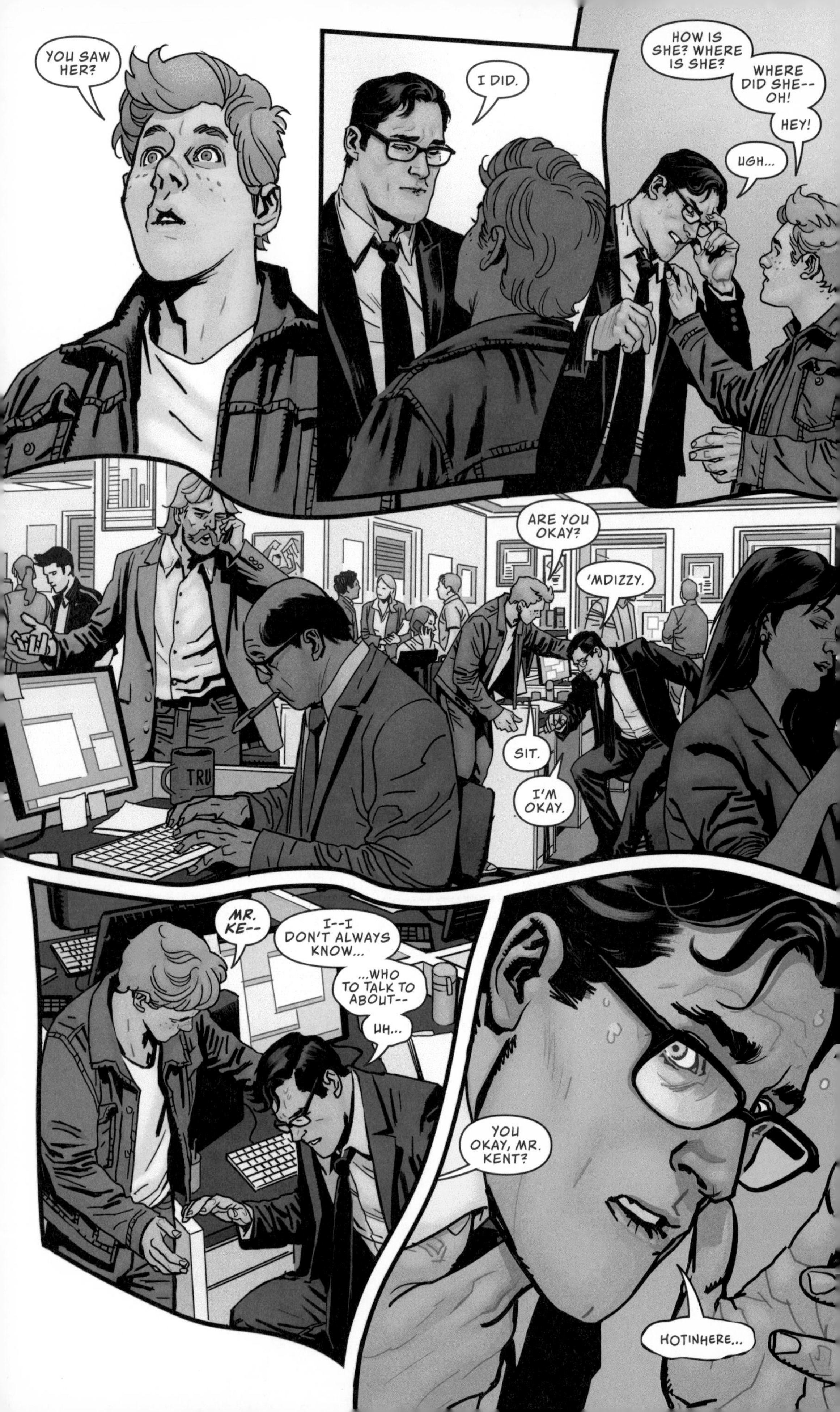
YOU SAW HER?
I DID.
HOW IS SHE? WHERE IS SHE?
WHERE DID SHE-- OH!
HEY!
UGH...
TRU
ARE YOU OKAY?
'MDIZZY.
SIT.
I'M OKAY.
MR. KE--
I--I DON'T ALWAYS KNOW...
...WHO TO TALK TO ABOUT--
UH...
YOU OKAY, MR. KENT?
HOTINHERE...

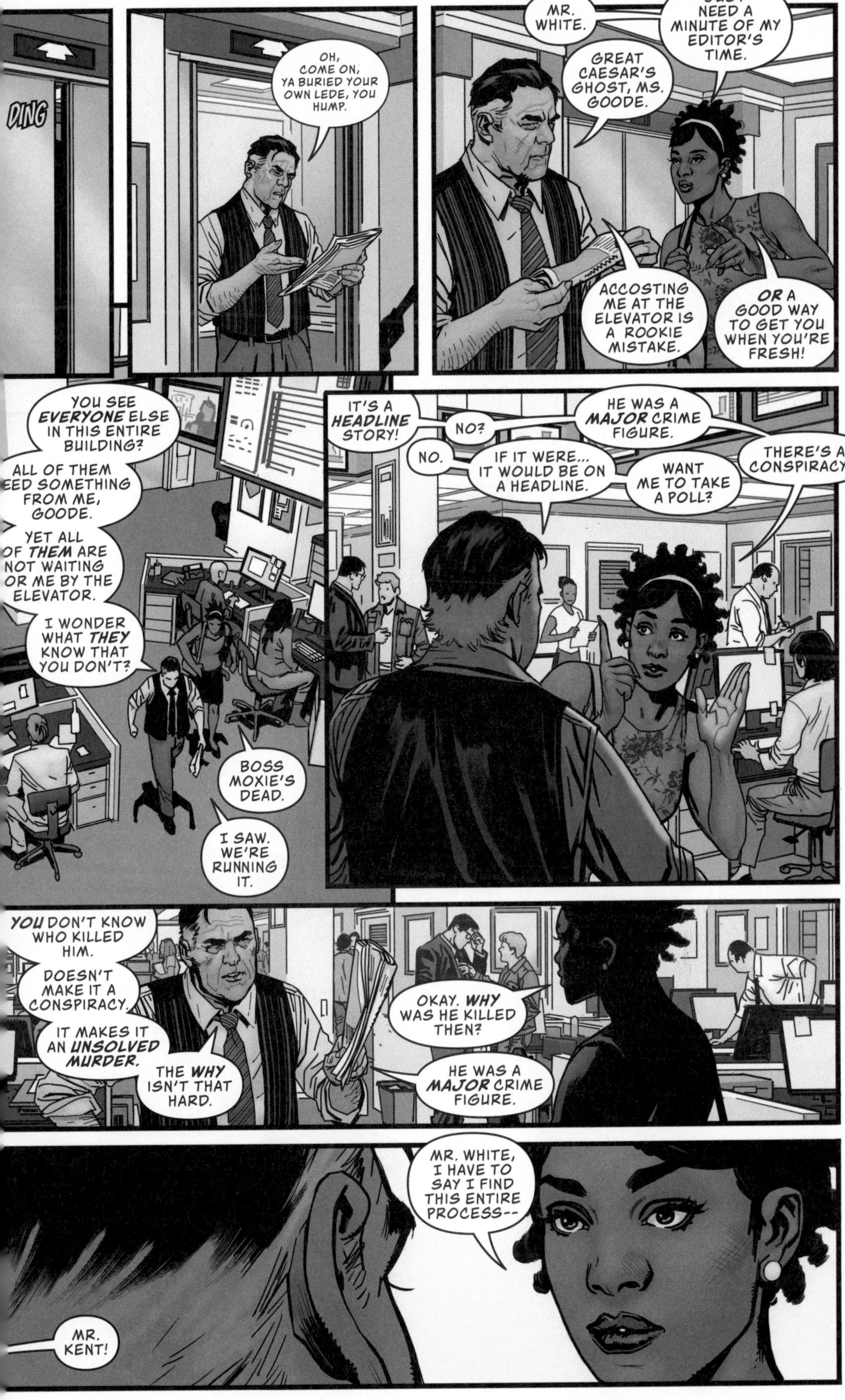
DING
OH, COME ON, YA BURIED YOUR OWN LEDE, YOU HUMP.
MR. WHITE.
JUST NEED A MINUTE OF MY EDITOR'S TIME.
GREAT CAESAR'S GHOST, MS. GOODE.
ACCOSTING ME AT THE ELEVATOR IS A ROOKIE MISTAKE.
OR A GOOD WAY TO GET YOU WHEN YOU'RE FRESH!
YOU SEE EVERYONE ELSE IN THIS ENTIRE BUILDING?
ALL OF THEM EED SOMETHING FROM ME, GOODE.
YET ALL OF THEM ARE NOT WAITING OR ME BY THE ELEVATOR.
I WONDER WHAT THEY KNOW THAT YOU DON'T?
BOSS MOXIE'S DEAD.
I SAW. WE'RE RUNNING IT.
IT'S A HEADLINE STORY!
NO?
NO.
IF IT WERE... IT WOULD BE ON A HEADLINE.
HE WAS A MAJOR CRIME FIGURE.
WANT ME TO TAKE A POLL?
THERE'S A CONSPIRACY...
YOU DON'T KNOW WHO KILLED HIM.
DOESN'T MAKE IT A CONSPIRACY.
IT MAKES IT AN UNSOLVED MURDER.
OKAY. WHY WAS HE KILLED THEN?
THE WHY ISN'T THAT HARD.
HE WAS A MAJOR CRIME FIGURE.
MR. WHITE, I HAVE TO SAY I FIND THIS ENTIRE PROCESS--
MR. KENT!

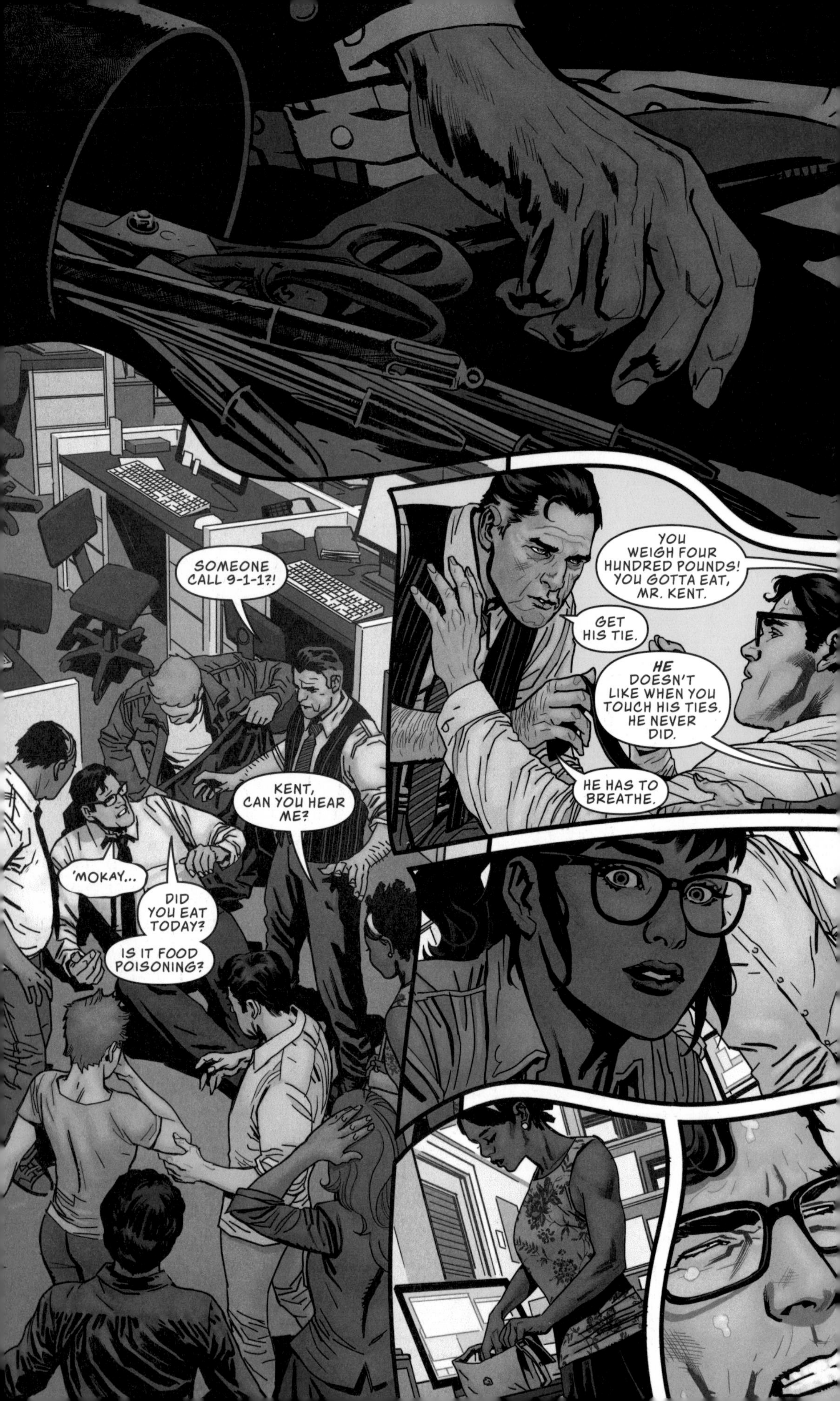
SOMEONE CALL 9-1-1?!
KENT, CAN YOU HEAR ME?
'MOKAY...
DID YOU EAT TODAY?
IS IT FOOD POISONING?
YOU WEIGH FOUR HUNDRED POUNDS! YOU GOTTA EAT, MR. KENT.
GET HIS TIE.
HE DOESN'T LIKE WHEN YOU TOUCH HIS TIES. HE NEVER DID.
HE HAS TO BREATHE.

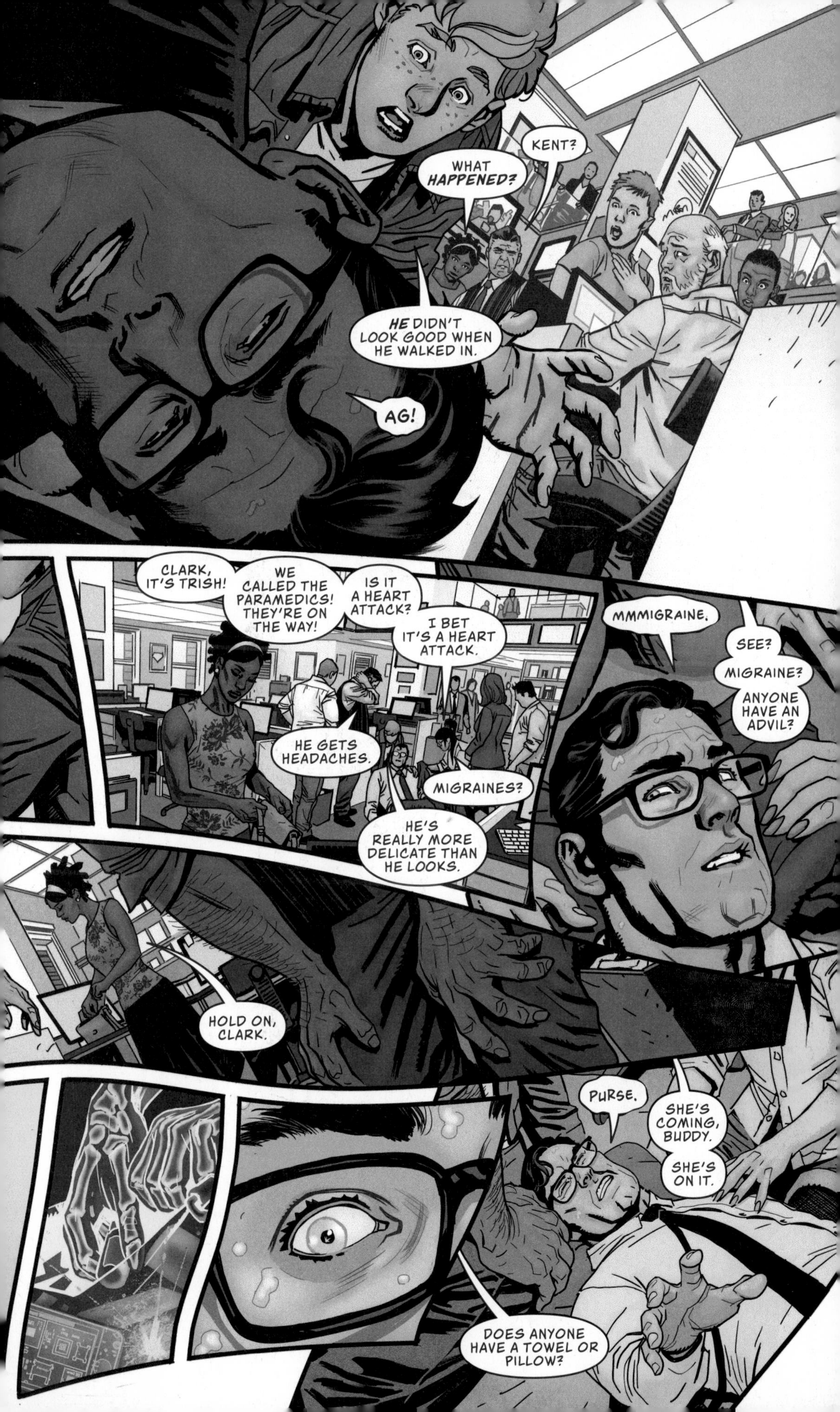
KENT?
WHAT HAPPENED?
HE DIDN'T LOOK GOOD WHEN HE WALKED IN.
AG!
CLARK, IT'S TRISH!
WE CALLED THE PARAMEDICS! THEY'RE ON THE WAY!
IS IT A HEART ATTACK?
I BET IT'S A HEART ATTACK.
HE GETS HEADACHES.
MIGRAINES?
HE'S REALLY MORE DELICATE THAN HE LOOKS.
MMMIGRAINE.
SEE?
MIGRAINE?
ANYONE HAVE AN ADVIL?
HOLD ON, CLARK.
PURSE.
SHE'S COMING, BUDDY.
SHE'S ON IT.
DOES ANYONE HAVE A TOWEL OR PILLOW?

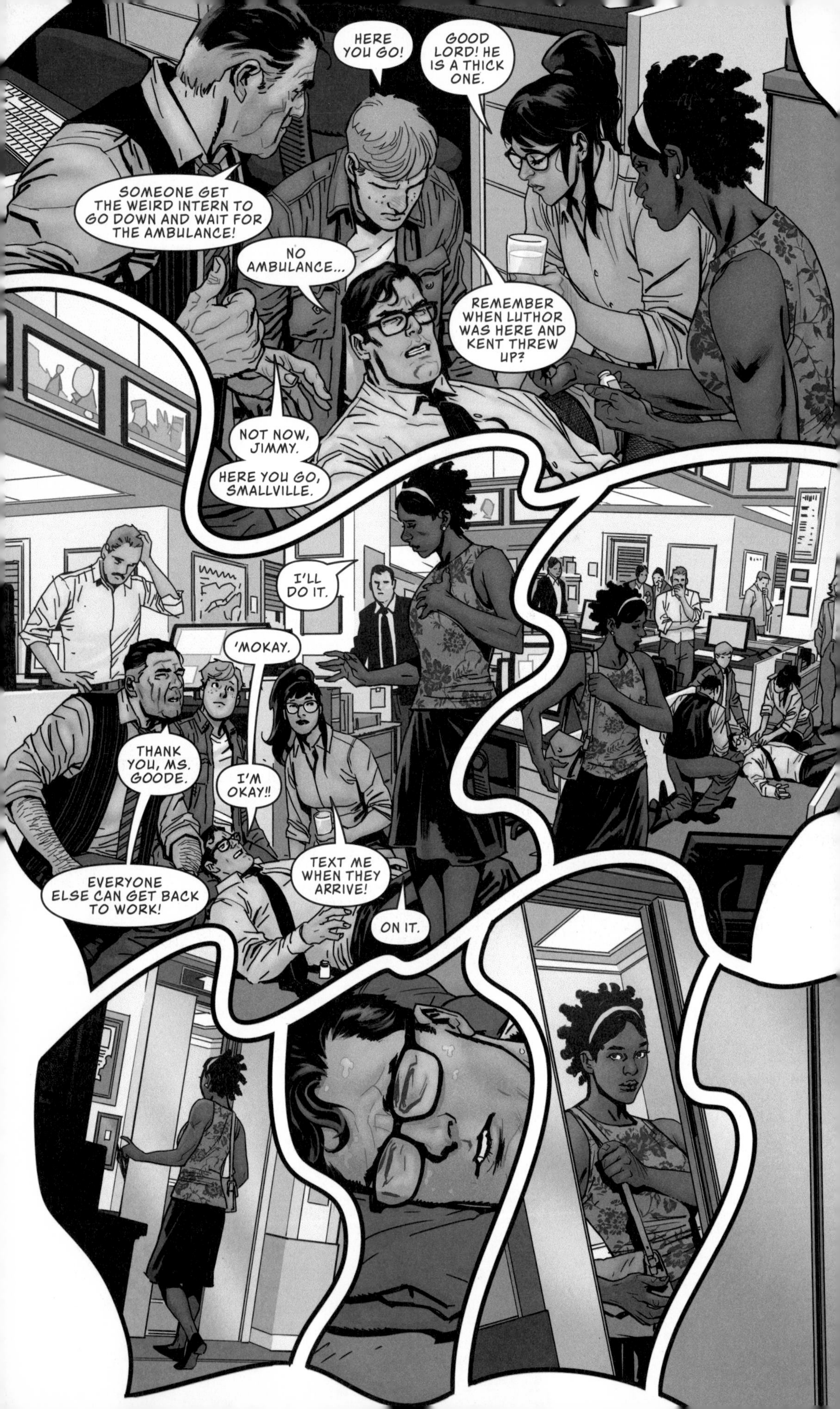

HERE YOU GO!
GOOD LORD! HE IS A THICK ONE.
SOMEONE GET THE WEIRD INTERN TO GO DOWN AND WAIT FOR THE AMBULANCE!
NO AMBULANCE...
REMEMBER WHEN LUTHOR WAS HERE AND KENT THREW UP?
NOT NOW, JIMMY.
HERE YOU GO, SMALLVILLE.
I'LL DO IT.
'MOKAY.
THANK YOU, MS. GOODE.
I'M OKAY!!
EVERYONE ELSE CAN GET BACK TO WORK!
TEXT ME WHEN THEY ARRIVE!
ON IT.

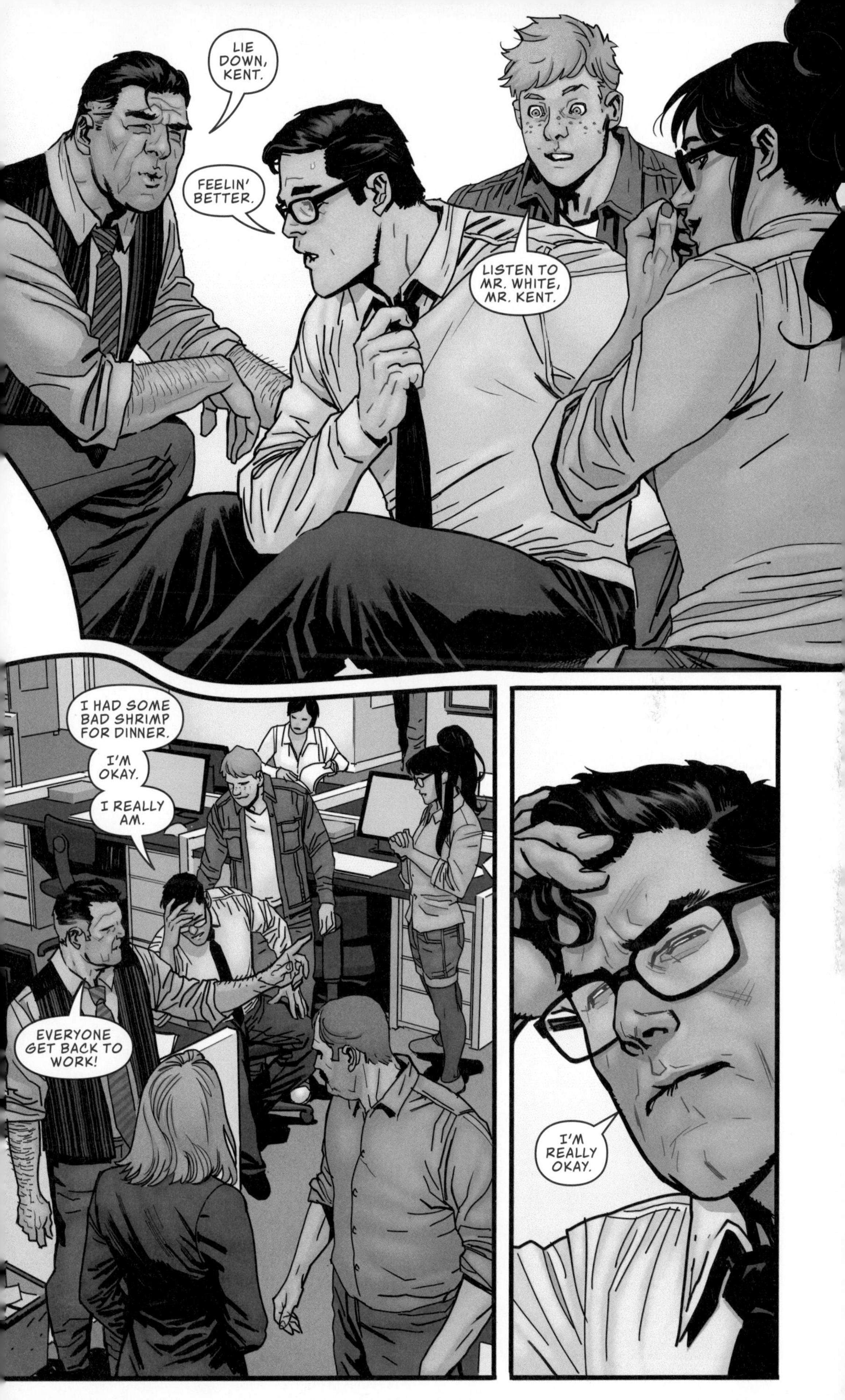
LIE DOWN, KENT.
FEELIN' BETTER.
LISTEN TO MR. WHITE, MR. KENT.
I HAD SOME BAD SHRIMP FOR DINNER.
I'M OKAY.
I REALLY AM.
EVERYONE GET BACK TO WORK!
I'M REALLY OKAY.

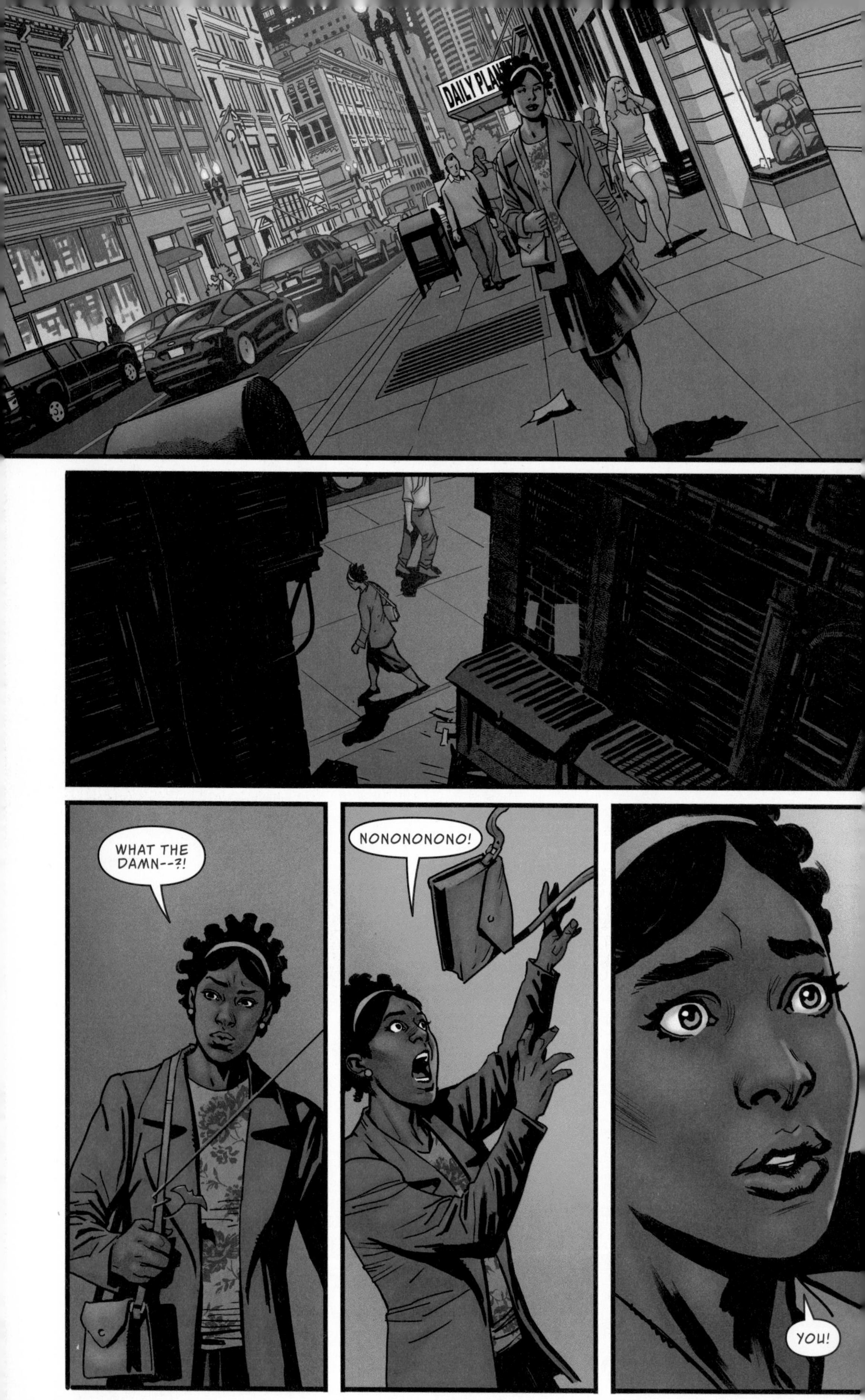
DAILY PLAN
WHAT THE DAMN--?!
NONONONONO!
YOU!

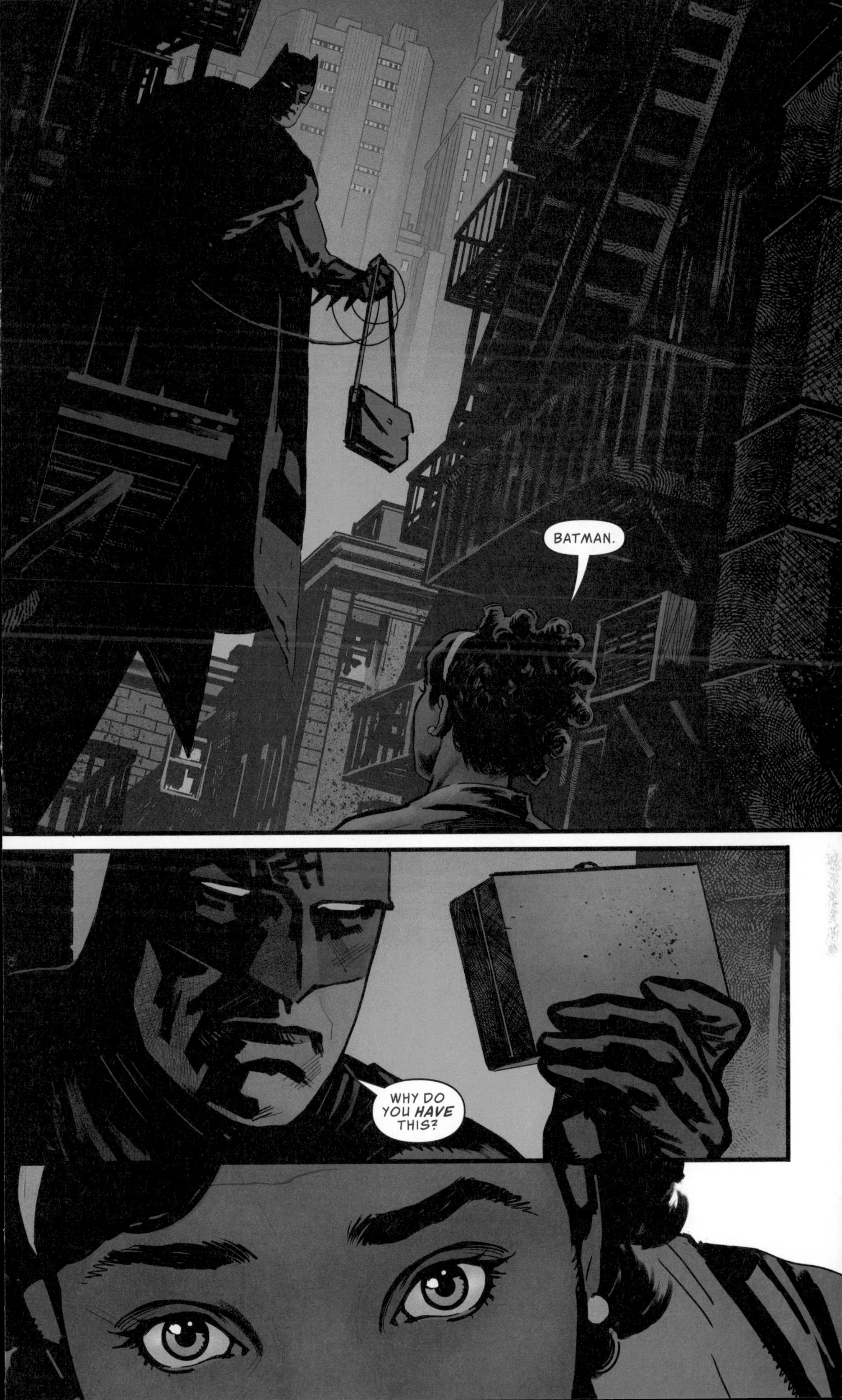
BATMAN.
WHY DO YOU HAVE THIS?

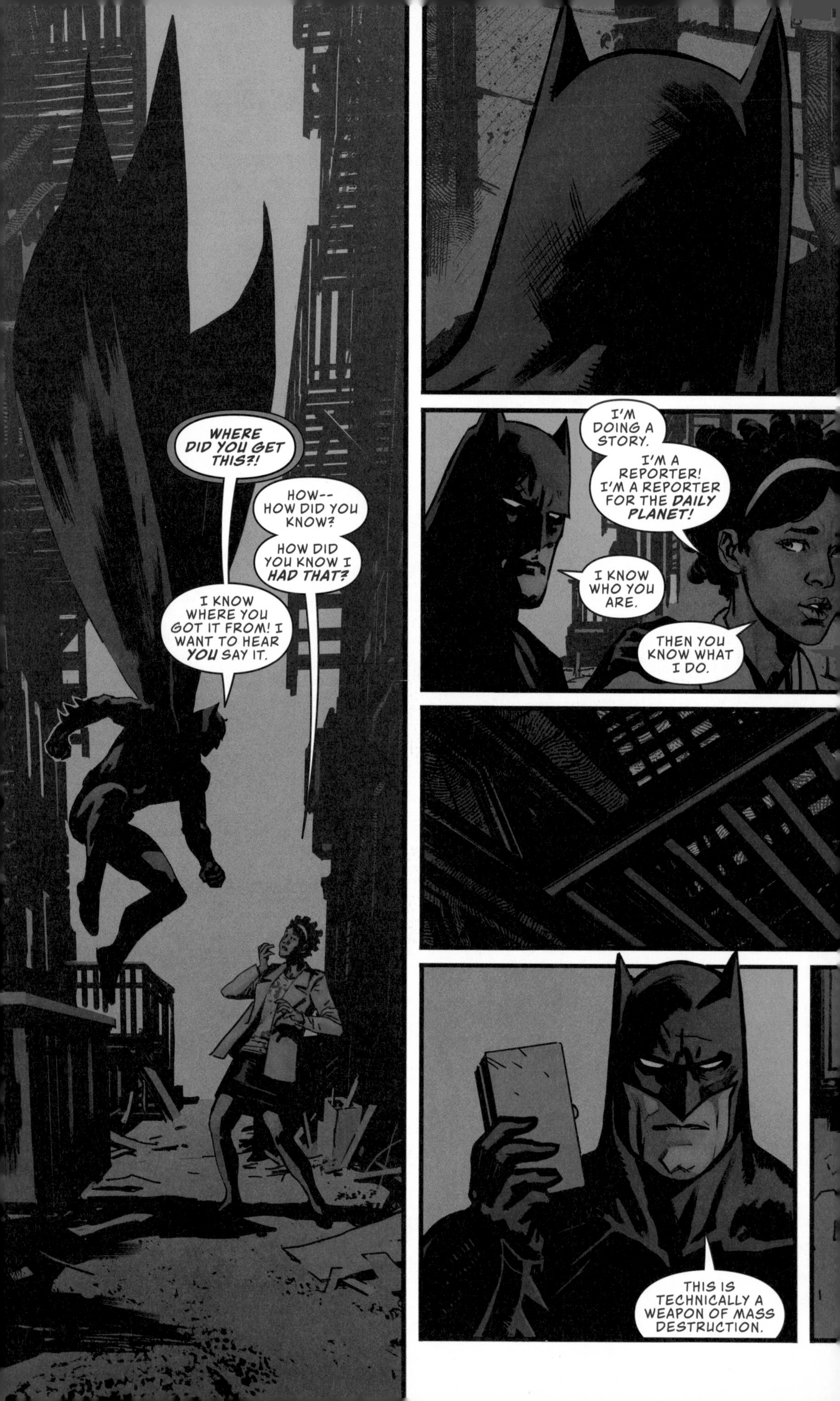

WHERE DID YOU GET THIS?!
HOW-- HOW DID YOU KNOW?
HOW DID YOU KNOW I HAD THAT?
I KNOW WHERE YOU GOT IT FROM! I WANT TO HEAR YOU SAY IT.
I'M DOING A STORY.
I'M A REPORTER! I'M A REPORTER FOR THE DAILY PLANET!
I KNOW WHO YOU ARE.
THEN YOU KNOW WHAT I DO.
THIS IS TECHNICALLY A WEAPON OF MASS DESTRUCTION.

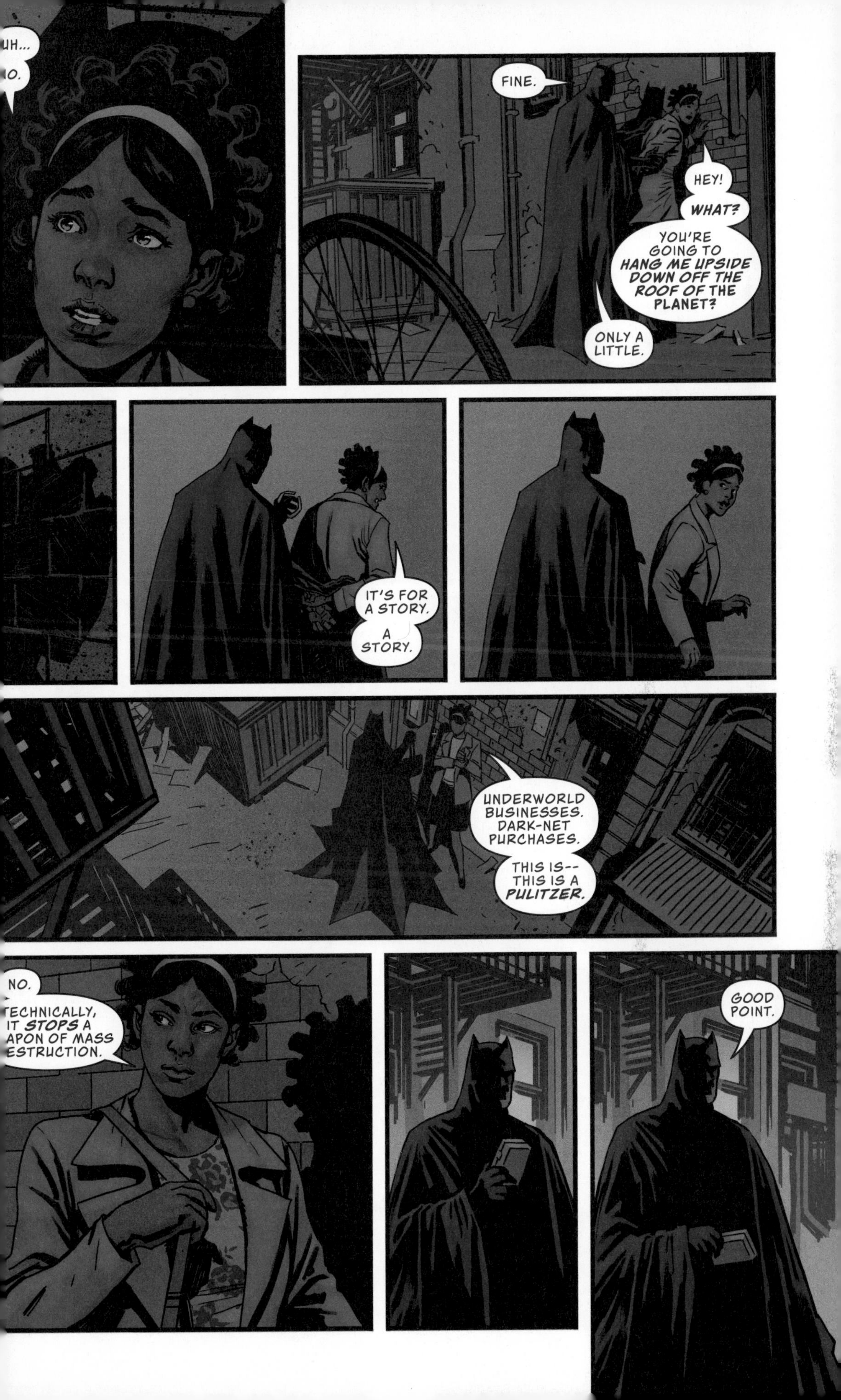
UH...
NO.
FINE.
HEY!
WHAT?
YOU'RE GOING TO HANG ME UPSIDE DOWN OFF THE ROOF OF THE PLANET?
ONLY A LITTLE.
IT'S FOR A STORY.
A STORY.
UNDERWORLD BUSINESSES. DARK-NET PURCHASES.
THIS IS-- THIS IS A PULITZER.
NO.
TECHNICALLY, IT STOPS A APON OF MASS ESTRUCTION.
GOOD POINT.

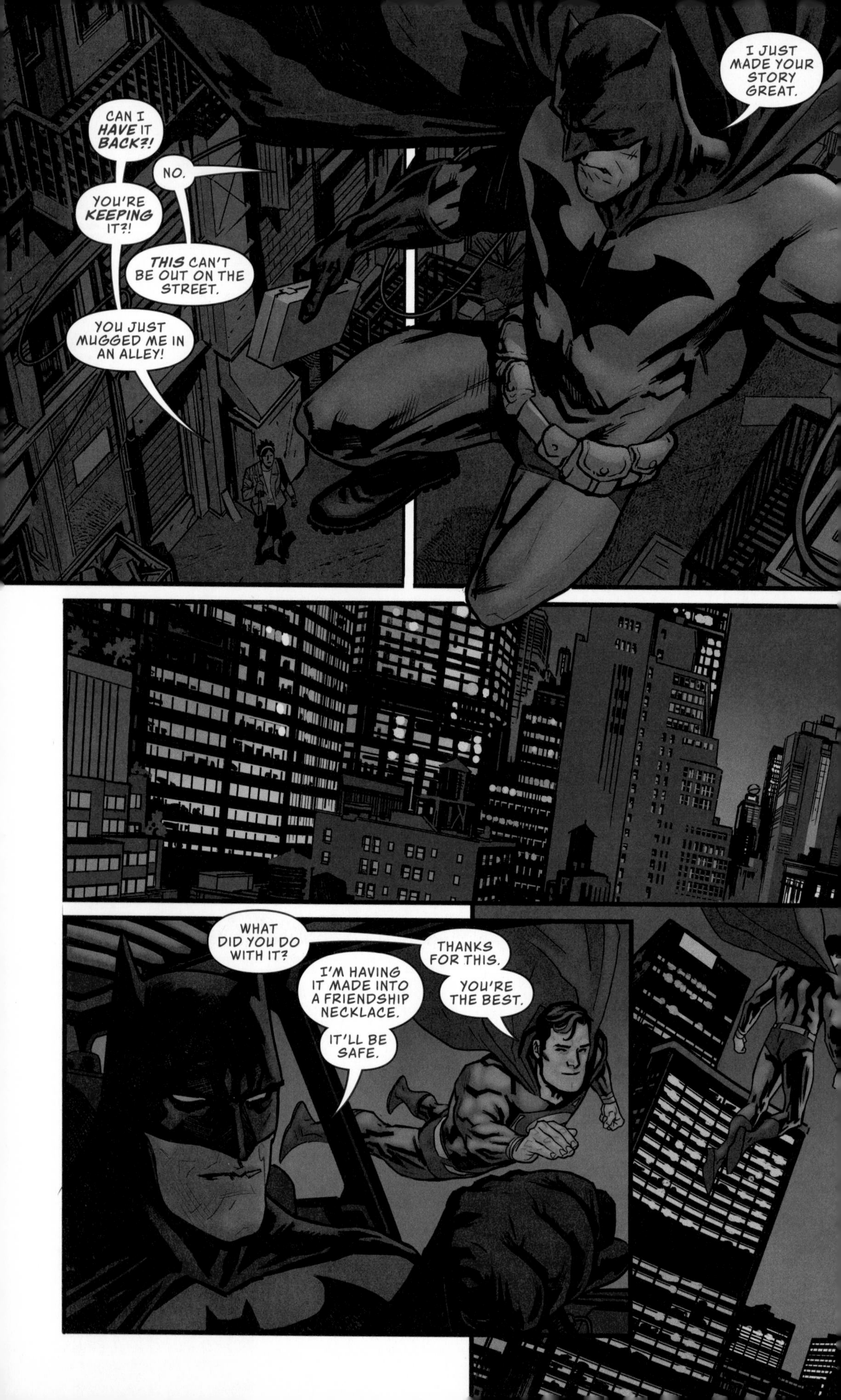
CAN I HAVE IT BACK?!
NO.
YOU'RE KEEPING IT?!
THIS CAN'T BE OUT ON THE STREET.
YOU JUST MUGGED ME IN AN ALLEY!
I JUST MADE YOUR STORY GREAT.
WHAT DID YOU DO WITH IT?
I'M HAVING IT MADE INTO A FRIENDSHIP NECKLACE.
IT'LL BE SAFE.
THANKS FOR THIS.
YOU'RE THE BEST.

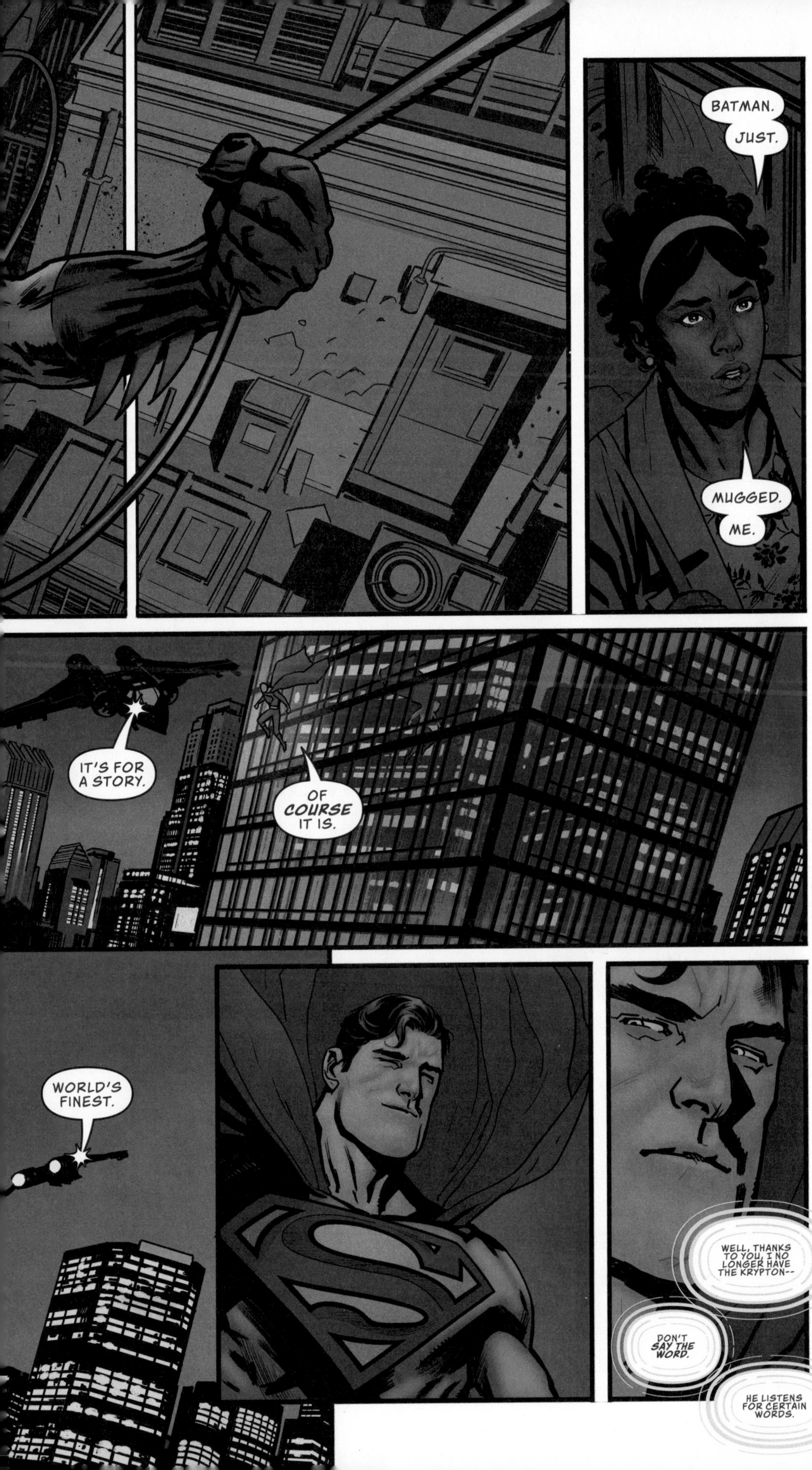
BATMAN. JUST.
MUGGED. ME.
IT'S FOR A STORY.
OF COURSE IT IS.
WORLD'S FINEST.
WELL, THANKS TO YOU, I NO LONGER HAVE THE KRYPTON--
DON'T SAY THE WORD.
HE LISTENS FOR CERTAIN WORDS.

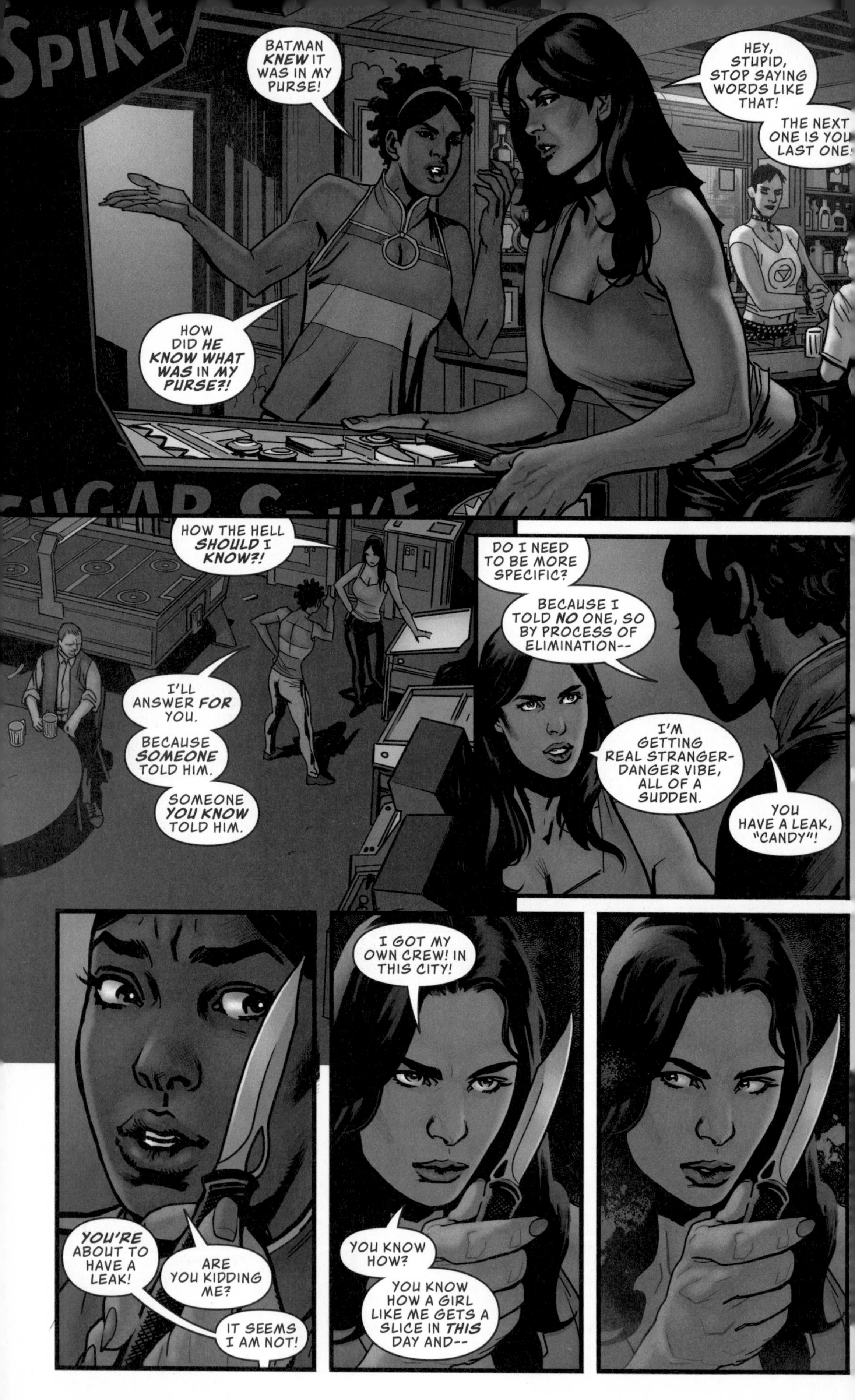
SPIKE
BATMAN KNEW IT WAS IN MY PURSE!
HEY, STUPID, STOP SAYING WORDS LIKE THAT!
THE NEXT ONE IS YOU LAST ONE
HOW DID HE KNOW WHAT WAS IN MY PURSE?!
HOW THE HELL SHOULD I KNOW?!
DO I NEED TO BE MORE SPECIFIC?
BECAUSE I TOLD NO ONE, SO BY PROCESS OF ELIMINATION--
I'LL ANSWER FOR YOU.
BECAUSE SOMEONE TOLD HIM.
SOMEONE YOU KNOW TOLD HIM.
I'M GETTING REAL STRANGER-DANGER VIBE, ALL OF A SUDDEN.
YOU HAVE A LEAK, "CANDY"!
YOU'RE ABOUT TO HAVE A LEAK!
ARE YOU KIDDING ME?
IT SEEMS I AM NOT!
I GOT MY OWN CREW! IN THIS CITY!
YOU KNOW HOW?
YOU KNOW HOW A GIRL LIKE ME GETS A SLICE IN THIS DAY AND--

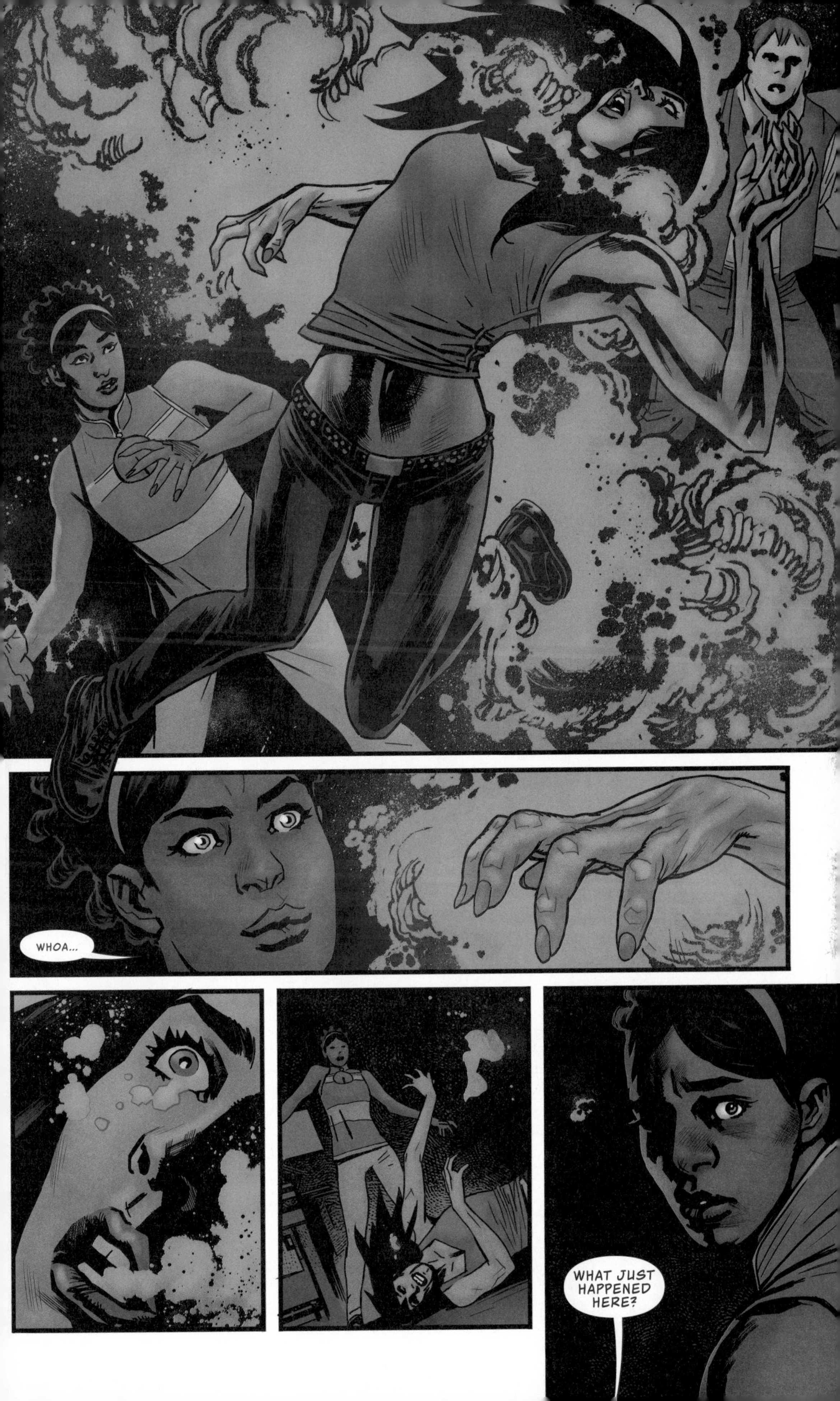
WHOA...
WHAT JUST HAPPENED HERE?

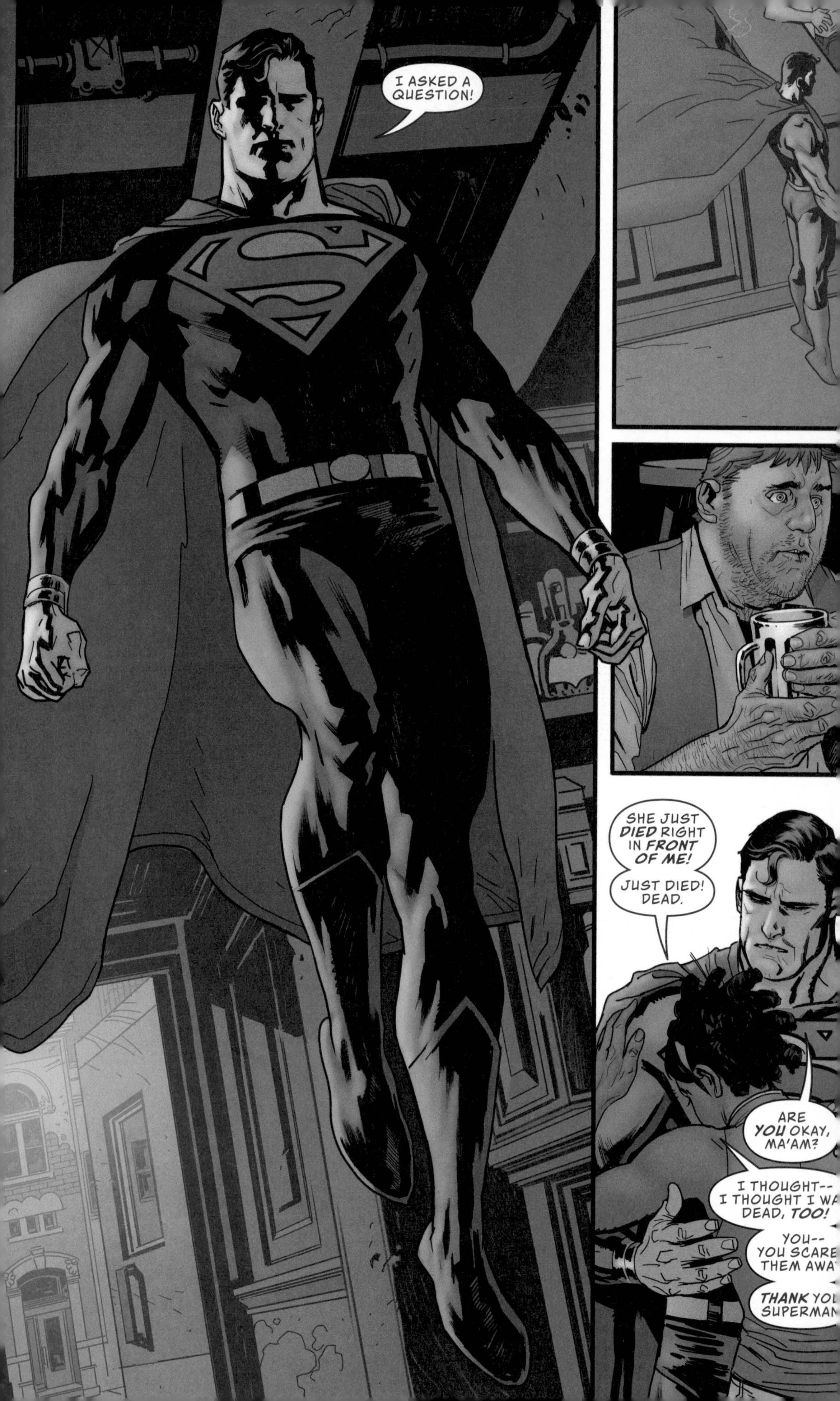
I ASKED A QUESTION!
SHE JUST DIED RIGHT IN FRONT OF ME!
JUST DIED! DEAD.
ARE YOU OKAY, MA'AM?
I THOUGHT-- I THOUGHT I WA DEAD, TOO!
YOU-- YOU SCARE THEM AWA
THANK YO SUPERMAN

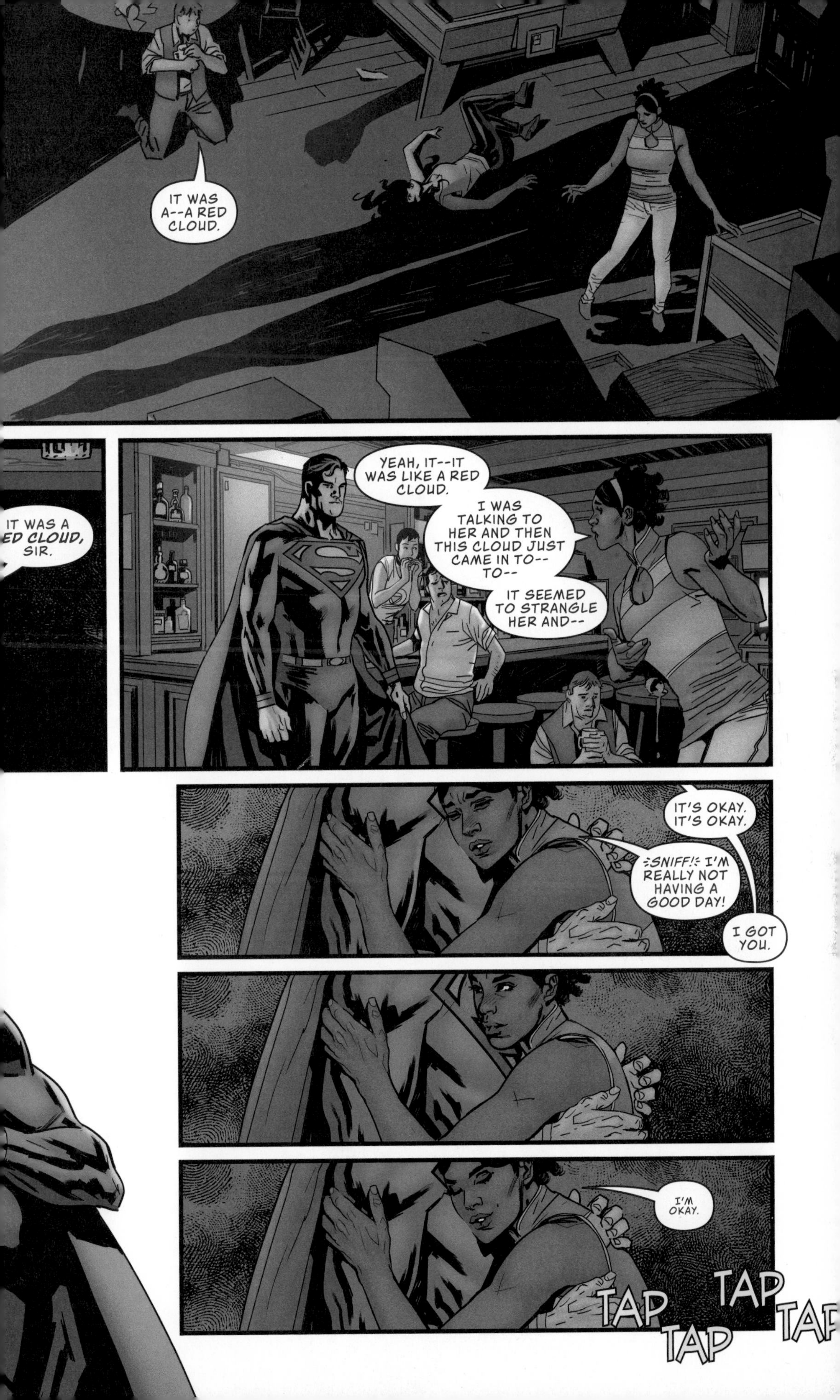
IT WAS A--A RED CLOUD.
IT WAS A ED CLOUD, SIR.
YEAH, IT--IT WAS LIKE A RED CLOUD.
I WAS TALKING TO HER AND THEN THIS CLOUD JUST CAME IN TO--TO--
IT SEEMED TO STRANGLE HER AND--
IT'S OKAY. IT'S OKAY.
SNIFF! I'M REALLY NOT HAVING A GOOD DAY!
I GOT YOU.
I'M OKAY.
TAP TAP TAP TAP

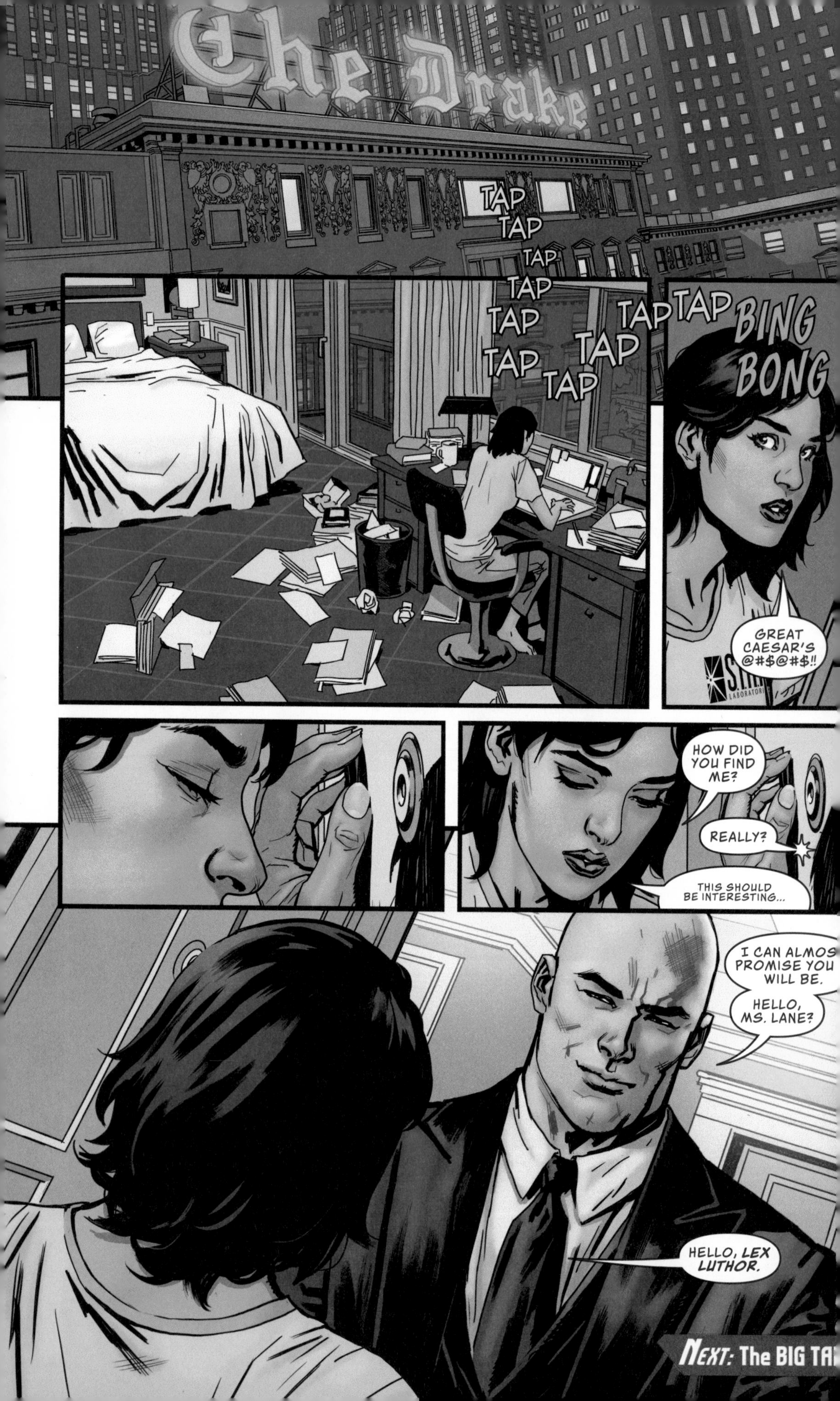
The Drake
TAP TAP TAP TAP TAP TAP TAP TAP TAP TAP
BING BONG
GREAT CAESAR'S @#$@#$!!
HOW DID YOU FIND ME?
REALLY?
THIS SHOULD BE INTERESTING...
I CAN ALMOS PROMISE YOU WILL BE.
HELLO, MS. LANE?
HELLO, LEX LUTHOR.
NEXT: The BIG TA

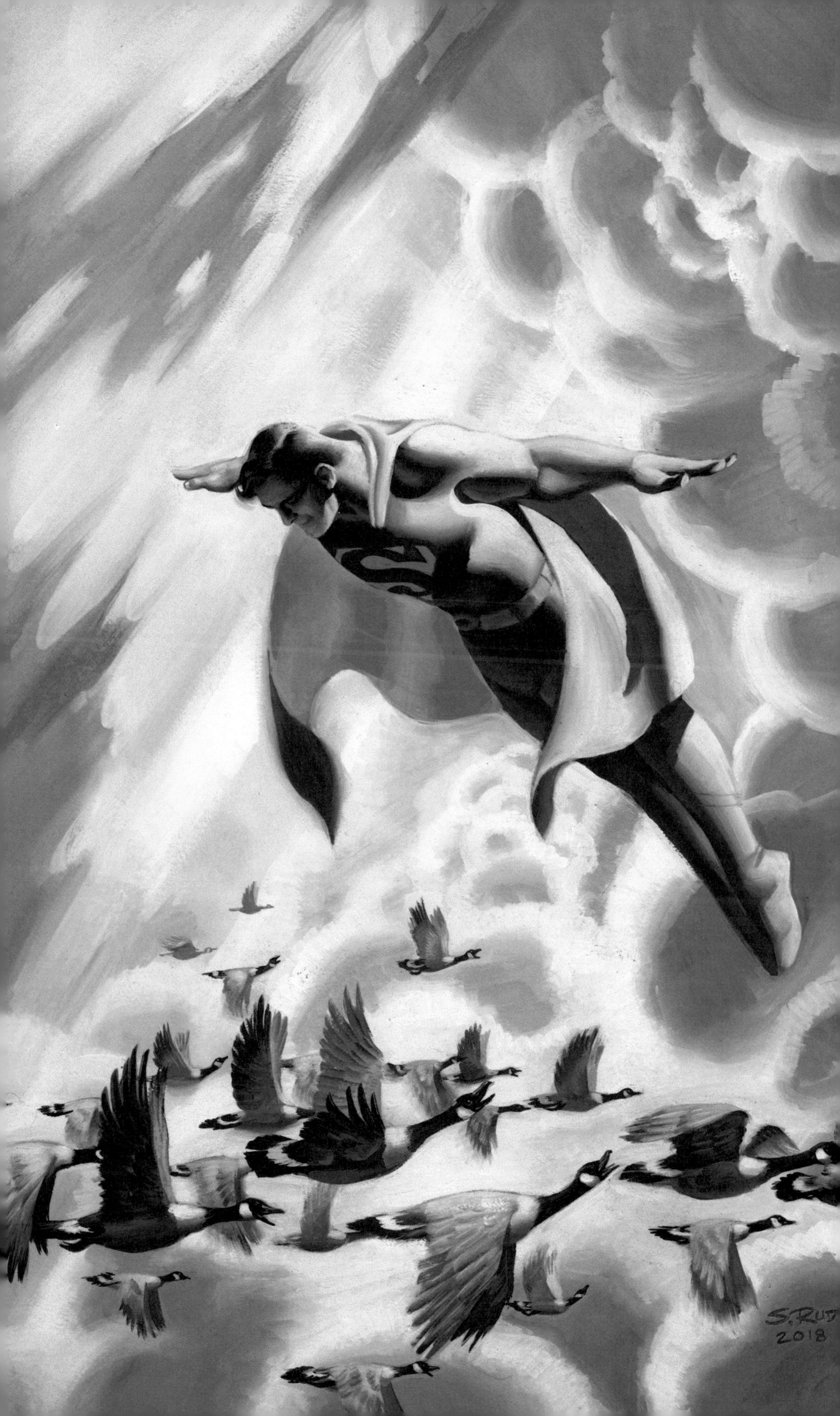

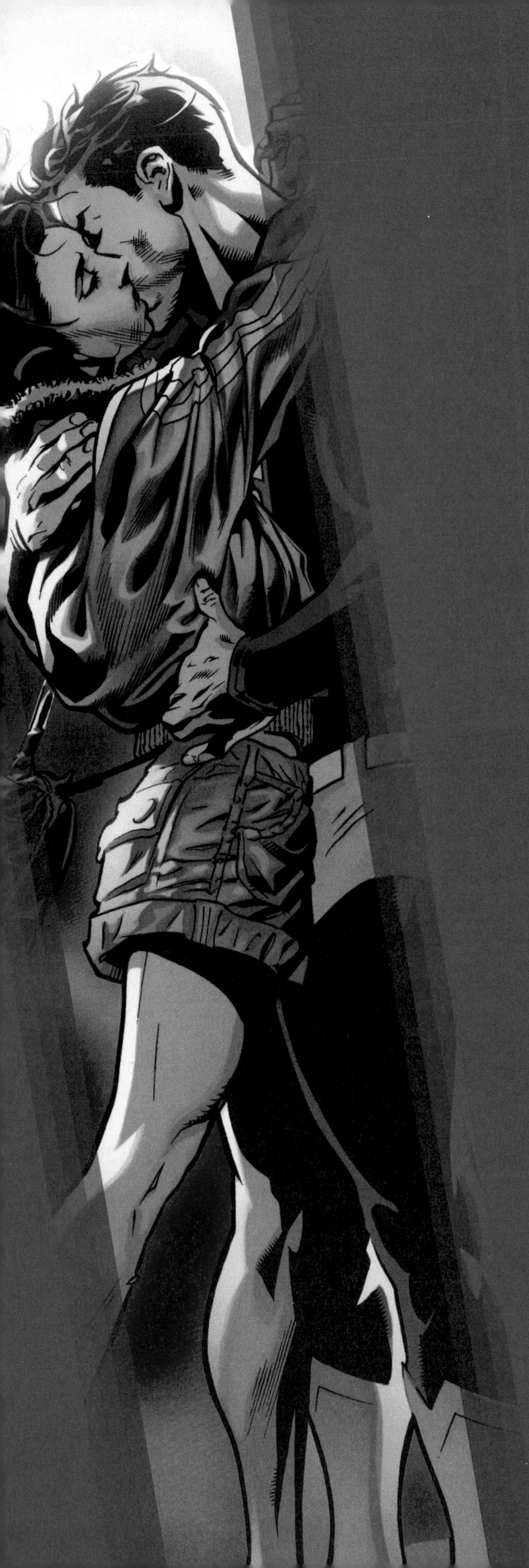

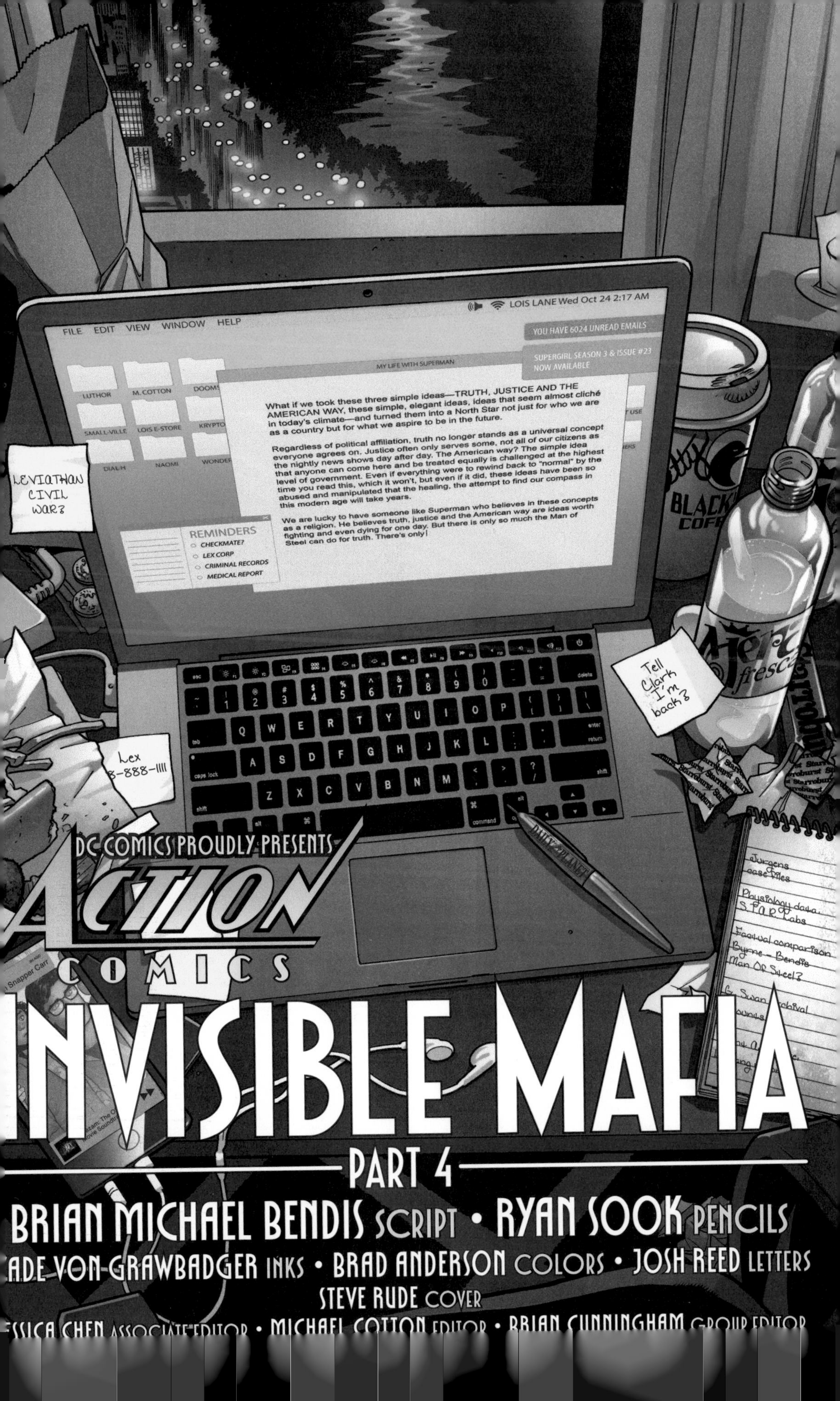

LOIS LANE Wed Oct 24 2:17 AM
FILE EDIT VIEW WINDOW HELP
YOU HAVE 6024 UNREAD EMAILS
SUPERGIRL SEASON 3 & ISSUE #23 NOW AVAILABLE
LUTHOR
M. COTTON
SMALLVILLE
LOIS E-STORE
DIAL H
NAOMI
MY LIFE WITH SUPERMAN
What if we took these three simple ideas—TRUTH, JUSTICE AND THE AMERICAN WAY, these simple, elegant ideas, ideas that seem almost cliché in today's climate—and turned them into a North Star not just for who we are as a country but for what we aspire to be in the future.
Regardless of political affiliation, truth no longer stands as a universal concept everyone agrees on. Justice often only serves some, not all of our citizens as the nightly news shows day after day. The American way? The simple idea that anyone can come here and be treated equally is challenged at the highest level of government. Even if everything were to rewind back to "normal" by the time you read this, which it won't, but even if it did, these ideas have been so abused and manipulated that the healing, the attempt to find our compass in this modern age will take years.
We are lucky to have someone like Superman who believes in these concepts as a religion. He believes truth, justice and the American way are ideas worth fighting and even dying for one day. But there is only so much the Man of Steel can do for truth. There's only
REMINDERS
CHECKMATE?
LEX CORP
CRIMINAL RECORDS
MEDICAL REPORT
LEVIATHAN CIVIL WAR?
Tell Clark I'm back?
Lex 8-888-1111
DAILY PLANET
Jurgens case files
Physiology data S.T.A.R. Labs
Factual comparison Byrne - Bendis Man Of Steel?
DC COMICS PROUDLY PRESENTS
ACTION COMICS
INVISIBLE MAFIA
PART 4
BRIAN MICHAEL BENDIS SCRIPT • RYAN SOOK PENCILS
ADE VON-GRAWBADGER INKS • BRAD ANDERSON COLORS • JOSH REED LETTERS
STEVE RUDE COVER
ESSICA CHEN ASSOCIATE EDITOR • MICHAEL COTTON EDITOR • BRIAN CUNNINGHAM GROUP EDITOR

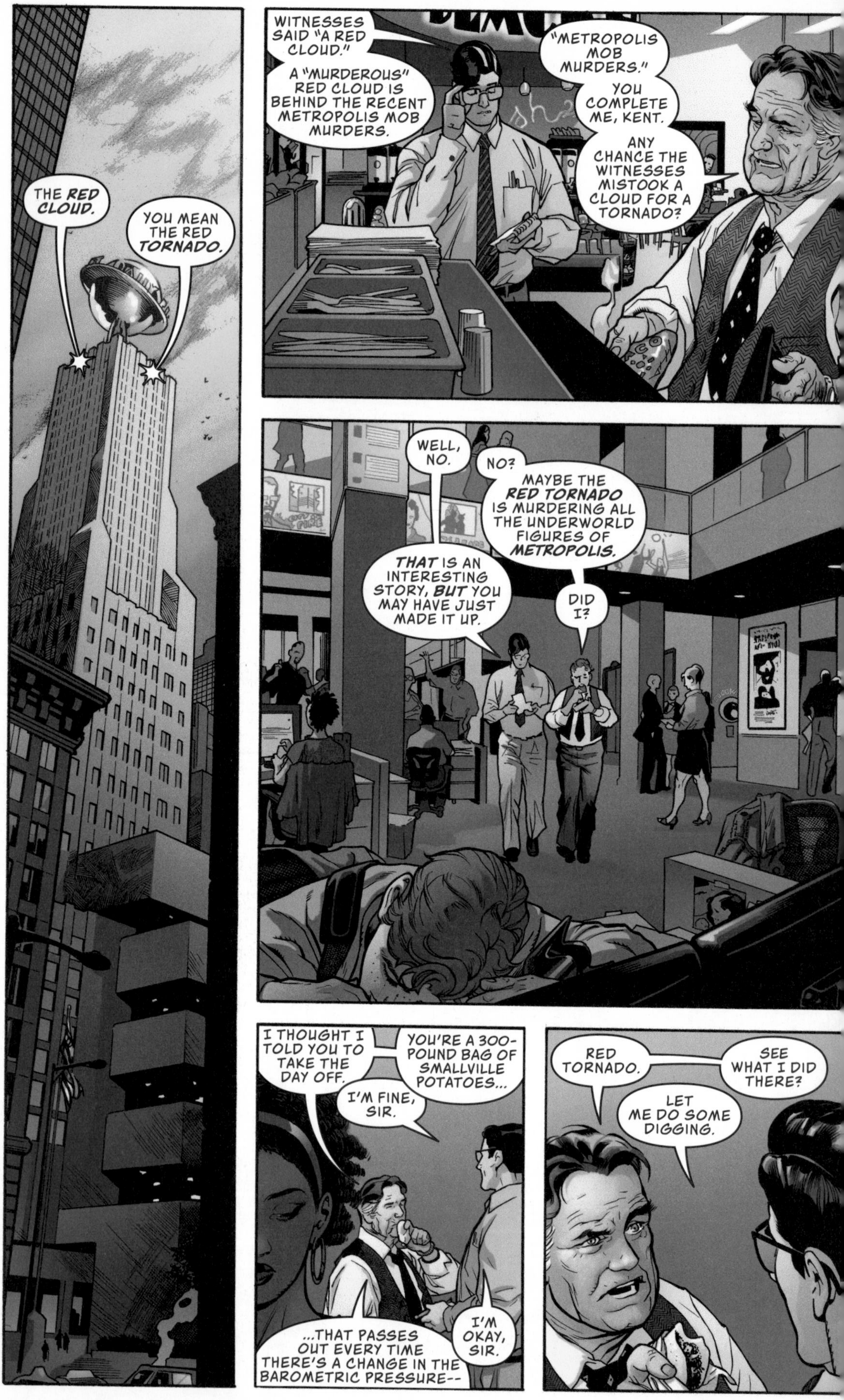

THE RED CLOUD.
YOU MEAN THE RED TORNADO.
WITNESSES SAID "A RED CLOUD."
A "MURDEROUS" RED CLOUD IS BEHIND THE RECENT METROPOLIS MOB MURDERS.
"METROPOLIS MOB MURDERS."
YOU COMPLETE ME, KENT.
ANY CHANCE THE WITNESSES MISTOOK A CLOUD FOR A TORNADO?
WELL, NO.
NO?
MAYBE THE RED TORNADO IS MURDERING ALL THE UNDERWORLD FIGURES OF METROPOLIS.
THAT IS AN INTERESTING STORY, BUT YOU MAY HAVE JUST MADE IT UP.
DID I?
I THOUGHT I TOLD YOU TO TAKE THE DAY OFF.
YOU'RE A 300-POUND BAG OF SMALLVILLE POTATOES...
I'M FINE, SIR.
...THAT PASSES OUT EVERY TIME THERE'S A CHANGE IN THE BAROMETRIC PRESSURE--
I'M OKAY, SIR.
RED TORNADO.
SEE WHAT I DID THERE?
LET ME DO SOME DIGGING.

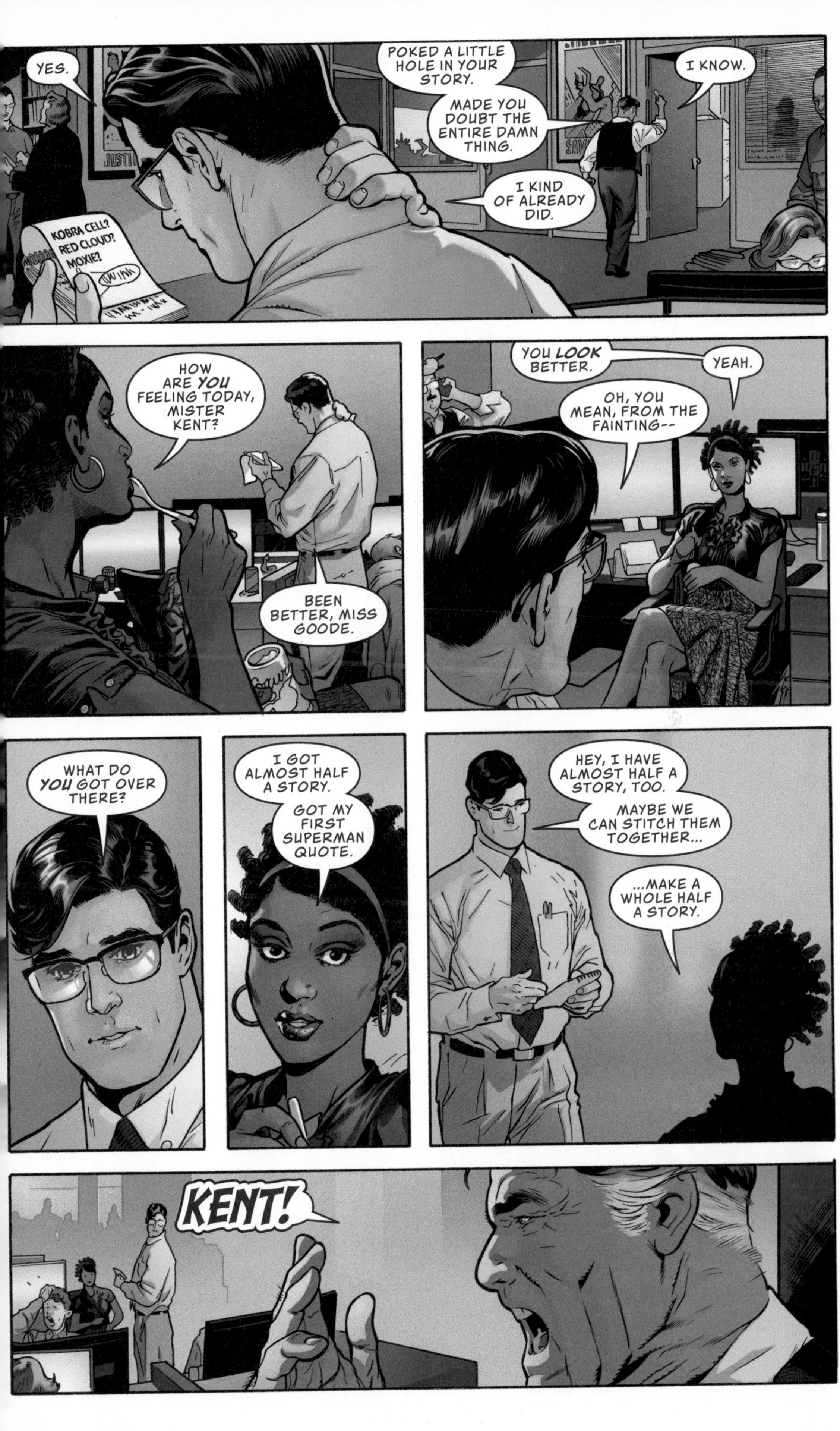
YES.
POKED A LITTLE HOLE IN YOUR STORY.
MADE YOU DOUBT THE ENTIRE DAMN THING.
I KNOW.
I KIND OF ALREADY DID.
KOBRA CELL? RED CLOUD? MOXIE?
HOW ARE *YOU* FEELING TODAY, MISTER KENT?
BEEN BETTER, MISS GOODE.
YOU *LOOK* BETTER.
YEAH.
OH, YOU MEAN, FROM THE FAINTING--
WHAT DO *YOU* GOT OVER THERE?
I GOT ALMOST HALF A STORY.
GOT MY FIRST SUPERMAN QUOTE.
HEY, I HAVE ALMOST HALF A STORY, TOO.
MAYBE WE CAN STITCH THEM TOGETHER...
...MAKE A WHOLE HALF A STORY.
KENT!

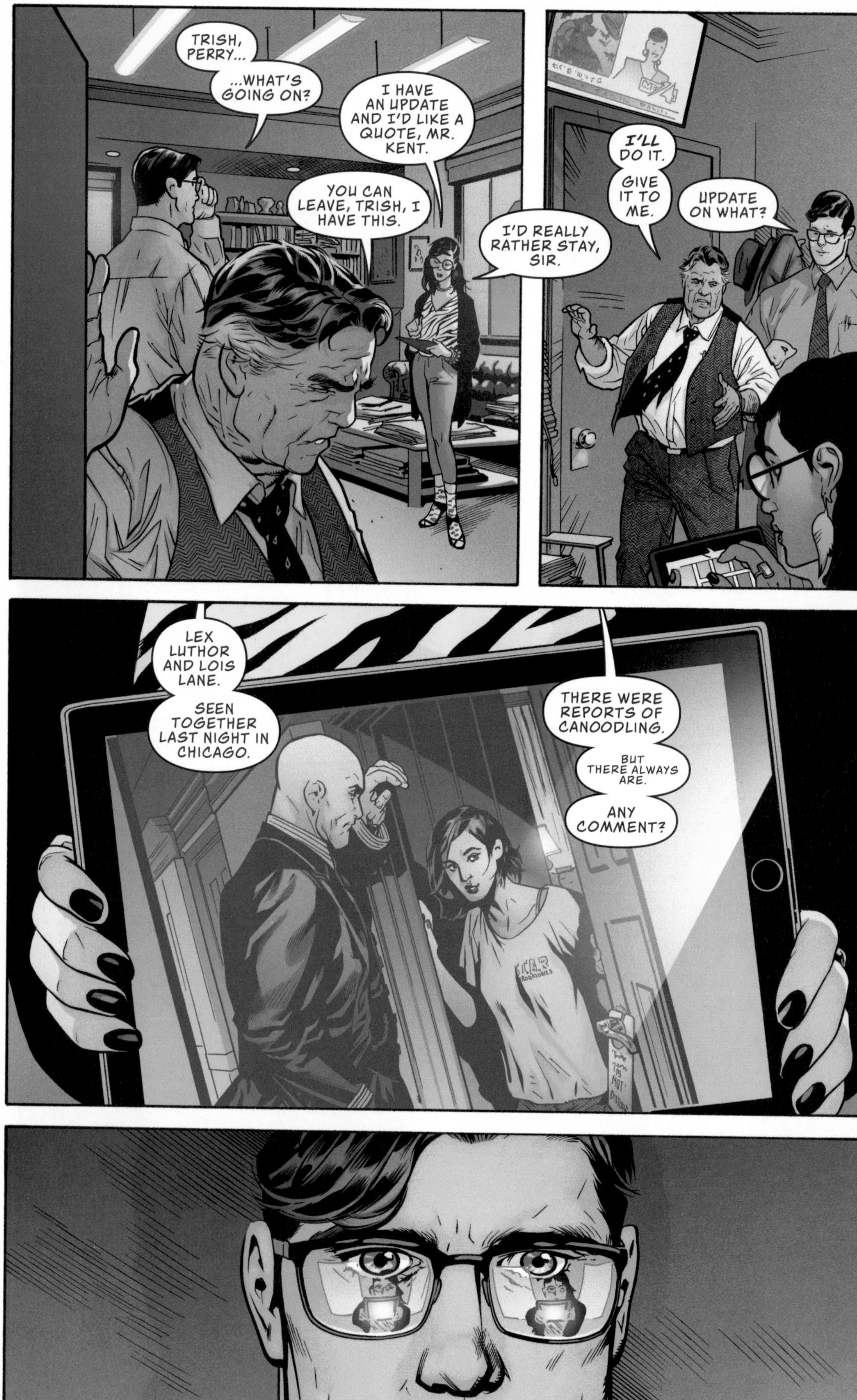
TRISH, PERRY...
...WHAT'S GOING ON?
I HAVE AN UPDATE AND I'D LIKE A QUOTE, MR. KENT.
YOU CAN LEAVE, TRISH, I HAVE THIS.
I'D REALLY RATHER STAY, SIR.
I'LL DO IT.
GIVE IT TO ME.
UPDATE ON WHAT?
LEX LUTHOR AND LOIS LANE.
SEEN TOGETHER LAST NIGHT IN CHICAGO.
THERE WERE REPORTS OF CANOODLING.
BUT THERE ALWAYS ARE.
ANY COMMENT?

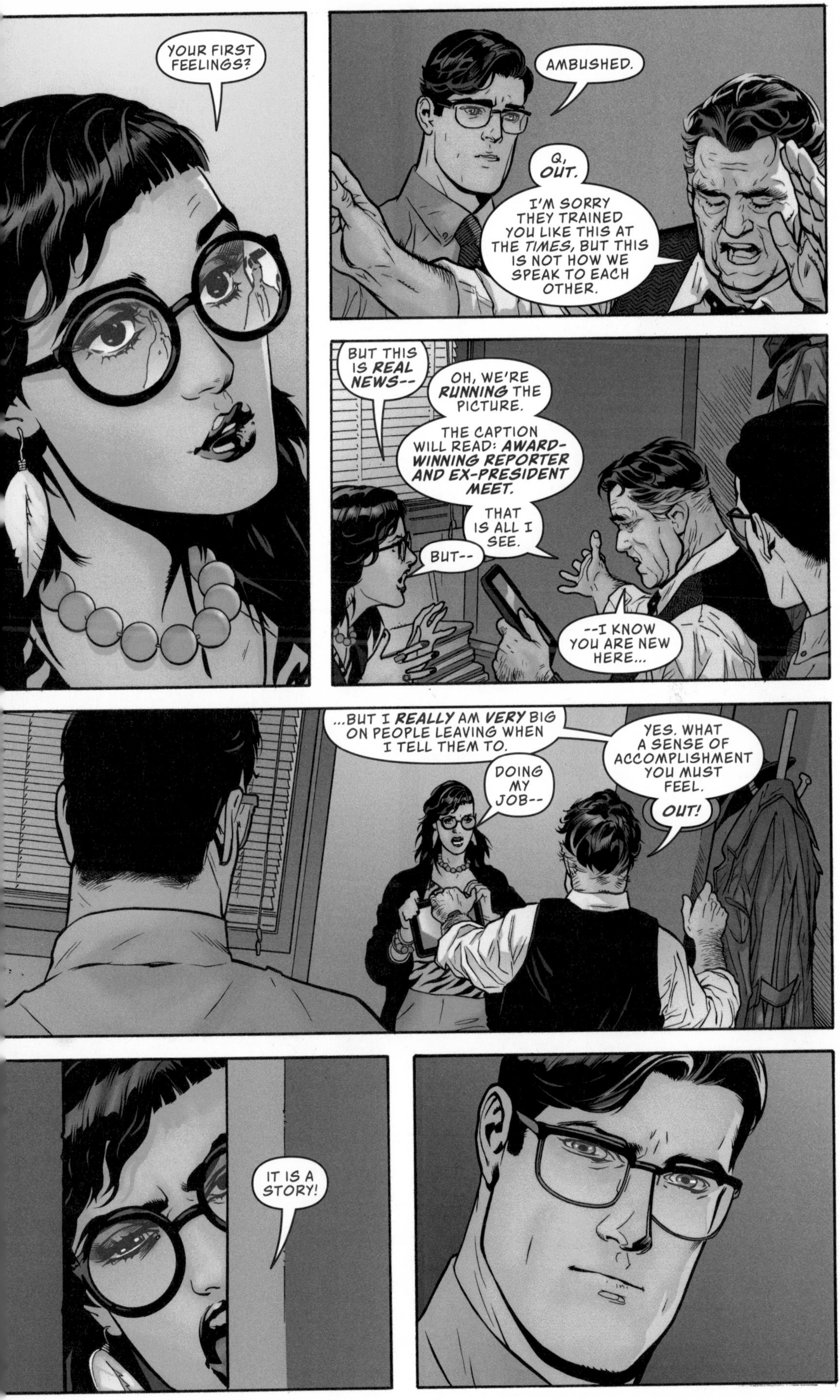
YOUR FIRST FEELINGS?
AMBUSHED.
Q, *OUT.*
I'M SORRY THEY TRAINED YOU LIKE THIS AT THE *TIMES*, BUT THIS IS NOT HOW WE SPEAK TO EACH OTHER.
BUT THIS IS *REAL NEWS--*
OH, WE'RE *RUNNING* THE PICTURE.
THE CAPTION WILL READ: *AWARD-WINNING REPORTER AND EX-PRESIDENT MEET.*
THAT IS ALL I SEE.
BUT--
--I KNOW YOU ARE NEW HERE...
...BUT I *REALLY* AM *VERY* BIG ON PEOPLE LEAVING WHEN I TELL THEM TO.
DOING MY JOB--
YES. WHAT A SENSE OF ACCOMPLISHMENT YOU MUST FEEL.
OUT!
IT IS A STORY!

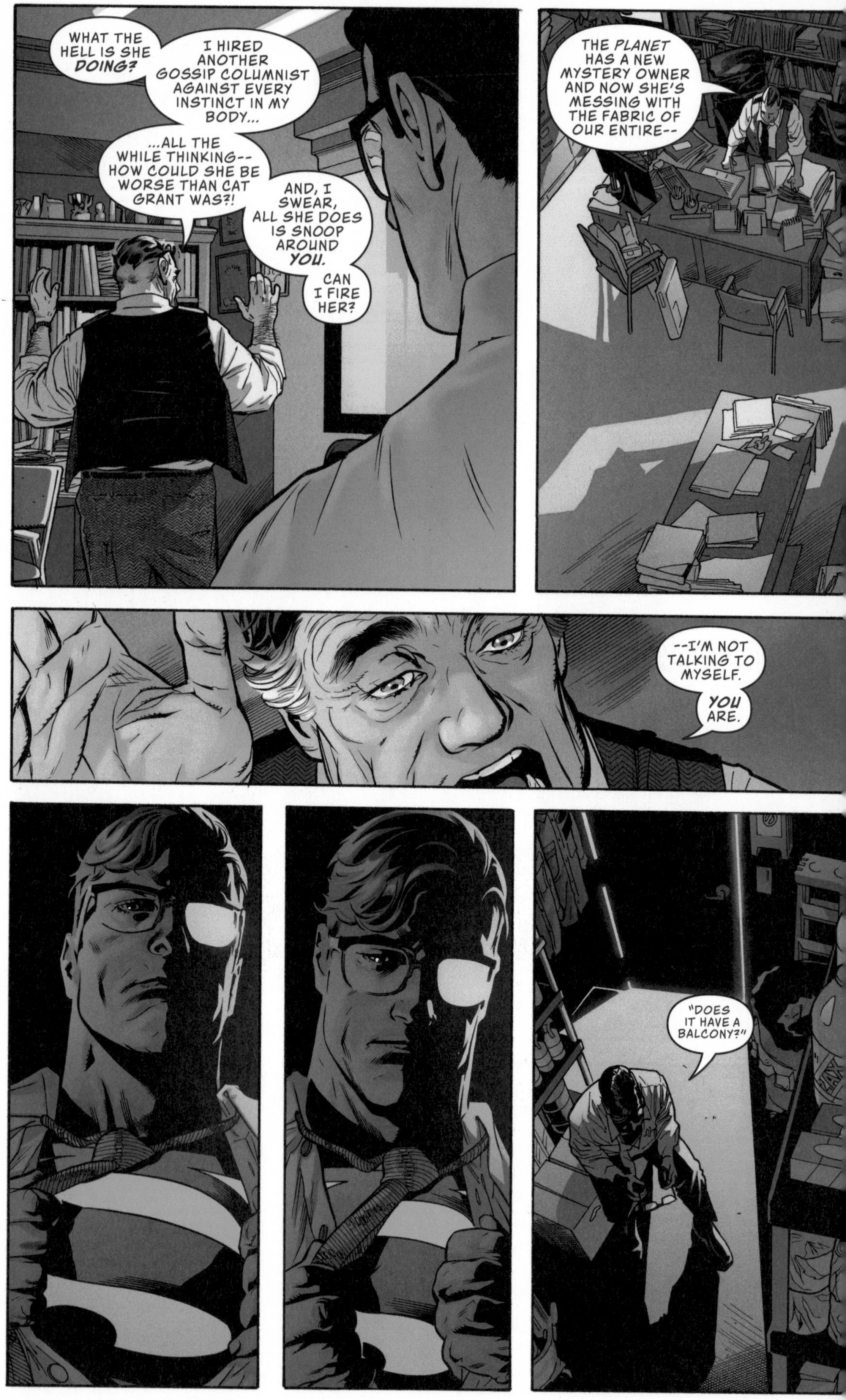
WHAT THE HELL IS SHE *DOING?*
I HIRED ANOTHER GOSSIP COLUMNIST AGAINST EVERY INSTINCT IN MY BODY...
...ALL THE WHILE THINKING--HOW COULD SHE BE WORSE THAN CAT GRANT WAS?!
AND, I SWEAR, ALL SHE DOES IS SNOOP AROUND *YOU.*
CAN I FIRE HER?
THE *PLANET* HAS A NEW MYSTERY OWNER AND NOW SHE'S MESSING WITH THE FABRIC OF OUR ENTIRE--
--I'M NOT TALKING TO MYSELF.
YOU ARE.
"DOES IT HAVE A BALCONY?"

LAST

NIGHT.

I ASKED
FOR NO
PICKLES...

LOIS?

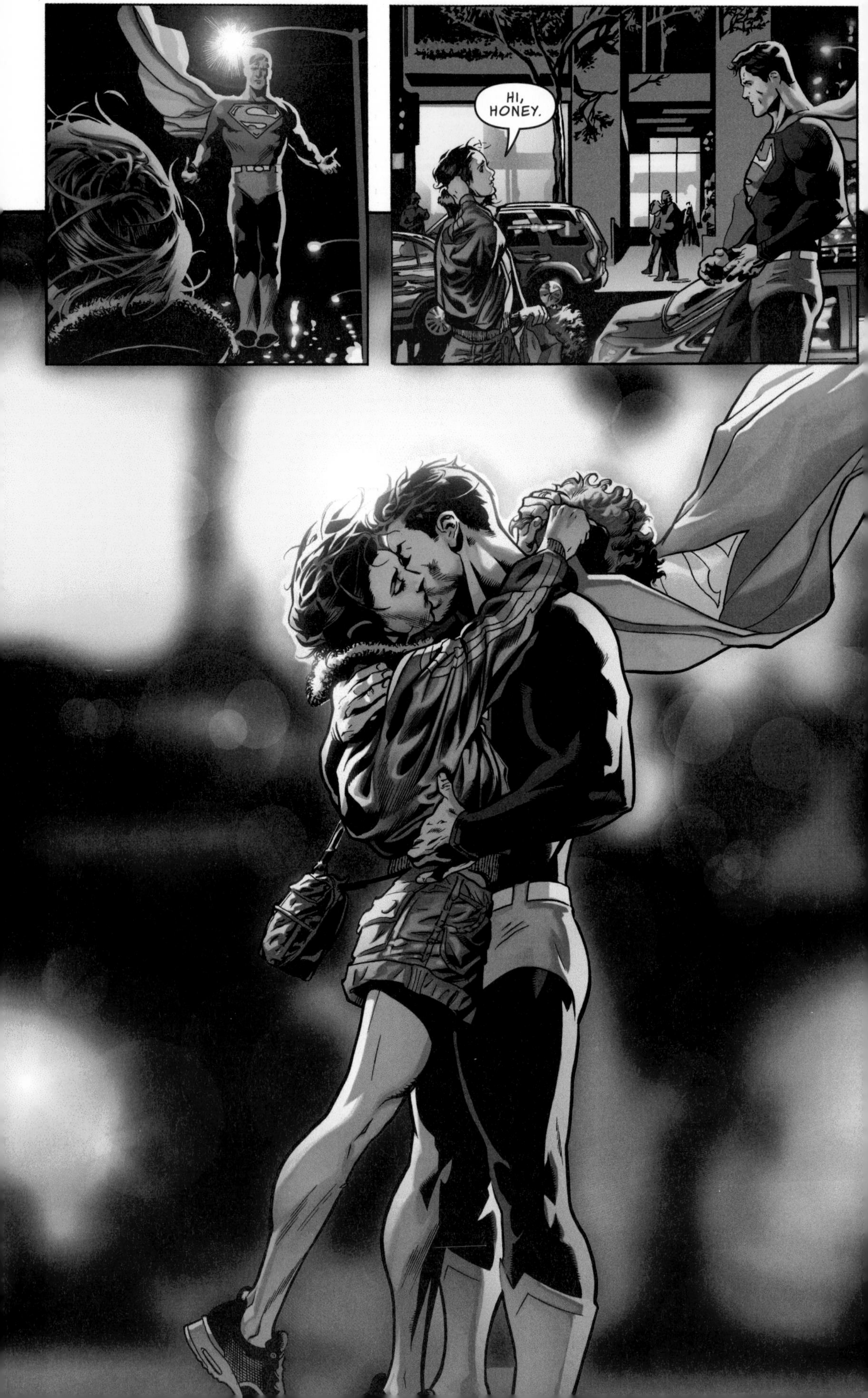
HI, HONEY.

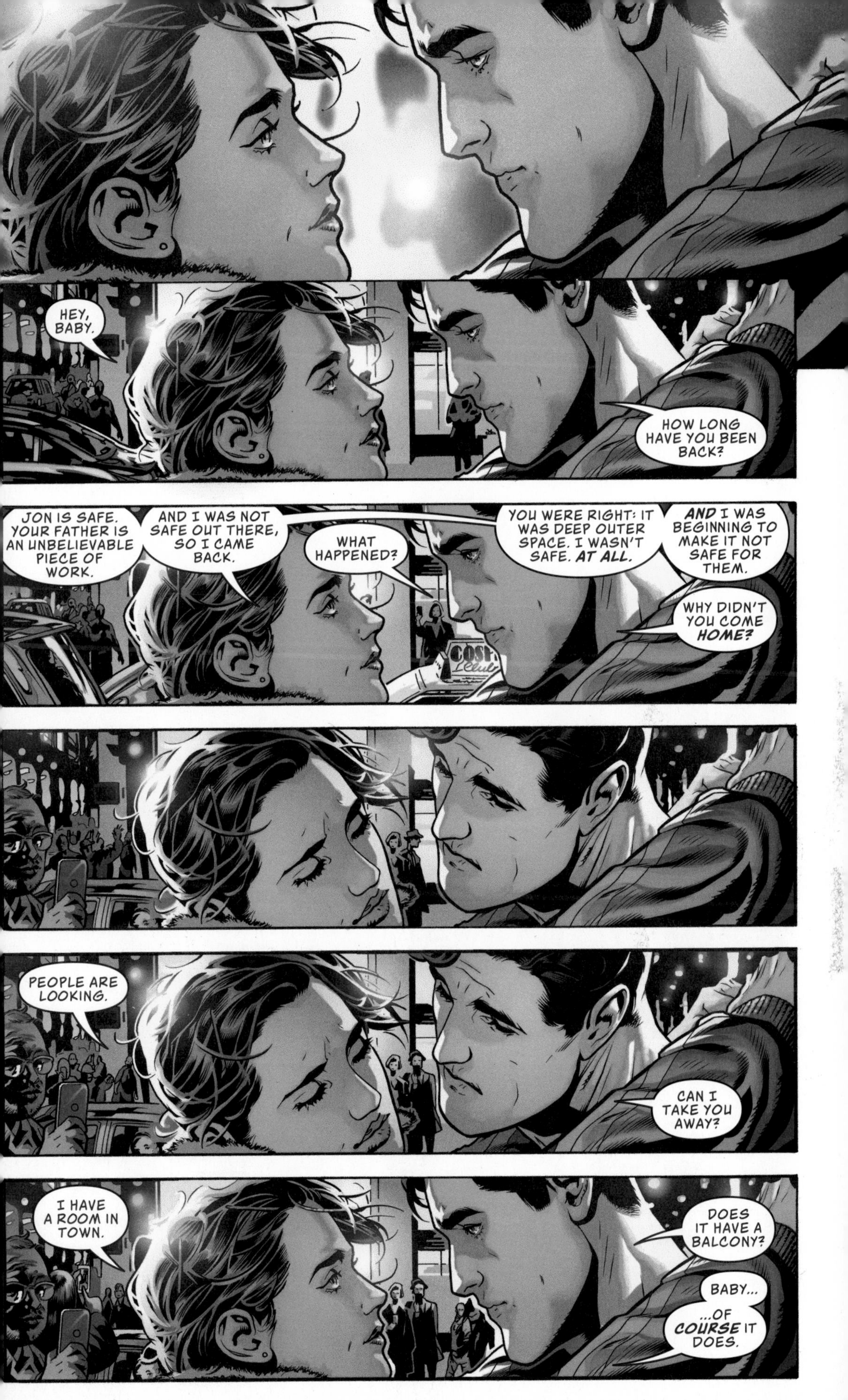
HEY, BABY.
HOW LONG HAVE YOU BEEN BACK?
JON IS SAFE. YOUR FATHER IS AN UNBELIEVABLE PIECE OF WORK.
AND I WAS NOT SAFE OUT THERE, SO I CAME BACK.
WHAT HAPPENED?
YOU WERE RIGHT: IT WAS DEEP OUTER SPACE. I WASN'T SAFE. AT ALL.
AND I WAS BEGINNING TO MAKE IT NOT SAFE FOR THEM.
WHY DIDN'T YOU COME HOME?
PEOPLE ARE LOOKING.
CAN I TAKE YOU AWAY?
I HAVE A ROOM IN TOWN.
DOES IT HAVE A BALCONY?
BABY...
...OF COURSE IT DOES.

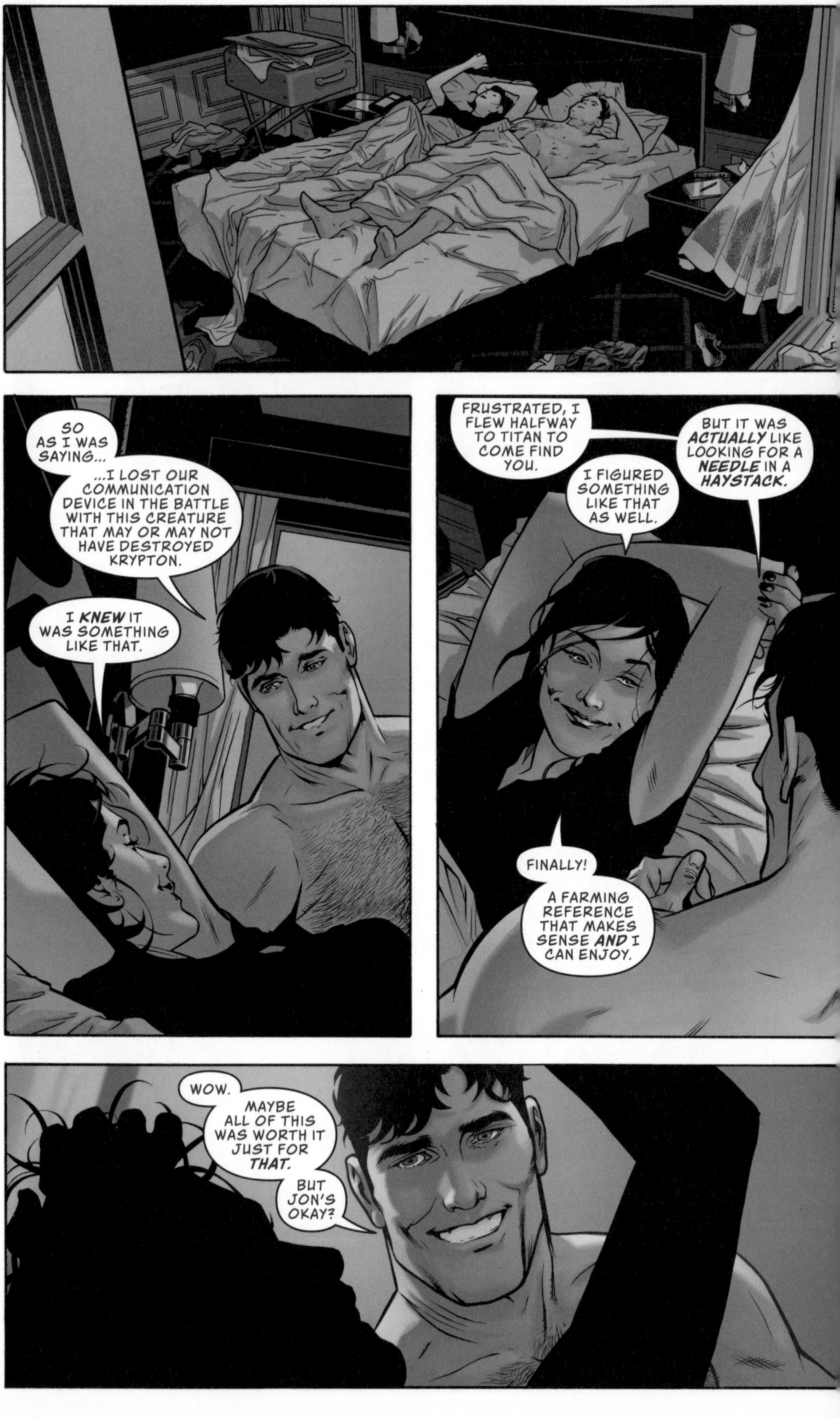
SO AS I WAS SAYING...
...I LOST OUR COMMUNICATION DEVICE IN THE BATTLE WITH THIS CREATURE THAT MAY OR MAY NOT HAVE DESTROYED KRYPTON.
I KNEW IT WAS SOMETHING LIKE THAT.
FRUSTRATED, I FLEW HALFWAY TO TITAN TO COME FIND YOU.
BUT IT WAS ACTUALLY LIKE LOOKING FOR A NEEDLE IN A HAYSTACK.
I FIGURED SOMETHING LIKE THAT AS WELL.
FINALLY!
A FARMING REFERENCE THAT MAKES SENSE AND I CAN ENJOY.
WOW.
MAYBE ALL OF THIS WAS WORTH IT JUST FOR THAT.
BUT JON'S OKAY?

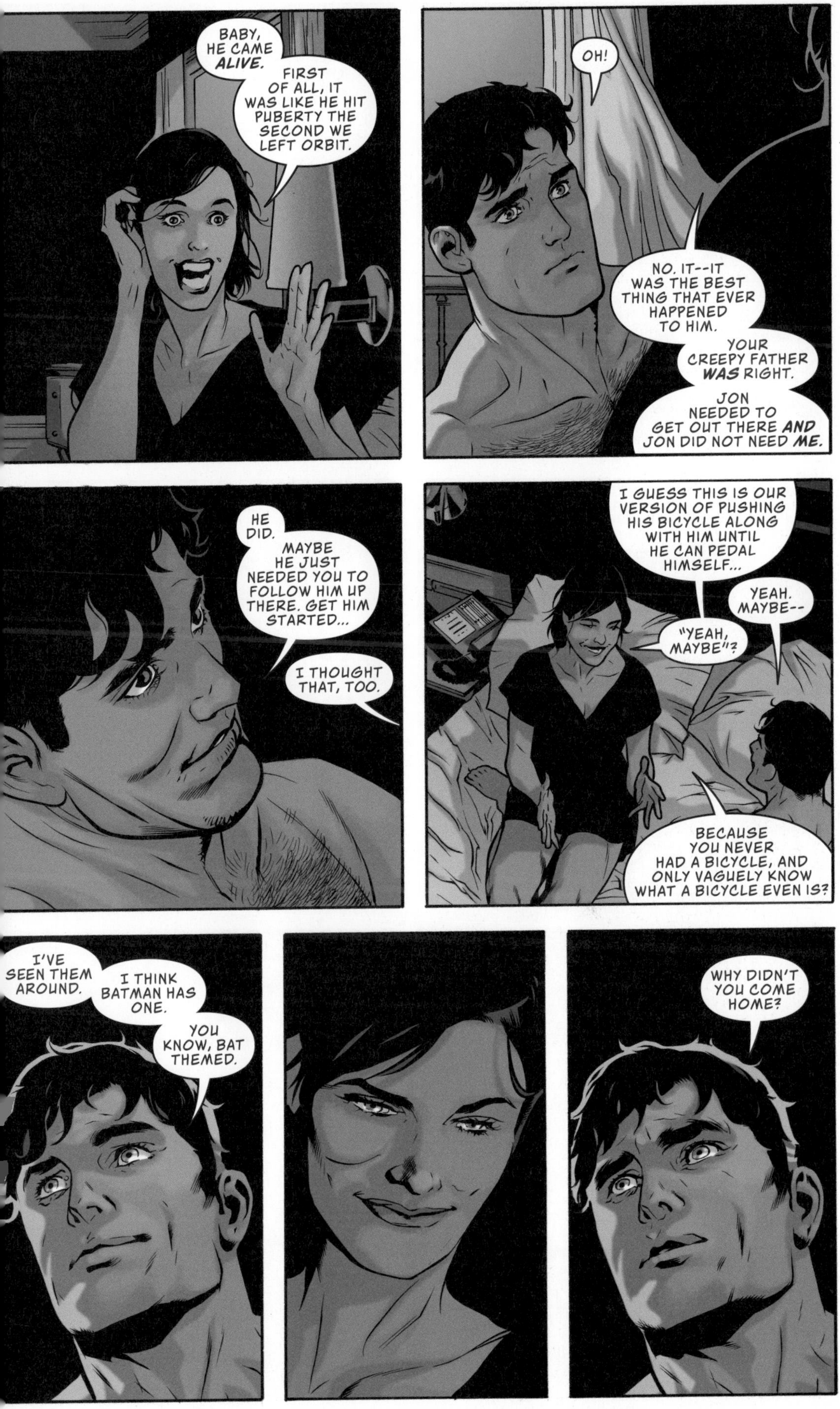
BABY, HE CAME ALIVE.
FIRST OF ALL, IT WAS LIKE HE HIT PUBERTY THE SECOND WE LEFT ORBIT.
OH!
NO. IT--IT WAS THE BEST THING THAT EVER HAPPENED TO HIM.
YOUR CREEPY FATHER WAS RIGHT.
JON NEEDED TO GET OUT THERE AND JON DID NOT NEED ME.
HE DID.
MAYBE HE JUST NEEDED YOU TO FOLLOW HIM UP THERE. GET HIM STARTED...
I THOUGHT THAT, TOO.
I GUESS THIS IS OUR VERSION OF PUSHING HIS BICYCLE ALONG WITH HIM UNTIL HE CAN PEDAL HIMSELF...
YEAH. MAYBE--
"YEAH, MAYBE"?
BECAUSE YOU NEVER HAD A BICYCLE, AND ONLY VAGUELY KNOW WHAT A BICYCLE EVEN IS?
I'VE SEEN THEM AROUND.
I THINK BATMAN HAS ONE.
YOU KNOW, BAT THEMED.
WHY DIDN'T YOU COME HOME?

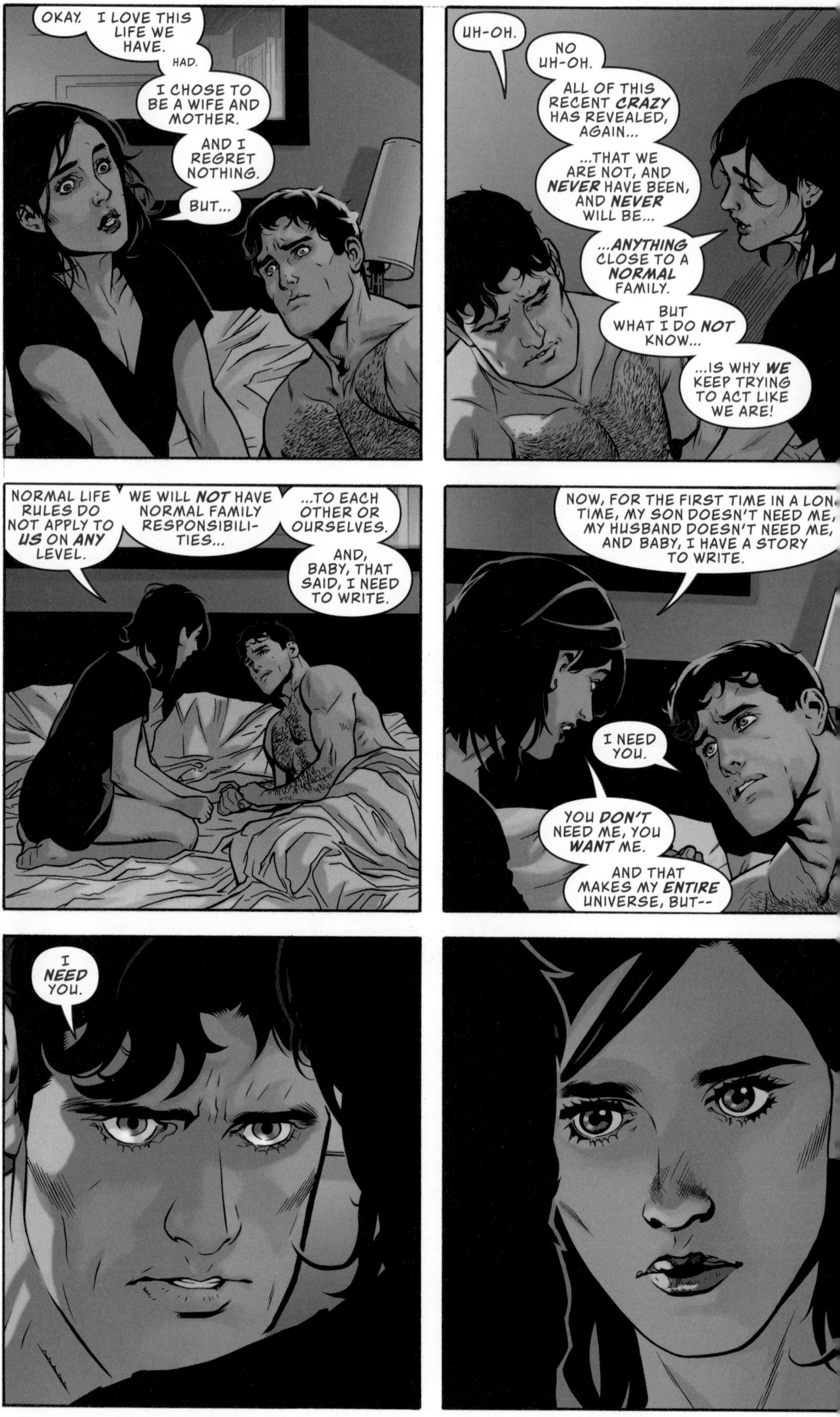
OKAY. I LOVE THIS LIFE WE HAVE.
HAD.
I CHOSE TO BE A WIFE AND MOTHER.
AND I REGRET NOTHING.
BUT...
UH-OH.
NO UH-OH.
ALL OF THIS RECENT CRAZY HAS REVEALED, AGAIN...
...THAT WE ARE NOT, AND NEVER HAVE BEEN, AND NEVER WILL BE...
...ANYTHING CLOSE TO A NORMAL FAMILY.
BUT WHAT I DO NOT KNOW...
...IS WHY WE KEEP TRYING TO ACT LIKE WE ARE!
NORMAL LIFE RULES DO NOT APPLY TO US ON ANY LEVEL.
WE WILL NOT HAVE NORMAL FAMILY RESPONSIBILI-TIES...
...TO EACH OTHER OR OURSELVES.
AND, BABY, THAT SAID, I NEED TO WRITE.
NOW, FOR THE FIRST TIME IN A LON TIME, MY SON DOESN'T NEED ME, MY HUSBAND DOESN'T NEED ME, AND BABY, I HAVE A STORY TO WRITE.
I NEED YOU.
YOU DON'T NEED ME, YOU WANT ME.
AND THAT MAKES MY ENTIRE UNIVERSE, BUT--
I NEED YOU.

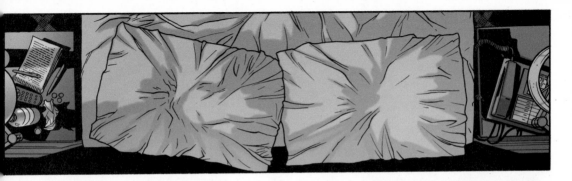

GREAT CAESAR'S--

GHOST.

HEY.

JUST SO WE'RE PERFECTLY, TOTALLY, 100 PERCENT CLEAR--

PLEASE!

WE'RE NOT BREAKING UP.

WE JUST BOTH HAVE *IMPORTANT* WORK TO DO.

I WAS ON MY WAY BACK THINKING ABOUT *ALL* OF THIS AND THEN I THOUGHT: IF I'M RUNNING AROUND AND *HE'S* RUNNING AROUND AND NORMAL DOESN'T APPLY, WHY ARE WE FIGHTING THE TIDE?

BUT I *WANT* THINGS TO BE NORMAL.

BABY...

HOLD ON...

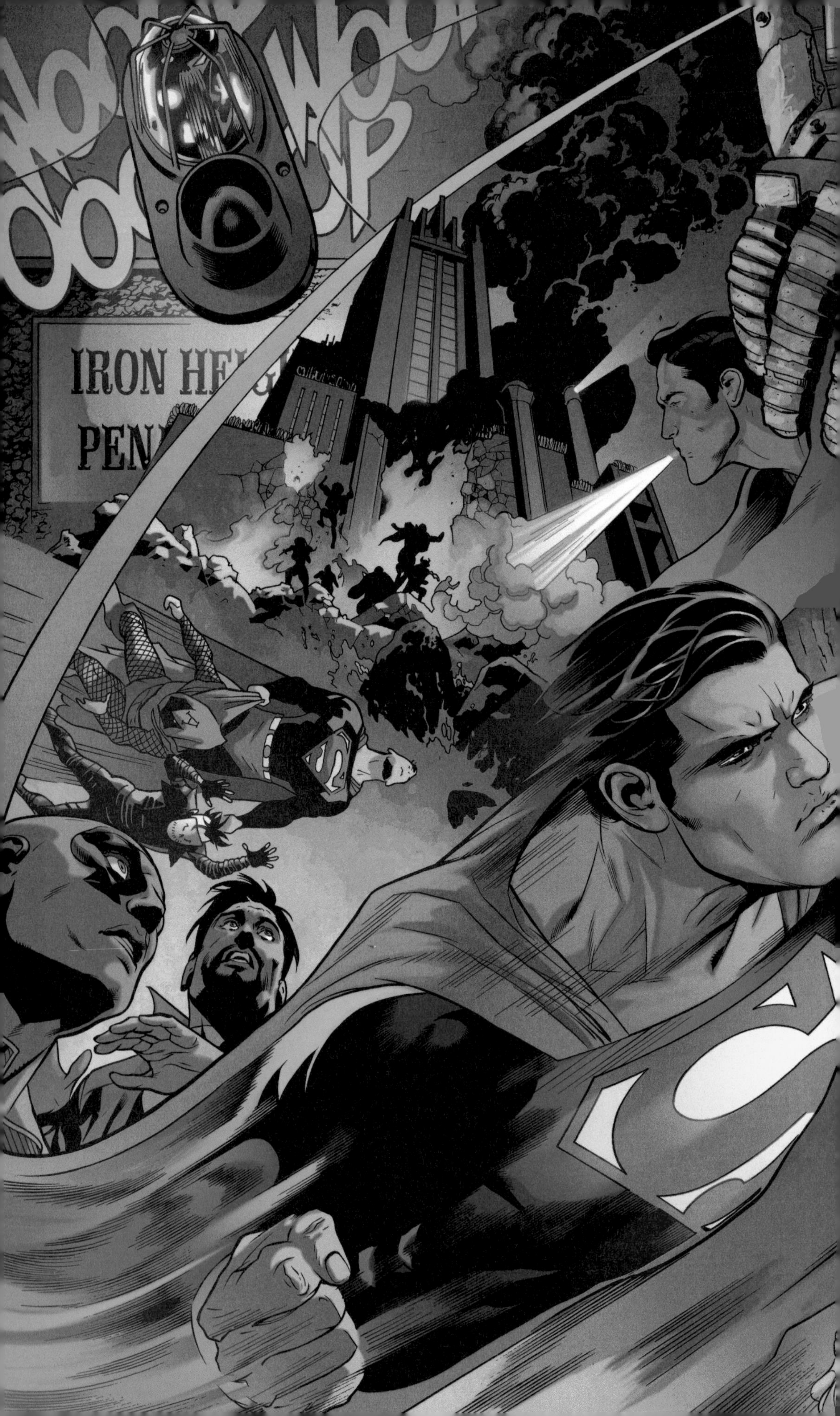
IRON HE
PEN

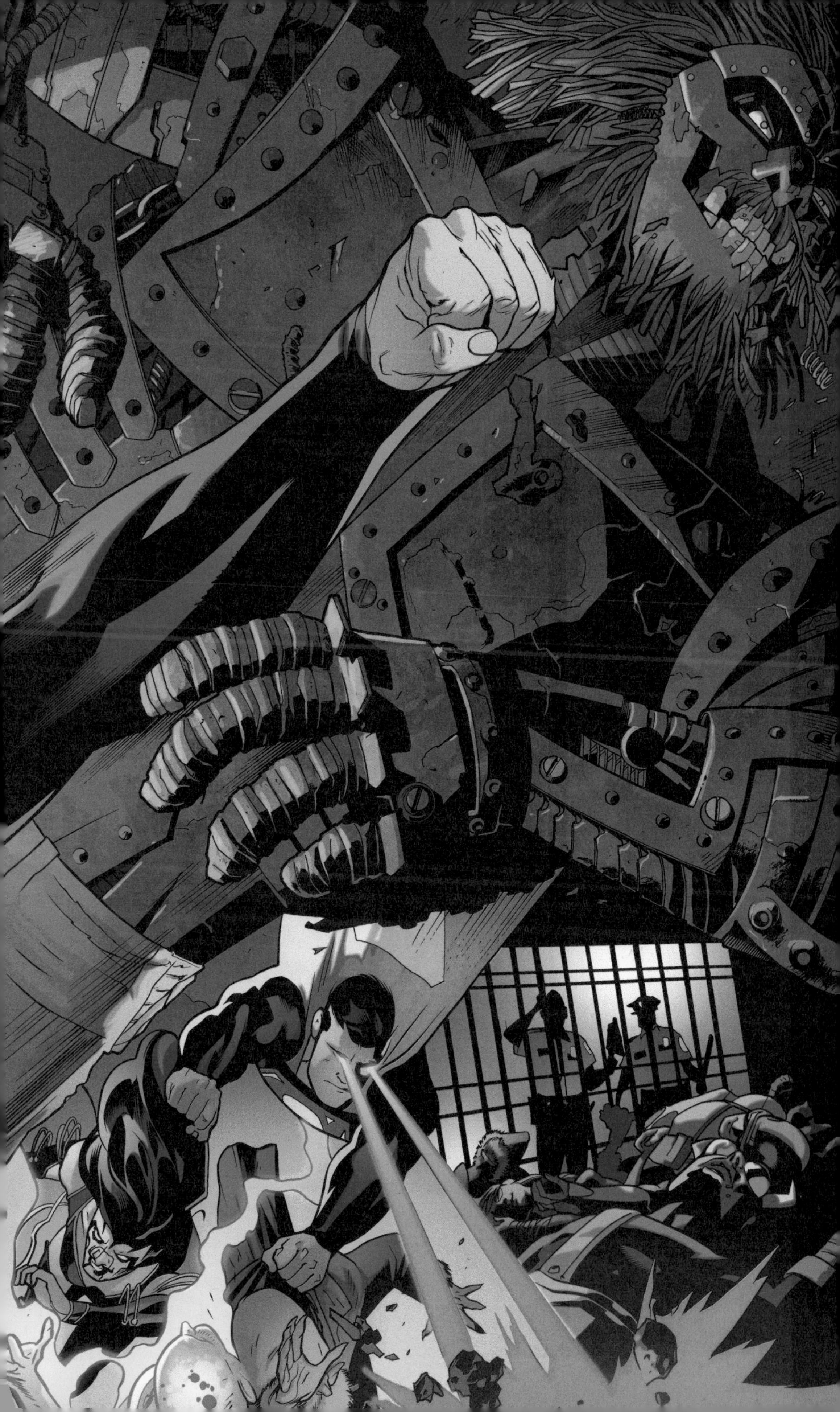

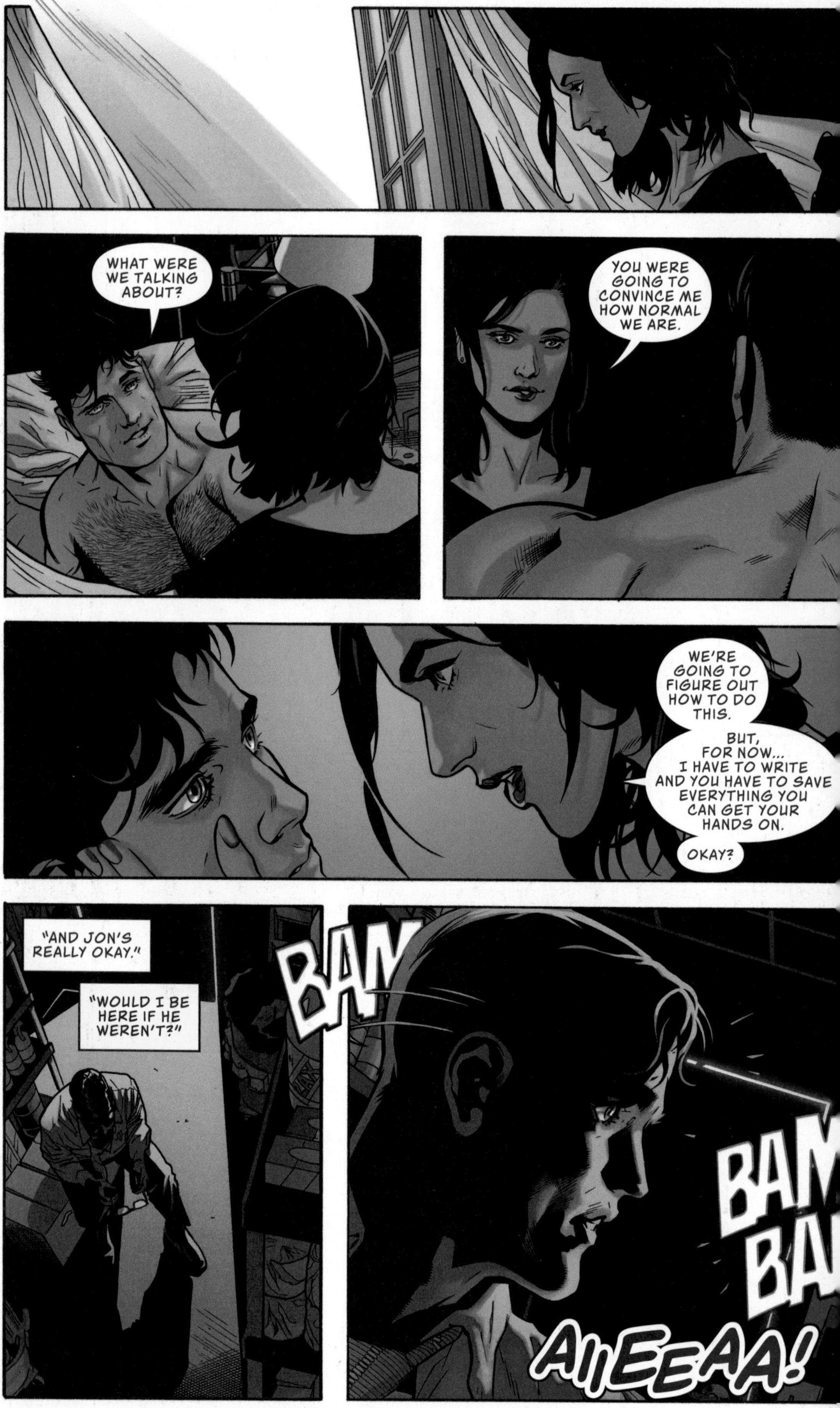

WHAT WERE WE TALKING ABOUT?
YOU WERE GOING TO CONVINCE ME HOW NORMAL WE ARE.
WE'RE GOING TO FIGURE OUT HOW TO DO THIS.
BUT, FOR NOW... I HAVE TO WRITE AND YOU HAVE TO SAVE EVERYTHING YOU CAN GET YOUR HANDS ON.
OKAY?
"AND JON'S REALLY OKAY."
"WOULD I BE HERE IF HE WEREN'T?"
AIIEEAA!

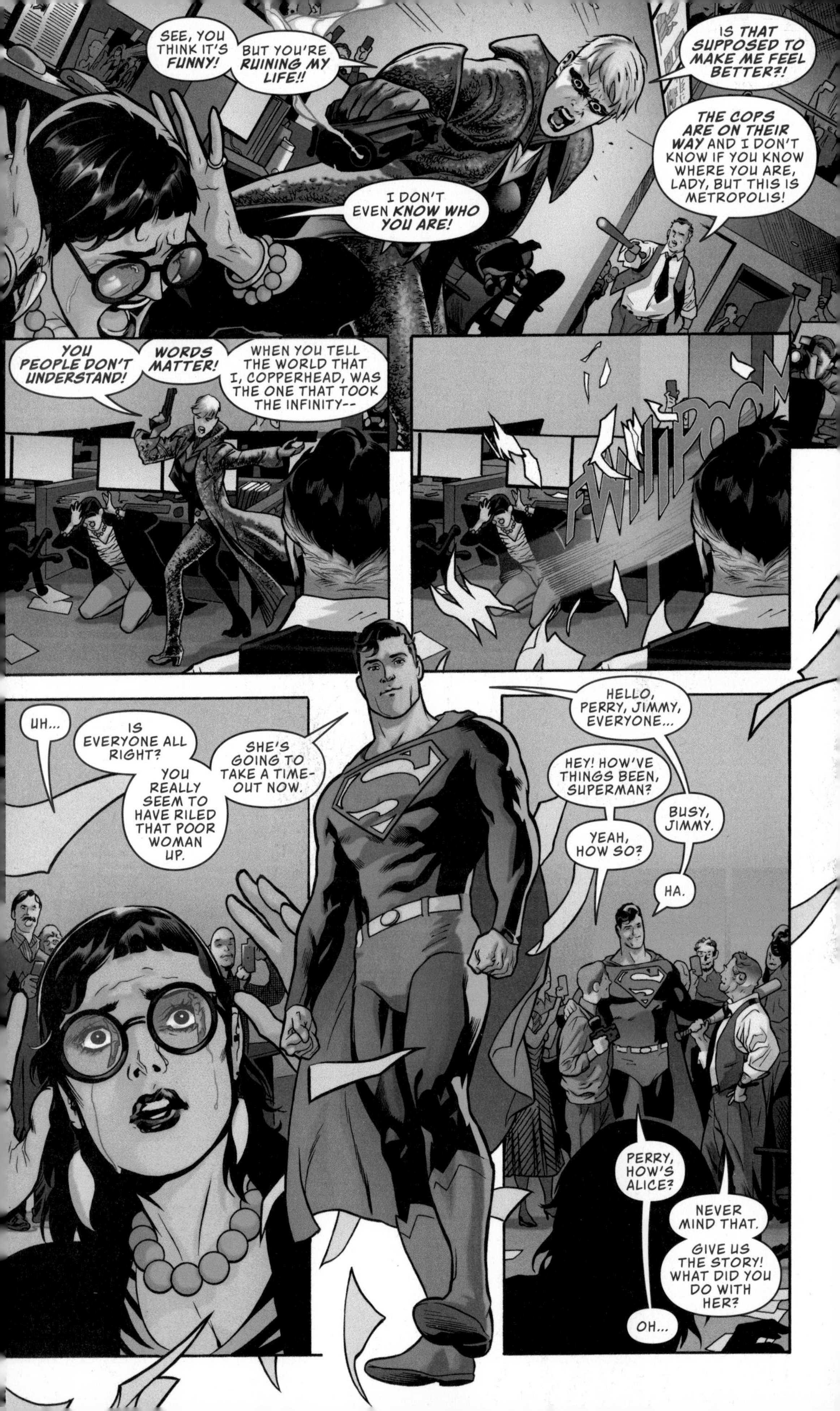
SEE, YOU THINK IT'S FUNNY!
BUT YOU'RE RUINING MY LIFE!!
IS THAT SUPPOSED TO MAKE ME FEEL BETTER?!
THE COPS ARE ON THEIR WAY AND I DON'T KNOW IF YOU KNOW WHERE YOU ARE, LADY, BUT THIS IS METROPOLIS!
I DON'T EVEN KNOW WHO YOU ARE!
YOU PEOPLE DON'T UNDERSTAND!
WORDS MATTER!
WHEN YOU TELL THE WORLD THAT I, COPPERHEAD, WAS THE ONE THAT TOOK THE INFINITY--
FWWIIPOOM
UH...
IS EVERYONE ALL RIGHT?
YOU REALLY SEEM TO HAVE RILED THAT POOR WOMAN UP.
SHE'S GOING TO TAKE A TIME-OUT NOW.
HELLO, PERRY, JIMMY, EVERYONE...
HEY! HOW'VE THINGS BEEN, SUPERMAN?
BUSY, JIMMY.
YEAH, HOW SO?
HA.
PERRY, HOW'S ALICE?
NEVER MIND THAT.
GIVE US THE STORY! WHAT DID YOU DO WITH HER?
OH...

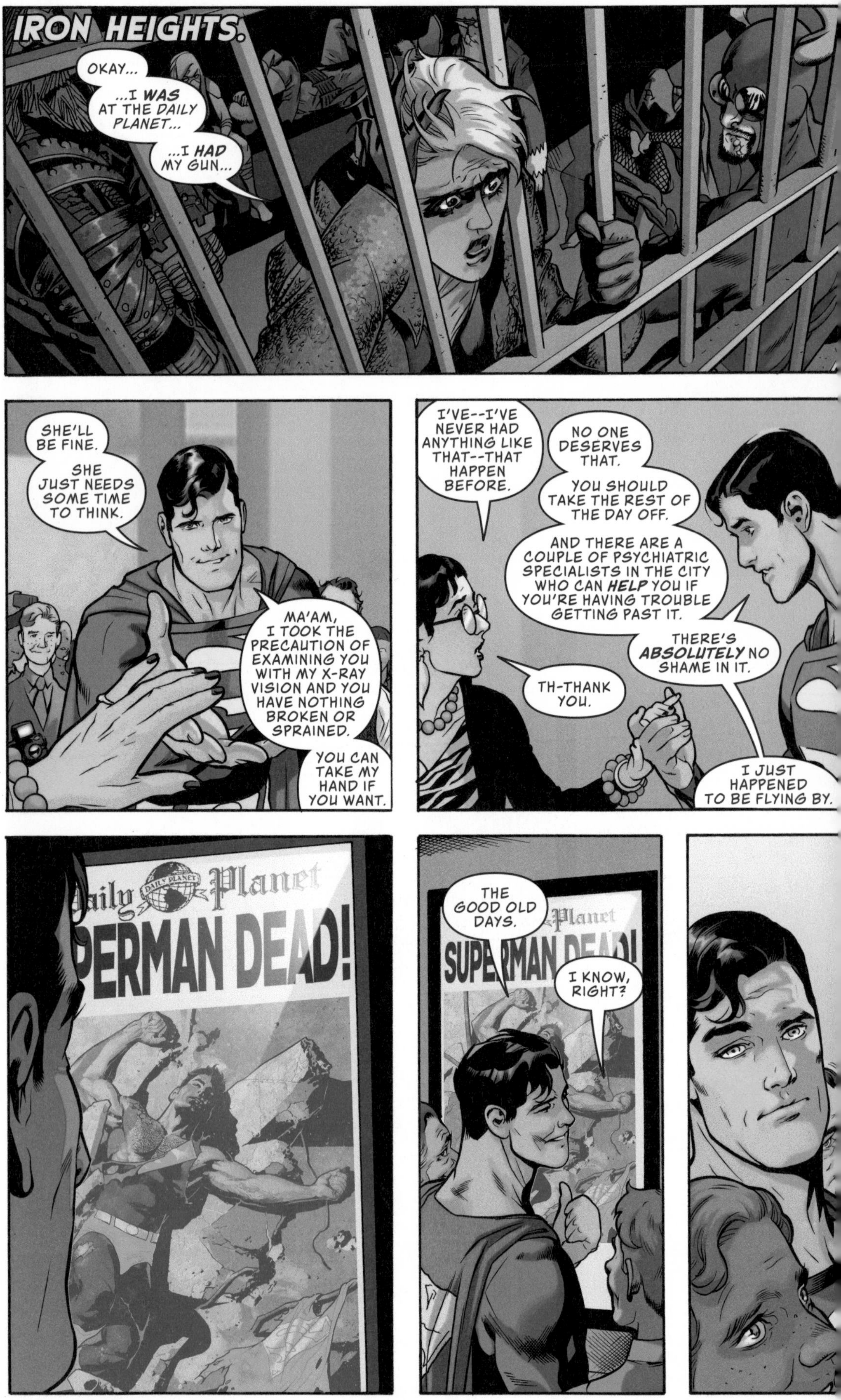
IRON HEIGHTS.
OKAY...
...I WAS AT THE DAILY PLANET...
...I HAD MY GUN...
SHE'LL BE FINE.
SHE JUST NEEDS SOME TIME TO THINK.
MA'AM, I TOOK THE PRECAUTION OF EXAMINING YOU WITH MY X-RAY VISION AND YOU HAVE NOTHING BROKEN OR SPRAINED.
YOU CAN TAKE MY HAND IF YOU WANT.
I'VE--I'VE NEVER HAD ANYTHING LIKE THAT--THAT HAPPEN BEFORE.
NO ONE DESERVES THAT.
YOU SHOULD TAKE THE REST OF THE DAY OFF.
AND THERE ARE A COUPLE OF PSYCHIATRIC SPECIALISTS IN THE CITY WHO CAN HELP YOU IF YOU'RE HAVING TROUBLE GETTING PAST IT.
THERE'S ABSOLUTELY NO SHAME IN IT.
TH-THANK YOU.
I JUST HAPPENED TO BE FLYING BY.
Daily Planet
PERMAN DEAD!
THE GOOD OLD DAYS.
I KNOW, RIGHT?
SUPERMAN DEAD!

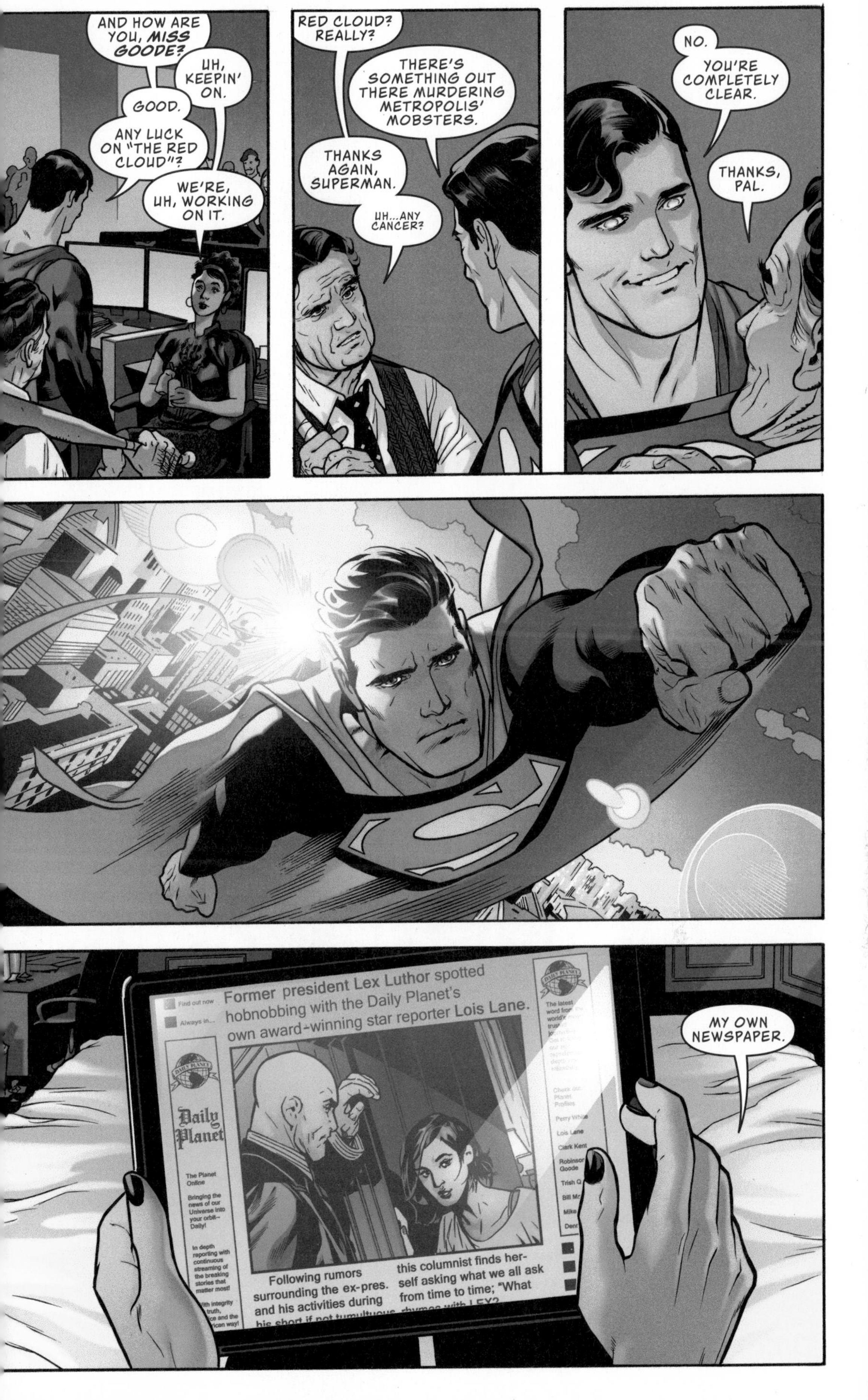
AND HOW ARE YOU, MISS GOODE?
UH, KEEPIN' ON.
GOOD.
ANY LUCK ON "THE RED CLOUD"?
WE'RE, UH, WORKING ON IT.
RED CLOUD? REALLY?
THERE'S SOMETHING OUT THERE MURDERING METROPOLIS' MOBSTERS.
THANKS AGAIN, SUPERMAN.
UH...ANY CANCER?
NO.
YOU'RE COMPLETELY CLEAR.
THANKS, PAL.
Former president Lex Luthor spotted hobnobbing with the Daily Planet's own award-winning star reporter Lois Lane.
Find out now
Always in...
Daily Planet
The Planet Online
Bringing the news of our Universe into your orbit– Daily!
In depth reporting with continuous streaming of the breaking stories that matter most!
Following rumors surrounding the ex-pres. and his activities during
this columnist finds herself asking what we all ask from time to time; "What
Check out Planet Profiles
Perry White
Lois Lane
Clark Kent
Robinson Goode
MY OWN NEWSPAPER.

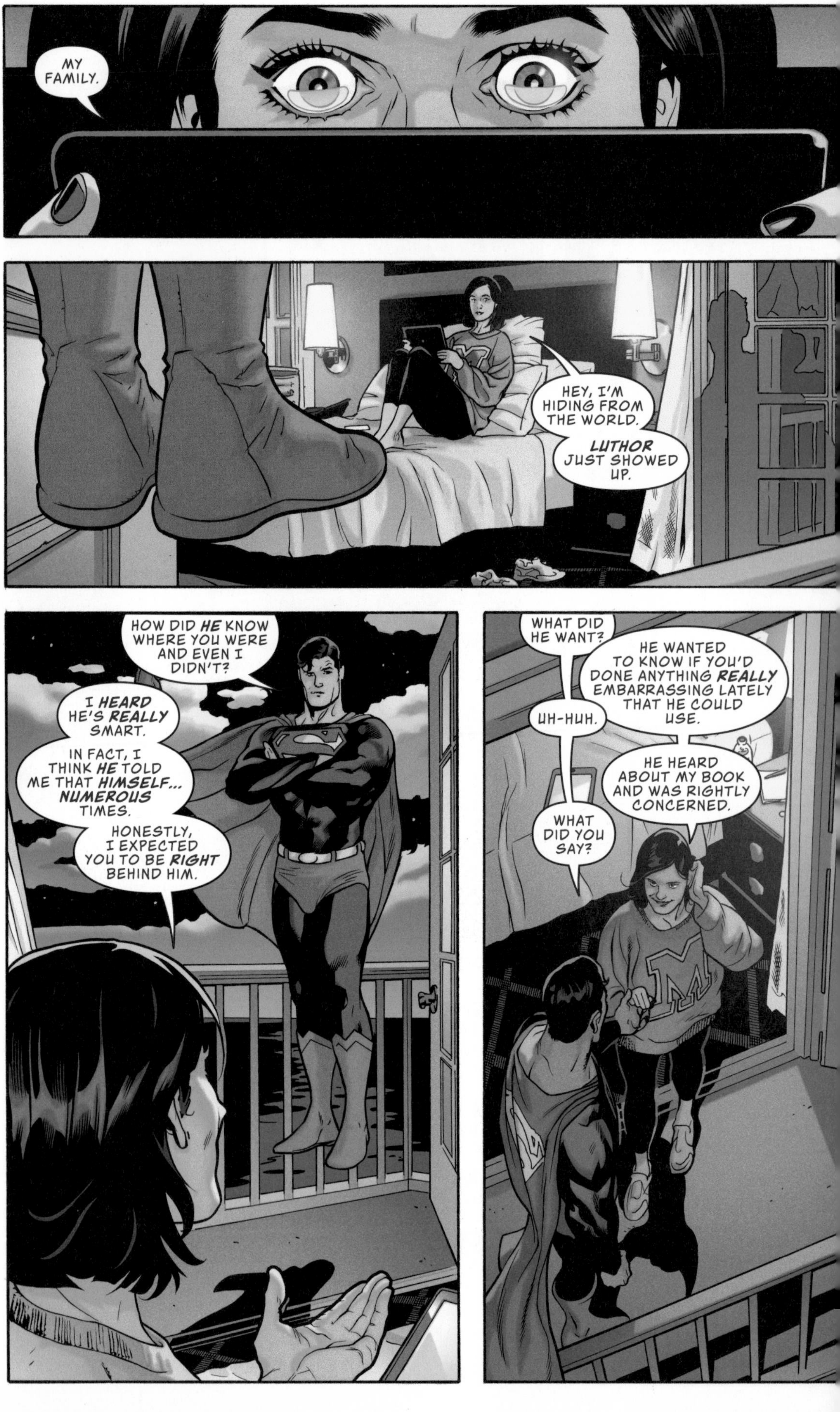
MY FAMILY.
HEY, I'M HIDING FROM THE WORLD.
LUTHOR JUST SHOWED UP.
HOW DID HE KNOW WHERE YOU WERE AND EVEN I DIDN'T?
I HEARD HE'S REALLY SMART.
IN FACT, I THINK HE TOLD ME THAT HIMSELF... NUMEROUS TIMES.
HONESTLY, I EXPECTED YOU TO BE RIGHT BEHIND HIM.
WHAT DID HE WANT?
HE WANTED TO KNOW IF YOU'D DONE ANYTHING REALLY EMBARRASSING LATELY THAT HE COULD USE.
UH-HUH.
HE HEARD ABOUT MY BOOK AND WAS RIGHTLY CONCERNED.
WHAT DID YOU SAY?

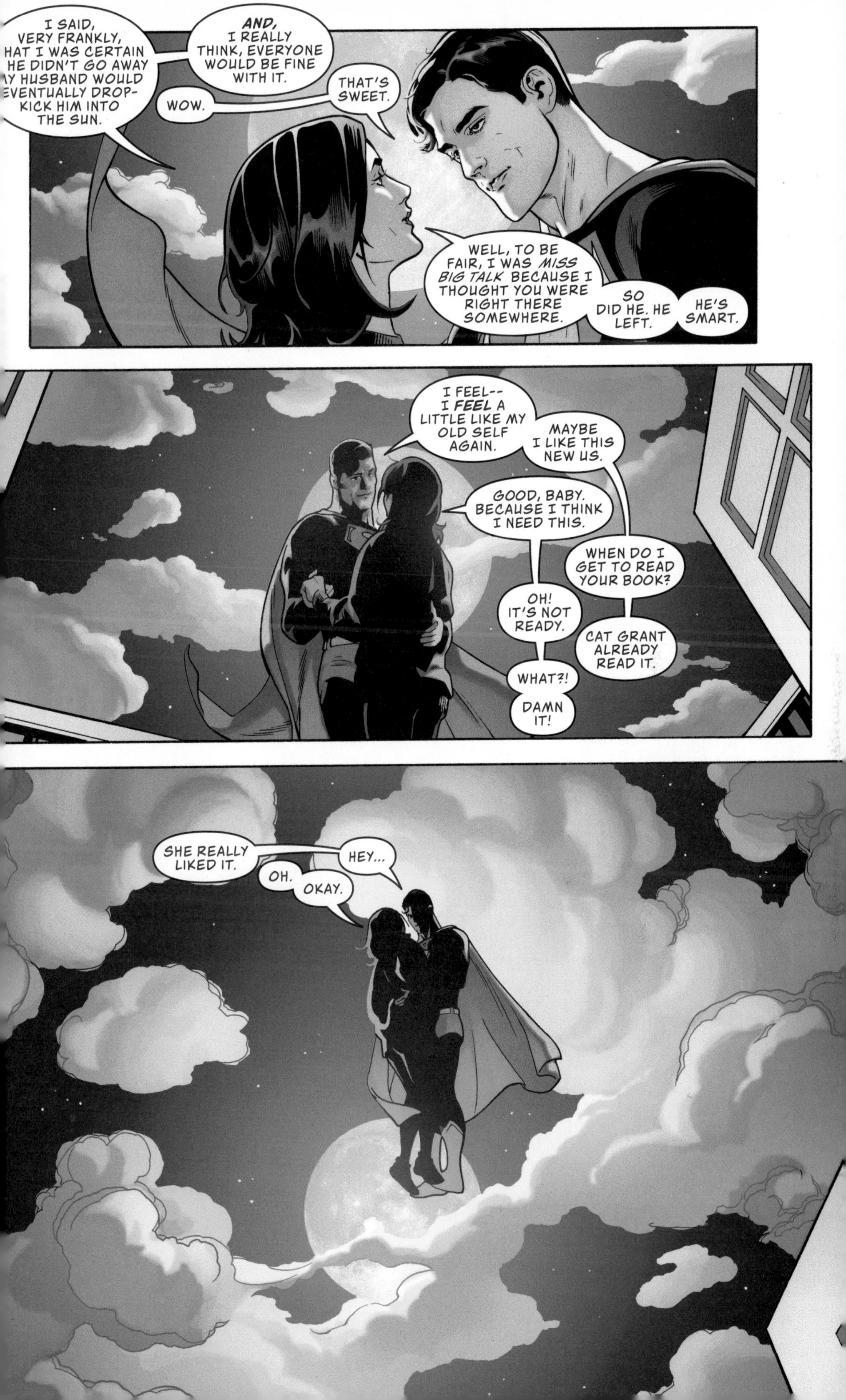

I SAID, VERY FRANKLY, HAT I WAS CERTAIN HE DIDN'T GO AWAY Y HUSBAND WOULD EVENTUALLY DROP-KICK HIM INTO THE SUN.
AND, I REALLY THINK, EVERYONE WOULD BE FINE WITH IT.
WOW.
THAT'S SWEET.
WELL, TO BE FAIR, I WAS MISS BIG TALK BECAUSE I THOUGHT YOU WERE RIGHT THERE SOMEWHERE.
SO DID HE. HE LEFT.
HE'S SMART.
I FEEL-- I FEEL A LITTLE LIKE MY OLD SELF AGAIN.
MAYBE I LIKE THIS NEW US.
GOOD, BABY. BECAUSE I THINK I NEED THIS.
WHEN DO I GET TO READ YOUR BOOK?
OH! IT'S NOT READY.
CAT GRANT ALREADY READ IT.
WHAT?!
DAMN IT!
SHE REALLY LIKED IT.
HEY...
OH.
OKAY.

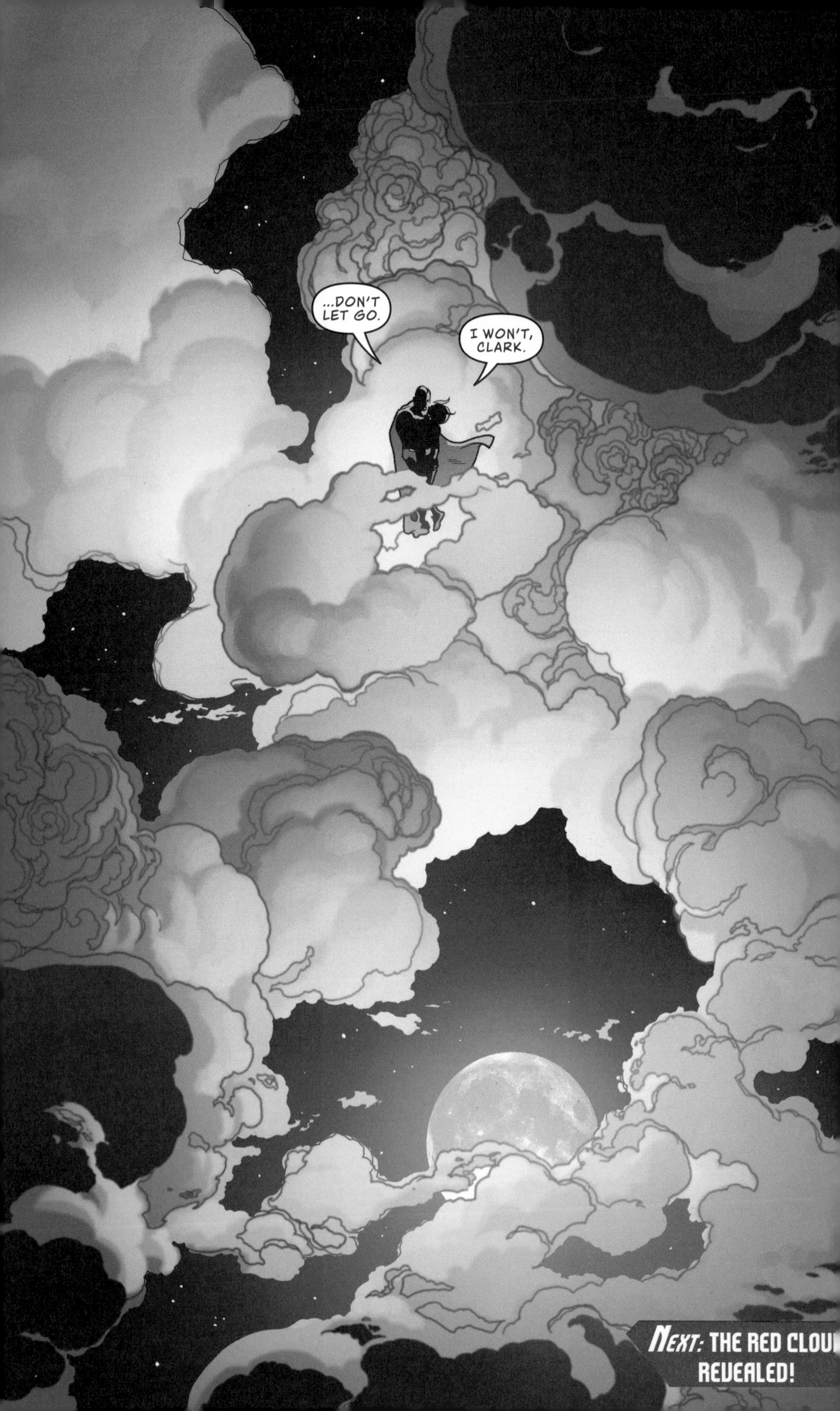

...DON'T LET GO.
I WON'T, CLARK.
NEXT: THE RED CLOU
REVEALED!

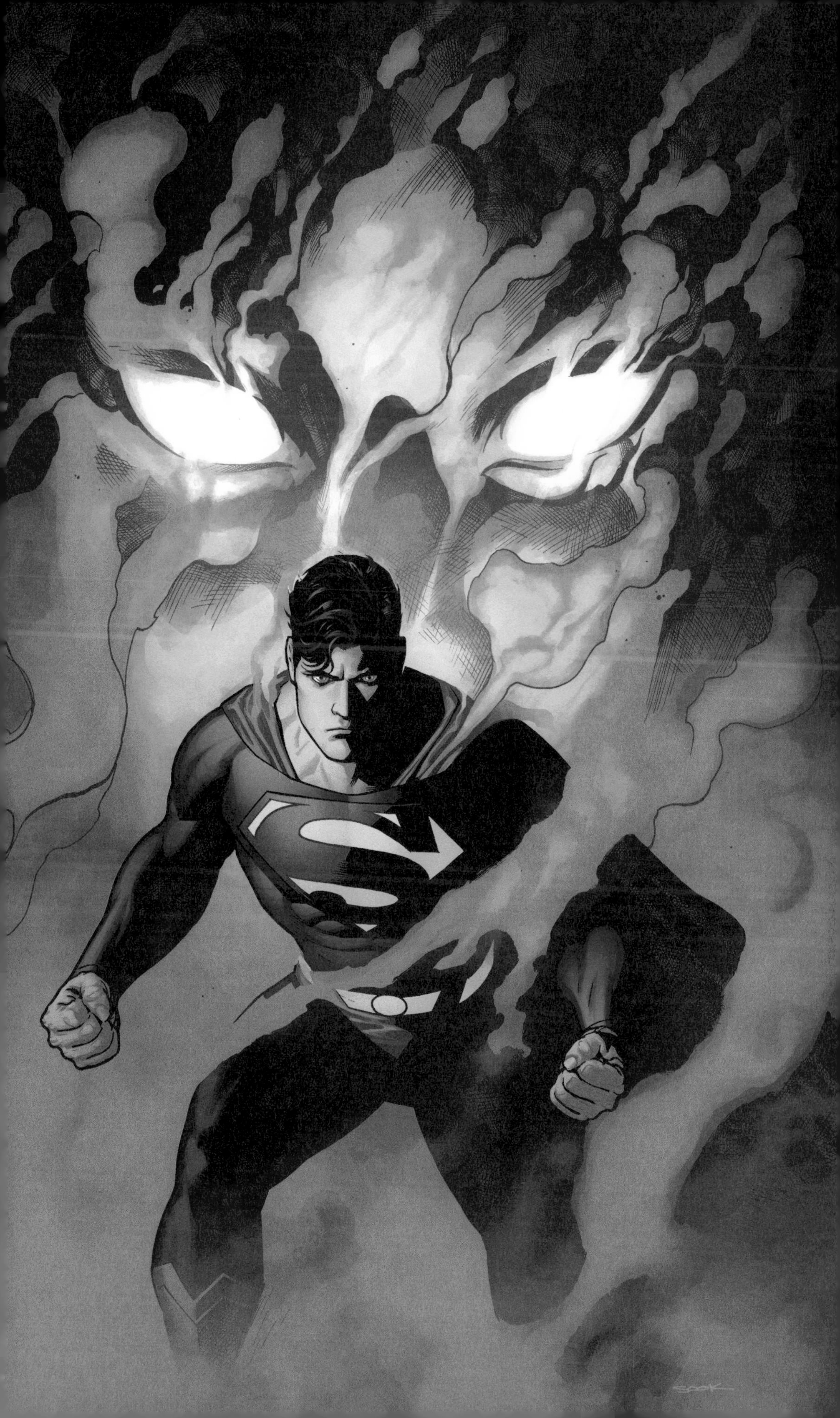

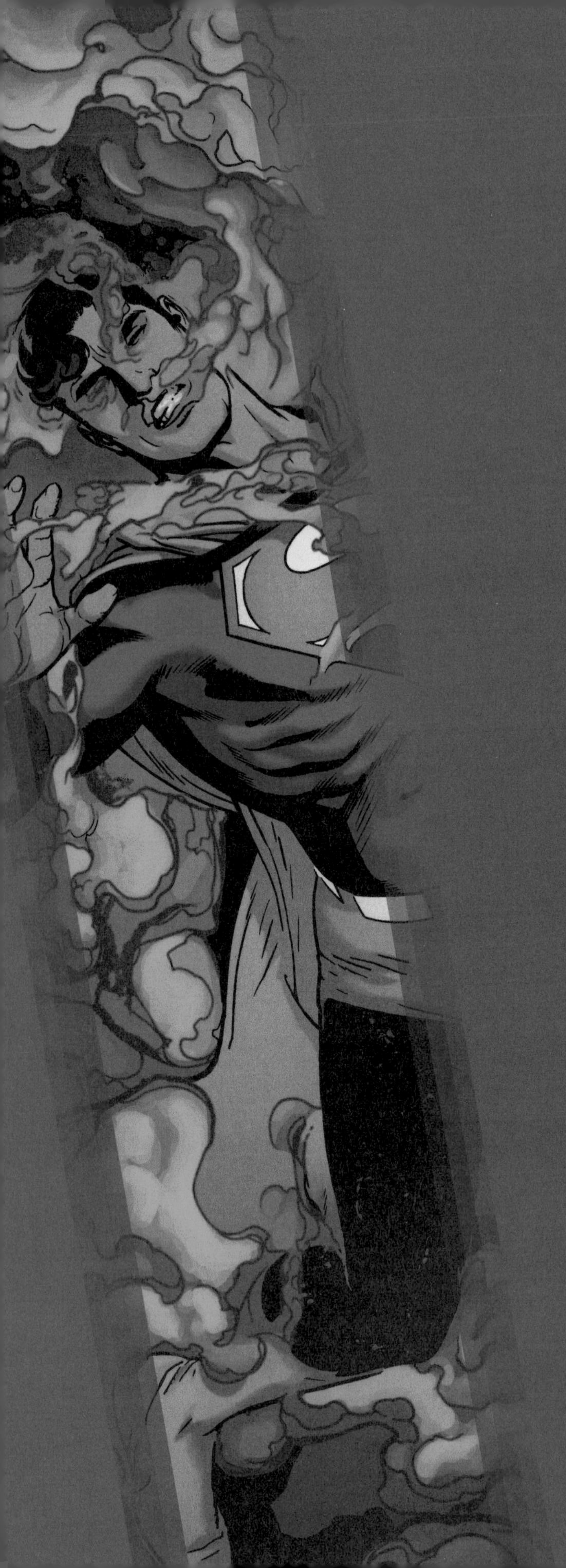

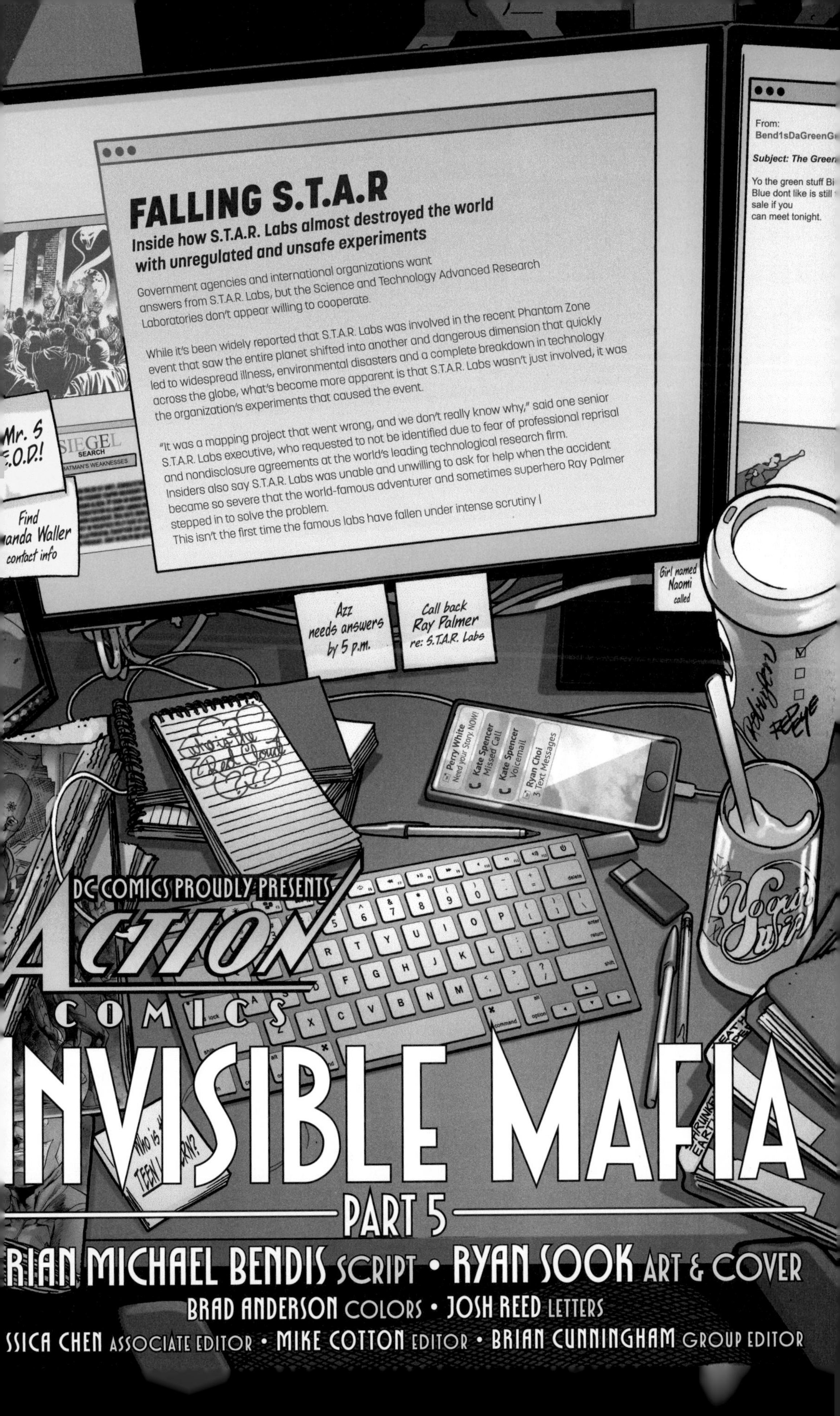
FALLING S.T.A.R
Inside how S.T.A.R. Labs almost destroyed the world with unregulated and unsafe experiments
Government agencies and international organizations want answers from S.T.A.R. Labs, but the Science and Technology Advanced Research Laboratories don't appear willing to cooperate.
While it's been widely reported that S.T.A.R. Labs was involved in the recent Phantom Zone event that saw the entire planet shifted into another and dangerous dimension that quickly led to widespread illness, environmental disasters and a complete breakdown in technology across the globe, what's become more apparent is that S.T.A.R. Labs wasn't just involved, it was the organization's experiments that caused the event.
"It was a mapping project that went wrong, and we don't really know why," said one senior S.T.A.R. Labs executive, who requested to not be identified due to fear of professional reprisal and nondisclosure agreements at the world's leading technological research firm.
Insiders also say S.T.A.R. Labs was unable and unwilling to ask for help when the accident became so severe that the world-famous adventurer and sometimes superhero Ray Palmer stepped in to solve the problem.
This isn't the first time the famous labs have fallen under intense scrutiny I
From:
Bend1sDaGreenG
Subject: The Green
Yo the green stuff Bi
Blue dont like is still
sale if you
can meet tonight.
SIEGEL
SEARCH
BATMAN'S WEAKNESSES
Mr. S
F.O.D.!
Find
anda Waller
contact info
Girl named
Naomi
called
Azz
needs answers
by 5 p.m.
Call back
Ray Palmer
re: S.T.A.R. Labs
Perry White
Need your Story. NOW!
Kate Spencer
Missed Call
Kate Spencer
Voicemail
Ryan Choi
3 Text Messages
Who is the Red Cloud???
Who is t TEEN ...RN?
DC COMICS PROUDLY PRESENTS
ACTION COMICS
INVISIBLE MAFIA
PART 5
RIAN MICHAEL BENDIS SCRIPT • RYAN SOOK ART & COVER
BRAD ANDERSON COLORS • JOSH REED LETTERS
SSICA CHEN ASSOCIATE EDITOR • MIKE COTTON EDITOR • BRIAN CUNNINGHAM GROUP EDITOR

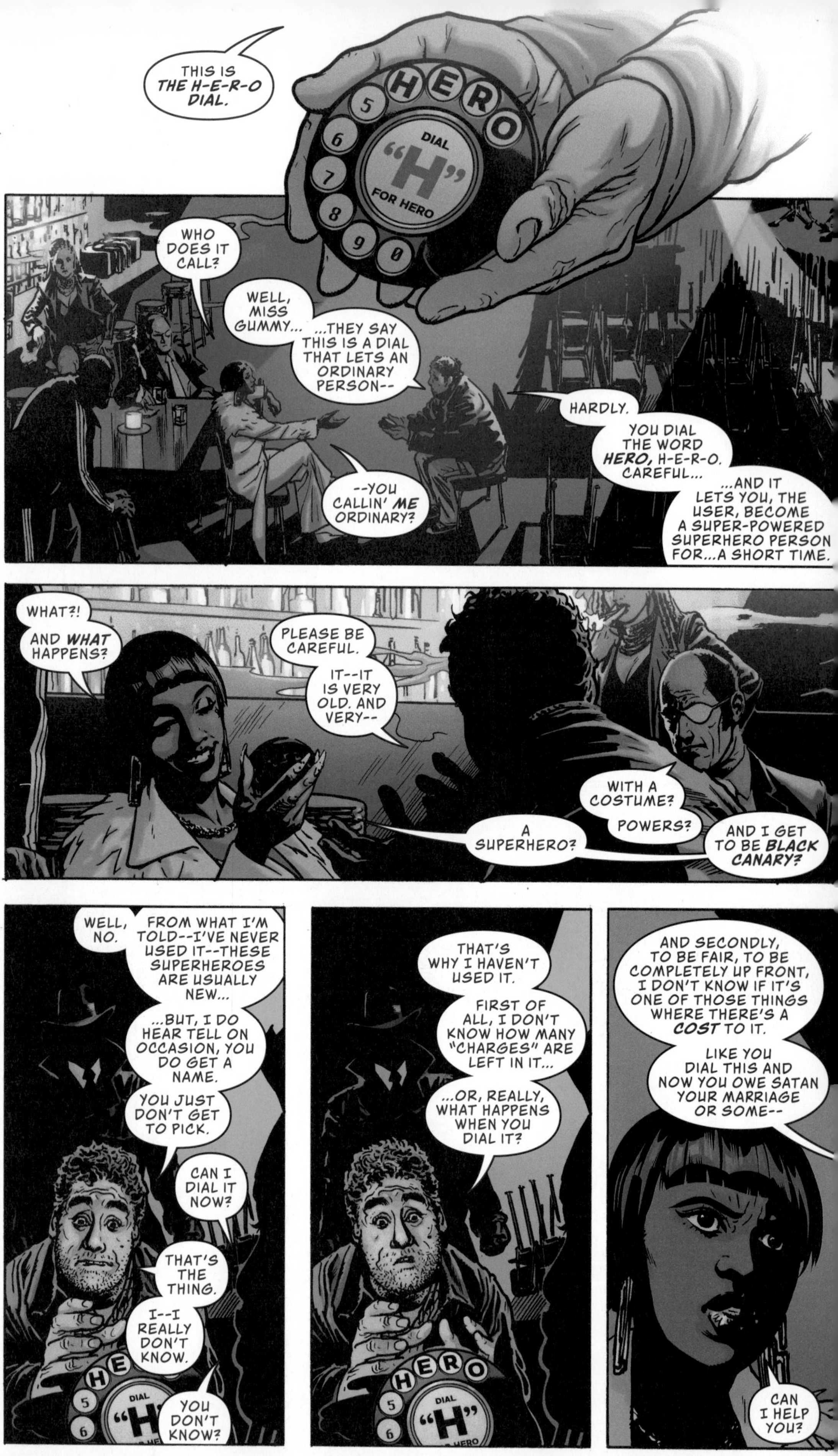
THIS IS THE H-E-R-O DIAL.
HERO
DIAL "H" FOR HERO
WHO DOES IT CALL?
WELL, MISS GUMMY...
...THEY SAY THIS IS A DIAL THAT LETS AN ORDINARY PERSON--
--YOU CALLIN' ME ORDINARY?
HARDLY.
YOU DIAL THE WORD HERO, H-E-R-O. CAREFUL...
...AND IT LETS YOU, THE USER, BECOME A SUPER-POWERED SUPERHERO PERSON FOR...A SHORT TIME.
WHAT?! AND WHAT HAPPENS?
PLEASE BE CAREFUL.
IT--IT IS VERY OLD. AND VERY--
A SUPERHERO?
WITH A COSTUME?
POWERS?
AND I GET TO BE BLACK CANARY?
WELL, NO.
FROM WHAT I'M TOLD--I'VE NEVER USED IT--THESE SUPERHEROES ARE USUALLY NEW...
...BUT, I DO HEAR TELL ON OCCASION, YOU DO GET A NAME.
YOU JUST DON'T GET TO PICK.
CAN I DIAL IT NOW?
THAT'S THE THING.
I--I REALLY DON'T KNOW.
YOU DON'T KNOW?
THAT'S WHY I HAVEN'T USED IT.
FIRST OF ALL, I DON'T KNOW HOW MANY "CHARGES" ARE LEFT IN IT...
...OR, REALLY, WHAT HAPPENS WHEN YOU DIAL IT?
AND SECONDLY, TO BE FAIR, TO BE COMPLETELY UP FRONT, I DON'T KNOW IF IT'S ONE OF THOSE THINGS WHERE THERE'S A COST TO IT.
LIKE YOU DIAL THIS AND NOW YOU OWE SATAN YOUR MARRIAGE OR SOME--
CAN I HELP YOU?

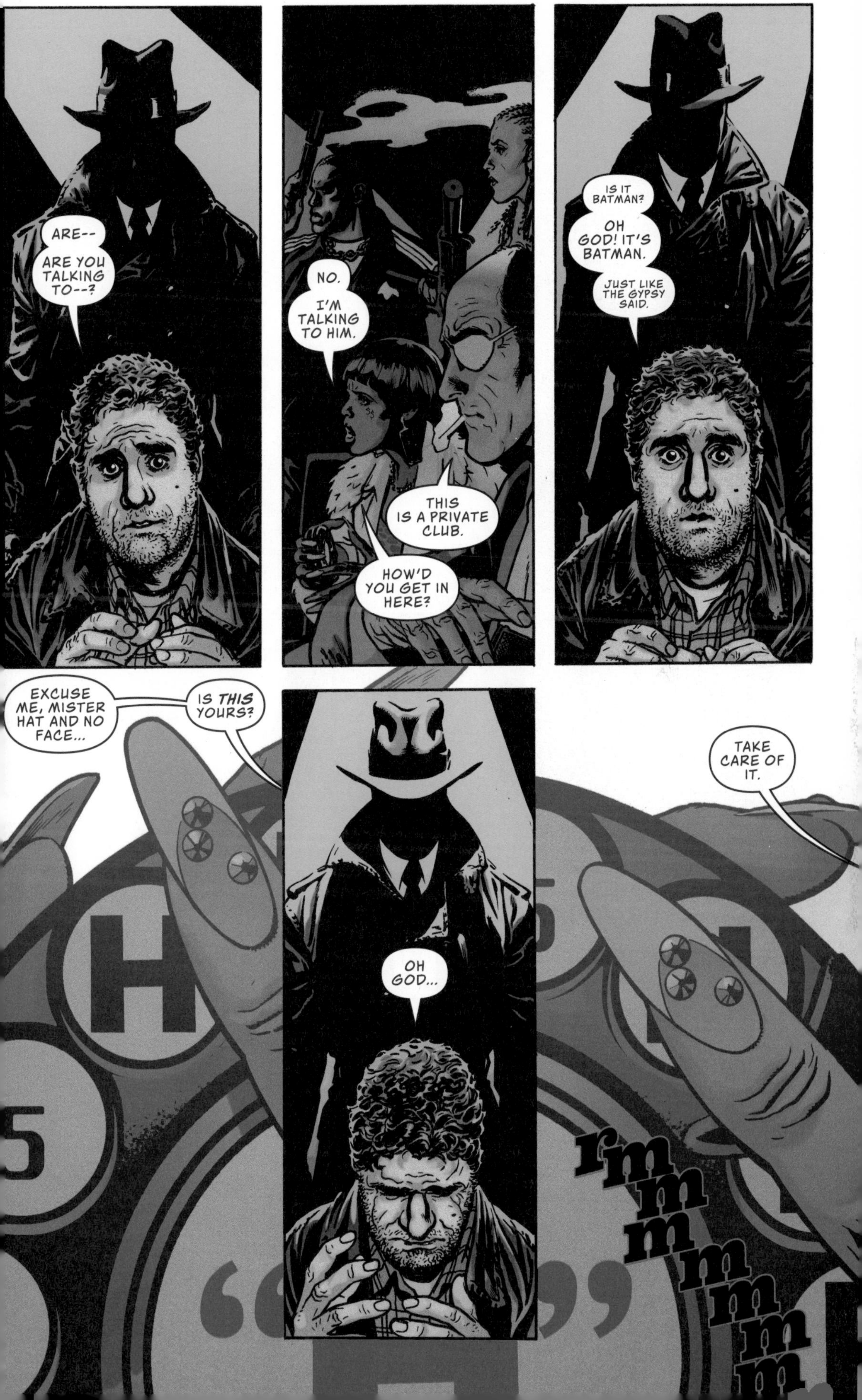
ARE--
ARE YOU TALKING TO--?
NO.
I'M TALKING TO HIM.
THIS IS A PRIVATE CLUB.
HOW'D YOU GET IN HERE?
IS IT BATMAN?
OH GOD! IT'S BATMAN.
JUST LIKE THE GYPSY SAID.
EXCUSE ME, MISTER HAT AND NO FACE...
IS THIS YOURS?
OH GOD...
TAKE CARE OF IT.
rmmmmmmm

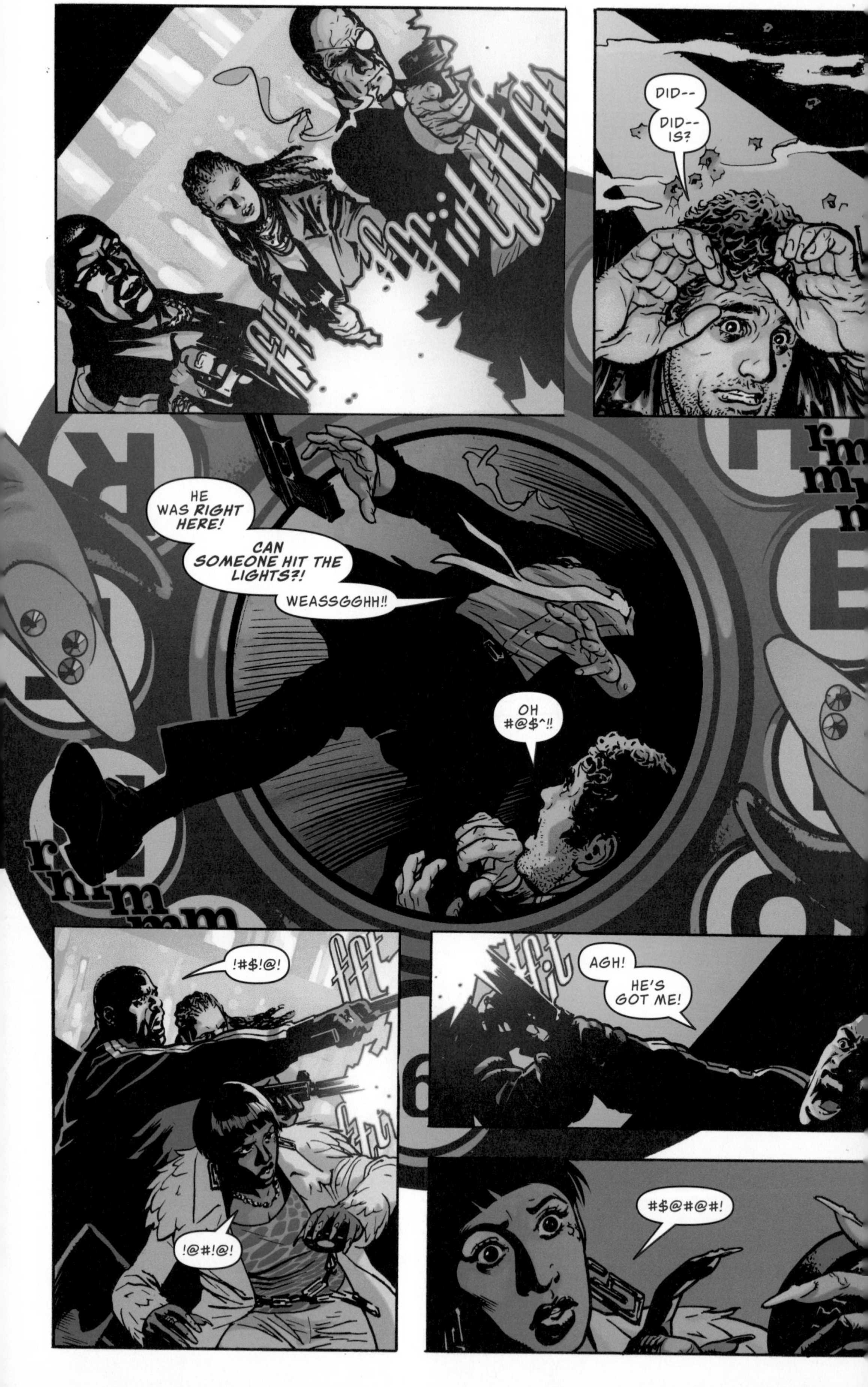

fft
DID--
DID--
IS?
rmm
HE WAS RIGHT HERE!
CAN SOMEONE HIT THE LIGHTS?!
WEASSGGHH!!
OH #@$^!!
rmm
!#$!@!
fft
!@#!@!
fft
AGH!
HE'S GOT ME!
#$@#@#!

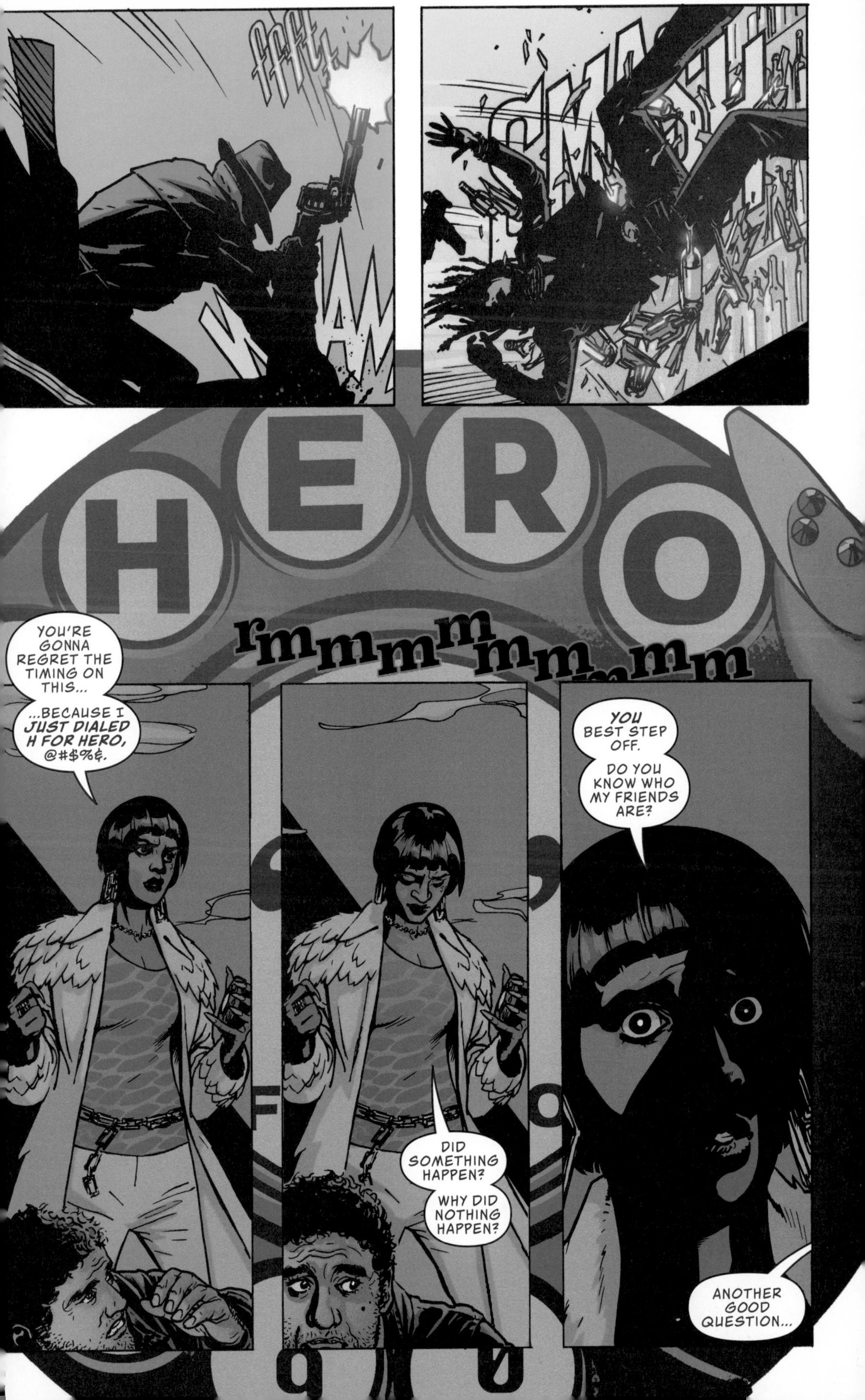

fffft
HERO
YOU'RE GONNA REGRET THE TIMING ON THIS...
...BECAUSE I JUST DIALED H FOR HERO, @#$%&.
rmmmmmmmmmm
DID SOMETHING HAPPEN?
WHY DID NOTHING HAPPEN?
YOU BEST STEP OFF.
DO YOU KNOW WHO MY FRIENDS ARE?
ANOTHER GOOD QUESTION...

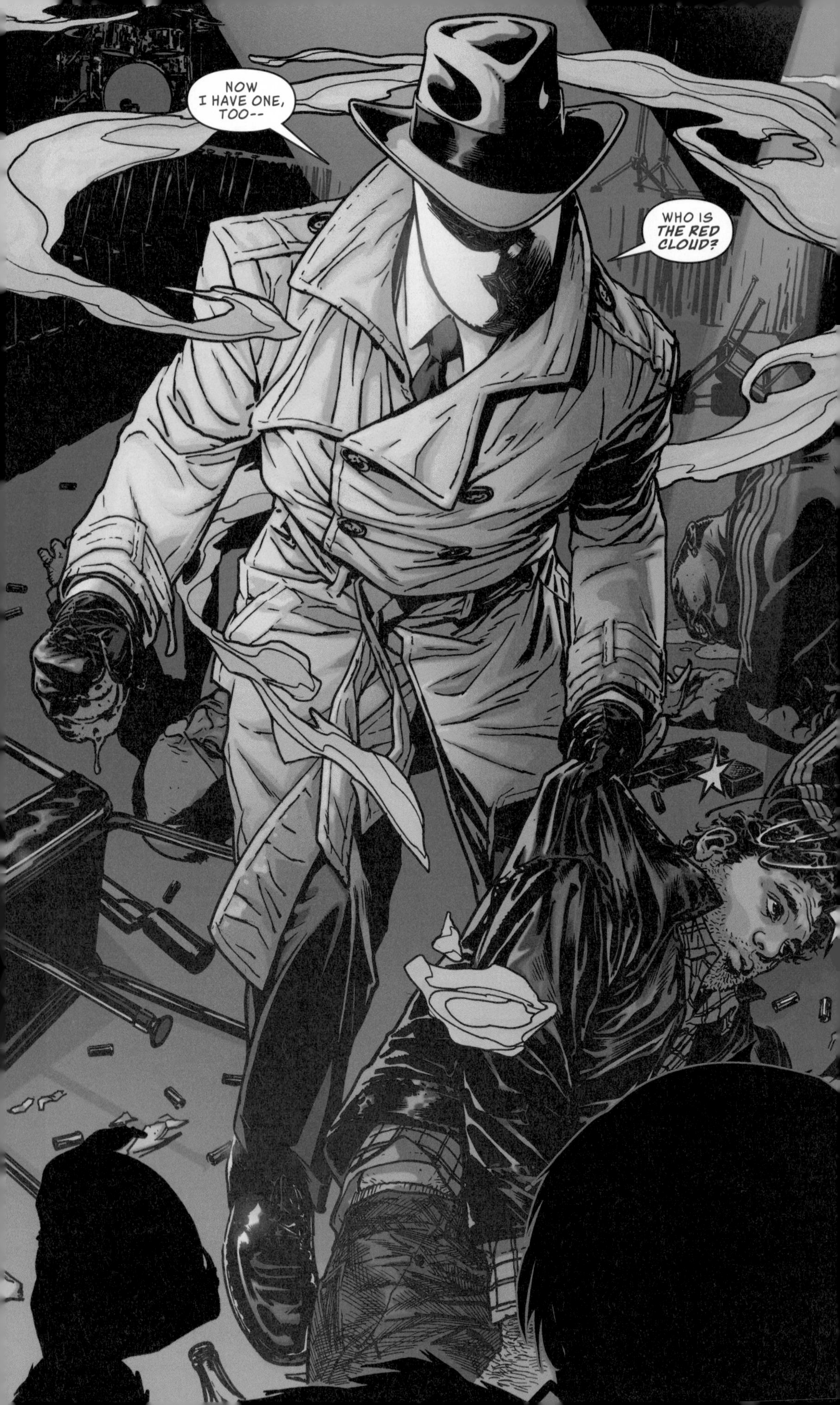
NOW I HAVE ONE, TOO--
WHO IS THE RED CLOUD?

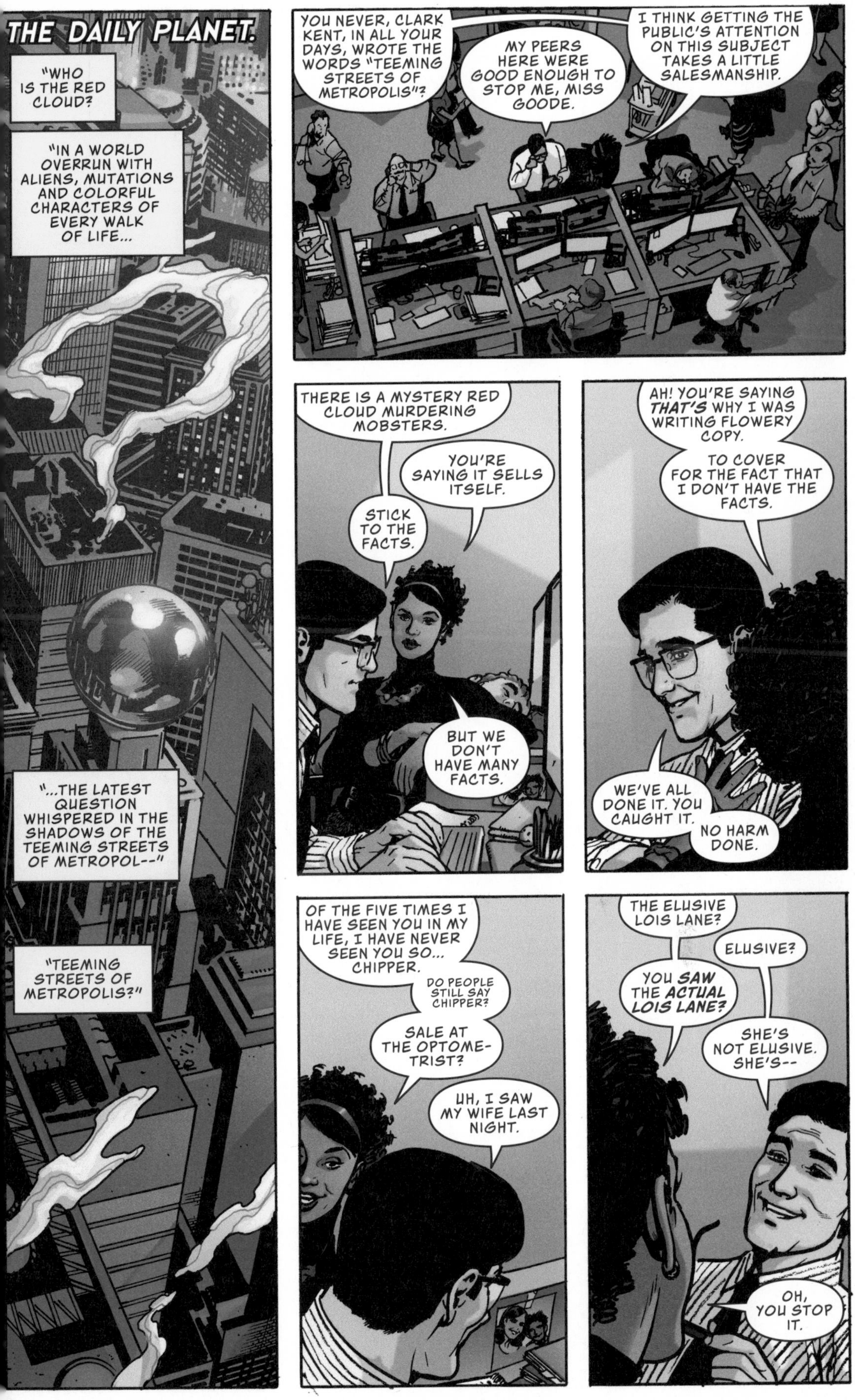
THE DAILY PLANET.
"WHO IS THE RED CLOUD?
"IN A WORLD OVERRUN WITH ALIENS, MUTATIONS AND COLORFUL CHARACTERS OF EVERY WALK OF LIFE...
"...THE LATEST QUESTION WHISPERED IN THE SHADOWS OF THE TEEMING STREETS OF METROPOL--"
"TEEMING STREETS OF METROPOLIS?"
YOU NEVER, CLARK KENT, IN ALL YOUR DAYS, WROTE THE WORDS "TEEMING STREETS OF METROPOLIS"?
MY PEERS HERE WERE GOOD ENOUGH TO STOP ME, MISS GOODE.
I THINK GETTING THE PUBLIC'S ATTENTION ON THIS SUBJECT TAKES A LITTLE SALESMANSHIP.
THERE IS A MYSTERY RED CLOUD MURDERING MOBSTERS.
STICK TO THE FACTS.
YOU'RE SAYING IT SELLS ITSELF.
BUT WE DON'T HAVE MANY FACTS.
AH! YOU'RE SAYING *THAT'S* WHY I WAS WRITING FLOWERY COPY.
TO COVER FOR THE FACT THAT I DON'T HAVE THE FACTS.
WE'VE ALL DONE IT. YOU CAUGHT IT.
NO HARM DONE.
OF THE FIVE TIMES I HAVE SEEN YOU IN MY LIFE, I HAVE NEVER SEEN YOU SO... CHIPPER.
DO PEOPLE STILL SAY CHIPPER?
SALE AT THE OPTOME-TRIST?
UH, I SAW MY WIFE LAST NIGHT.
THE ELUSIVE LOIS LANE?
ELUSIVE?
YOU *SAW* THE *ACTUAL LOIS LANE?*
SHE'S NOT ELUSIVE. SHE'S--
OH, YOU STOP IT.

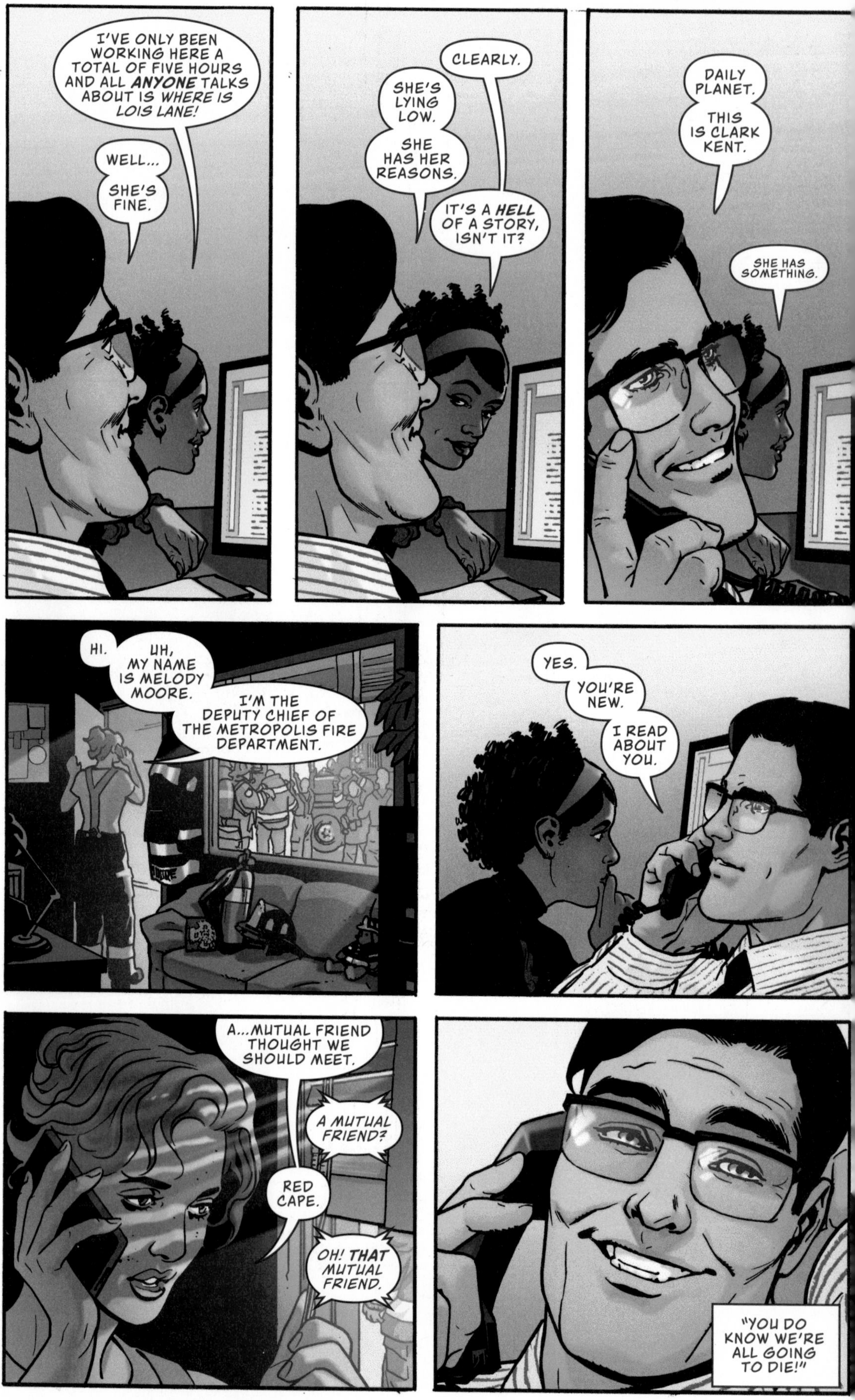

I'VE ONLY BEEN WORKING HERE A TOTAL OF FIVE HOURS AND ALL ANYONE TALKS ABOUT IS WHERE IS LOIS LANE!
WELL...
SHE'S FINE.
CLEARLY.
SHE'S LYING LOW.
SHE HAS HER REASONS.
IT'S A HELL OF A STORY, ISN'T IT?
DAILY PLANET.
THIS IS CLARK KENT.
SHE HAS SOMETHING.
HI.
UH, MY NAME IS MELODY MOORE.
I'M THE DEPUTY CHIEF OF THE METROPOLIS FIRE DEPARTMENT.
YES.
YOU'RE NEW.
I READ ABOUT YOU.
A...MUTUAL FRIEND THOUGHT WE SHOULD MEET.
A MUTUAL FRIEND?
RED CAPE.
OH! THAT MUTUAL FRIEND.
"YOU DO KNOW WE'RE ALL GOING TO DIE!"

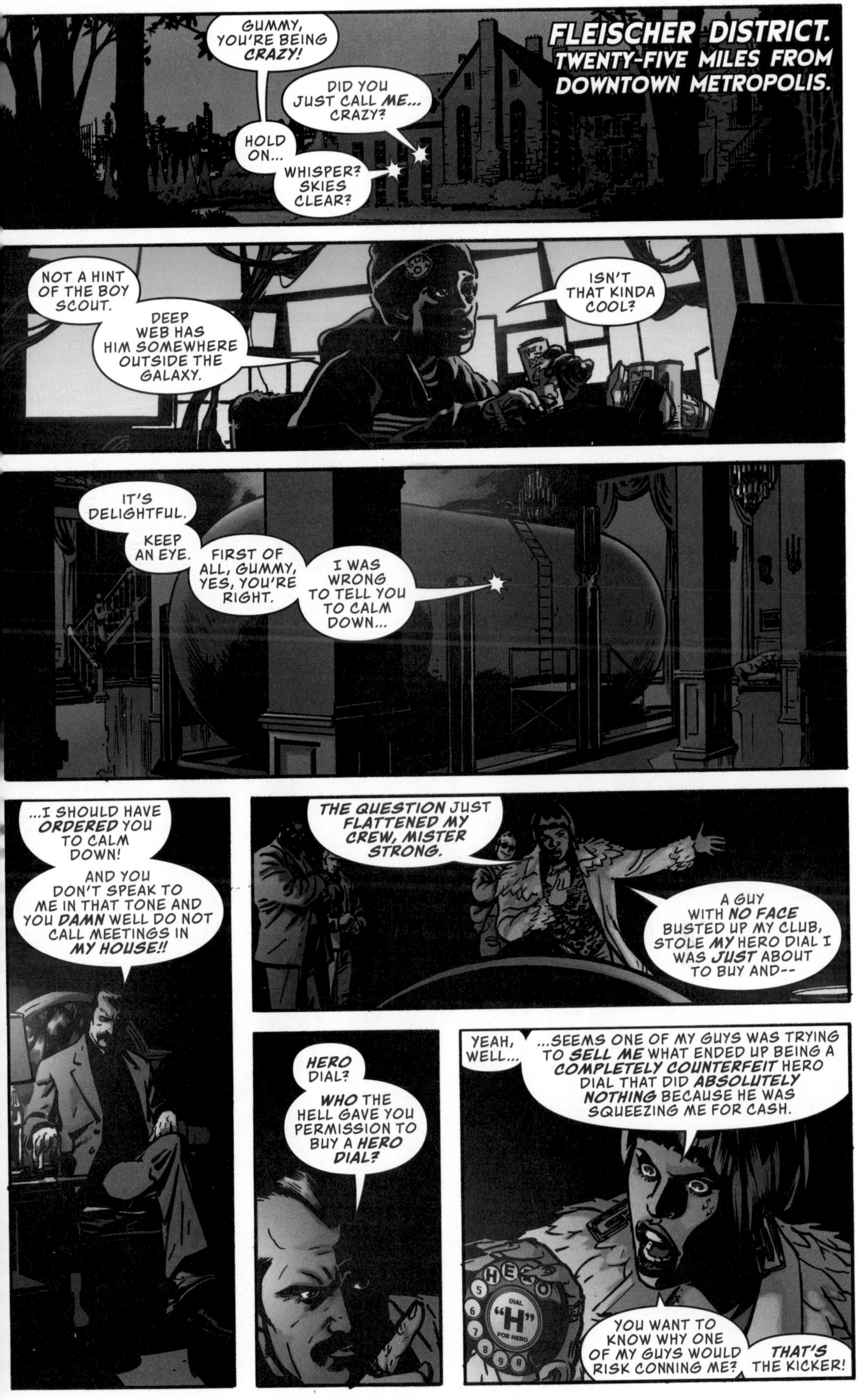
FLEISCHER DISTRICT. TWENTY-FIVE MILES FROM DOWNTOWN METROPOLIS.
GUMMY, YOU'RE BEING CRAZY!
DID YOU JUST CALL ME... CRAZY?
HOLD ON...
WHISPER? SKIES CLEAR?
NOT A HINT OF THE BOY SCOUT.
DEEP WEB HAS HIM SOMEWHERE OUTSIDE THE GALAXY.
ISN'T THAT KINDA COOL?
IT'S DELIGHTFUL.
KEEP AN EYE.
FIRST OF ALL, GUMMY, YES, YOU'RE RIGHT.
I WAS WRONG TO TELL YOU TO CALM DOWN...
...I SHOULD HAVE ORDERED YOU TO CALM DOWN!
AND YOU DON'T SPEAK TO ME IN THAT TONE AND YOU DAMN WELL DO NOT CALL MEETINGS IN MY HOUSE!!
THE QUESTION JUST FLATTENED MY CREW, MISTER STRONG.
A GUY WITH NO FACE BUSTED UP MY CLUB, STOLE MY HERO DIAL I WAS JUST ABOUT TO BUY AND--
HERO DIAL?
WHO THE HELL GAVE YOU PERMISSION TO BUY A HERO DIAL?
YEAH, WELL...
...SEEMS ONE OF MY GUYS WAS TRYING TO SELL ME WHAT ENDED UP BEING A COMPLETELY COUNTERFEIT HERO DIAL THAT DID ABSOLUTELY NOTHING BECAUSE HE WAS SQUEEZING ME FOR CASH.
DIAL "H" FOR HERO
YOU WANT TO KNOW WHY ONE OF MY GUYS WOULD RISK CONNING ME?
THAT'S THE KICKER!

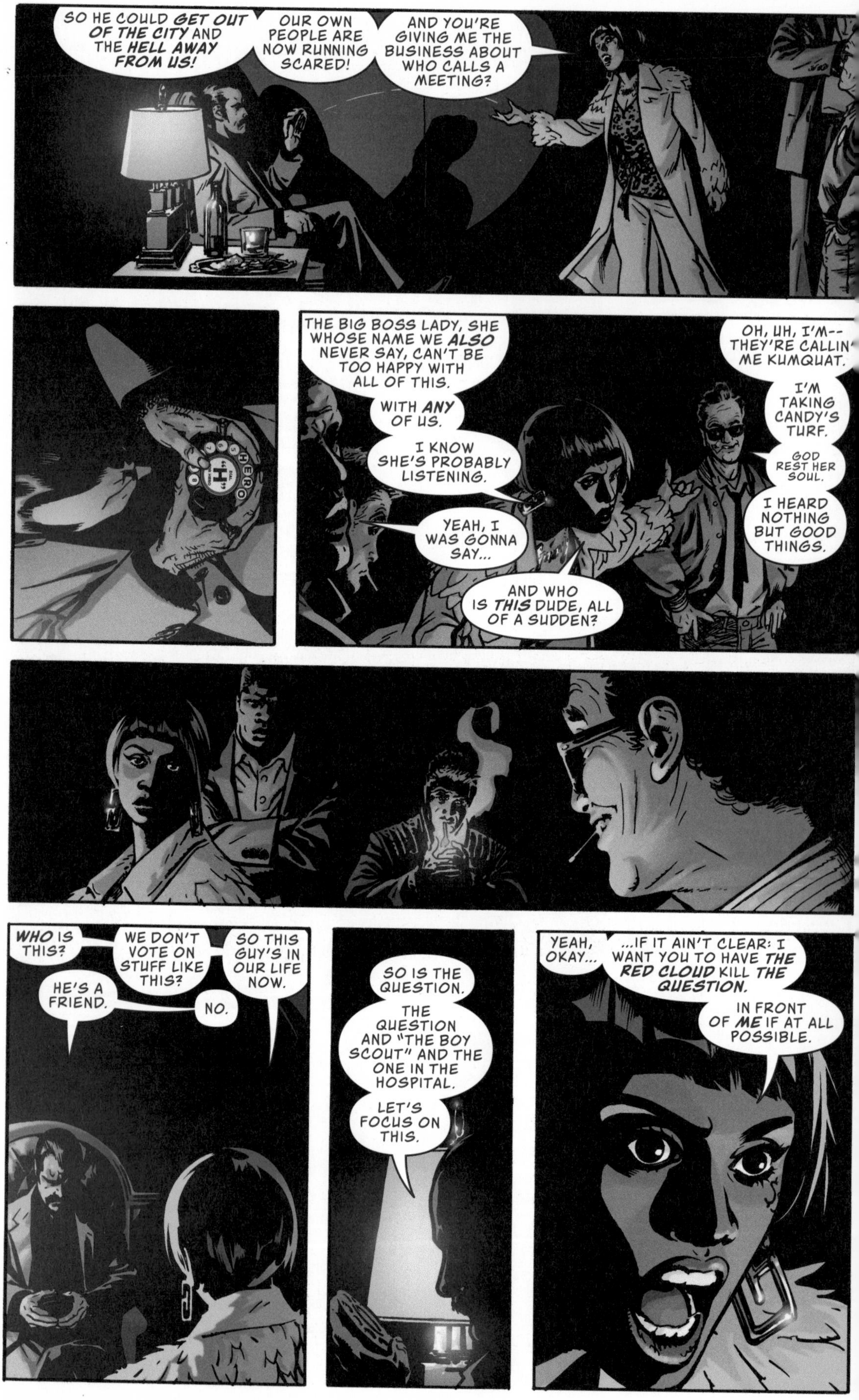
SO HE COULD GET OUT OF THE CITY AND THE HELL AWAY FROM US!
OUR OWN PEOPLE ARE NOW RUNNING SCARED!
AND YOU'RE GIVING ME THE BUSINESS ABOUT WHO CALLS A MEETING?
HERO
H
THE BIG BOSS LADY, SHE WHOSE NAME WE ALSO NEVER SAY, CAN'T BE TOO HAPPY WITH ALL OF THIS.
WITH ANY OF US.
I KNOW SHE'S PROBABLY LISTENING.
YEAH, I WAS GONNA SAY...
AND WHO IS THIS DUDE, ALL OF A SUDDEN?
OH, UH, I'M-- THEY'RE CALLIN' ME KUMQUAT.
I'M TAKING CANDY'S TURF.
GOD REST HER SOUL.
I HEARD NOTHING BUT GOOD THINGS.
WHO IS THIS?
HE'S A FRIEND.
WE DON'T VOTE ON STUFF LIKE THIS?
NO.
SO THIS GUY'S IN OUR LIFE NOW.
SO IS THE QUESTION.
THE QUESTION AND "THE BOY SCOUT" AND THE ONE IN THE HOSPITAL.
LET'S FOCUS ON THIS.
YEAH, OKAY...
...IF IT AIN'T CLEAR: I WANT YOU TO HAVE THE RED CLOUD KILL THE QUESTION.
IN FRONT OF ME IF AT ALL POSSIBLE.

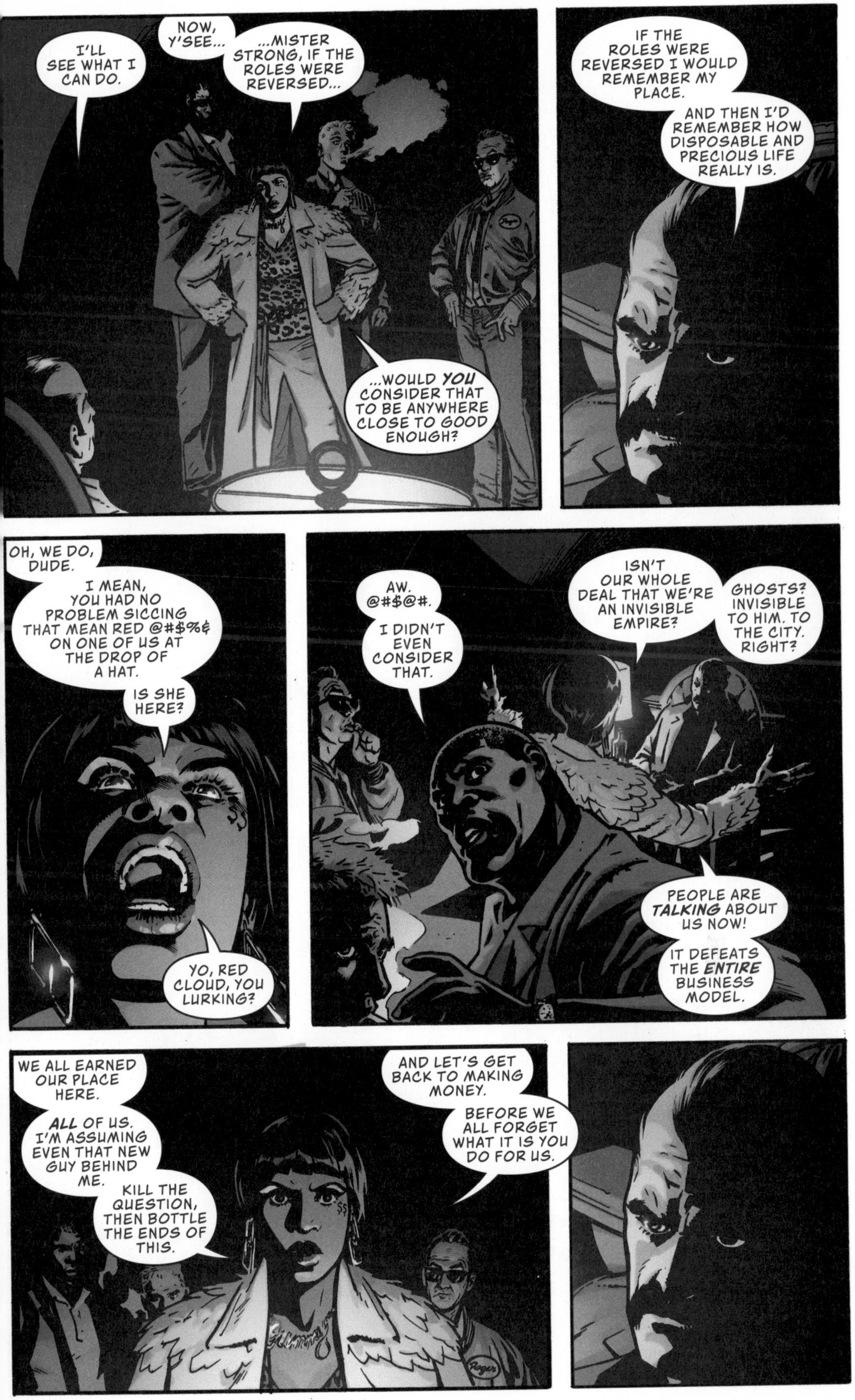
I'LL SEE WHAT I CAN DO.
NOW, Y'SEE...
...MISTER STRONG, IF THE ROLES WERE REVERSED...
...WOULD YOU CONSIDER THAT TO BE ANYWHERE CLOSE TO GOOD ENOUGH?
IF THE ROLES WERE REVERSED I WOULD REMEMBER MY PLACE.
AND THEN I'D REMEMBER HOW DISPOSABLE AND PRECIOUS LIFE REALLY IS.
OH, WE DO, DUDE.
I MEAN, YOU HAD NO PROBLEM SICCING THAT MEAN RED @#$%& ON ONE OF US AT THE DROP OF A HAT.
IS SHE HERE?
YO, RED CLOUD, YOU LURKING?
AW. @#$@#.
I DIDN'T EVEN CONSIDER THAT.
ISN'T OUR WHOLE DEAL THAT WE'RE AN INVISIBLE EMPIRE?
GHOSTS? INVISIBLE TO HIM. TO THE CITY. RIGHT?
PEOPLE ARE TALKING ABOUT US NOW!
IT DEFEATS THE ENTIRE BUSINESS MODEL.
WE ALL EARNED OUR PLACE HERE.
ALL OF US. I'M ASSUMING EVEN THAT NEW GUY BEHIND ME.
KILL THE QUESTION, THEN BOTTLE THE ENDS OF THIS.
AND LET'S GET BACK TO MAKING MONEY.
BEFORE WE ALL FORGET WHAT IT IS YOU DO FOR US.

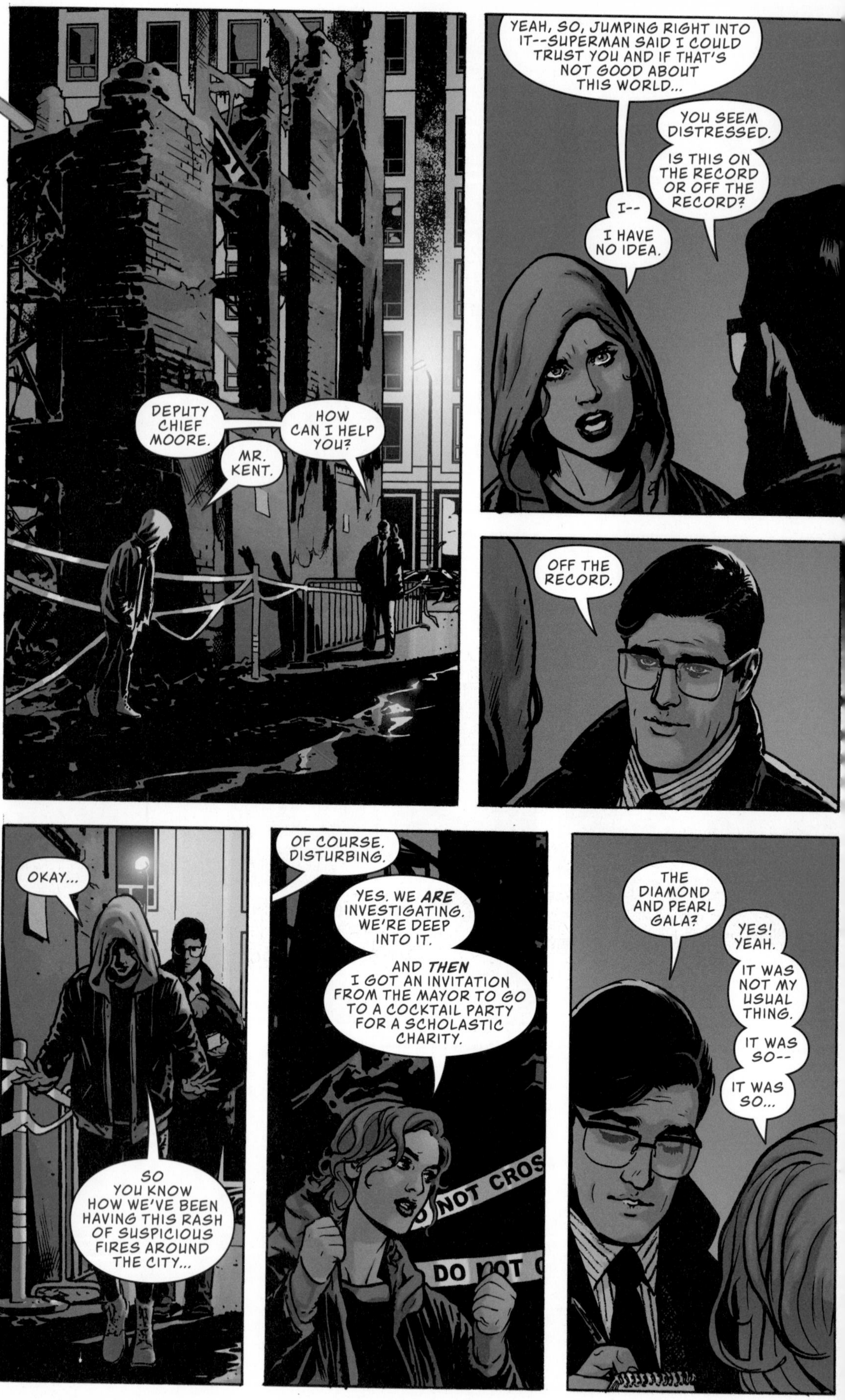
DEPUTY CHIEF MOORE.
MR. KENT.
HOW CAN I HELP YOU?
YEAH, SO, JUMPING RIGHT INTO IT--SUPERMAN SAID I COULD TRUST YOU AND IF THAT'S NOT GOOD ABOUT THIS WORLD...
YOU SEEM DISTRESSED.
IS THIS ON THE RECORD OR OFF THE RECORD?
I--
I HAVE NO IDEA.
OFF THE RECORD.
OKAY...
SO YOU KNOW HOW WE'VE BEEN HAVING THIS RASH OF SUSPICIOUS FIRES AROUND THE CITY...
OF COURSE. DISTURBING.
YES. WE *ARE* INVESTIGATING. WE'RE DEEP INTO IT.
AND *THEN* I GOT AN INVITATION FROM THE MAYOR TO GO TO A COCKTAIL PARTY FOR A SCHOLASTIC CHARITY.
DO NOT CROS
DO NOT C
THE DIAMOND AND PEARL GALA?
YES! YEAH.
IT WAS NOT MY USUAL THING.
IT WAS SO--
IT WAS SO...

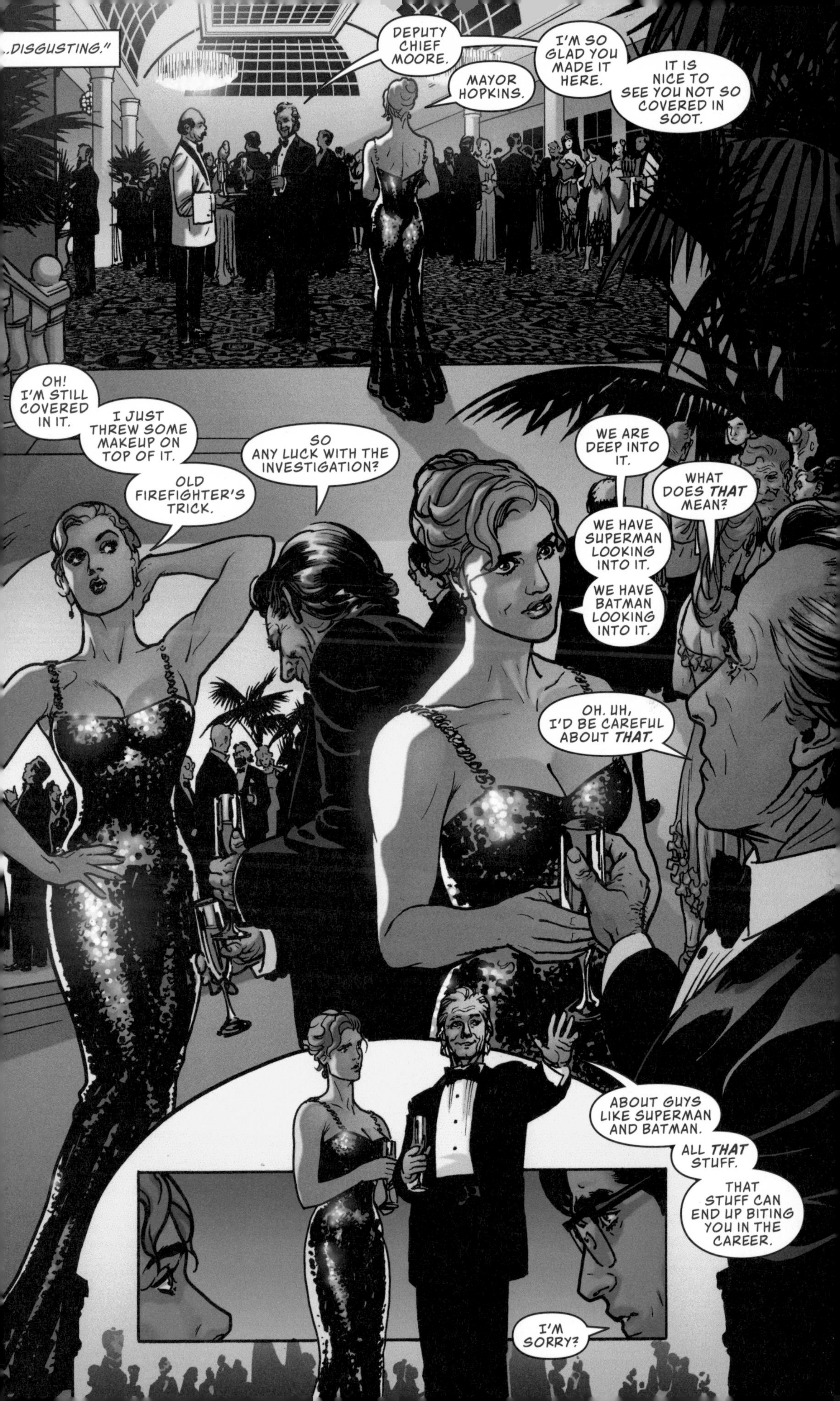

..DISGUSTING."
DEPUTY CHIEF MOORE.
MAYOR HOPKINS.
I'M SO GLAD YOU MADE IT HERE.
IT IS NICE TO SEE YOU NOT SO COVERED IN SOOT.
OH! I'M STILL COVERED IN IT.
I JUST THREW SOME MAKEUP ON TOP OF IT.
OLD FIREFIGHTER'S TRICK.
SO ANY LUCK WITH THE INVESTIGATION?
WE ARE DEEP INTO IT.
WE HAVE SUPERMAN LOOKING INTO IT.
WE HAVE BATMAN LOOKING INTO IT.
WHAT DOES THAT MEAN?
OH. UH, I'D BE CAREFUL ABOUT THAT.
ABOUT GUYS LIKE SUPERMAN AND BATMAN.
ALL THAT STUFF.
THAT STUFF CAN END UP BITING YOU IN THE CAREER.
I'M SORRY?

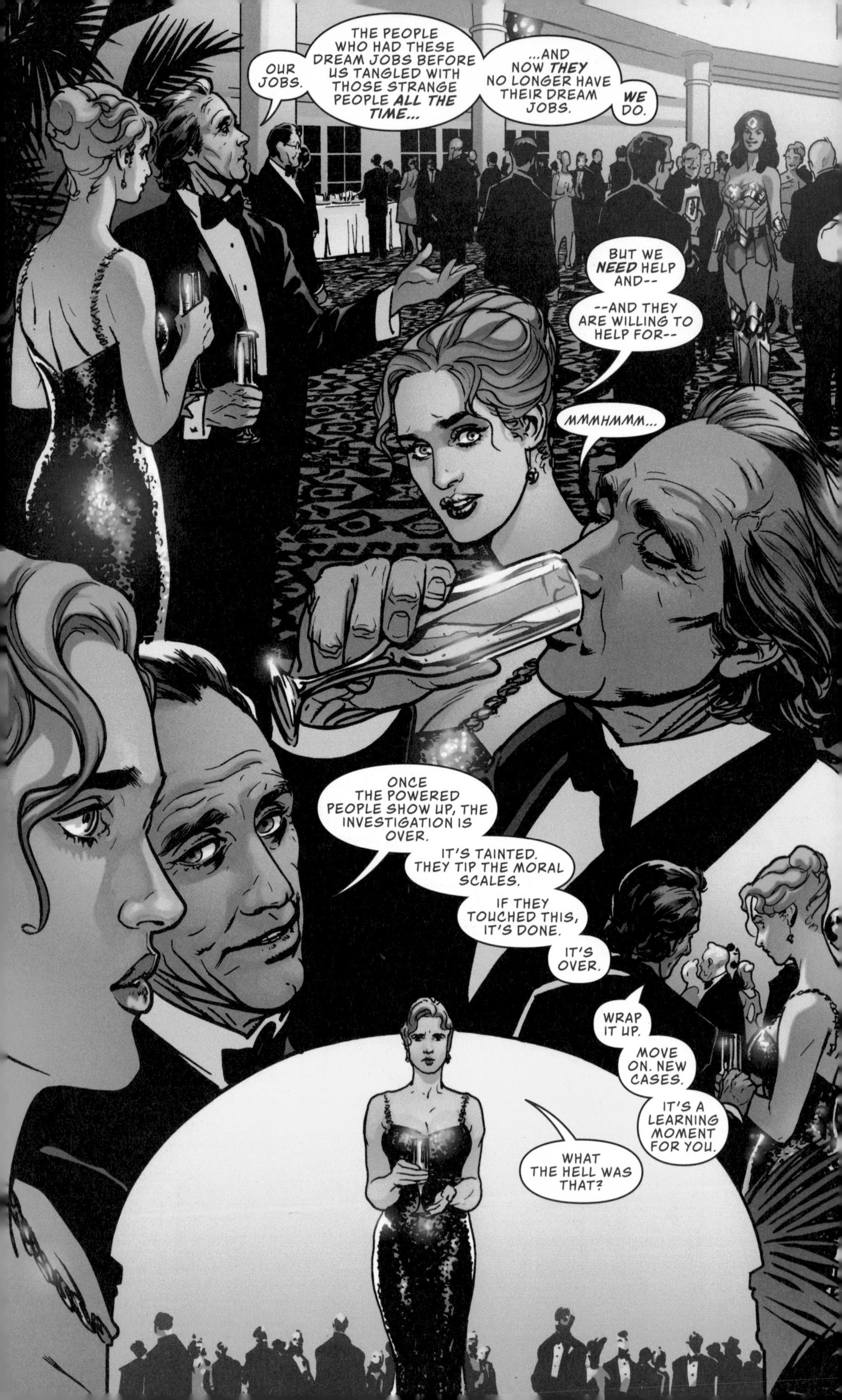

OUR JOBS.
THE PEOPLE WHO HAD THESE DREAM JOBS BEFORE US TANGLED WITH THOSE STRANGE PEOPLE ALL THE TIME...
...AND NOW THEY NO LONGER HAVE THEIR DREAM JOBS.
WE DO.
BUT WE NEED HELP AND--
--AND THEY ARE WILLING TO HELP FOR--
MMMHMMM...
ONCE THE POWERED PEOPLE SHOW UP, THE INVESTIGATION IS OVER.
IT'S TAINTED. THEY TIP THE MORAL SCALES.
IF THEY TOUCHED THIS, IT'S DONE.
IT'S OVER.
WRAP IT UP.
MOVE ON. NEW CASES.
IT'S A LEARNING MOMENT FOR YOU.
WHAT THE HELL WAS THAT?

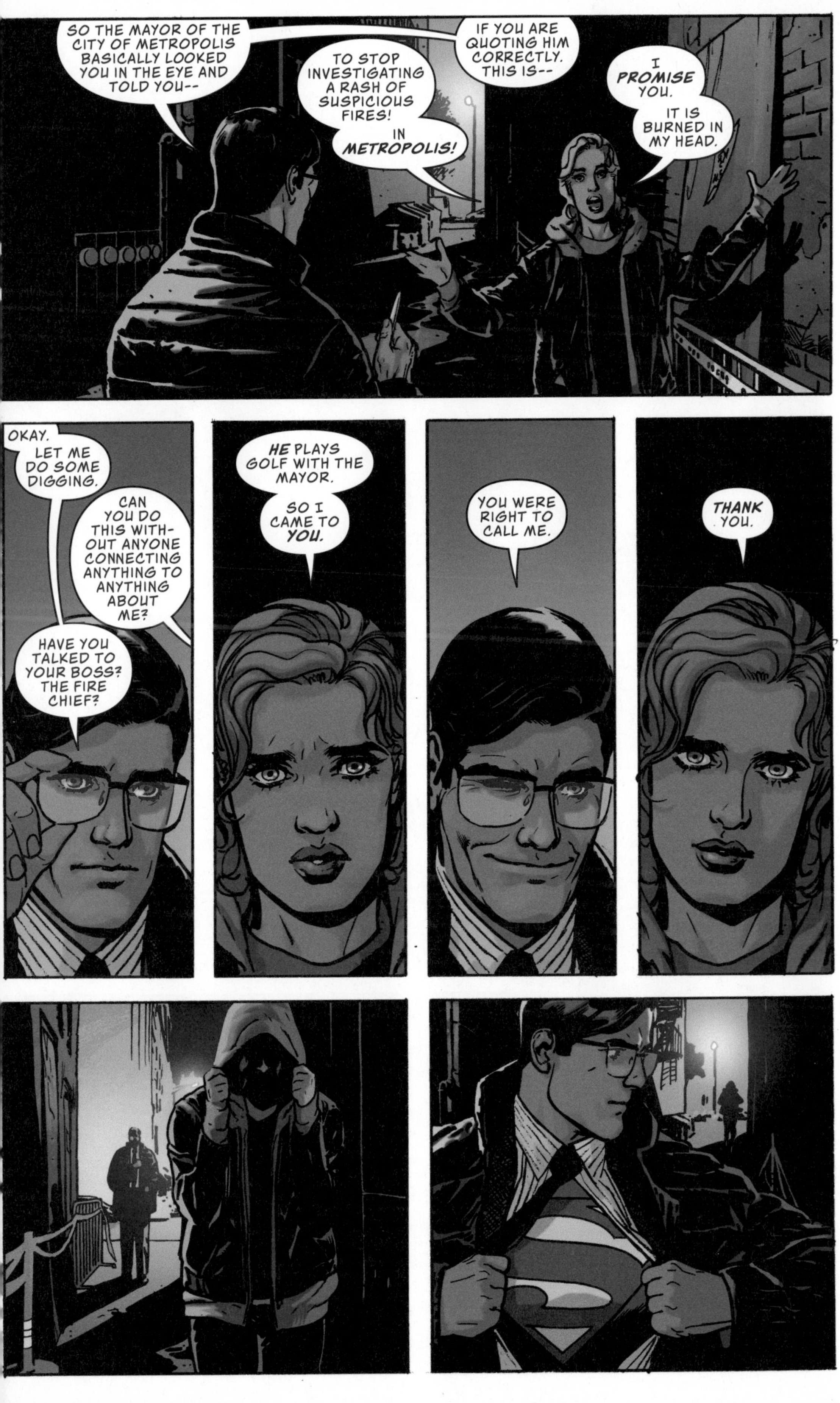
SO THE MAYOR OF THE CITY OF METROPOLIS BASICALLY LOOKED YOU IN THE EYE AND TOLD YOU--
TO STOP INVESTIGATING A RASH OF SUSPICIOUS FIRES!
IN METROPOLIS!
IF YOU ARE QUOTING HIM CORRECTLY. THIS IS--
I PROMISE YOU.
IT IS BURNED IN MY HEAD.
OKAY. LET ME DO SOME DIGGING.
CAN YOU DO THIS WITH-OUT ANYONE CONNECTING ANYTHING TO ANYTHING ABOUT ME?
HAVE YOU TALKED TO YOUR BOSS? THE FIRE CHIEF?
HE PLAYS GOLF WITH THE MAYOR.
SO I CAME TO YOU.
YOU WERE RIGHT TO CALL ME.
THANK YOU.

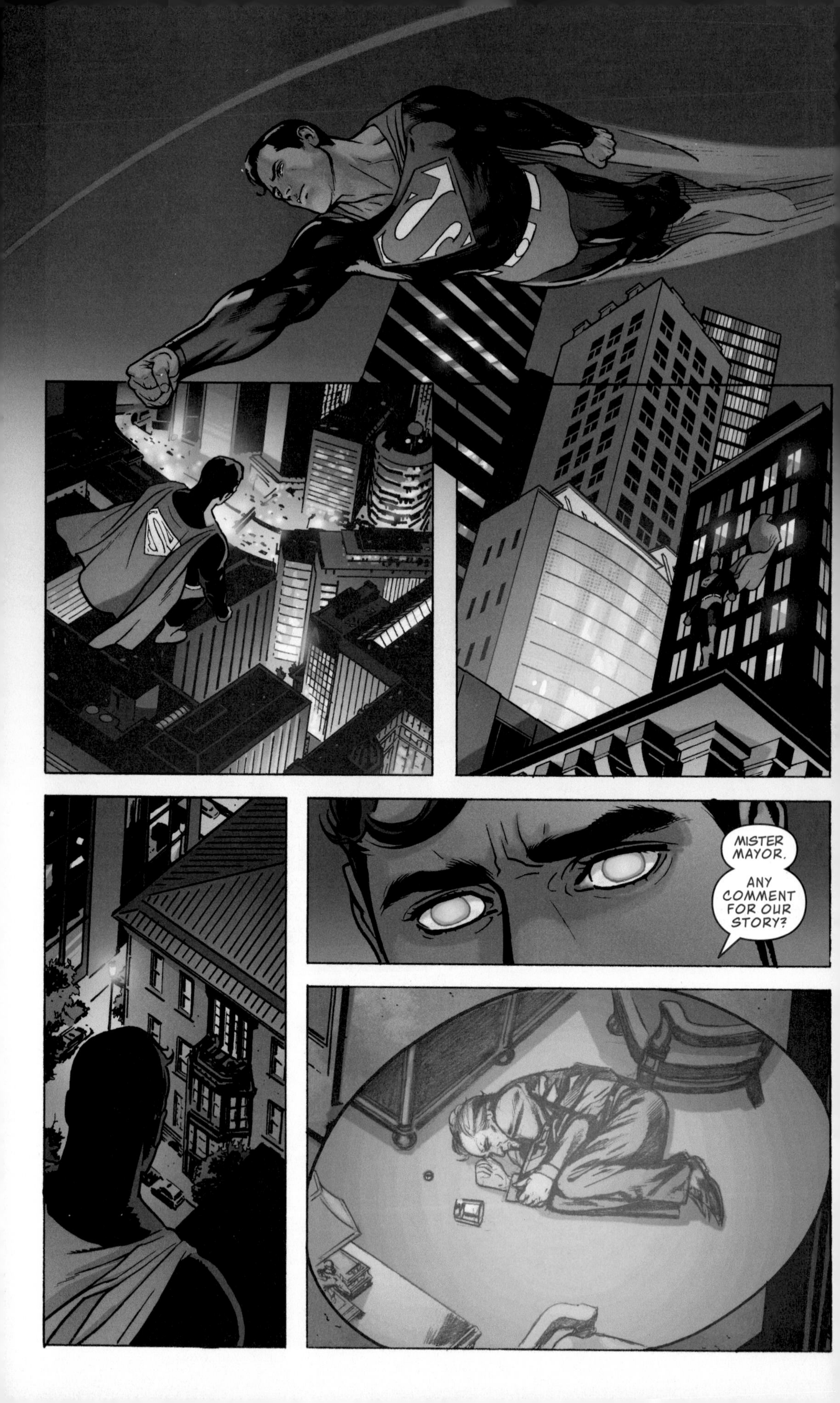
MISTER MAYOR.
ANY COMMENT FOR OUR STORY?

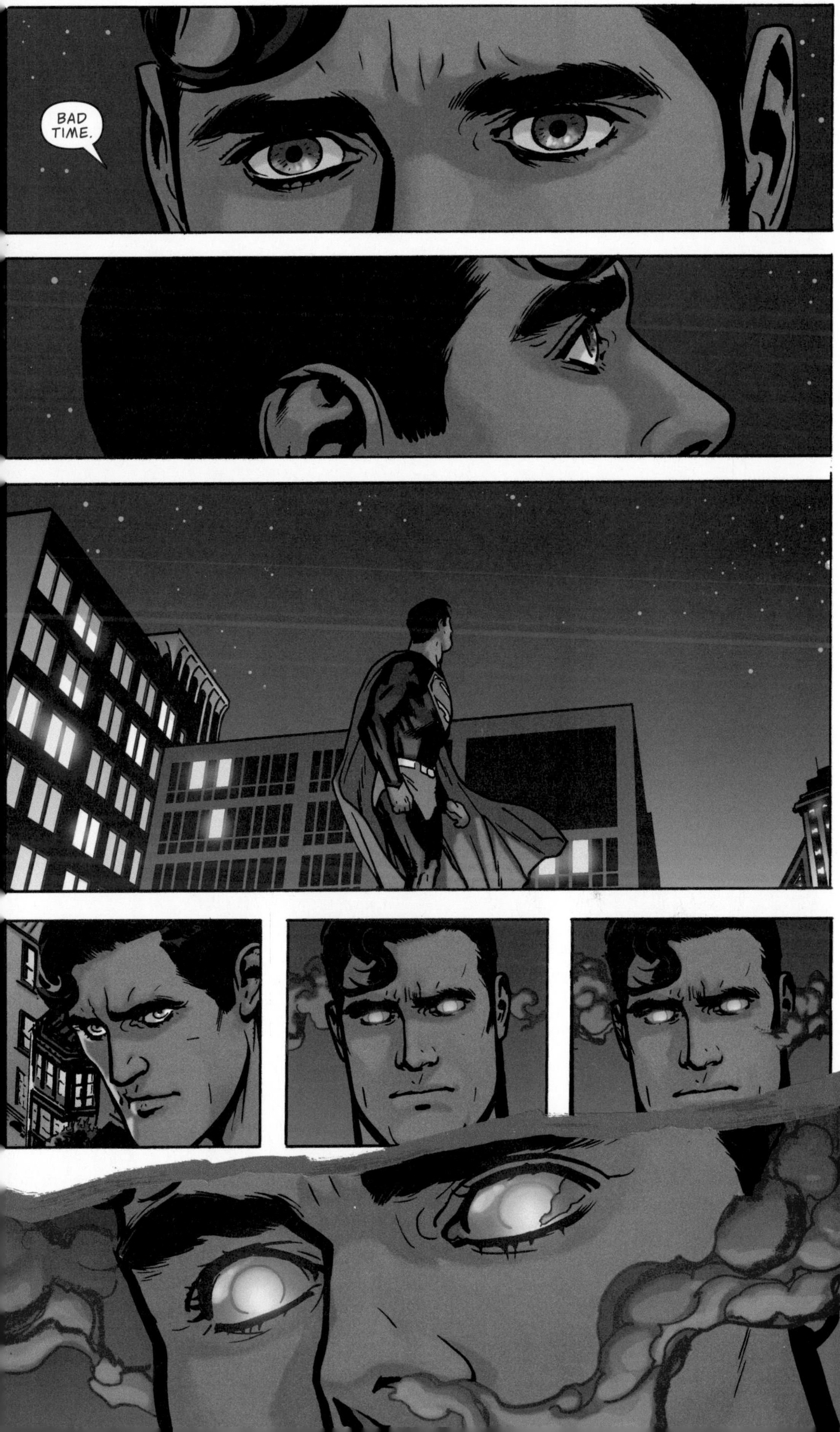
BAD TIME.

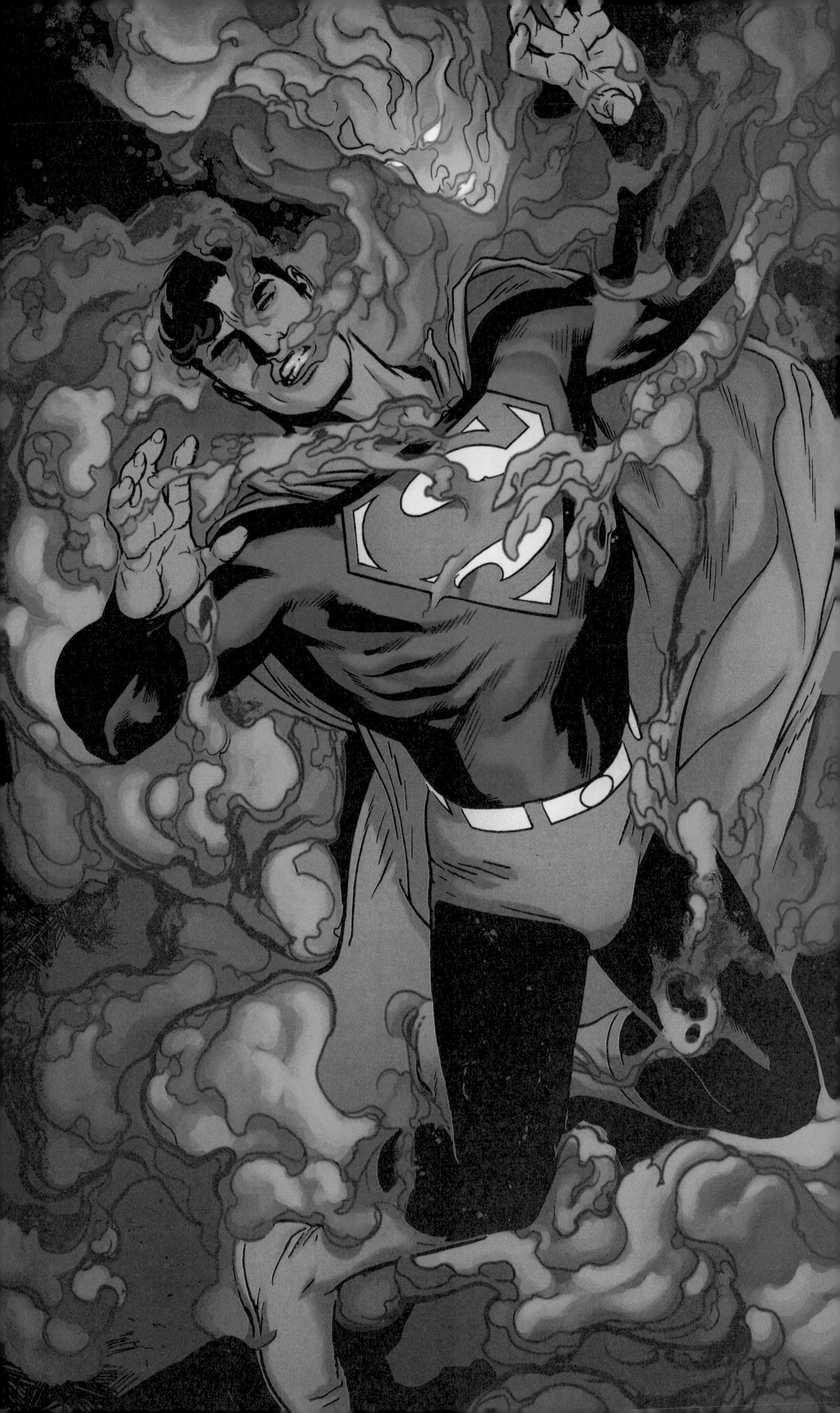

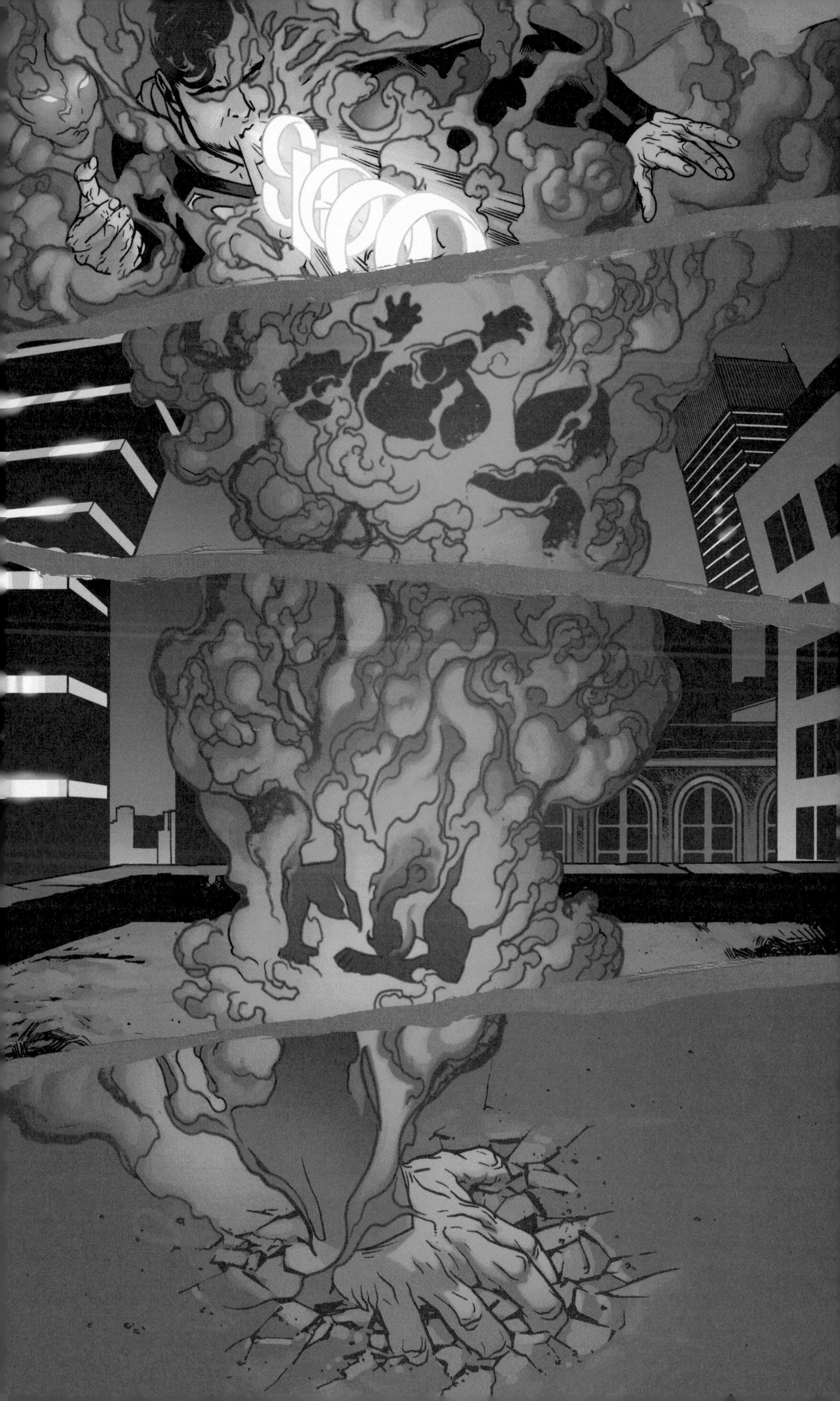
SHOOO

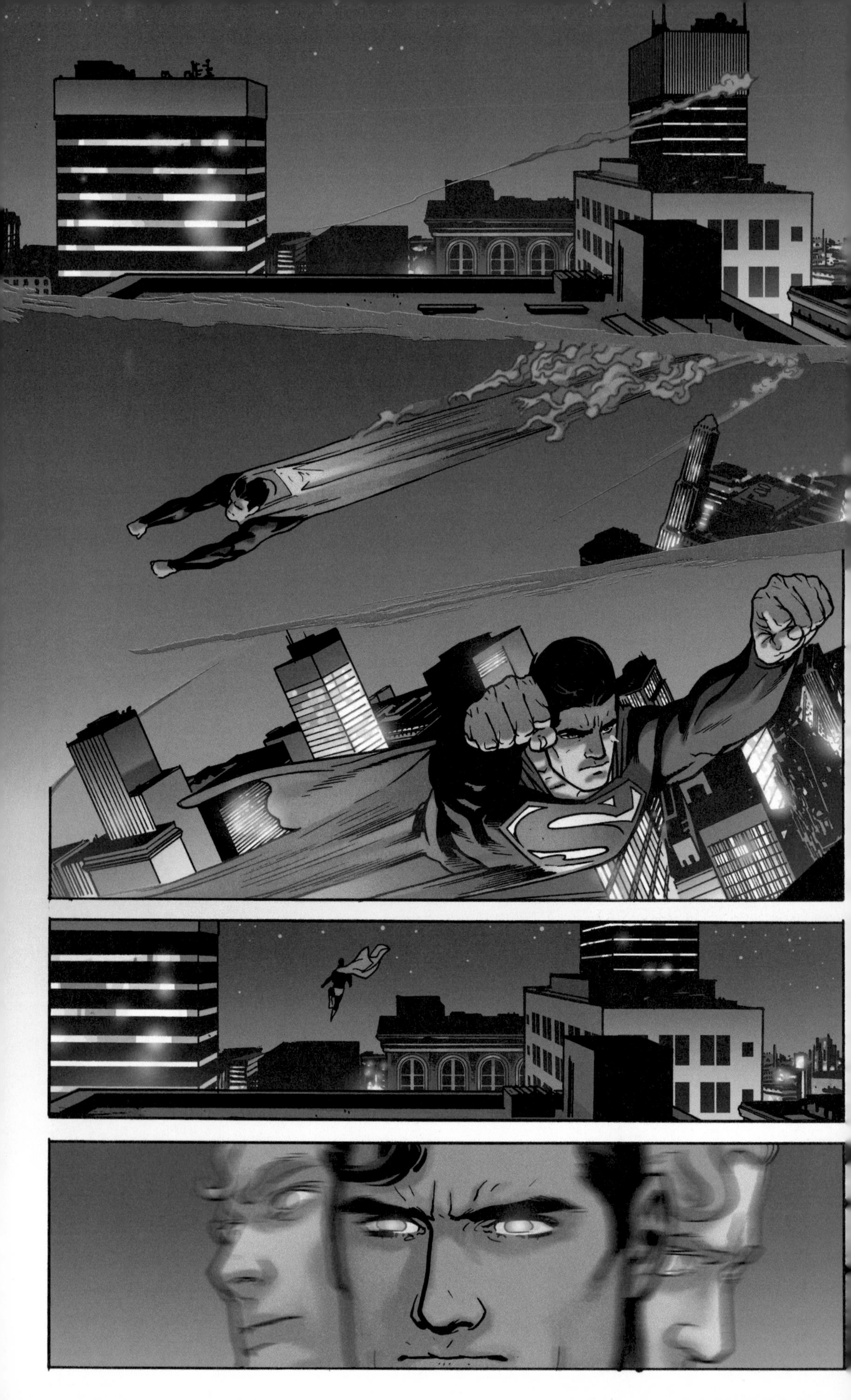

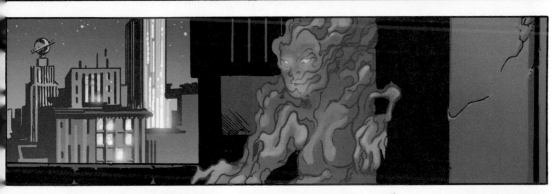

WELL, DAMN...

...I JUST WENT FACE TO FACE AGAINST THE GREATEST OF ALL TIME...

...AND I LIVED TO TELL THE TALE.

I CAN CHASE OFF SUPERMAN...

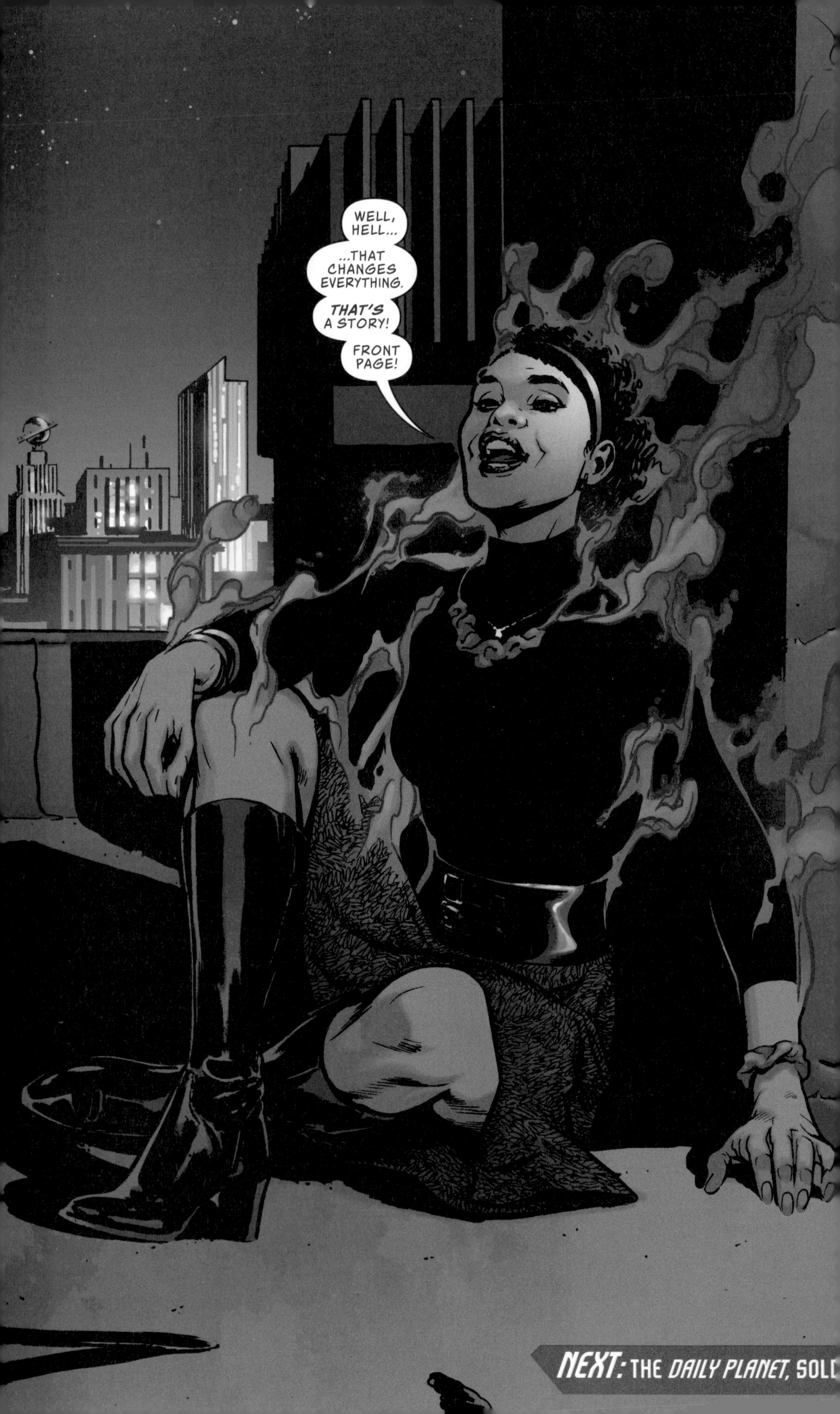
WELL, HELL...
...THAT CHANGES EVERYTHING.
THAT'S A STORY!
FRONT PAGE!
NEXT: THE DAILY PLANET, SOLD

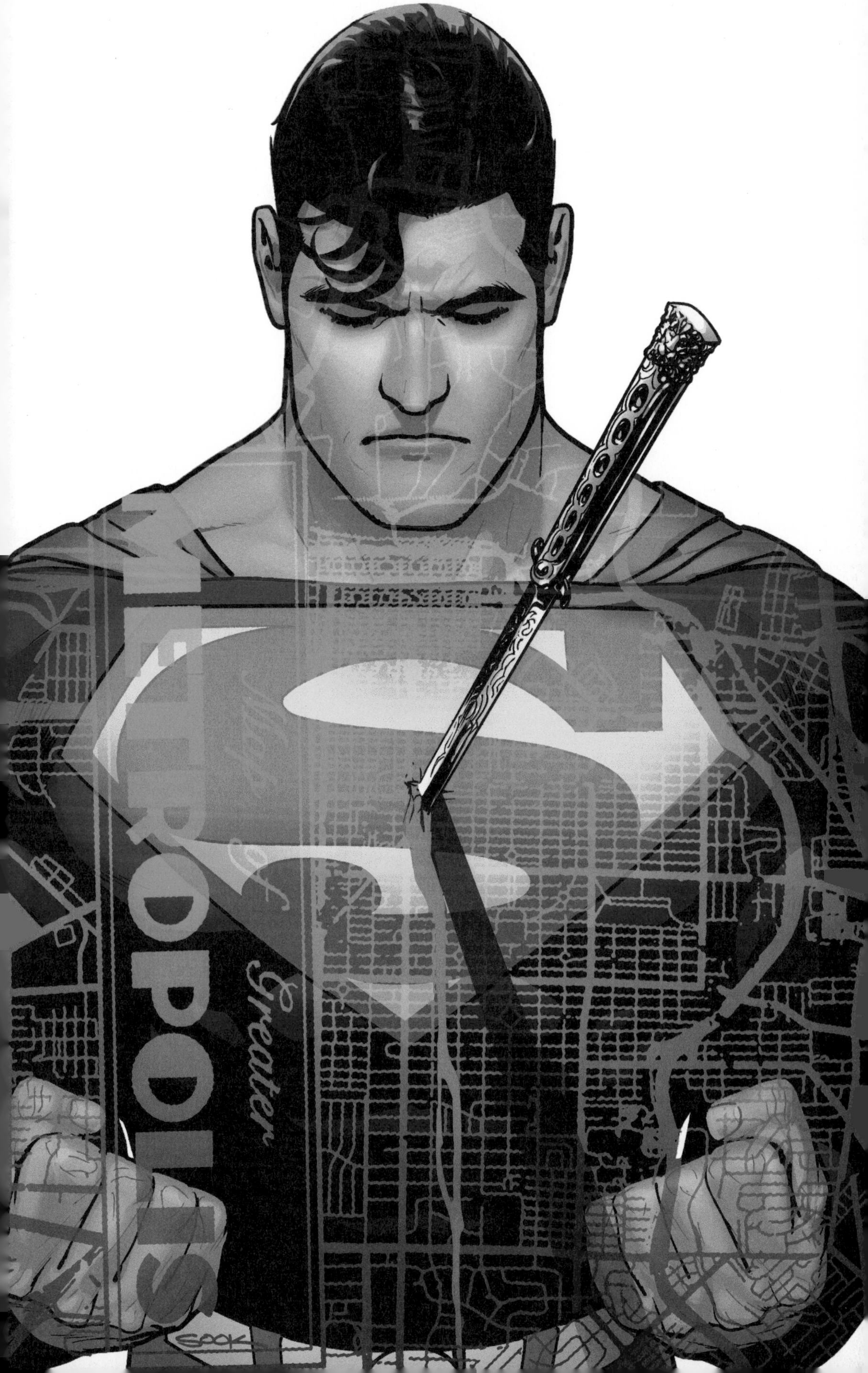
Greater

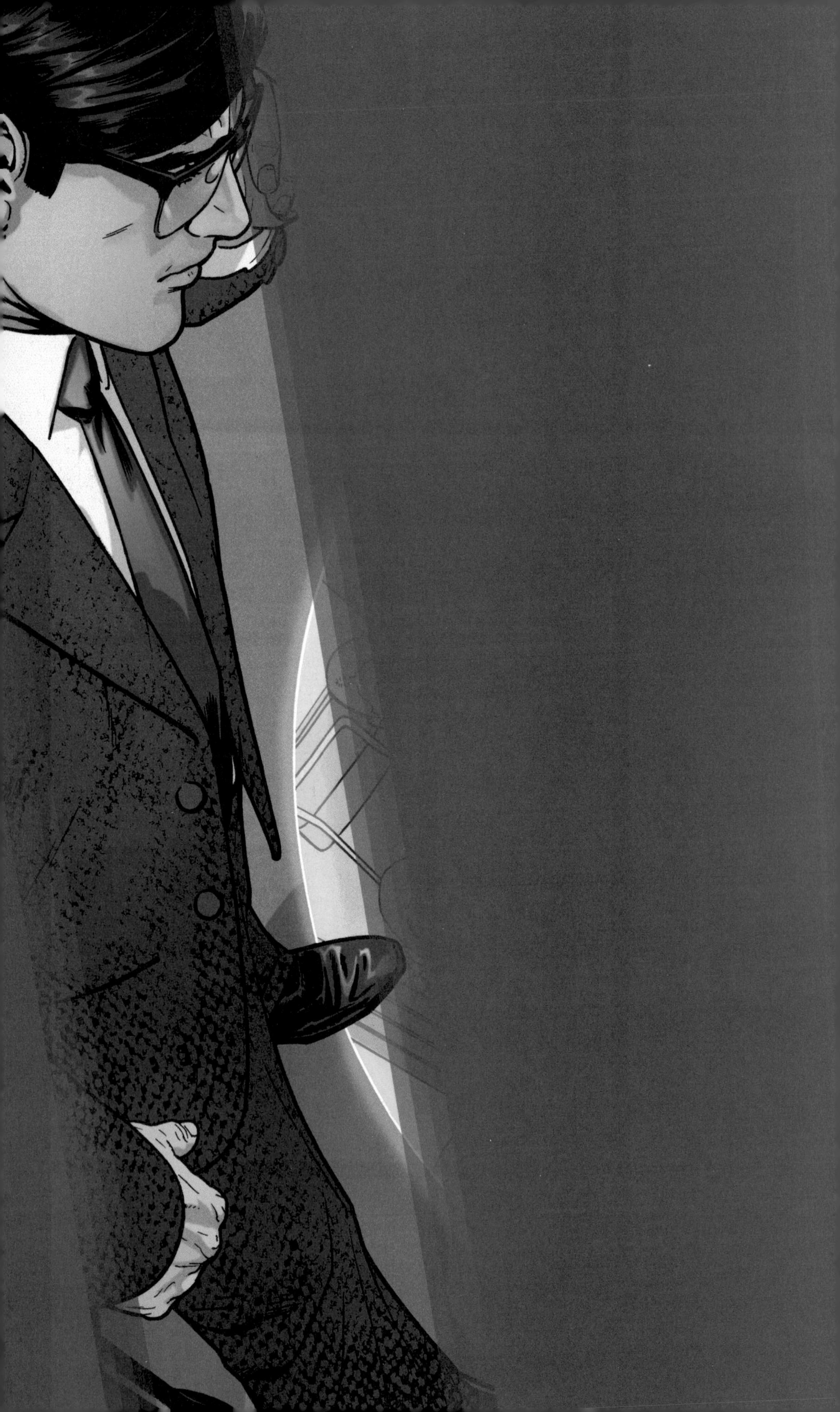

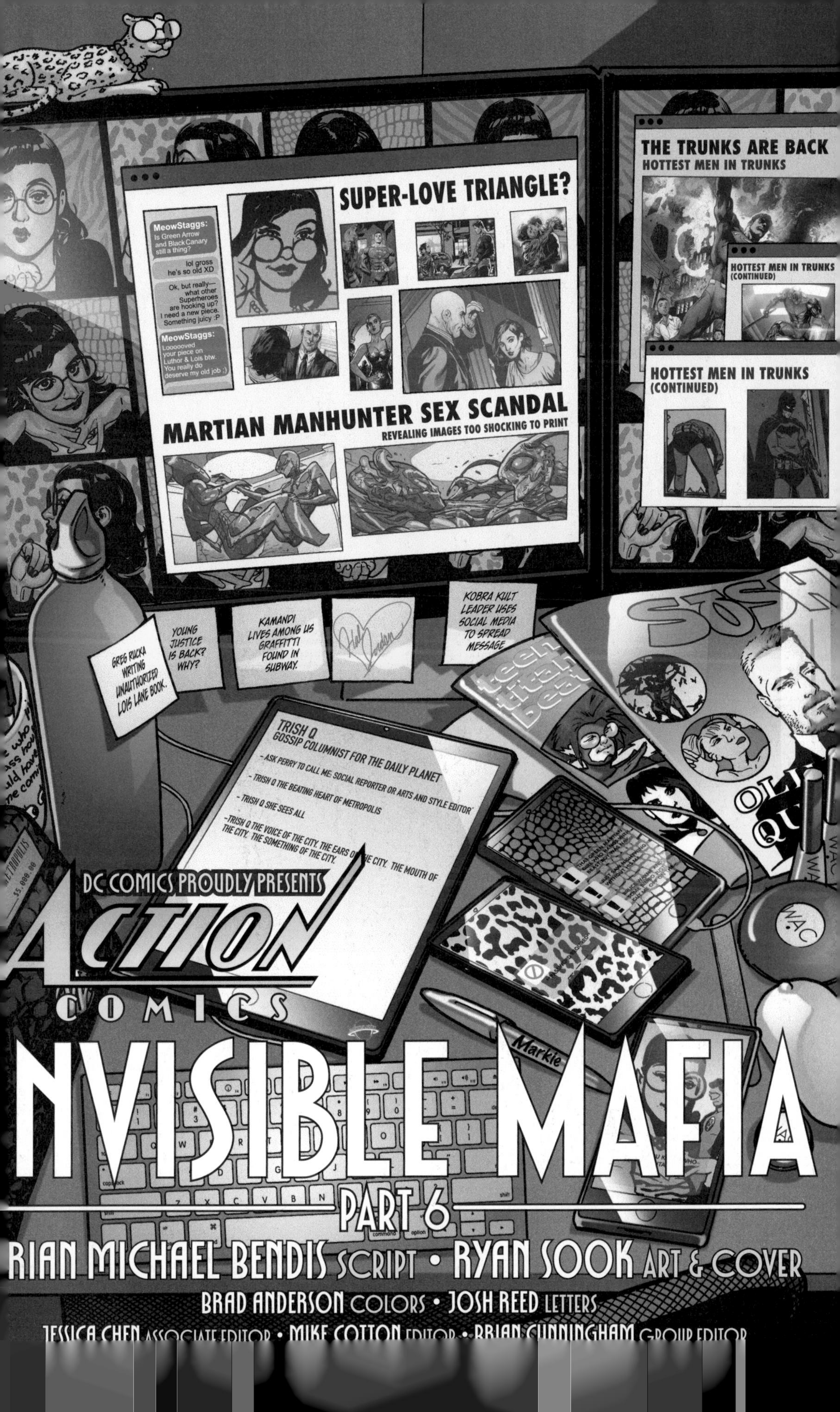

THE TRUNKS ARE BACK
HOTTEST MEN IN TRUNKS
HOTTEST MEN IN TRUNKS (CONTINUED)
HOTTEST MEN IN TRUNKS (CONTINUED)
SUPER-LOVE TRIANGLE?
MeowStaggs: Is Green Arrow and Black Canary still a thing?
lol gross he's so old XD
Ok, but really—what other Superheroes are hooking up? I need a new piece. Something juicy :P
MeowStaggs: Loooooved your piece on Luthor & Lois btw. You really do deserve my old job ;)
MARTIAN MANHUNTER SEX SCANDAL
REVEALING IMAGES TOO SHOCKING TO PRINT
GREG RUCKA WRITING UNAUTHORIZED LOIS LANE BOOK.
YOUNG JUSTICE IS BACK? WHY?
KAMANDI LIVES AMONG US GRAFFITTI FOUND IN SUBWAY.
KOBRA KULT LEADER USES SOCIAL MEDIA TO SPREAD MESSAGE.
teen titan beat
TRISH Q
GOSSIP COLUMNIST FOR THE DAILY PLANET
- ASK PERRY TO CALL ME: SOCIAL REPORTER OR ARTS AND STYLE EDITOR
- TRISH Q THE BEATING HEART OF METROPOLIS
- TRISH Q SHE SEES ALL
-TRISH Q THE VOICE OF THE CITY. THE EARS OF THE CITY. THE MOUTH OF THE CITY. THE SOMETHING OF THE CITY.
Markie
DC COMICS PROUDLY PRESENTS
ACTION COMICS
NVISIBLE MAFIA
PART 6
RIAN MICHAEL BENDIS SCRIPT • RYAN SOOK ART & COVER
BRAD ANDERSON COLORS • JOSH REED LETTERS
JESSICA CHEN ASSOCIATE EDITOR • MIKE COTTON EDITOR • BRIAN CUNNINGHAM GROUP EDITOR

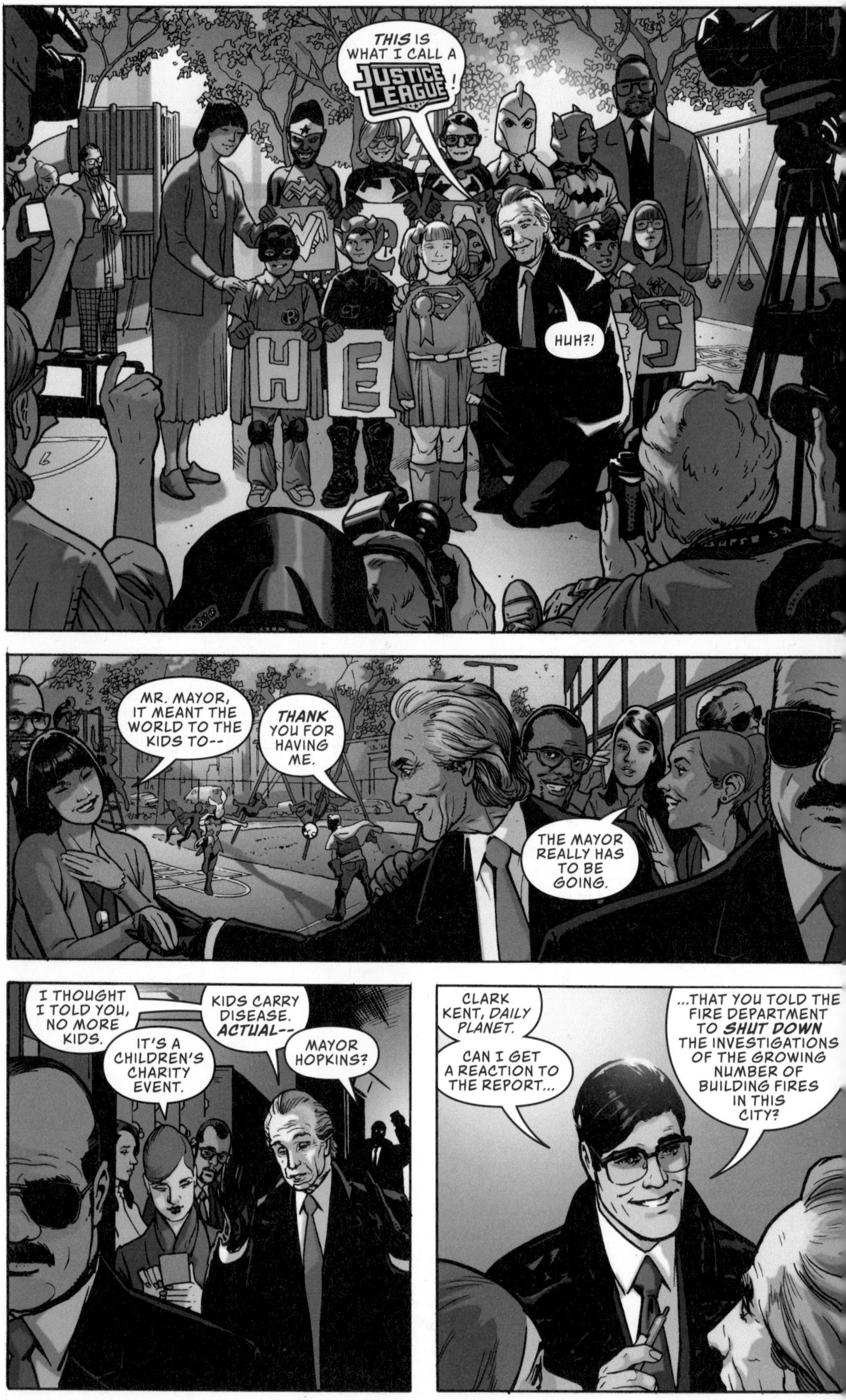
THIS IS WHAT I CALL A JUSTICE LEAGUE!
HUH?!
MR. MAYOR, IT MEANT THE WORLD TO THE KIDS TO--
THANK YOU FOR HAVING ME.
THE MAYOR REALLY HAS TO BE GOING.
I THOUGHT I TOLD YOU, NO MORE KIDS.
IT'S A CHILDREN'S CHARITY EVENT.
KIDS CARRY DISEASE. ACTUAL--
MAYOR HOPKINS?
CLARK KENT, DAILY PLANET.
CAN I GET A REACTION TO THE REPORT...
...THAT YOU TOLD THE FIRE DEPARTMENT TO SHUT DOWN THE INVESTIGATIONS OF THE GROWING NUMBER OF BUILDING FIRES IN THIS CITY?

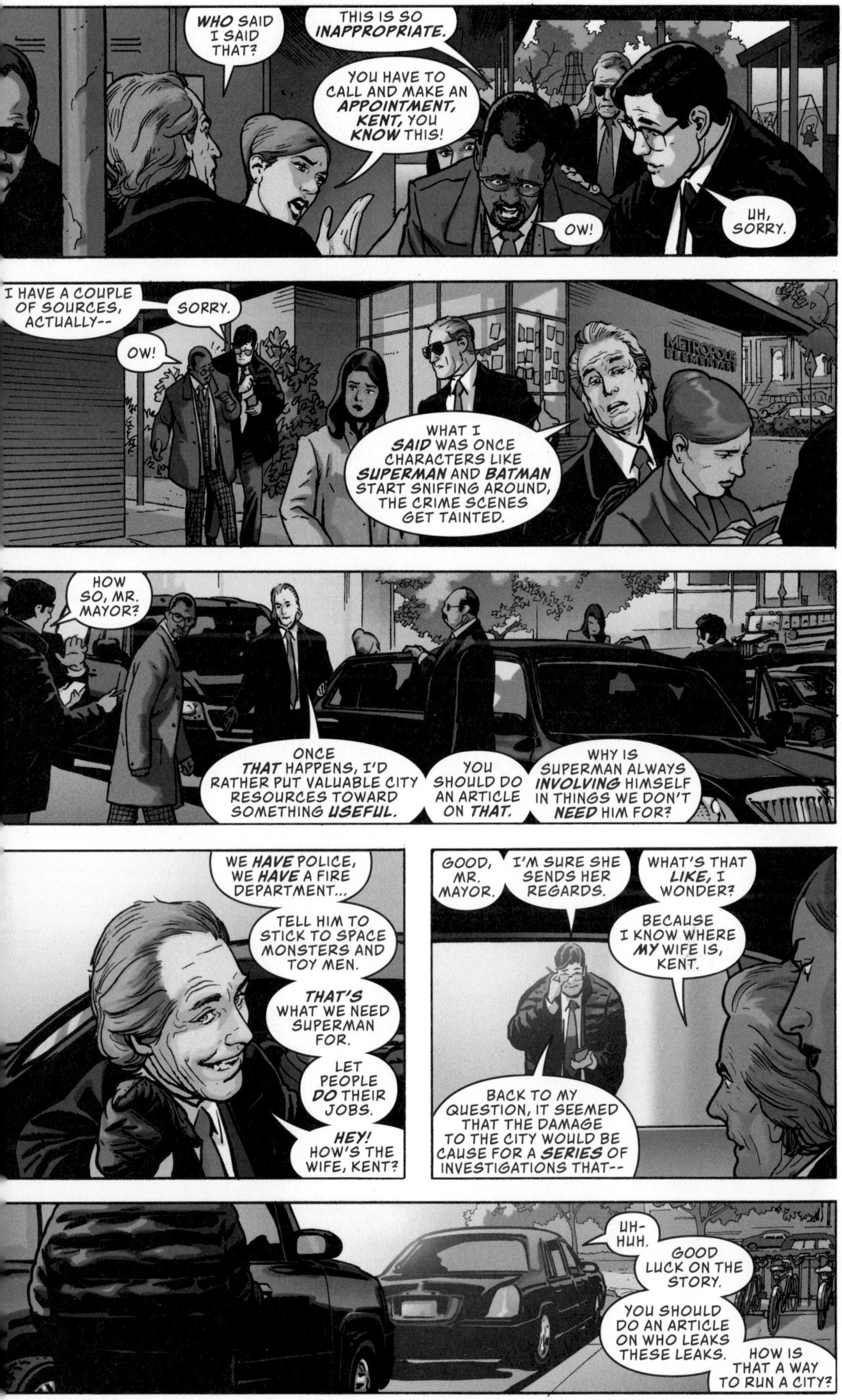
WHO SAID I SAID THAT?
THIS IS SO INAPPROPRIATE.
YOU HAVE TO CALL AND MAKE AN APPOINTMENT, KENT, YOU KNOW THIS!
OW!
UH, SORRY.
I HAVE A COUPLE OF SOURCES, ACTUALLY--
SORRY.
OW!
METROPOLIS ELEMENTARY
WHAT I SAID WAS ONCE CHARACTERS LIKE SUPERMAN AND BATMAN START SNIFFING AROUND, THE CRIME SCENES GET TAINTED.
HOW SO, MR. MAYOR?
ONCE THAT HAPPENS, I'D RATHER PUT VALUABLE CITY RESOURCES TOWARD SOMETHING USEFUL.
YOU SHOULD DO AN ARTICLE ON THAT.
WHY IS SUPERMAN ALWAYS INVOLVING HIMSELF IN THINGS WE DON'T NEED HIM FOR?
WE HAVE POLICE, WE HAVE A FIRE DEPARTMENT...
TELL HIM TO STICK TO SPACE MONSTERS AND TOY MEN.
THAT'S WHAT WE NEED SUPERMAN FOR.
LET PEOPLE DO THEIR JOBS.
HEY! HOW'S THE WIFE, KENT?
GOOD, MR. MAYOR.
I'M SURE SHE SENDS HER REGARDS.
WHAT'S THAT LIKE, I WONDER?
BECAUSE I KNOW WHERE MY WIFE IS, KENT.
BACK TO MY QUESTION, IT SEEMED THAT THE DAMAGE TO THE CITY WOULD BE CAUSE FOR A SERIES OF INVESTIGATIONS THAT--
UH-HUH.
GOOD LUCK ON THE STORY.
YOU SHOULD DO AN ARTICLE ON WHO LEAKS THESE LEAKS.
HOW IS THAT A WAY TO RUN A CITY?

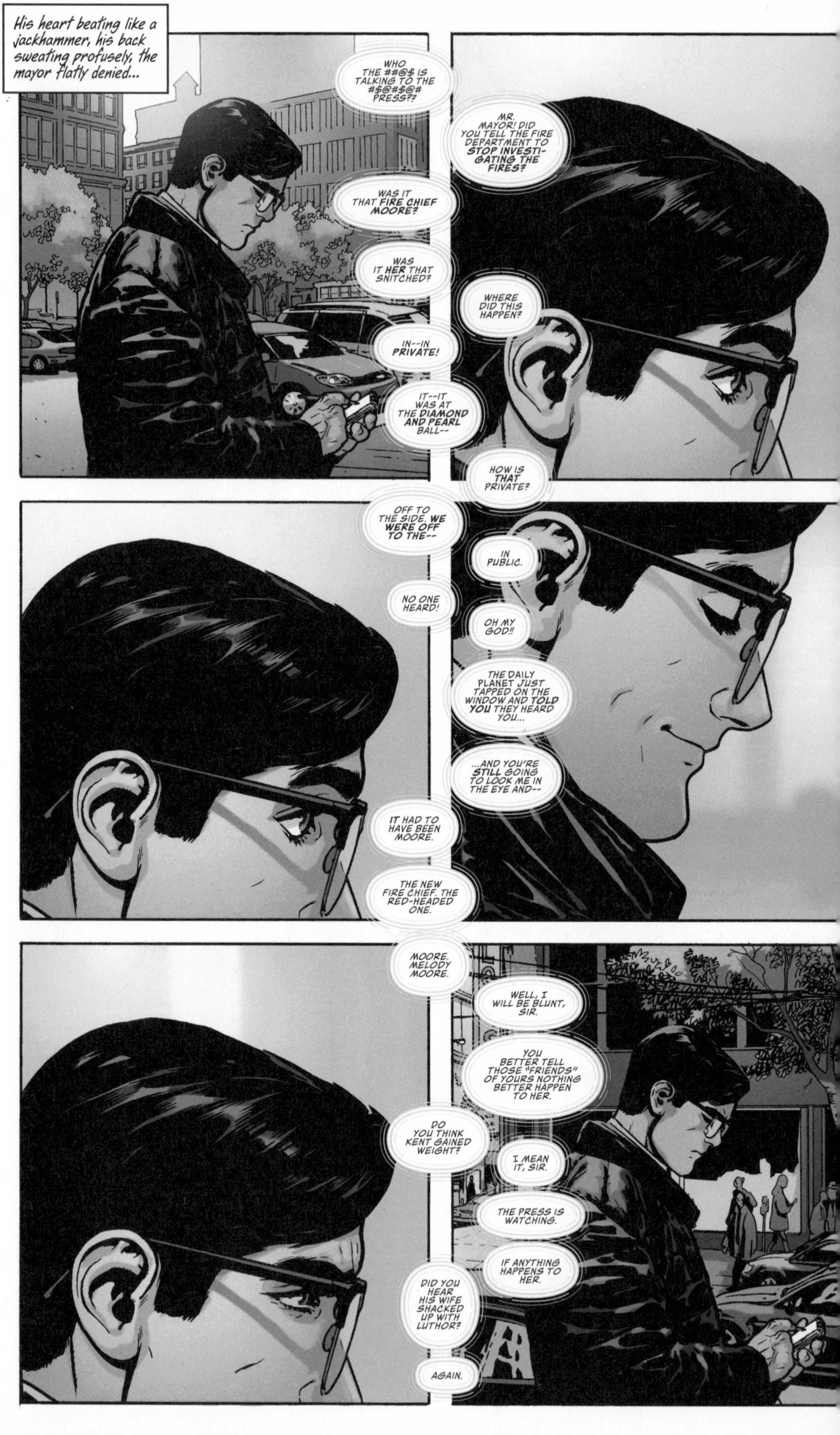
His heart beating like a jackhammer, his back sweating profusely, the mayor flatly denied...
WHO THE ##@$ IS TALKING TO THE #$@#$@# PRESS??
MR. MAYOR! DID YOU TELL THE FIRE DEPARTMENT TO STOP INVESTI-GATING THE FIRES?
WAS IT THAT FIRE CHIEF MOORE?
WAS IT HER THAT SNITCHED?
WHERE DID THIS HAPPEN?
IN--IN PRIVATE!
IT--IT WAS AT THE DIAMOND AND PEARL BALL--
HOW IS THAT PRIVATE?
OFF TO THE SIDE. WE WERE OFF TO THE--
IN PUBLIC.
NO ONE HEARD!
OH MY GOD!!
THE DAILY PLANET JUST TAPPED ON THE WINDOW AND TOLD YOU THEY HEARD YOU...
...AND YOU'RE STILL GOING TO LOOK ME IN THE EYE AND--
IT HAD TO HAVE BEEN MOORE.
THE NEW FIRE CHIEF. THE RED-HEADED ONE.
MOORE. MELODY MOORE.
WELL, I WILL BE BLUNT, SIR.
YOU BETTER TELL THOSE "FRIENDS" OF YOURS NOTHING BETTER HAPPEN TO HER.
DO YOU THINK KENT GAINED WEIGHT?
I MEAN IT, SIR.
THE PRESS IS WATCHING.
IF ANYTHING HAPPENS TO HER.
DID YOU HEAR HIS WIFE SHACKED UP WITH LUTHOR?
AGAIN.

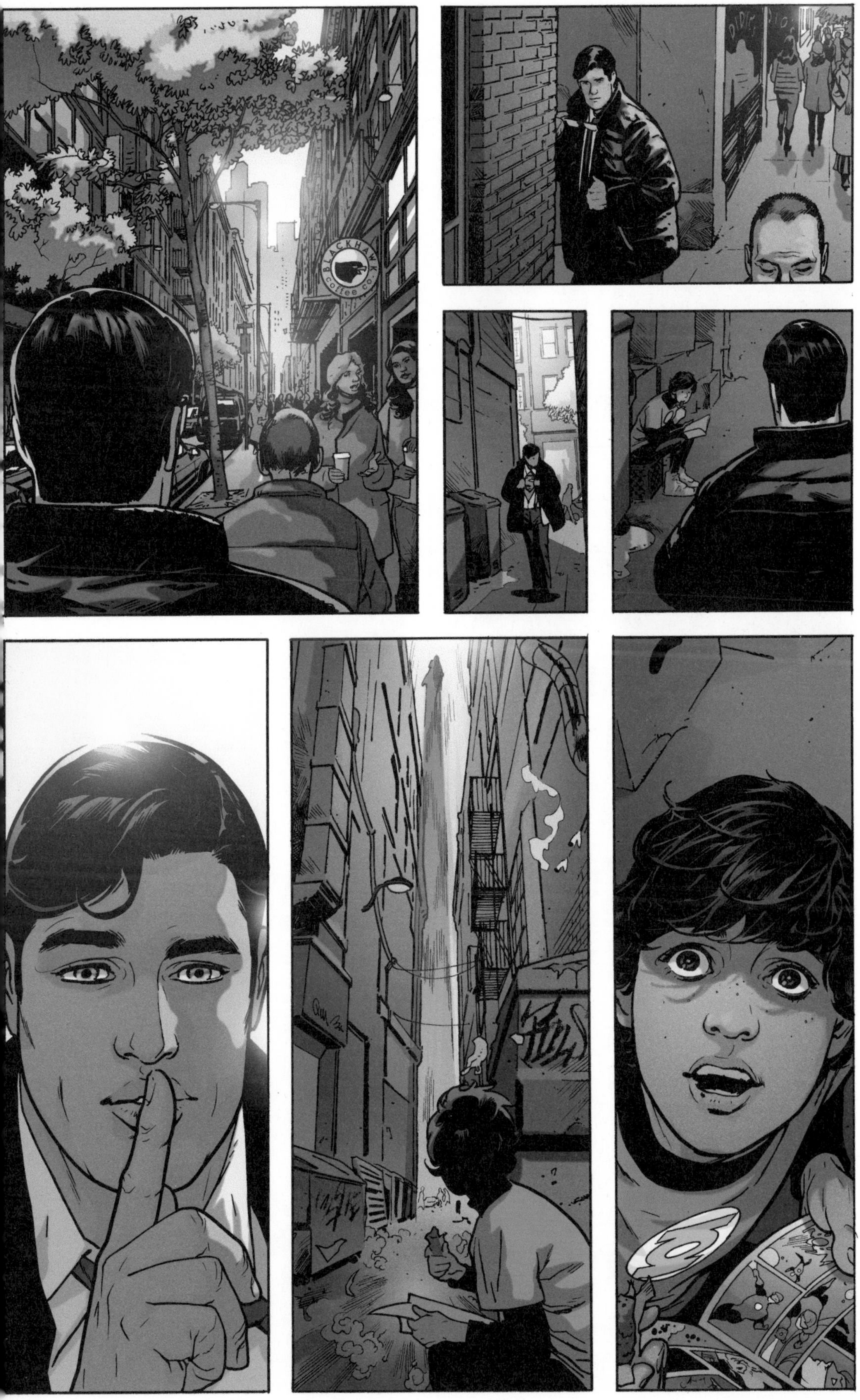
BLACKHAWK
coffee co.

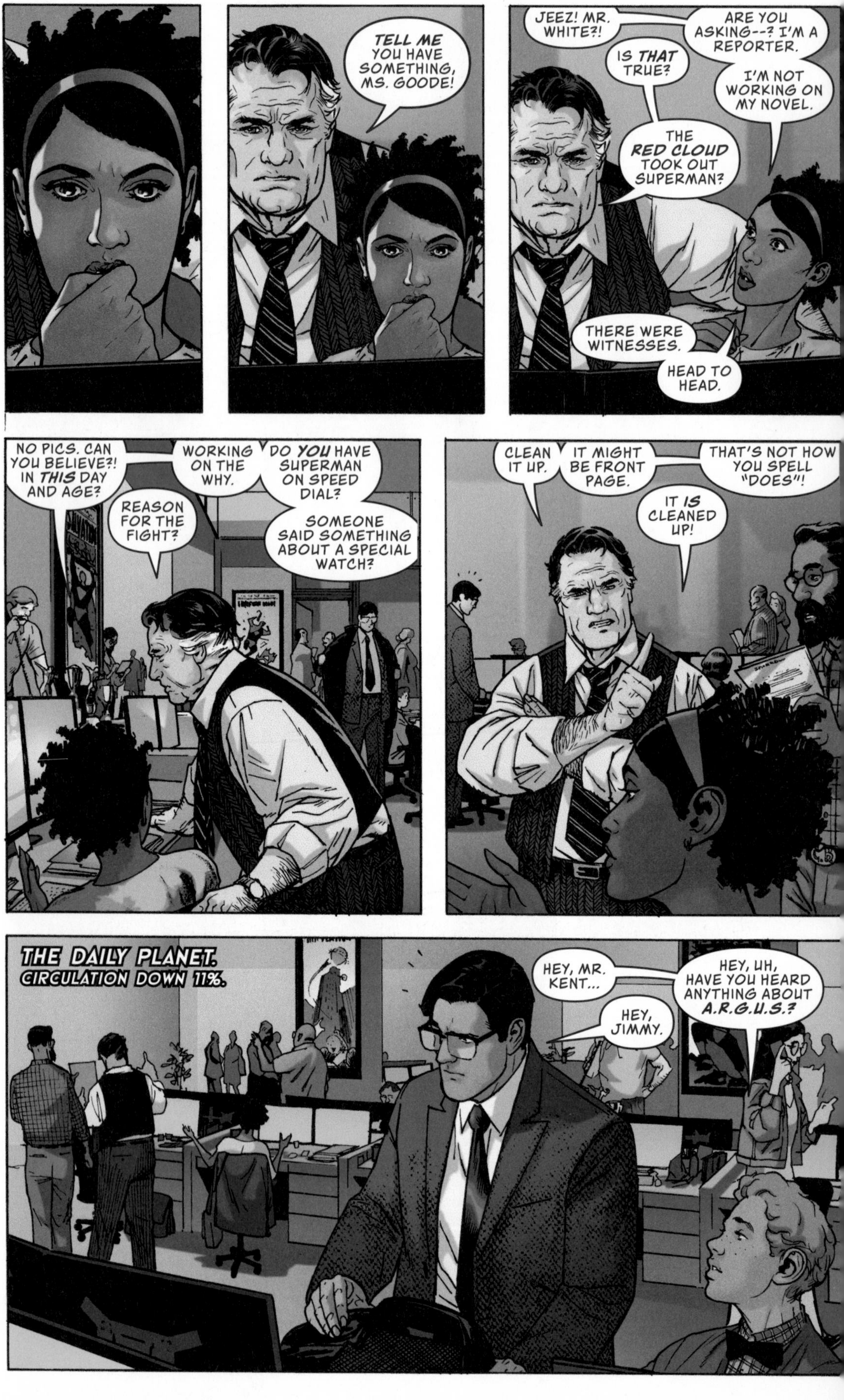

TELL ME YOU HAVE SOMETHING, MS. GOODE!
JEEZ! MR. WHITE?!
IS THAT TRUE?
ARE YOU ASKING--? I'M A REPORTER.
I'M NOT WORKING ON MY NOVEL.
THE RED CLOUD TOOK OUT SUPERMAN?
THERE WERE WITNESSES.
HEAD TO HEAD.
NO PICS. CAN YOU BELIEVE?! IN THIS DAY AND AGE?
REASON FOR THE FIGHT?
WORKING ON THE WHY.
DO YOU HAVE SUPERMAN ON SPEED DIAL?
SOMEONE SAID SOMETHING ABOUT A SPECIAL WATCH?
CLEAN IT UP.
IT MIGHT BE FRONT PAGE.
IT IS CLEANED UP!
THAT'S NOT HOW YOU SPELL "DOES"!
THE DAILY PLANET.
CIRCULATION DOWN 11%.
HEY, MR. KENT...
HEY, JIMMY.
HEY, UH, HAVE YOU HEARD ANYTHING ABOUT A.R.G.U.S.?

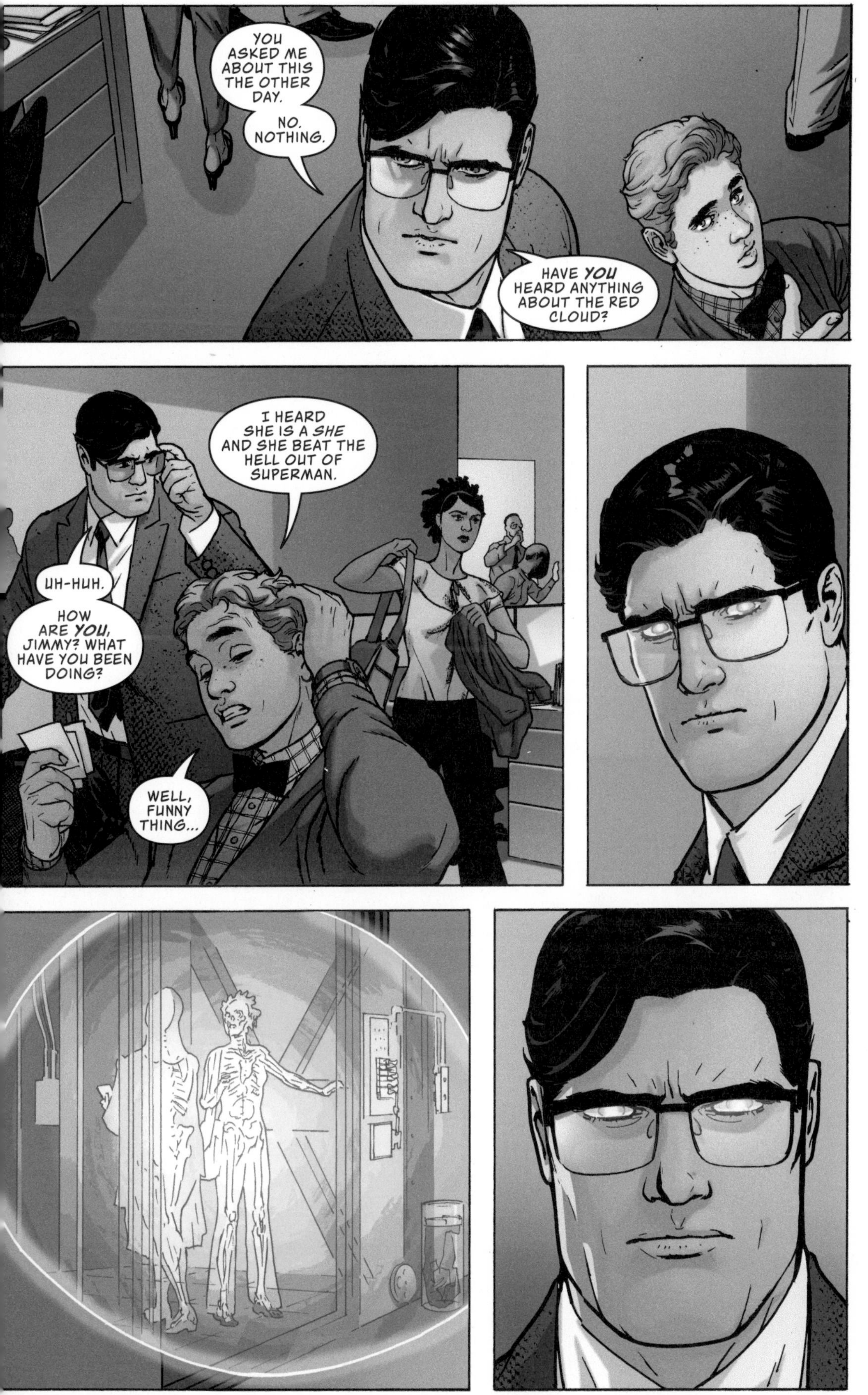
YOU ASKED ME ABOUT THIS THE OTHER DAY.
NO. NOTHING.
HAVE YOU HEARD ANYTHING ABOUT THE RED CLOUD?
I HEARD SHE IS A SHE AND SHE BEAT THE HELL OUT OF SUPERMAN.
UH-HUH.
HOW ARE YOU, JIMMY? WHAT HAVE YOU BEEN DOING?
WELL, FUNNY THING...

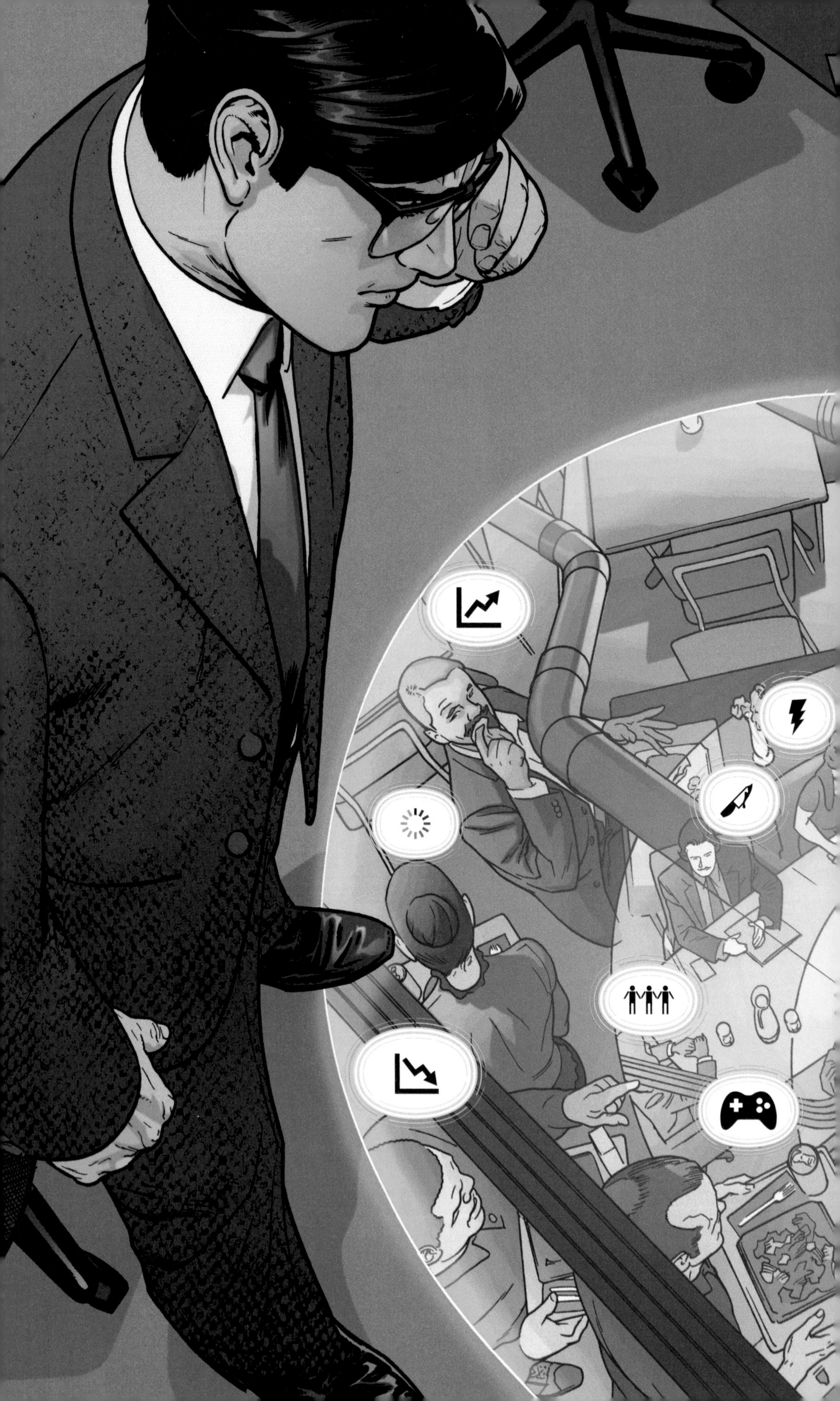

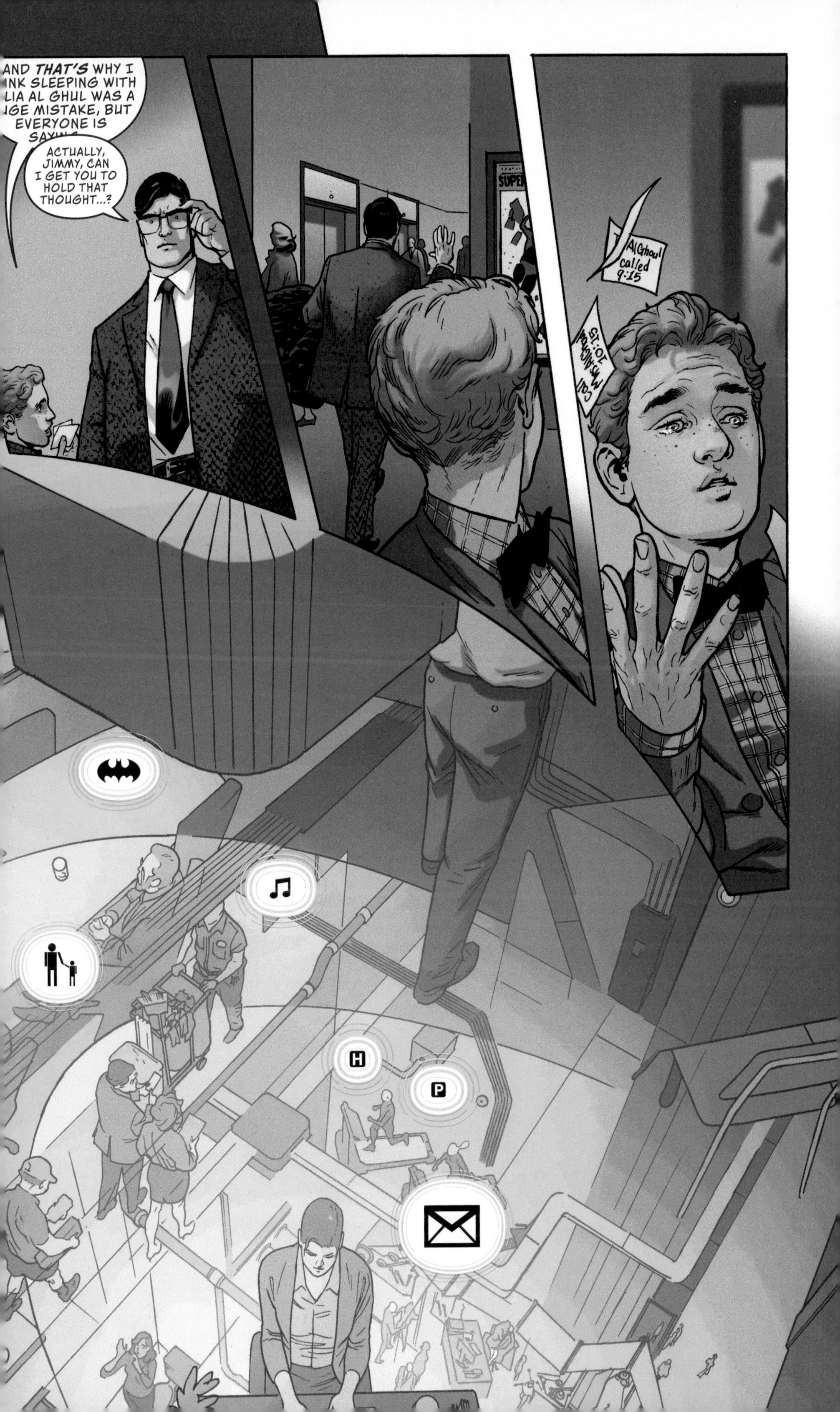
AND THAT'S WHY I
INK SLEEPING WITH
LIA AL GHUL WAS A
IGE MISTAKE, BUT
EVERYONE IS
ACTUALLY, JIMMY, CAN I GET YOU TO HOLD THAT THOUGHT...?
SUPER
Al Ghoul called 9:15

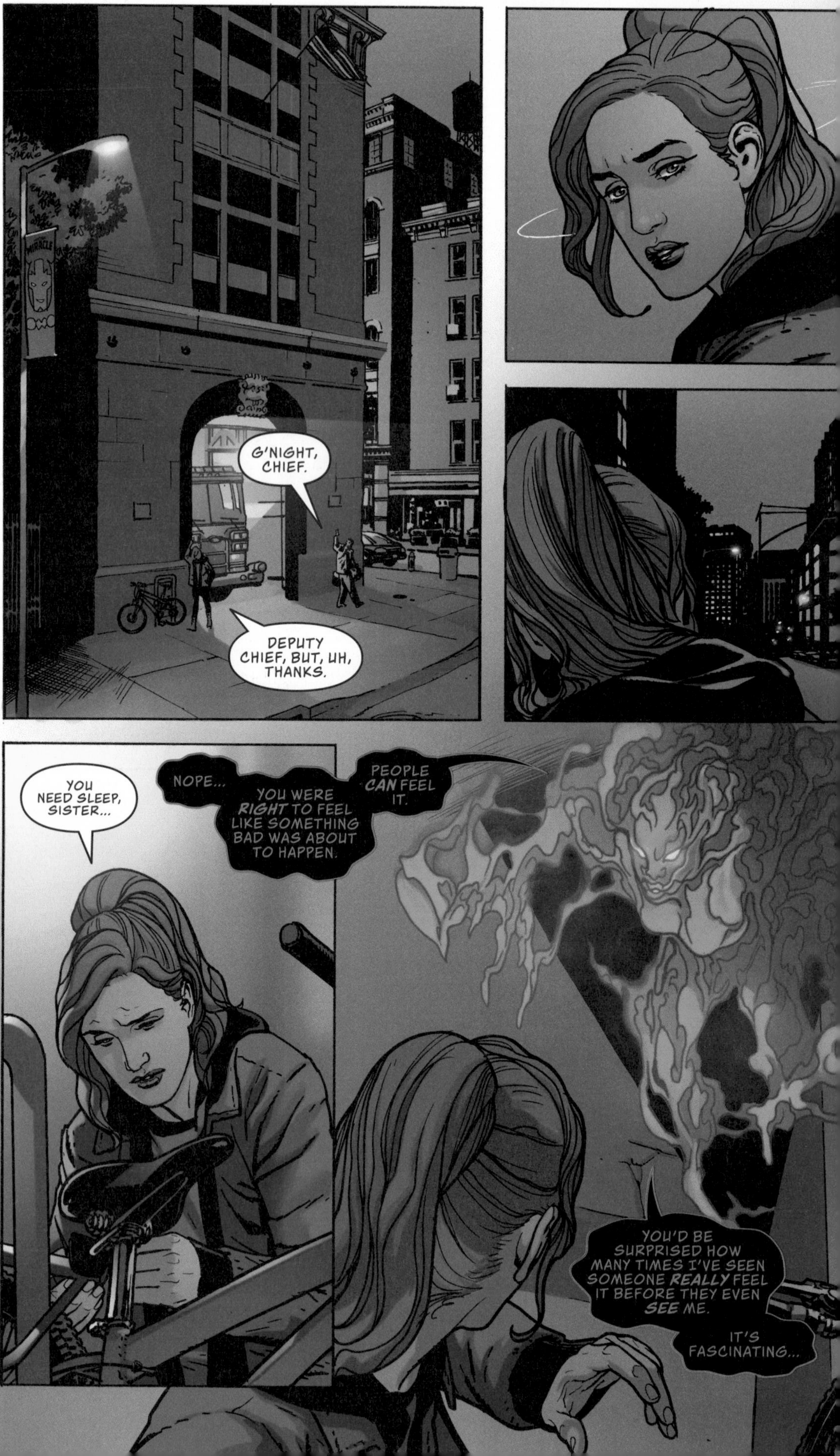

G'NIGHT, CHIEF.
DEPUTY CHIEF, BUT, UH, THANKS.
YOU NEED SLEEP, SISTER...
NOPE...
YOU WERE RIGHT TO FEEL LIKE SOMETHING BAD WAS ABOUT TO HAPPEN.
PEOPLE CAN FEEL IT.
YOU'D BE SURPRISED HOW MANY TIMES I'VE SEEN SOMEONE REALLY FEEL IT BEFORE THEY EVEN SEE ME.
IT'S FASCINATING...

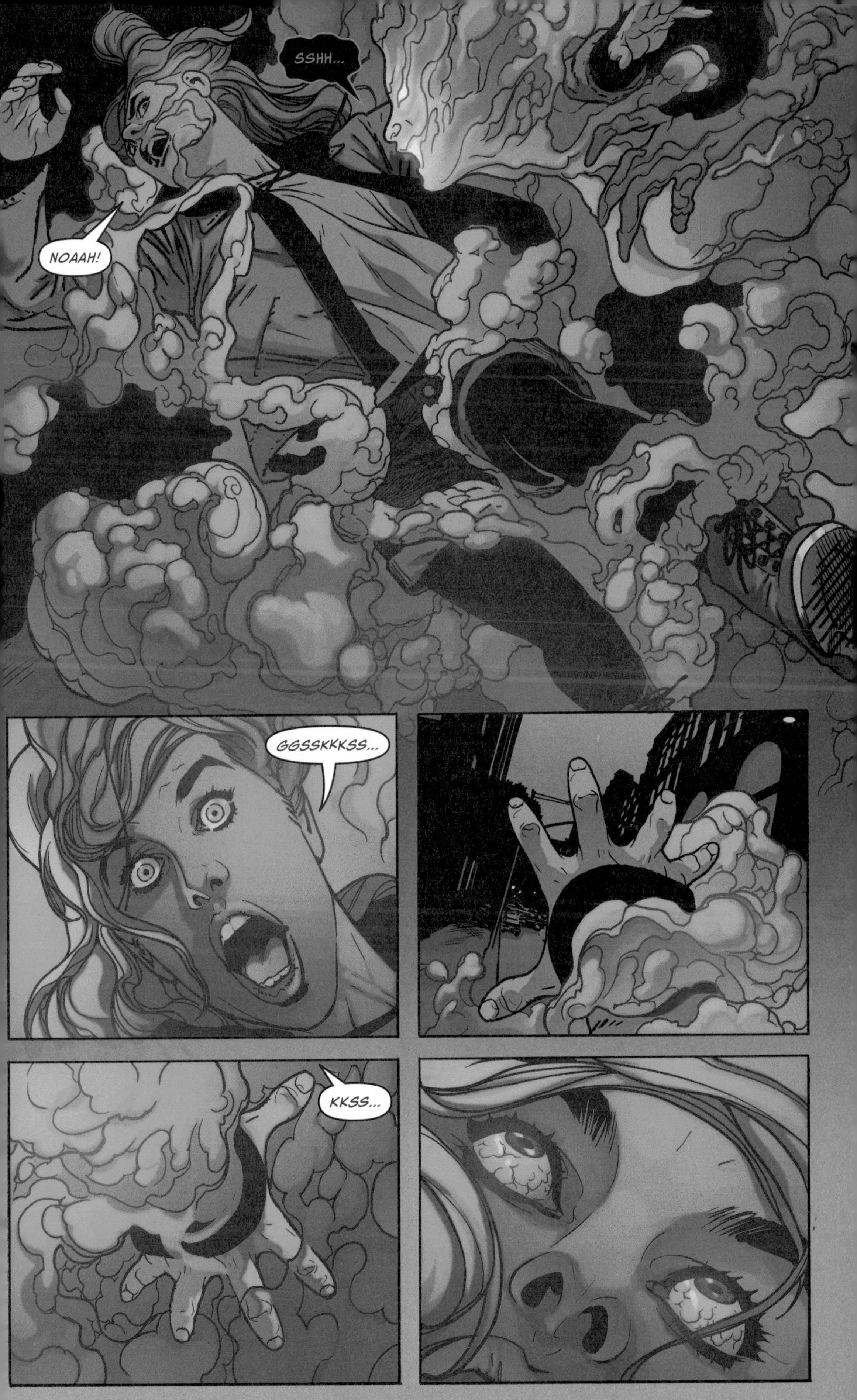
SSHH...
NOAAH!
GGSSKKKSS...
KKSS...

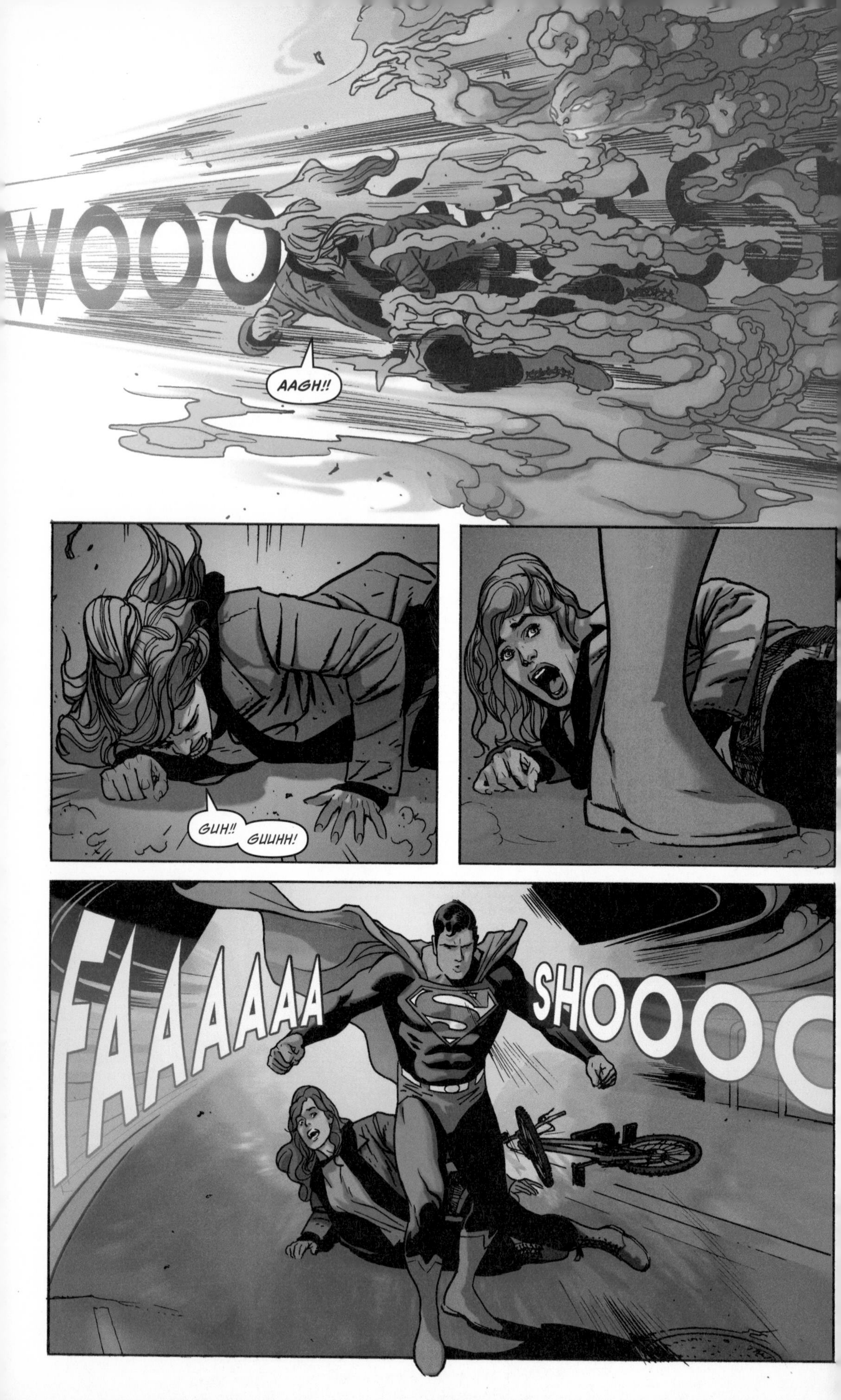
WOOOOSH
AAGH!!
GUH!!
GUUHH!
FAAAAAA
SHOOOO

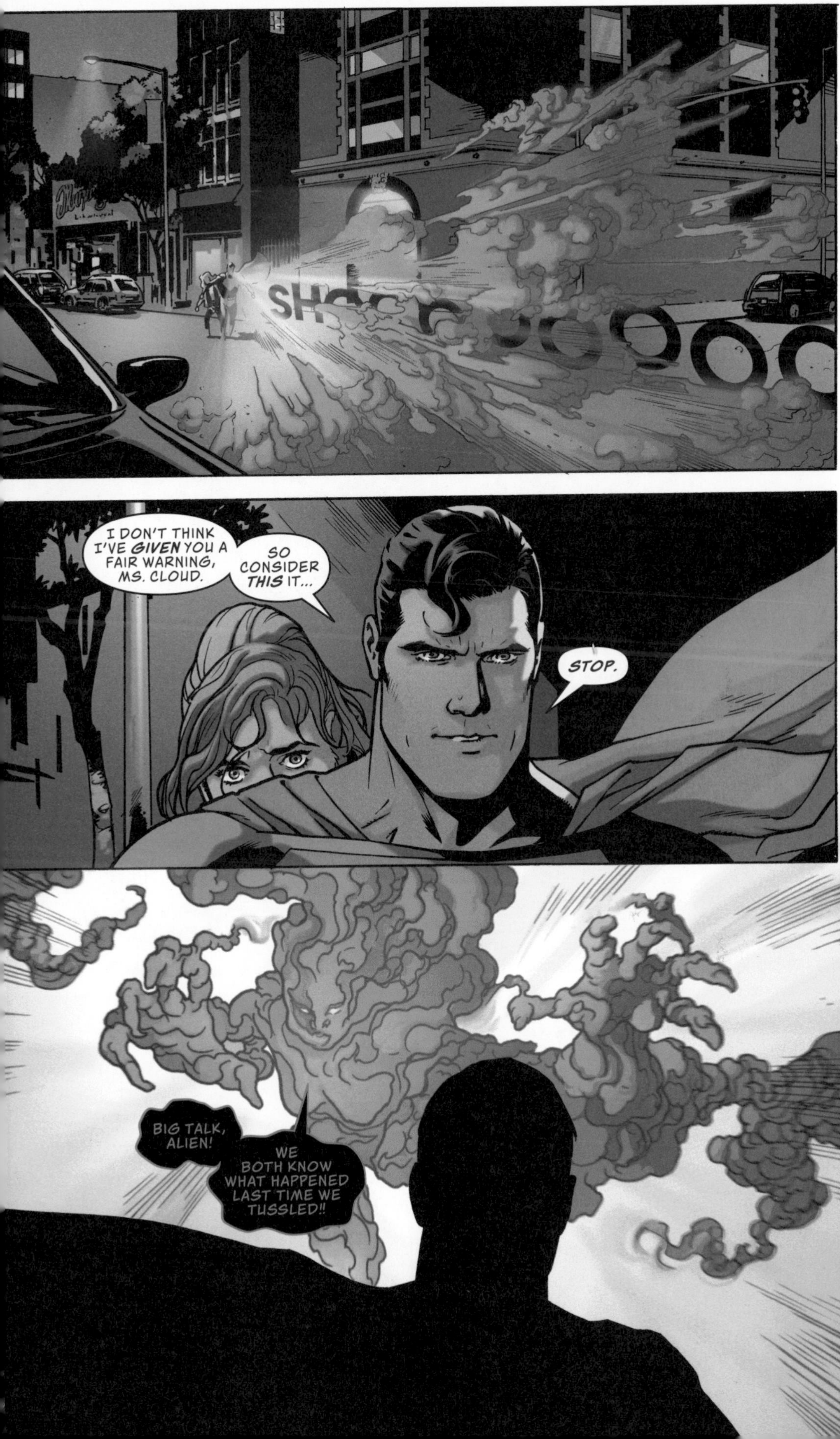
I DON'T THINK I'VE GIVEN YOU A FAIR WARNING, MS. CLOUD.
SO CONSIDER THIS IT...
STOP.
BIG TALK, ALIEN!
WE BOTH KNOW WHAT HAPPENED LAST TIME WE TUSSLED!!

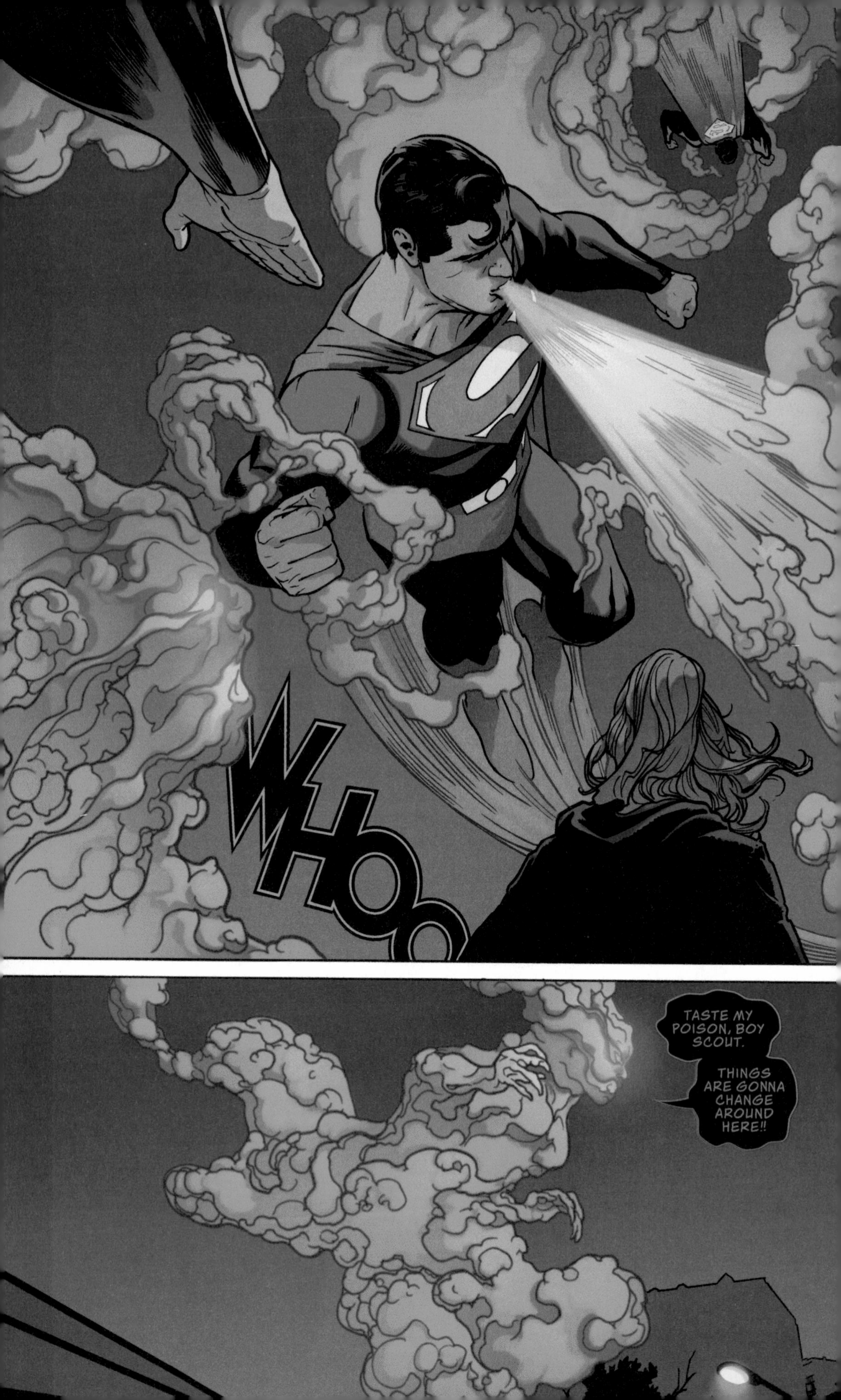
WHOO
TASTE MY POISON, BOY SCOUT.
THINGS ARE GONNA CHANGE AROUND HERE!!

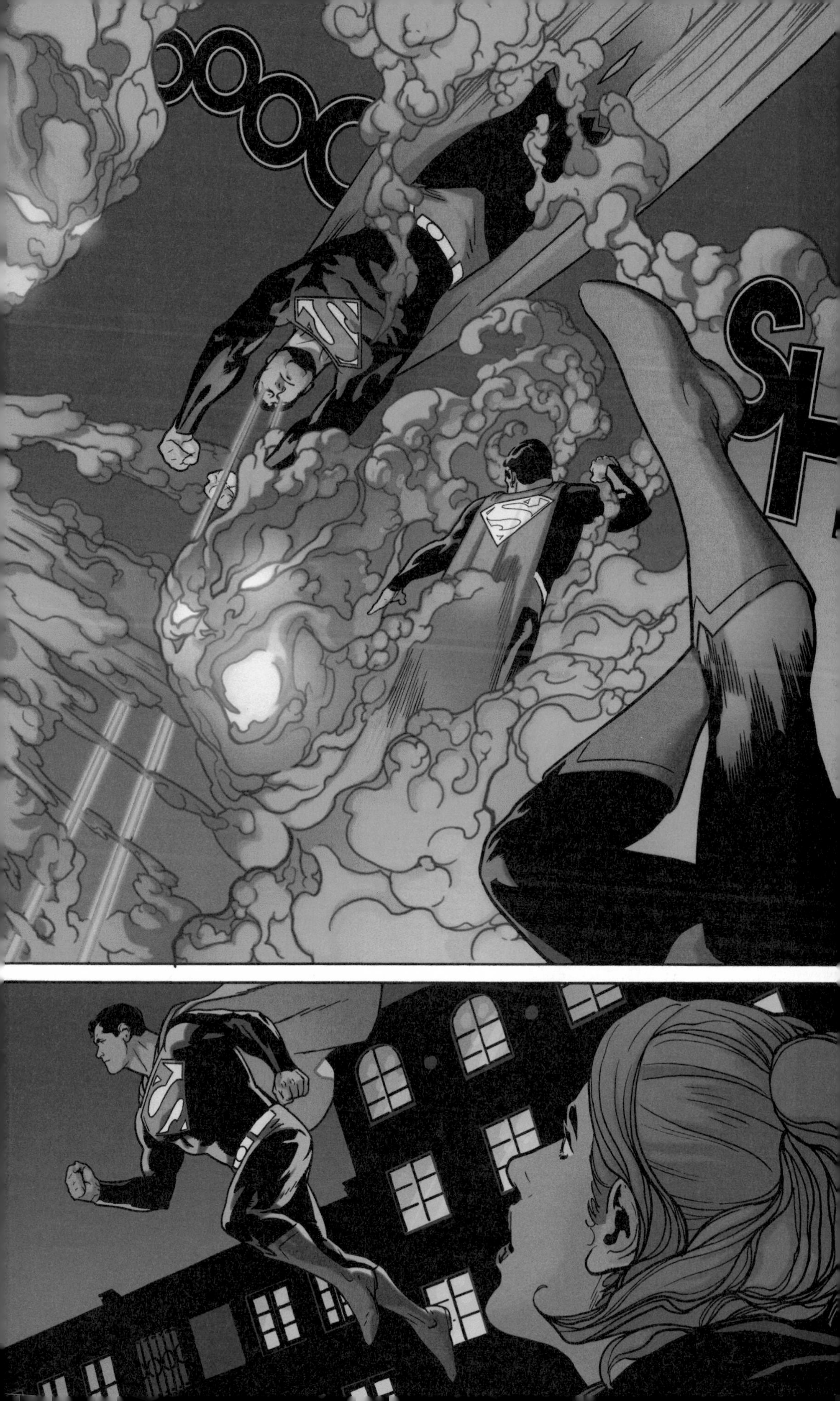

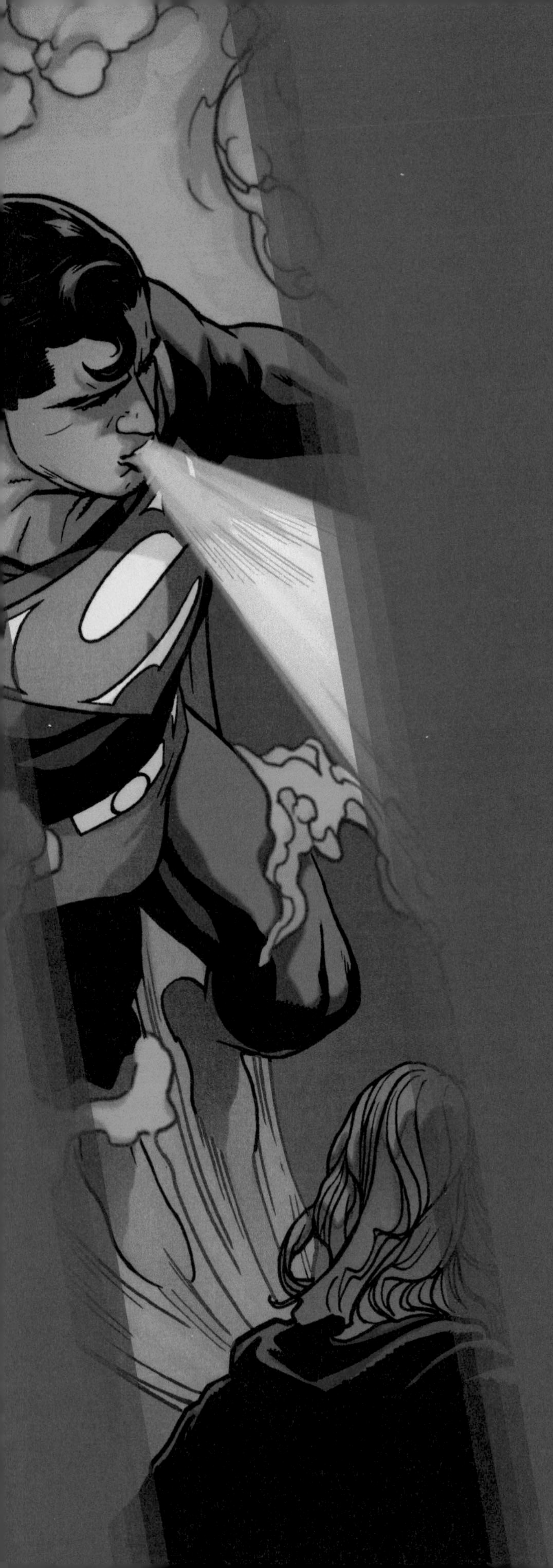

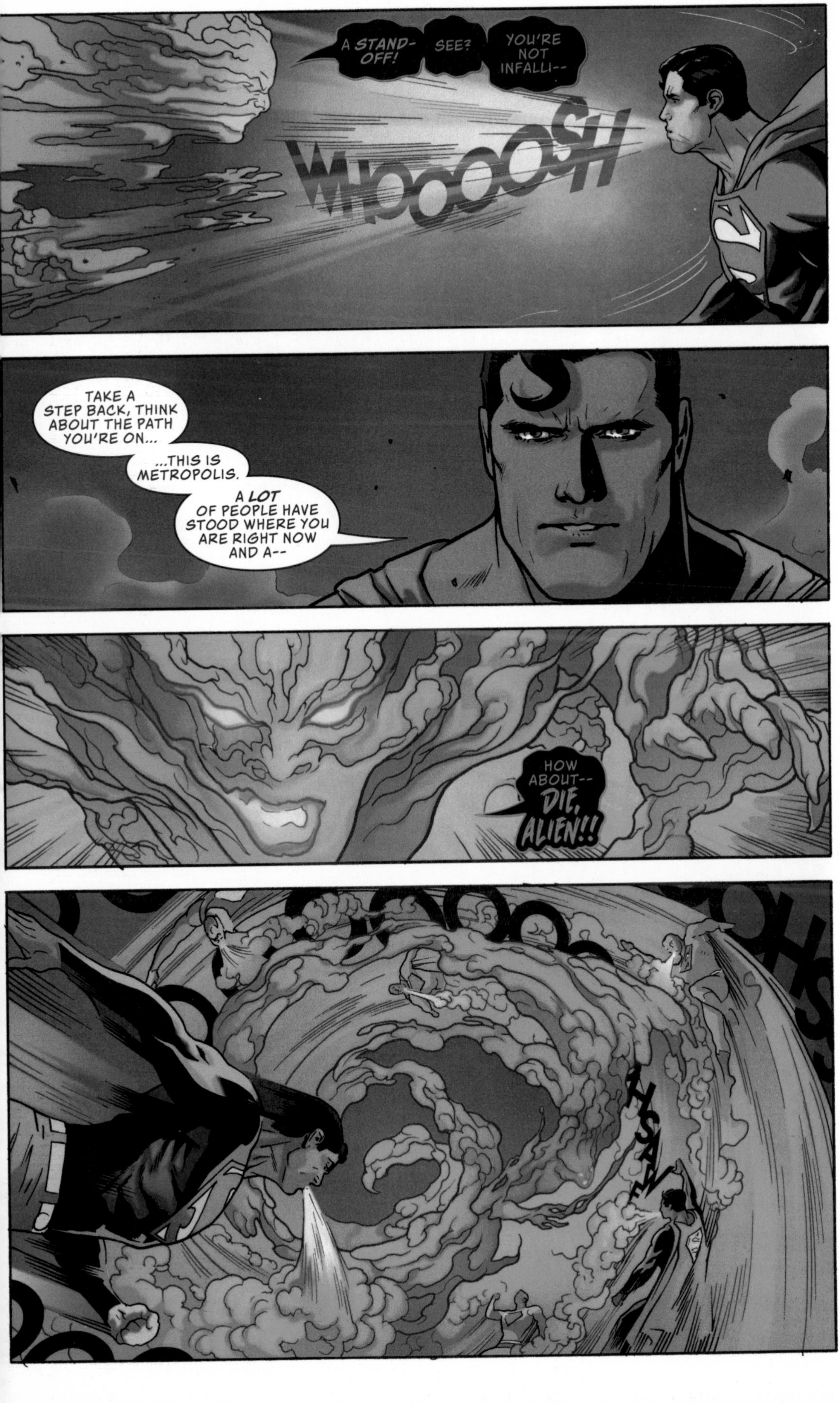
A STAND-OFF!
SEE?
YOU'RE NOT INFALLI--
WHOOOOSH
TAKE A STEP BACK, THINK ABOUT THE PATH YOU'RE ON...
...THIS IS METROPOLIS.
A LOT OF PEOPLE HAVE STOOD WHERE YOU ARE RIGHT NOW AND A--
HOW ABOUT-- DIE, ALIEN!!

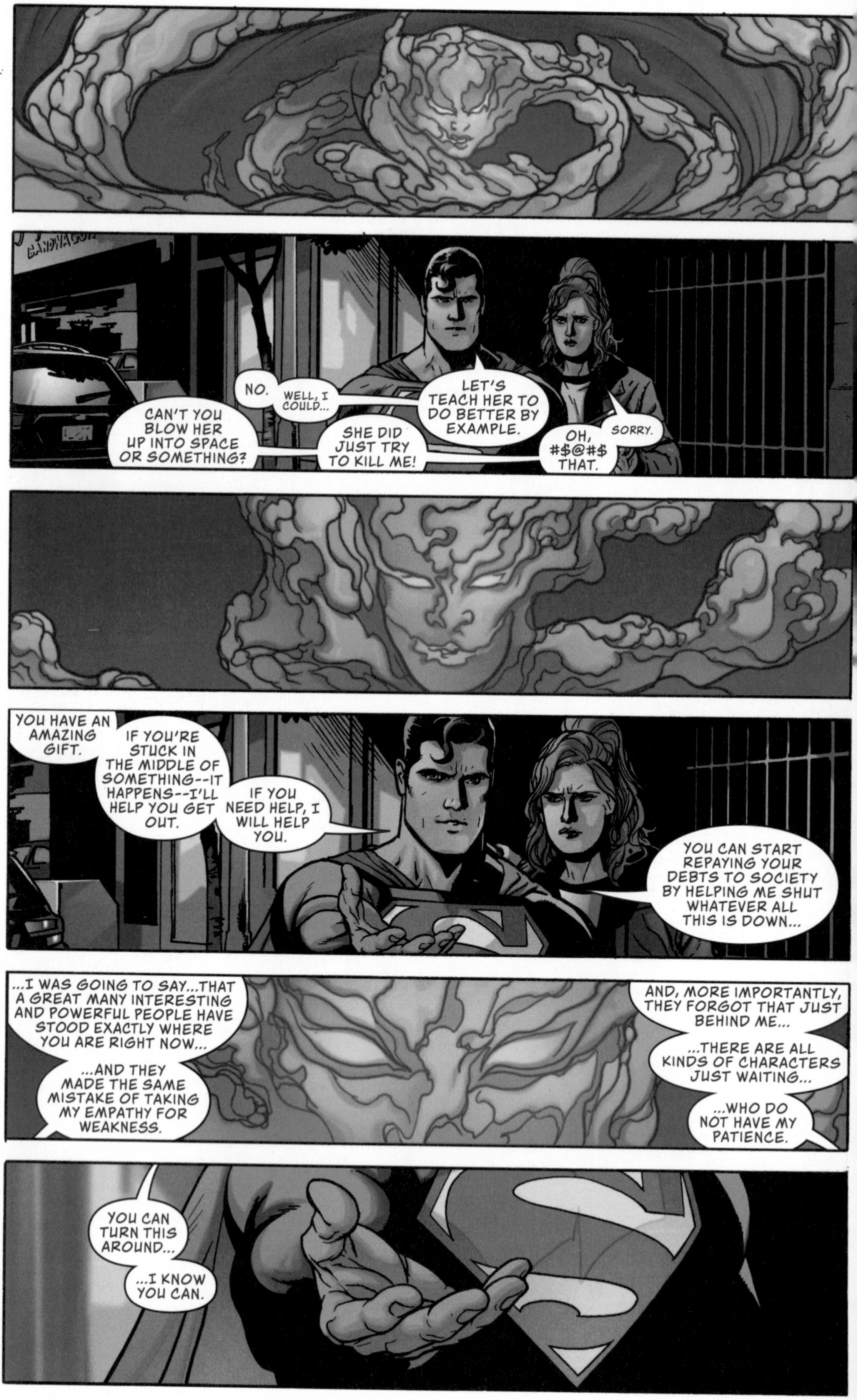

CAN'T YOU BLOW HER UP INTO SPACE OR SOMETHING?
NO.
WELL, I COULD...
SHE DID JUST TRY TO KILL ME!
LET'S TEACH HER TO DO BETTER BY EXAMPLE.
OH, #$@#$ THAT.
SORRY.
YOU HAVE AN AMAZING GIFT.
IF YOU'RE STUCK IN THE MIDDLE OF SOMETHING--IT HAPPENS--I'LL HELP YOU GET OUT.
IF YOU NEED HELP, I WILL HELP YOU.
YOU CAN START REPAYING YOUR DEBTS TO SOCIETY BY HELPING ME SHUT WHATEVER ALL THIS IS DOWN...
...I WAS GOING TO SAY...THAT A GREAT MANY INTERESTING AND POWERFUL PEOPLE HAVE STOOD EXACTLY WHERE YOU ARE RIGHT NOW...
...AND THEY MADE THE SAME MISTAKE OF TAKING MY EMPATHY FOR WEAKNESS.
AND, MORE IMPORTANTLY, THEY FORGOT THAT JUST BEHIND ME...
...THERE ARE ALL KINDS OF CHARACTERS JUST WAITING...
...WHO DO NOT HAVE MY PATIENCE.
YOU CAN TURN THIS AROUND...
...I KNOW YOU CAN.

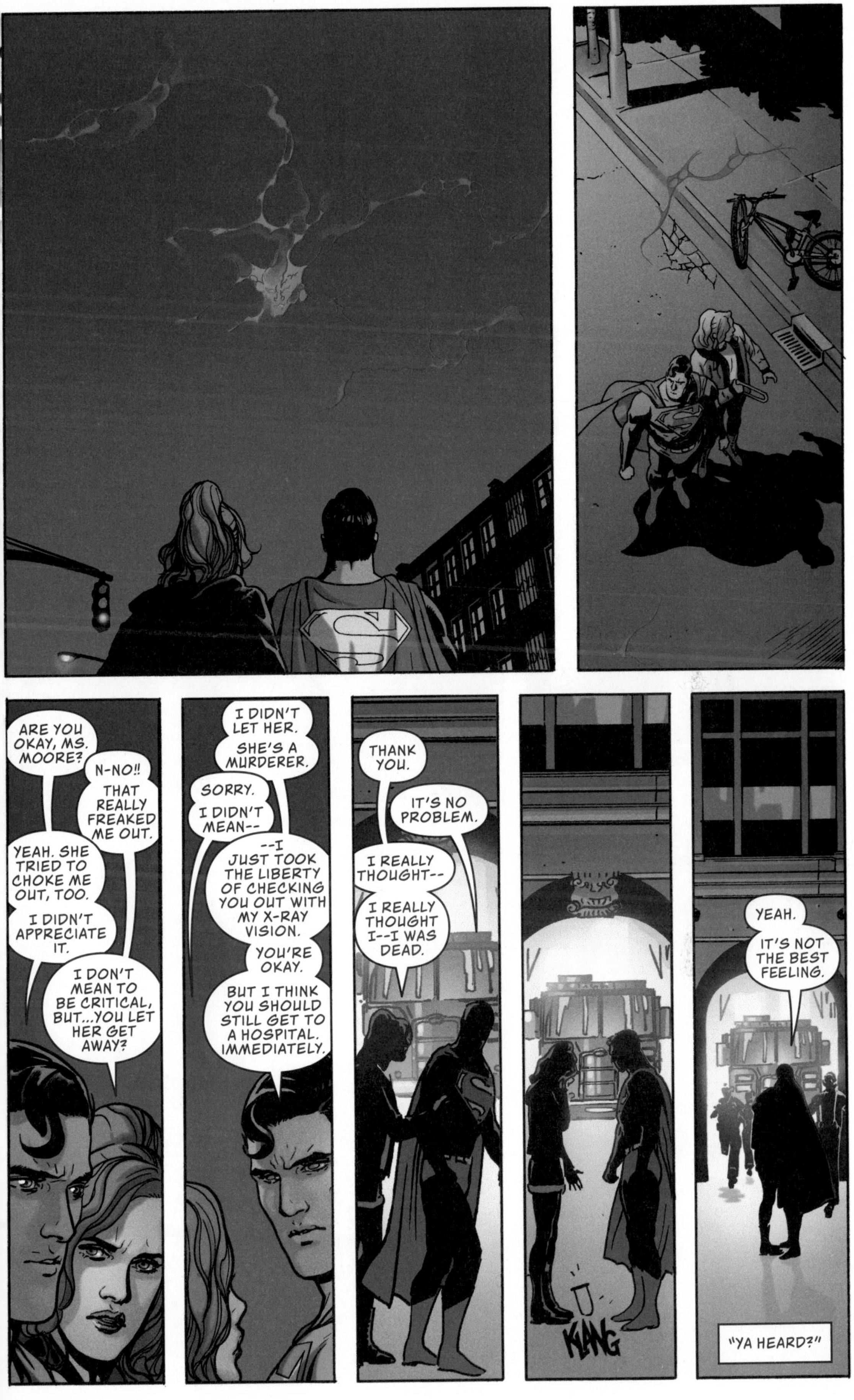
ARE YOU OKAY, MS. MOORE?
N-NO!! THAT REALLY FREAKED ME OUT.
YEAH. SHE TRIED TO CHOKE ME OUT, TOO.
I DIDN'T APPRECIATE IT.
I DON'T MEAN TO BE CRITICAL, BUT...YOU LET HER GET AWAY?
I DIDN'T LET HER.
SHE'S A MURDERER.
SORRY.
I DIDN'T MEAN--
--I JUST TOOK THE LIBERTY OF CHECKING YOU OUT WITH MY X-RAY VISION.
YOU'RE OKAY.
BUT I THINK YOU SHOULD STILL GET TO A HOSPITAL. IMMEDIATELY.
THANK YOU.
IT'S NO PROBLEM.
I REALLY THOUGHT--
I REALLY THOUGHT I--I WAS DEAD.
KLANG
YEAH.
IT'S NOT THE BEST FEELING.
"YA HEARD?"

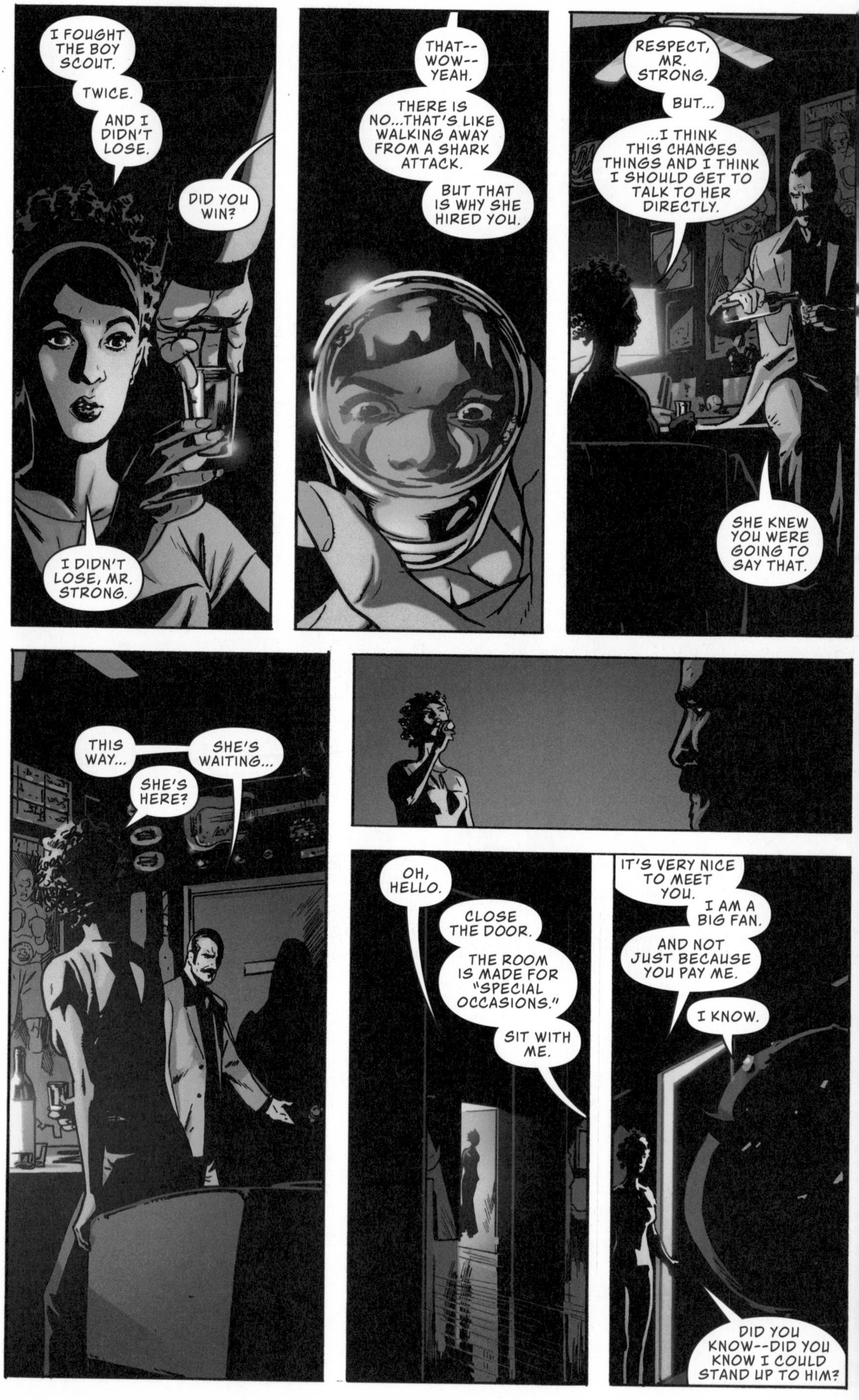
I FOUGHT THE BOY SCOUT.
TWICE.
AND I DIDN'T LOSE.
DID YOU WIN?
I DIDN'T LOSE, MR. STRONG.
THAT-- WOW-- YEAH.
THERE IS NO...THAT'S LIKE WALKING AWAY FROM A SHARK ATTACK.
BUT THAT IS WHY SHE HIRED YOU.
RESPECT, MR. STRONG.
BUT...
...I THINK THIS CHANGES THINGS AND I THINK I SHOULD GET TO TALK TO HER DIRECTLY.
SHE KNEW YOU WERE GOING TO SAY THAT.
THIS WAY...
SHE'S WAITING...
SHE'S HERE?
OH, HELLO.
CLOSE THE DOOR.
THE ROOM IS MADE FOR "SPECIAL OCCASIONS."
SIT WITH ME.
IT'S VERY NICE TO MEET YOU.
I AM A BIG FAN.
AND NOT JUST BECAUSE YOU PAY ME.
I KNOW.
DID YOU KNOW--DID YOU KNOW I COULD STAND UP TO HIM?

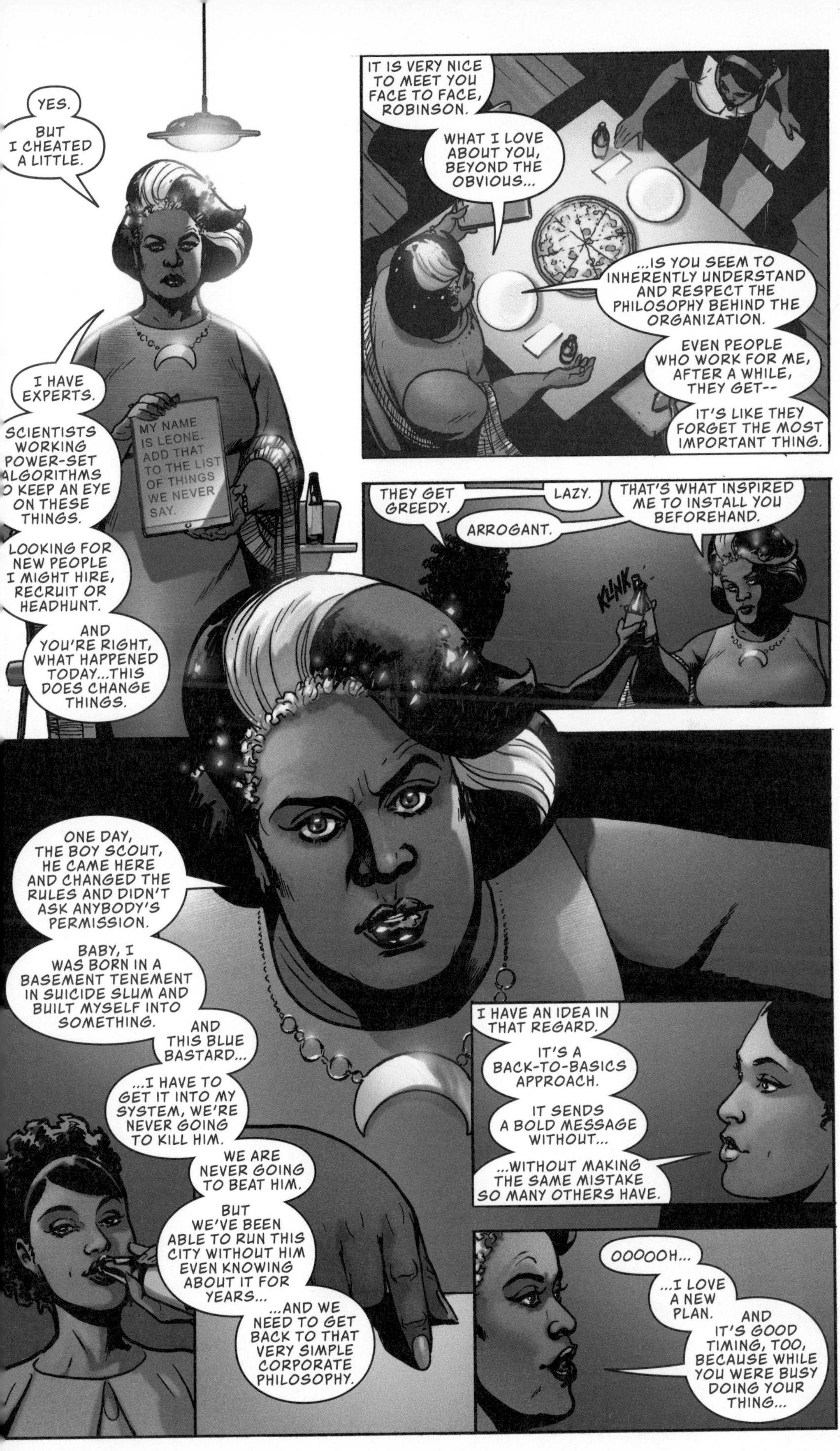
YES.
BUT I CHEATED A LITTLE.
I HAVE EXPERTS.
SCIENTISTS WORKING POWER-SET ALGORITHMS TO KEEP AN EYE ON THESE THINGS.
LOOKING FOR NEW PEOPLE I MIGHT HIRE, RECRUIT OR HEADHUNT.
AND YOU'RE RIGHT, WHAT HAPPENED TODAY...THIS DOES CHANGE THINGS.
MY NAME IS LEONE. ADD THAT TO THE LIST OF THINGS WE NEVER SAY.
IT IS VERY NICE TO MEET YOU FACE TO FACE, ROBINSON.
WHAT I LOVE ABOUT YOU, BEYOND THE OBVIOUS...
...IS YOU SEEM TO INHERENTLY UNDERSTAND AND RESPECT THE PHILOSOPHY BEHIND THE ORGANIZATION.
EVEN PEOPLE WHO WORK FOR ME, AFTER A WHILE, THEY GET--
IT'S LIKE THEY FORGET THE MOST IMPORTANT THING.
THEY GET GREEDY.
LAZY.
ARROGANT.
THAT'S WHAT INSPIRED ME TO INSTALL YOU BEFOREHAND.
KLINK
ONE DAY, THE BOY SCOUT, HE CAME HERE AND CHANGED THE RULES AND DIDN'T ASK ANYBODY'S PERMISSION.
BABY, I WAS BORN IN A BASEMENT TENEMENT IN SUICIDE SLUM AND BUILT MYSELF INTO SOMETHING.
AND THIS BLUE BASTARD...
...I HAVE TO GET IT INTO MY SYSTEM, WE'RE NEVER GOING TO KILL HIM.
WE ARE NEVER GOING TO BEAT HIM.
BUT WE'VE BEEN ABLE TO RUN THIS CITY WITHOUT HIM EVEN KNOWING ABOUT IT FOR YEARS...
...AND WE NEED TO GET BACK TO THAT VERY SIMPLE CORPORATE PHILOSOPHY.
I HAVE AN IDEA IN THAT REGARD.
IT'S A BACK-TO-BASICS APPROACH.
IT SENDS A BOLD MESSAGE WITHOUT...
...WITHOUT MAKING THE SAME MISTAKE SO MANY OTHERS HAVE.
OOOOOH...
...I LOVE A NEW PLAN.
AND IT'S GOOD TIMING, TOO, BECAUSE WHILE YOU WERE BUSY DOING YOUR THING...

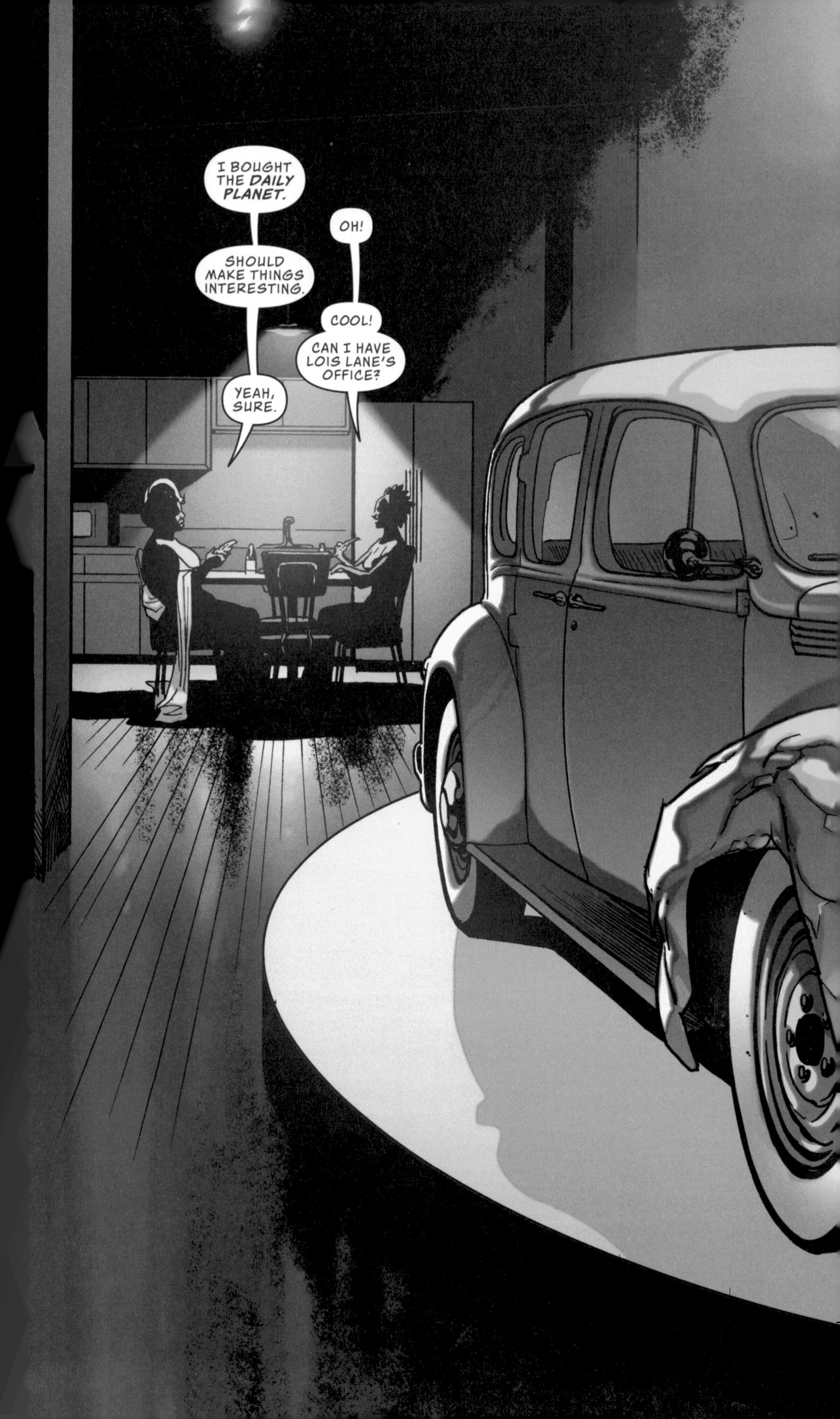
I BOUGHT THE *DAILY PLANET.*
OH!
SHOULD MAKE THINGS INTERESTING.
COOL!
CAN I HAVE LOIS LANE'S OFFICE?
YEAH, SURE.

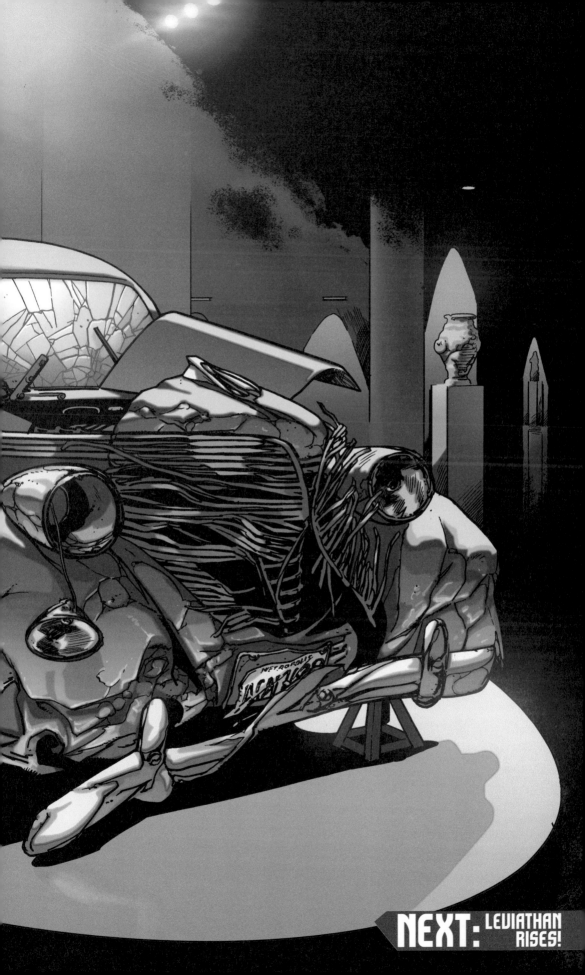

NEXT: LEVIATHAN RISES!

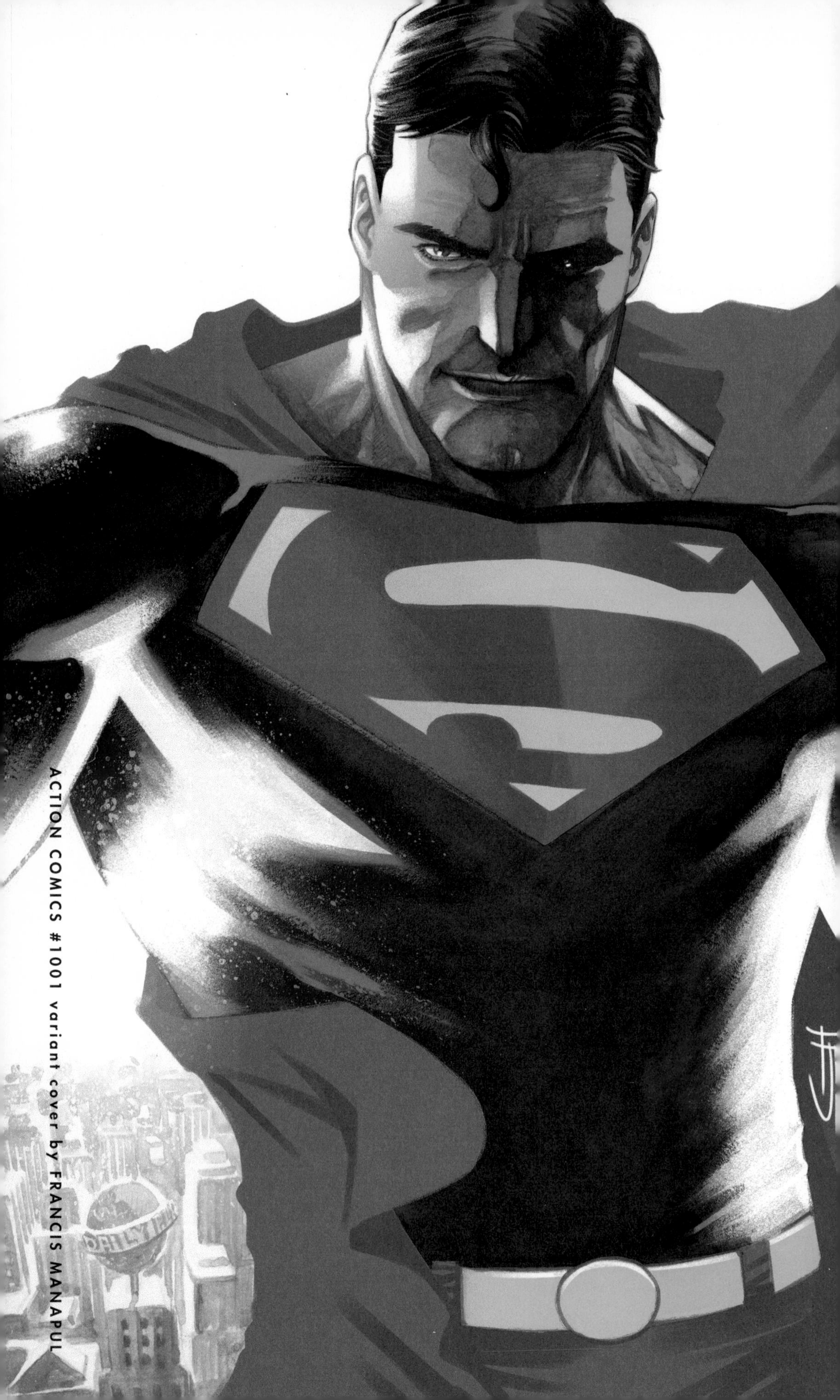

ACTION COMICS #1001 variant cover by FRANCIS MANAPUL

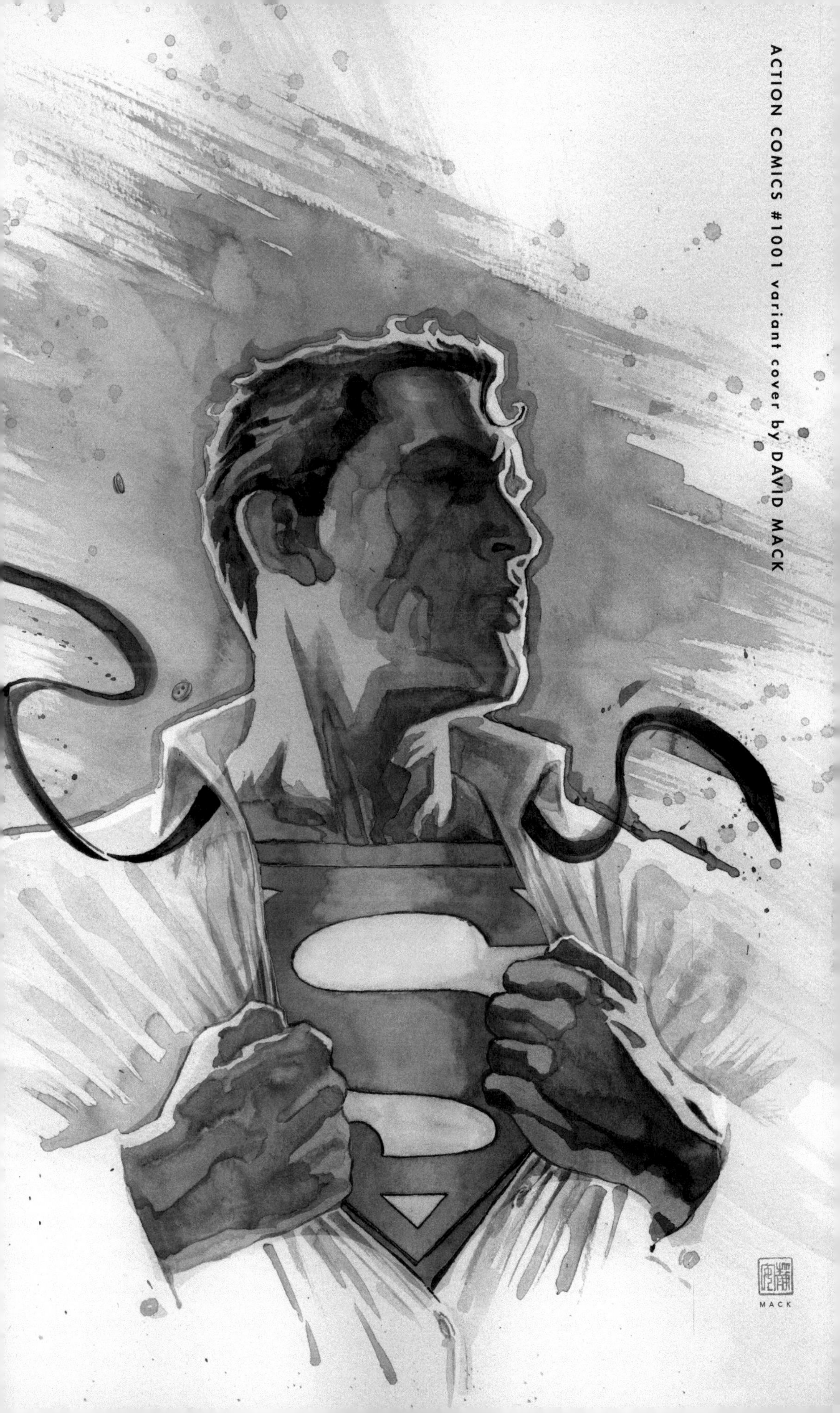
MACK
ACTION COMICS #1001 variant cover by DAVID MACK

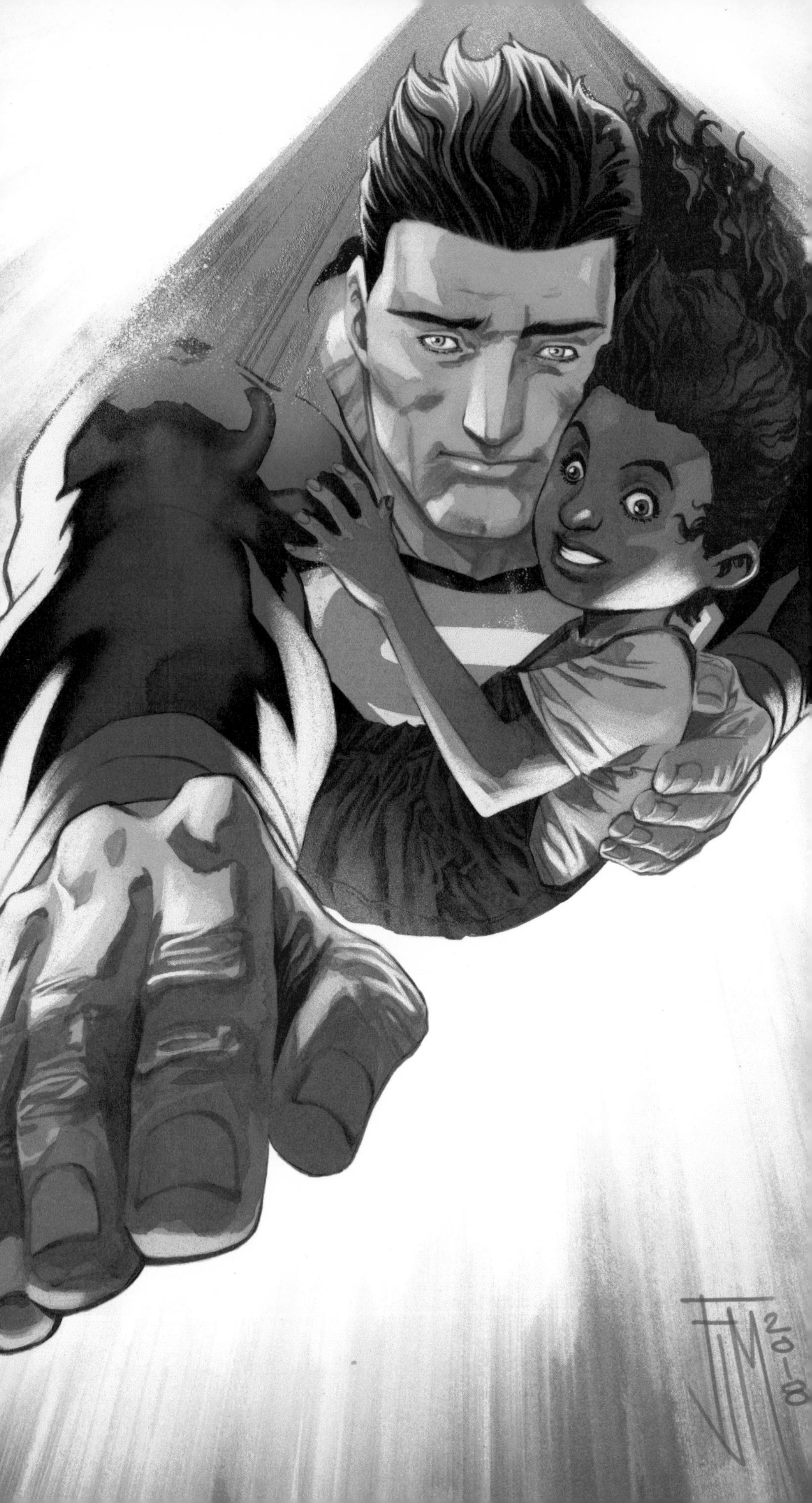

ACTION COMICS #1002 variant cover by FRANCIS MANAPUL

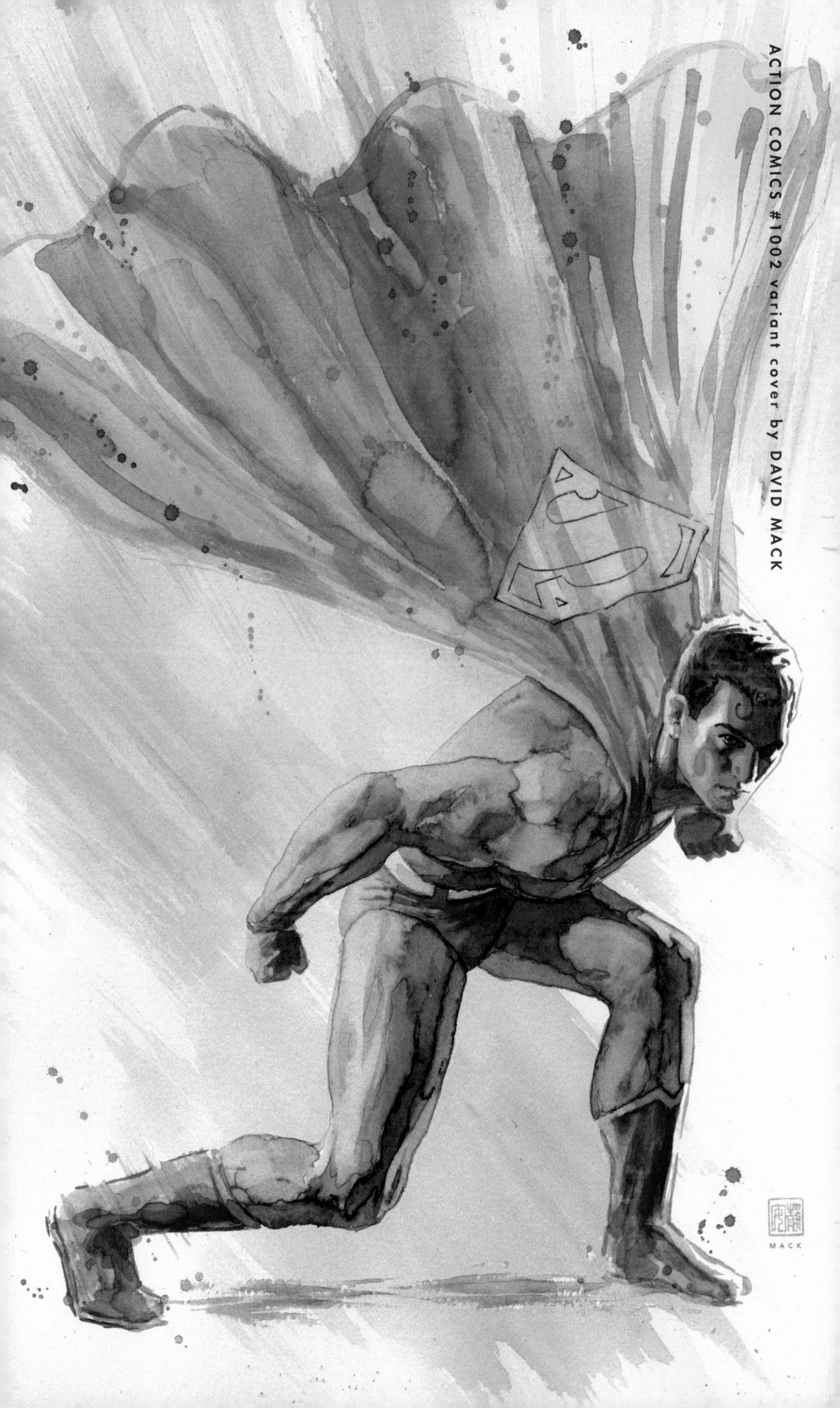
MACK
ACTION COMICS #1002 variant cover by DAVID MACK

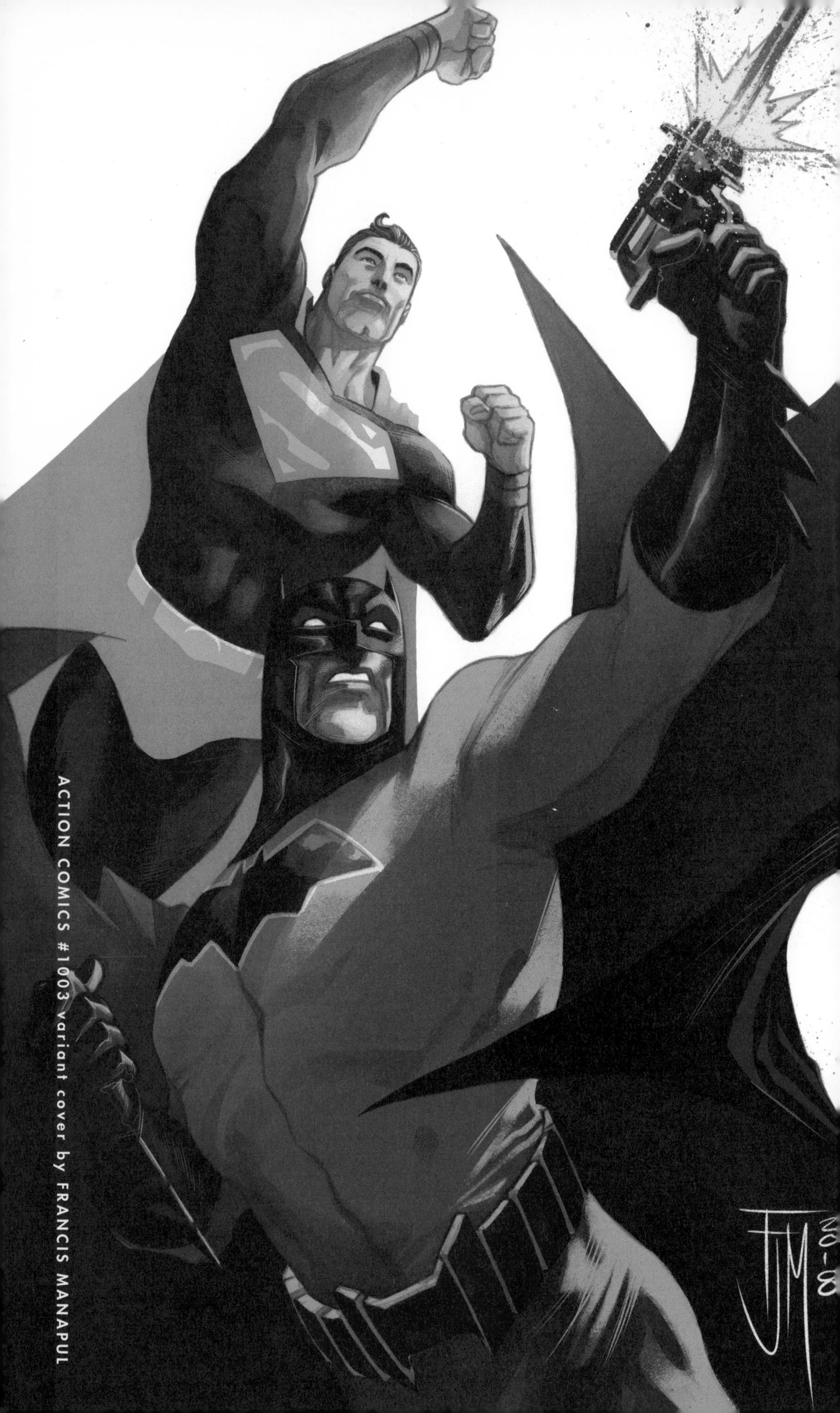

ACTION COMICS #1003 variant cover by FRANCIS MANAPUL

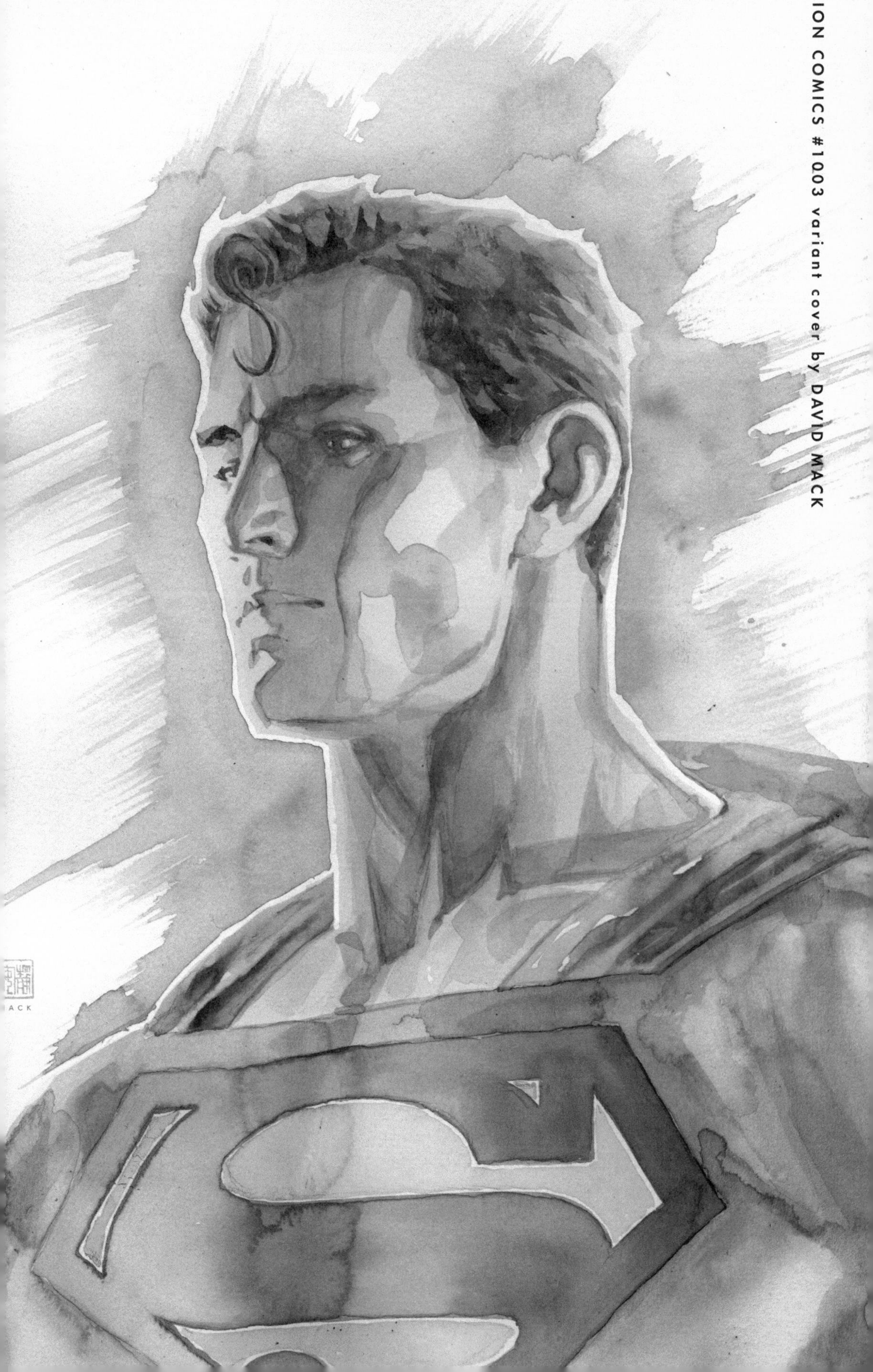

ACTION COMICS #1003 variant cover by DAVID MACK

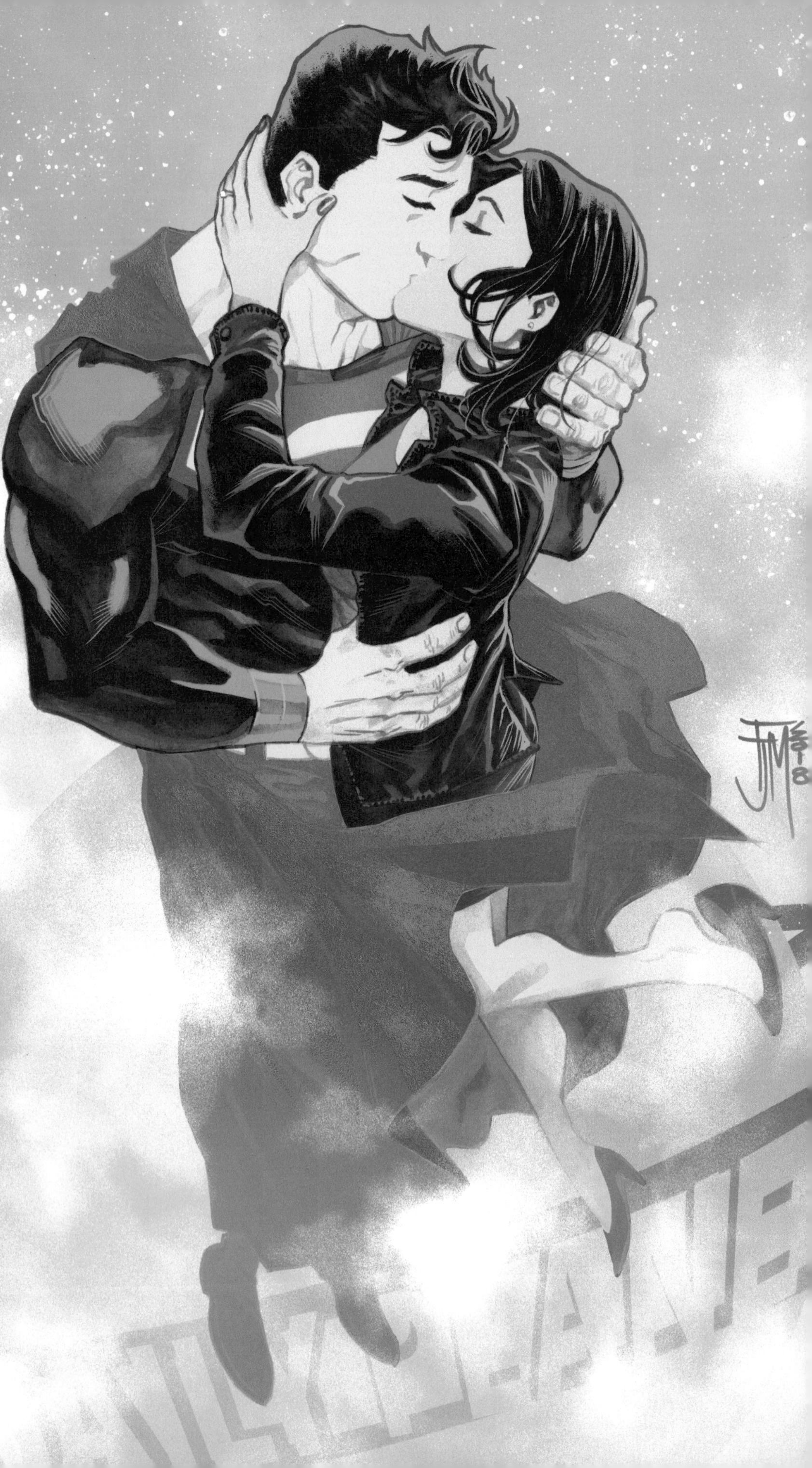

ACTION COMICS #1004 variant cover by FRANCIS MANAPUL

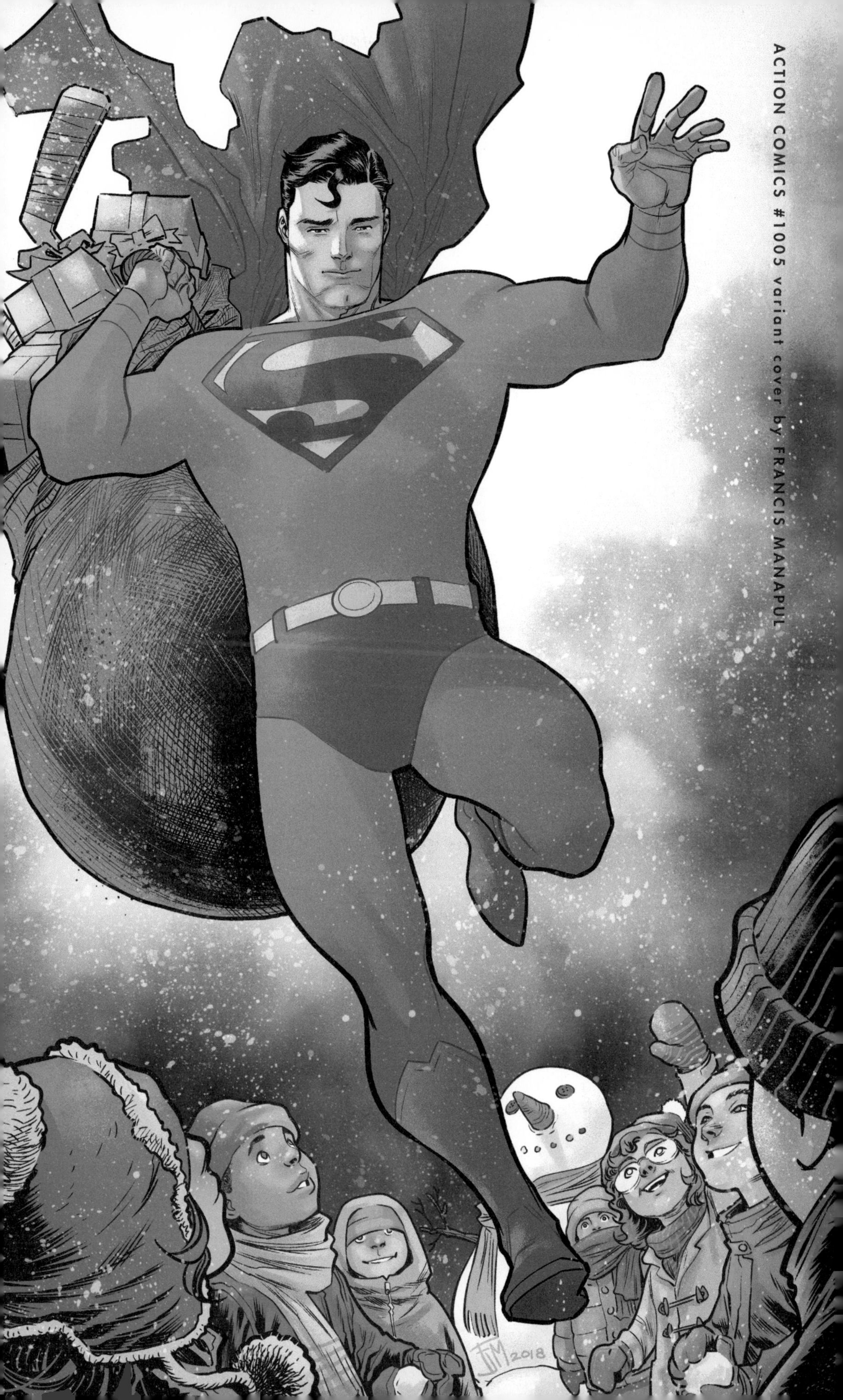

ACTION COMICS #1005 variant cover by FRANCIS MANAPUL

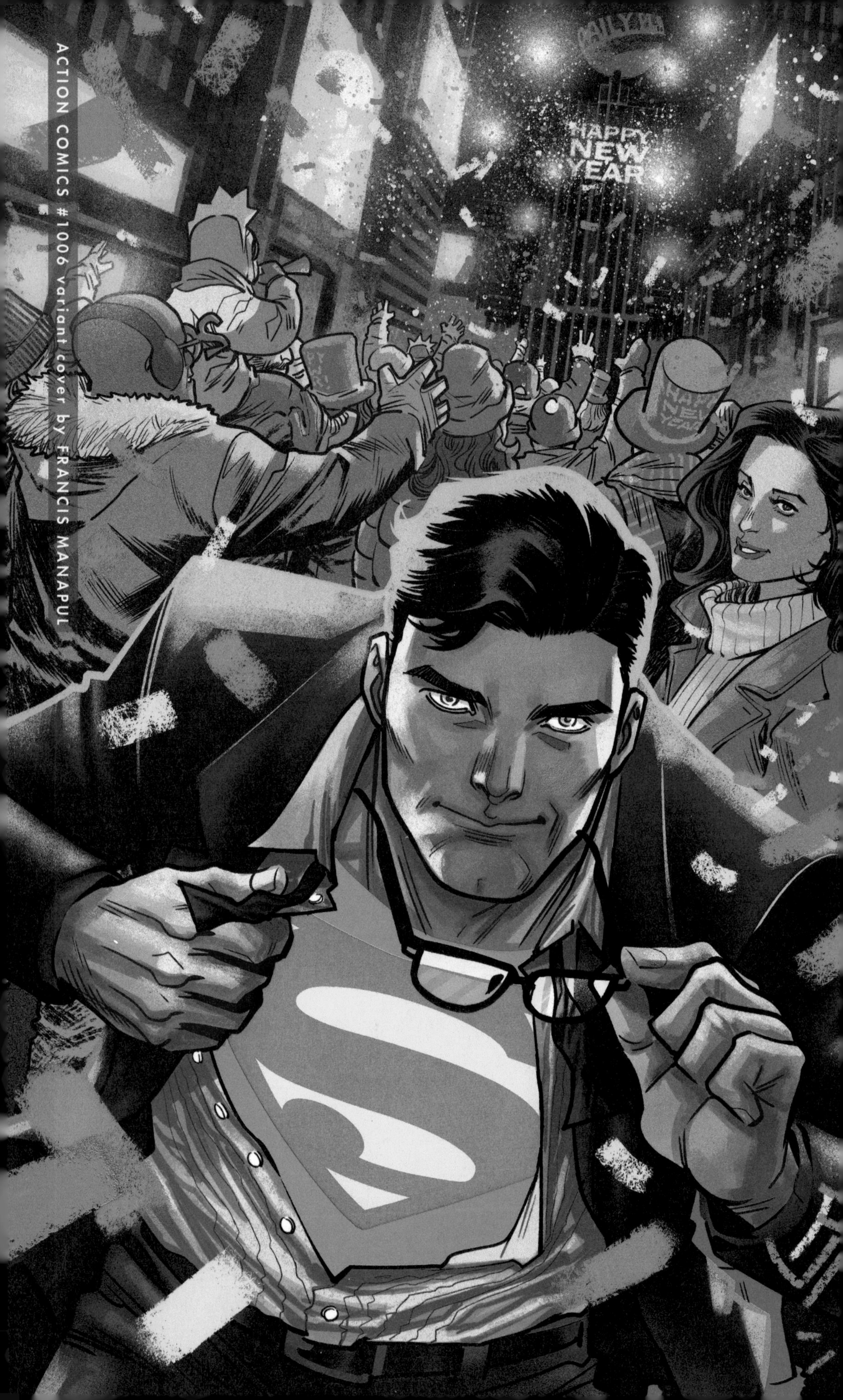
HAPPY
NEW
YEAR

ACTION COMICS #1006 variant cover by FRANCIS MANAPUL